'Graham Davey, one of the foremost experts on anxiety in the world, alerts us that "if you're alive you'll experience anxiety". But is it good or bad for you? Where does it come from? Is it worse now than it used to be in prior ages? And what is there to do about it? Answers to these and many other questions are forthcoming in this highly readable, entertaining book. Everyone wrestling with anxiety in their lives will benefit from the up-to-date information provided'

– Prof. David H. Barlow, PhD, ABPP, Professor of Psychology
and Psychiatry Emeritus at Boston University

'Drawing on personal and extensive academic experience as a leading anxiety researcher, Professor Davey addresses one of the major but neglected sources of suffering in our time. Everyone should pay attention to his engaging, informative and at times controversial discourse on anxiety. This book is a must-read for all those interested in one of the most fundamental but disruptive human emotions'

– Prof. Adrian Wells, PhD, Professor of Clinical and
Experimental Psychopathology, University of Manchester

THE
ANXIETY
EPIDEMIC

The Causes of Our Modern-Day Anxieties

Graham Davey

ROBINSON

ROBINSON

First published in Great Britain in 2018 by Robinson

Copyright © Graham Davey, 2018

1 3 5 7 9 8 6 4 2

A CIP catalogue record for this book is available from the British Library

p.113: © Craig RJD
p.165: © Konstantin Tronin/Shutterstock.com
p.295: © NiDer Lander

ISBN: 978-1-47214-096-8

Typeset by Initial Typesetting Services
Printed and bound in Great Britain by CPI Group (UK) Ltd, Croydon CR0 4YY

Papers used by Robinson are from well-managed forests and
other responsible sources

Robinson
An imprint of
Little, Brown Book Group
Carmelite House
50 Victoria Embankment
London EC4Y 0DZ

An Hachette UK Company
www.hachette.co.uk

www.littlebrown.co.uk

For my mother Betty,
a lifelong devotee of anxiety and its various conditions

CONTENTS

PREFACE

In 2014 'what is anxiety?' became one of the top ten most Googled 'What is . . . ?' search phrases in the UK. More people are seeking treatment for anxiety than ever before, and one in nine people worldwide will experience a diagnosable anxiety disorder in any one year – that's over seven million people in the UK and over thirty-five million people in the USA alone. For those people suffering an anxiety disorder it's a distressing and disabling experience that prevents them undertaking many ordinary day-to-day activities such as going to work, educating themselves, looking after their families and socialising. So prevalent is anxiety in the world that we're now told that it's at epidemic proportions and it rivals depression as the major mental health problem worldwide. In June 2017 the *New York Times* ran the headline 'THE PROZAC NATION IS NOW THE UNITED STATES OF XANAX'![1]; 'the silent epidemic' has eclipsed the black dog[2].

This book has two main aims. The first is to describe the many ways in which the modern world creates stress and anxiety. The second is to provide an engaging and accessible account of the causes of anxiety and its disorders.

1 https://www.nytimes.com/2017/06/10/style/anxiety-is-the-new-depression-xanax.html
2 http://www.telegraph.co.uk/health-fitness/mind/how-anxiety-became-a-modern-epidemic-greater-than-depression/

The way that anxiety manifests itself has not really changed over the centuries and we're still plagued by the same forms of anxiety disorder as our ancient ancestors, but the things that trigger our anxiety have certainly changed. We still experience many traditional causes of anxiety such as poor health, difficult relationships, unemployment, poverty and disadvantage, loneliness, work stress, and exposure to violence, trauma and conflict, but even in our modern world, some of these traditional sources of anxiety have been on the increase. These include loneliness; relationship factors such as divorce; violence and abuse – including childhood abuse and neglect; increased working hours and more stressful work procedures; and a general sense of lack of control over our own destinies – especially amongst our youngsters who are introduced to the possibility of failure earlier and earlier in their lives as a result of increased systematic educational testing.

But modern technology has provided some entirely new sources of anxiety for the present generation. These include twenty-four-hour perpetual connectivity, the need to multitask across a range of different activities, and regular increasingly emotive news alerts and doomsday scenarios. Even that bastion of modern-day living, the computer, brings with it daily worrisome hassles that include crashing hard drives, forgotten passwords, and the frustration of daily transactions that begin to seem strangely distant when all we'd like to do is speak to a real person. Connecting to the Internet merely adds fears of identity theft, data hacking, phishing, grooming and trolling. And then there's social media. The first recognisable social media sites were created in the mid-1990s, so most youngsters under the age of twenty will never have lived without the curse of social media. And a curse it can be. Social media use is closely associated with social anxiety and loneliness and can generate feelings of disconnectedness when we view what seem like the rich lives and social successes of others. A consequence of social media use is that youngsters count their social success in terms of metrics such as the number of friends they have on sites like Facebook, not the number of genuine confidants they have – confidants who would be true friends in times of difficulty and need.

Anxiety is a shape-shifter that can appear in several very different guises and this book will tell the story of the many-headed beast from its inception as a helpful ramshackle emotion to its seduction by the dark side as it becomes a distressing and debilitating condition and gives life to anxiety disorders such as phobias, social anxiety, panic disorder, obsessive-compulsive disorder, pathological worrying and post-traumatic stress disorder. I started life as an anxious child, developed into an anxious adolescent, and then became an anxious adult, but I was fortunate enough to spend most of my working lifetime as a research psychologist involved at the forefront of our endeavour to understand anxiety – basically my day job paid the mortgage *and* helped me to understand myself! So you'll be reading plenty of my own anxiety anecdotes along the way as well as some insights into the research we conducted that cast new light on what anxiety is and how it is that many of us come to suffer it. Much of the battle against anxiety is won if you understand the causes of your anxiety – the external factors that give rise to your anxieties and worries, and the cognitive and physiological processes that generate your anxiety. They're all in this book.

Graham C. L. Davey
Brighton, UK
December 2017

Follow me on Twitter at:
http://twitter.com/GrahamCLDavey

CHAPTER ONE

'A Swarm of Rats Is Eating My Soul'

The Nature and Purpose of Anxiety

'Anxiety's like a rocking chair. It gives you something to do, but it doesn't get you very far.'

— Jodi Picoult, *Sing You Home*

In 1968 I headed to university to study psychology at the University College of North Wales in Bangor. I had a single suitcase full of clothes, and my mother stood tearfully on the platform as I boarded the train for the rain-soaked mountains and valleys of North Wales. I was pale with anxiety – it was my first time away from home. But to allay my separation fears, my father gave me a wad of blank postcards. He said he'd write to me every week if I wrote to him. After ten weeks I returned home at the end of term with the same suitcase, but this time full of dirty clothes and a trophy I'd won as the brand-new students' union table football champion. I didn't return with good grades, but instead with memories of a good time. My first question on returning was why my father hadn't written to me as he'd faithfully promised. As it turned out, he had written to me every week – but in his ignorance of many things, he'd addressed the letters to the Department of Physiology at the University of Bognor. He knew how to spell 'physiology' but not that new-fangled thing called 'psychology', and he'd heard of bloody Bognor, but not Bangor. We managed to laugh at this communication failure purely because in 1968 it was perfectly normal to go weeks without communicating with anyone who was more than a short bus or car journey away.

These primitive and imperfect ways we communicated in 1968 may seem prehistoric to today's generations of university freshers. They're not cursed with communication famine like I was; they're cursed with perpetual connectivity. Unlike today's freshers, I wasn't anxious about how many friends I had on Facebook, I wasn't anxious about the need to get a good degree in order to secure a future career, and I wasn't worried about 'FOMO' – fear of missing out. But I was anxious – anxious about very different things. I was anxious about leaving home. I was anxious about having no regular link with my family for the next ten weeks. I was even more anxious when I arrived at Bangor station to discover I could only get directions to my digs if I spoke Welsh! And I was still scared of heights, socially anxious and fearful of what the Cold War might bring. Are people just full of anxiety all the time – regardless of what they do or when they lived? Is anxiety just an inevitable consequence of being alive?

Almost fifty years after the day I left for university, journalist Jonathan Gornall wrote a lengthy article in March 2015 with the title 'The Puzzling Growth of Anxiety in the Modern Age'[1]. He's far from alone in believing that the modern age has brought with it more sources of anxiety and stress – some of which may be unique to our modern world. The so-called anxiety epidemic is reflected in growing concern about mental health (especially the mental health

1 Gornall, J (2015) 'The Long Read: The Puzzling Growth of Anxiety in the Modern Age.' *The National.* http://www.thenational.ae/arts-lifestyle/well-being/the-long-read-the-puzzling-growth-of-anxiety-in-the-modern-age

of our children in an age of pervasive social media and intensive schooling). It's reflected in new influences on modern life that require multitasking, that generate addictions to connectivity, a sensitisation to risk, and result in a constant bombardment of twenty-four-hour, sound-bite negative news. As Gornall points out, anxiety has not only become the norm, it's almost become fashionable. In his best-selling book, *My Age of Anxiety*, Scott Stossel wrote 'On ordinary days, doing ordinary things – reading a book, lying in bed, talking on the phone, sitting in a meeting, playing tennis – I have thousands of times been stricken by a pervasive sense of existential dread', and in a blog post that recently caught my eye called *Why anxiety is the plague of the modern world* the first sentence read 'Anxiety is feeling like a swarm of rats is eating your soul. Depression is feeling like it's already been eaten'.

This set me thinking about plagues, epidemics and what it meant to imply that anxiety really was a plague in the modern world[2]. One of the reasons why the plagues that swept across Europe from the tenth century onwards were so devastating was because no one at the time understood how they were caused or transmitted. They were effectively inexplicable, and so effectively unstoppable. So if we do live in times of a modern anxiety plague, why is it spreading and why aren't we stopping it? What, indeed, are the harbingers of the anxiety plague and how can we quell this epidemic? Have the causes of anxiety become so pervasive that they're now a swarm of rats eating away at our souls every minute of every day – a twenty-four-hour 'existential dread'?

Anxiety is an emotion – one that we experience like many other emotions in life. Let's be clear, emotions are not part of us simply to

2 http://www.cracked.com/blog/how-other-people-are-getting-rich-off-your-anxiety/

3

be 'felt' or 'experienced', they're not with us simply as a 'different' way of experiencing the world. Emotions have evolved as a central feature of human nature because they almost certainly serve a function – an evolutionary function. Individual emotions facilitate reproductive success or help us to identify and deal with specific challenges to reproductive fitness, and that's why, after thousands of years of human evolution, we still experience emotions. And anxiety is no exception to this.

The chapters in this book address four important questions about the role of anxiety in our modern-day world. First, what is anxiety good for? If it serves a useful purpose, surely it would be beneficial for everyone to experience it – regardless of whether they live today or lived centuries ago, and regardless of whether they're confronted by the stresses of the twenty-first century or live in peaceful retirement away from the hurly-burly of modern life?

Second, do we really experience more anxiety today than we've ever done before? It's a difficult question to answer. Who's more anxious, an eleven-year-old sitting a forty-five-minute SATs exam in 2018, or an eleven-year-old working eleven hours a day in 1840 scrambling under convulsing machinery to retrieve cotton bobs?

Thirdly, what are the brand-new shiny anxieties that the modern world has delivered to our doorsteps? Are Generations X, Y and Z experiencing anxieties that their parents will never have suffered and can hardly conceive of?

Finally, where does anxiety come from? How does that swarm of rats get into your soul – and more importantly, how does anxiety turn from a simple emotion into the many-headed beast that's a disabling diagnosable anxiety disorder, rearing its various heads as an incapacitating phobia, a panic attack, an uncontrollable worry, or an obsession or a compulsion. I hope the later chapters in this book will give you an accessible insight into how anxiety problems develop and how they can be managed. To truly conquer anxiety we need to understand how that swarm of rats gets into our soul.

The Waiting Room

Since the age of seven I've been severely dental phobic. I was taken out of class at primary school and briskly escorted across the school playground to a room painted hospital cream. In it was a large padded chair, some medical-looking instruments, and a man with a neat moustache and hair plastered strictly back across his head. Now, if you and your family enjoy a modern-day trip to the dentist, just let me finish. In those days there were no consent forms, no soothing pan-pipe music in the background, and most significantly, no anaesthetic to numb the grind of the dentist's drill as it hits your tooth. Does it sound bad already? Well, now imagine you're seven years old and have no idea what's going on. Since that day, my most intense of anxieties have been experienced in dentists' waiting rooms – whenever anyone has managed to get me into one, that is (I'm also not that keen when I meet men with neat moustaches either!).

The waiting room is an interesting phenomenon because it condenses the whole gamut of an anxious experience into those ten or fifteen minutes before the receptionist calls your name, you rise to your feet, and totter petrified to the butchery your mind has vividly invented with every tick of the waiting-room clock.

But my experience of anxiety is just one of many. Anxiety is a many-headed beast that eats its way out of your soul and appears to the world in many different forms. The waiting room is a good place to observe the forms taken by this beast. In our hypothetically constructed waiting room, let's just take a look at seven different people, each one fearful of the dentist's drill.

Amy is the first one we meet – she chats manically to everyone around her about nothing in particular.

Bruce feels sick, and is certain he's about to pass out – he thinks he's going crazy and can't seem to control what's happening to him. He has to make another trip to the toilet.

Caitlin is jittery – continuously tapping a foot on the floor to the annoyance of all the other clients. She periodically grips the magazine she's holding in her hands – the magazine she doesn't seem to be reading.

Damian is silently negotiating a string of intrusive thoughts about dentists' drills. What if the drill should slip? What if the anaesthetic fails to work? What if . . . ?

Edna can no longer stand the feelings she's experiencing, and suddenly gets up from her chair, rushes to the door, and disappears into the outside world with the door slamming behind her.

Frank has been here before – many times. But it still doesn't get any better. The flashbacks and memories are fresh and crystal clear, real, uncontrollable, and paralysing.

Gabriella stares into the middle distance, interrupted only by regular trips to the water dispenser.

These are seven faces of anxiety – yet it's best to think of them not as faces but as masks that the user can wear in the face of threat. You can see from these scenarios that those who suffer anxiety are future gazers – continually trying to define the future terrors that they believe the world will undoubtedly toss into their path.

For instance, the only way that *Amy* can cope with the events the world is about to subject her to is to babble herself into distraction by attempting to make trivial conversation about anything with anyone. She could babble incessantly as a child, but now she's found a real use for the unfettered verbosity her family used to berate her for. But it doesn't endear her to others in the waiting room, each of whom are focused on hiding behind their own masks.

In contrast, *Bruce*'s anxious thoughts crystallise into uncontrollable physical reactions. He feels nauseous and faint, as though the terror he's experiencing has decided to physically overwhelm him – just to show him who's boss and how little control he has over himself. And now, as if this were not enough, he's not just worrying about the dentist's drill, he's also worrying about how embarrassing it would be if he were to throw up in front of everyone! The more he struggles to control his mind and body, the more he feels as if he's becoming detached from himself – watching the whole terrifying affair as a depersonalised observer. He thinks he's going crazy! But he's not – he's experiencing a particular form of anxiety that manifests as a panic attack.

Caitlin's mask is a simple one, and one that many folk will wear in the face of anticipated threat or challenge. It's that contagious jig known as the 'anxiety tremble'. Her body is gripped by a convulsive tremble driven by the adrenaline pumping through her veins. She can feel her arms, hands, legs, feet, sides, chest, back and head shaking and vibrating. She can feel it, so she believes that everyone else must be able to see it, and to disguise her trembling she jigs her leg, taps her feet and rhythmically squeezes the life out of the magazine in her hand. And it's not just the outside of her body – she can feel her stomach trembling, and if she knew exactly where it was, she'd even say her liver was shaking! Caitlin's body is reacting to the physical threat of the dentist's drill, tightening her muscles so they're more resilient to damage – it's a natural part of our fight-fright-flight response to physical threats. But that's cold comfort to Caitlin right now.

Damian is the worrier. 'I'm a born worrier,' he tells everyone at the earliest opportunity. That's not because he's proud of this talent, but because he has to explain to everyone that they mustn't try to stop him worrying. He feels he has to worry otherwise the trillion bad things he's worked out in his head might happen – no, will indeed happen! Contrary to what he proclaims, he wasn't a worrier born with the words 'what if . . . ?' on his lips, but he's practised his worrying so incessantly it's now so automatic he has no option but to succumb to the stream of intrusive thoughts queuing to enter his head during every waking day. It's exhausting work!

Some of the anxiety masks are attempts to cover up uncontrollable mental and physical reactions to the dentist's drill, but other masks represent active attempts to cope with the impending horror. *Edna*'s is one of the most typical coping responses, but one that looks quite extreme in the context of the waiting room as she jumps up and runs out of the door. How might you eliminate the impending horror of the dentist's drill? Why not run away? Avoidance is the solution of choice for many anxiety sufferers – but it represents a very sharp, double-edged sword. Avoiding what you fear simply feeds the beast called anxiety, and the beast merely grows bigger and bigger!

Frank is slightly different to our other clients in the waiting room. Frank is the only one who's previously had frightening and painful dental experiences – a string of them in fact, all with different dentists. They've left him experiencing nightmares that interrupt his sleep and vivid flashbacks that force him to relive the sights, sounds and feelings of his previous traumas. Now every time he visits the dentist's waiting room he suffers these uncontrollable terrifying flashbacks. Frank's condition is so much like post-traumatic stress disorder (PTSD) that some experts have even suggested a name for it – post-traumatic dental-care anxiety (PTDA)[3]!

3 Bracha, H. S., Vega, E. M. & Vega, C. B. (2006) 'Posttraumatic dental-care anxiety (PTDA): Is "dental phobia" a misnomer?' *Hawaiian Dental Journal*, 37, 17–19.

Finally we have *Gabriella*, who experiences anxiety in a very particular way – she has a dry mouth and continually feels the urge to drink water. For me, as life has gone on and I've learned to cope with many kinds of potentially anxiety-provoking situations, I often think of myself now as a non-anxious person. But I know that I'm lying to myself, because no matter who you are, there will always be events and situations that will cause you to anticipate the possibility of difficult threats or challenges – and that, by definition, is anxiety. So for me, nowadays a dry mouth is the only way I know I'm experiencing anxiety. Have you ever found yourself repeatedly taking that water bottle from your bag and sipping from it? Yes? Then maybe you're anxious.

These are common manifestations of anxiety – the masks that anxious people wear. You can see from these examples that they're a mixture of active responding to the threat ahead and a resigned acceptance of the physical and mental reactions to those threats – in the latter case, it's an acceptance that requires a lot of work to hide what seem like embarrassing symptoms from the eyes of others. Anxiety appears in these many different forms, but they're all called 'anxiety' – so what exactly is anxiety, and is it just a curse imposed on us by an unforgiving world, or does it really have a purpose?

What in Hell *Is* Anxiety?

Before we can begin to understand anxiety, we have to understand what fear is. Fear is a very basic emotion, and many of our fear reactions to *immediate* threats are reflexive responses that have been biologically pre-wired over many thousands of years of selective evolution. You're bound to be familiar with these basic fear reactions. The sudden startle reactions and physiological arousal as a result of things like loud noises, looming shadows, sudden sharp pain, rapid

9

movements towards you, and even staring eyes![4] We all get startled by loud noises at firework displays (and so do our dogs and cats); attention is immediately grabbed when we see an animal darting backwards and forwards in our peripheral vision, and how weird is that rush of adrenaline when we dare to look up when riding on the Tube and see someone sitting opposite staring at us. You don't learn these reactions, you're born with them – but did you spot the common link between all those diverse triggers for our startle response?

If you did, you'd know that many of the triggers are characteristics possessed by most predatory animals when they're about to pounce – the looming shadow, the rapid movement towards you, and the staring eyes as the predator fixates its prey. With survival against predators being a very urgent business indeed, pre-wired reflexive responses that make you alert to and avoid these physical threats have evolved. And evolution is a very efficient process, so it wouldn't necessarily give you built-in reflexes that respond to every individual predator you might possibly encounter, but it selects out those characteristics that are common to most predators and provides you with immediate reactions to these universal features. But if evolution has only provided us with generalised responses to predators, why is it that some people become distressingly fearful of specific animals, such as spiders or snakes? More of that in later chapters.

All of that is fear, but anxiety is a little different. The modern world is made up of many more potential threats and challenges than the threat posed by predatory animals and their like, so we've developed a more flexible system for managing potential threats, and this is what anxiety is. Anxiety isn't a response to immediate threats (like avoiding a charging bull in a field), but a response to future

4 Russell, P. A. (1979) 'Fear-evoking stimuli', in W. Sluckin (Ed.) *Fear in Animals and Man*. New York: Van Nostrand Reinhold.

anticipated threats (like a surgical operation you're due to have in the next few months). It's a bit like fear, but with enough added bells and whistles to fill a book like this! So what is this many-headed beast called anxiety?

Most of us seem to understand what other people mean when they use the word 'anxiety', and most people also seem to know when they're experiencing anxiety. So at the very least, anxiety must be a socially constructed label that conveys some form of meaning between those who use the term. But let's be honest, there's still a real lack of consensus amongst experts and researchers about what kind of *thing* anxiety actually is. By thing, I mean 'Is it something that has a specific location in the brain?', 'Is it an emotion that we feel, in the same way that we can feel sad, for example?', or 'Is it a learnt set of responses that we deploy whenever we're confronted by an anticipated threat or challenge?' The most recognised approach to understanding anxiety is that it's a rather complex emotion, but it's one that has a rather awkward place within the study of emotions – suggesting that we're still not quite sure what it is.

For example, in a special issue of the journal *Emotion Review* in 2011, psychologists Jessica Tracy and Daniel Randles asked some of the most influential modern-day emotion researchers to define their list of basic emotions[5]. Surprisingly, none included anxiety in their lists, and only one, Carroll Izard, mentioned anxiety in their article at all. Why is that surprising, you might ask? Well, from a clinical perspective, it's astounding that anxiety as an emotion receives such little scientific acknowledgement. We are becoming more aware each year that anxiety-based problems are a significant mental health issue. For instance, clinical projections suggest that

5 Tracy, J. L. & Randles, D. (2011) Four models of basic emotions: A review of Ekman and Cordaro, Izard, Levenson, and Panksepp and Watt. *Emotion Review*, 3, 397–405.

in the late 2010s around 30–40 per cent of individuals in Western societies will develop a problem that is anxiety-related and will need treatment for this at some point in their lives[6]. So it's clear that when anxiety becomes a problem it imposes a high individual and social burden, it tends to be more chronic than many other psychological problems, and can be as disabling as a physical illness. In the UK alone, more than eight million people suffer from anxiety disorders which is estimated to cost the country £10 billion a year[7] (that's roughly equivalent to providing 1.5 million state pensions a year). Much of this continuing increase in the prevalence of anxiety as a mental health problem has been attributed to changes in modern lifestyles that have led to more stress and pressure being placed on people – and we'll examine that in detail in Chapters 2 and 3.

So, we know for sure that anxiety is out there with a vengeance, so why are emotion researchers so reticent to acknowledge it as a common and fundamental emotion? The answer probably lies in two important facts, and these facts give us some insight into why anxiety is such a slippery customer when it comes to defining it and understanding it.

First, try and imagine yourself feeling anxious or try to recall an instance when you were anxious. Now, what was your facial expression at that time? Most basic emotions are characterised by very distinctive and easily recognisable facial expressions – examples are fear, disgust, surprise, anger, happiness to name just a few. But there's little or no consensus about what represents a characteristic facial expression for anxiety. Just go back and have a look through the descriptions of anxiety exhibited by our clients in the waiting room –

6 Shepherd, M., Cooper, B., Brown, A. & Kalton, C. W. (1996). *Psychiatric Illness in General Practice*. London: Oxford University Press.
7 http://www.telegraph.co.uk/news/health/news/10200562/Anxiety-disorders-cost-10-billion-a-year.html

are there any obvious facial expressions that would be associated with any of these manifestations of anxiety? Whatever you come up with, I think you'd be severely challenged to be able to identify anxiety purely from a facial expression. Studies that have investigated the facial expressions of highly anxious people have tended to find that they don't have a particular facial expression, but they exhibit more facial movements, more eye blinks, 'non-enjoyment' smiles, and raised brows that are drawn together (frowns)[8]. The accepted view of this is that all of these expressions represent attenuated forms of other emotional facial expressions such as fear, disgust, sadness and anger, and one conclusion is that anxiety is a hybrid emotion that 'hijacks' expressions from other, more basic, emotions.

One compelling reason for why this happens is because most basic emotions represent in-built, reflexive reactions to relatively briefly presented stimuli – fear to the sudden noise, surprise to the face at the window, happiness to the sight of a close friend, anger in response to a critical remark. In contrast, anxiety is an emotion generated in anticipation of an event not as a reaction to an event – and this anticipated event could be months, or even years away. Given that your anxiety can hang around for so long waiting for the anticipated event, it's perhaps not surprising that you'll also feel elements of other emotions during this time. Sadness that you've felt anxious for so long, anger that you've been confronted with this threat or challenge, and of course, fear when you think of what the outcome of that threat or challenge might be. Depending on how that anticipated event is represented in your head at any one time is likely to trigger more basic emotions and the responses and facial expressions associated with those emotions.

8 Harrigan, J. A. & O'Connell, D. M. (1996) 'How do you look when feeling anxious? Facial displays of anxiety.' *Personality & Individual Differences*, 21, 205–212.

Furthermore, what's also perplexing about anxiety as a coherently experienced emotion is that there appears to be no physical basis for the existence of an entity called 'anxiety'. That is, you won't be able to point to any specific area of the brain and say 'this is a brain area where only anxiety is generated'. To be fair, this is also true of many other emotions. Kristen Lindquist and colleagues from the University of North Carolina have argued that there's no consistent evidence for particular brain locations for many of the basic emotions, including fear, anger, sadness, disgust and happiness[9]. They found that every brain region that was activated for at least one basic emotion was also activated for at least one other basic emotion.

In the case of anxiety, functional neuroimaging studies show that a number of anxiety disorders with quite different symptoms are associated with activation of specific brain areas such as the amygdala and insular[10]. The amygdala is an almond-shaped structure located deep within the temporal lobes of the brain and performs a primary role in processing memories and decision-making in relation to fear. It's considered a key element in the human alarm system, and facilitates attention to incoming emotional information, and assigns emotional value to stimuli. Its projections to the brainstem evoke autonomic threat responses and initiate the release of stress hormones, and in this way it plays a pivotal role in determining fear and anxiety responses[11].

9 Lindquist, K. A., Wager, T. D., Kober, H., Bliss-Moreau, E. & Barrett, L. F. (2012) 'The brain basis of emotion: A meta-analytic review.' *Behavioral & Brain Sciences*, 35, 121–202.

10 Etkin, A. & Wager, T. D. (2007) 'Functional neuroimaging of anxiety: A meta-analysis of emotional processing in PTSD, social anxiety disorder, and specific phobia.' *American Journal of Psychiatry*, 164, 1476–1488.

11 Shin, L. M. & Liberzon, I. (2010) 'The neurocircuitry of fear, stress, and anxiety disorders.' *Neuropsychopharmacology: Official Publication of the American College of Neuropsychopharmacology*, 35, 169–191.

The insular cortex is located in the cerebral cortex and plays a diverse role in the experience of emotions. Its functions include perception, motor control and self-awareness, amongst others. Involvement of just these two brain areas alone tells you something about what a complex business it is for the brain to generate anxiety and anxiety experiences. However, rather than being specific to anxiety, these two areas are also activated during the experience of many other negative emotions, particularly fear and disgust. In effect, no brain areas have been consistently identified that appear to be specific solely to the processing of stimuli and events that give rise to the experience of anxiety, and this is a testimony to the complexity of the biological and cognitive processes needed to generate anxiety.

As you can see from this discussion, evidence for anxiety as a physical entity with a distinct and unique neural location continues to be elusive. This suggests that anxiety may not be a hard-wired physical brain entity at all, but a collection of responses and feelings opportunistically harvested from other more basic emotions. They are then thrown together in our desperate attempts to deal with the diverse collection of anticipated threats and challenges posed by the modern world. If this is so, then anxiety is almost certainly an emotion that is in part learnt during the individual's lifetime, and not wholly an innate one.

While you can think of fear as a bunch of reflexes evolved to deal effectively with immediate threats, anxiety is best conceived as an emotion that does have a basis in the motivational systems devoted to fear, but develops into a broader 'precautionary system' by adding further higher-level cognitive activities to these reflexes. For instance, the basic fear ingredients involved in anxiety include heart rate increases, cortical arousal, high autonomic nervous system reactivity, and partial freezing and inhibition of ongoing responses. To these fundamental defining features are then added a range of basic psychological processes that influence attentional focus, and cautious, defensive interpretations of ongoing events[12]. These higher-level cognitive processes involved in anxiety have a number of effects that result in us being much more cautious in what we think and what we do. For example, when we're anxious our attention becomes drawn towards potential threats, we are more likely to interpret ambiguous events as being threatening, we deploy reasoning processes that maintain threatening interpretations of events, and we adopt a much more systematic way of making decisions rather than jumping to conclusions about things. In this way, anxiety becomes a mixture of ingredients, some of which are quite specific to threat and fear, but others of which are representative of more general psychological processes that serve many functional purposes other than just resolving threats (such as attentional, perceptual and decision-making processes). This latter fact is probably the reason why it's so difficult to identify a specific brain area or pathway dedicated to anxiety – because anxiety uses a broad range of brain processes, many of which are also used for purposes other than dealing with threats and challenges.

The fact that anxiety is a hybrid emotion built out of a combination of fear reflexes and higher-level cognitive processes suggests two important things. First, that anxiety is almost certainly a learnt emotion rather than an innate one. For example, your developmental experiences will probably determine the kinds of responses and feelings that you'll eventually include under the term 'anxiety', and which are activated when future threats and challenges are perceived. Some people will become worriers when confronted with anticipated threats, others will become avoiders, depending on how successful

12 Ouimet, A. J., Gawronski, B. & Dozois, D. J. A. (2009) 'Cognitive vulnerability to anxiety: A review and integrative model.' *Clinical Psychology Review*, 29, 459–470.

they believe these strategies have been in helping them to deal with threats in the past, or how such responses have been modelled for them in the past (see Chapter 4 on this). Different people will also evolve quite different conceptions of what a threat or a challenge is. Some will have a very narrow conception, and so experience anxiety much less than those who develop a much broader conception of threats and challenges. Given that this learning process may differ significantly across individuals, this leads to the second point, that anxiety will mean different things to different people and will be experienced differently by different people. We can see this in one form in our sample clients in the waiting room. Anxiety is expressed differently in each of them. For some of them, the basic elements of fear make up the anxiety response they exhibit (e.g. increased physiological arousal); for others, specific cognitive elements are prominent (e.g. worrying).

But this learning process doesn't mean that you can pick and choose the way in which you develop your conception of anxiety, nor does it mean that it's something you can control by turning it on and off when required. Anxiety develops into what psychologists call a 'cognitive schema'[13]. A schema is a high-level conceptual structure or network in the brain that enables rapid, effective and efficient responding to important everyday situations. Your own anxiety 'schema' could be activated by almost anything that you've identified as being threat-related, such as your own physiological changes associated with threat (your heart rate increasing, beginning to perspire), suddenly evoked memories of future threatening or challenging events, or simply appraising something as being potentially threatening or problematic. Once triggered, the anxiety schema is rapidly and automatically activated, and this gives rise to

13 Izard, C. E. (2007) 'Basic emotions, natural kinds, emotion schemas, and a new paradigm.' *Perspectives on Psychological Science*, 2, 260–269.

that 'gut' feeling of anxiety that we each experience as individuals. Imagine this as a champagne cascade. Once you've started pouring bottles of champagne into the glass at the top of the pyramid, it becomes impossible to stop it cascading down to the glasses below. That's the same with the brain network associated with your own anxiety schema in which all the elements within the network (physiological and cognitive) become activated automatically, effortlessly, and instantaneously. But unlike non-human animals, who are usually able to restore normal functioning after threat has passed, humans can often find themselves locked into the same recurring pattern of neural activation[14]. You have little or no conscious control over that, and it's one of the things that makes the experience of anxiety a negative and often repetitive one.

What's the Difference Between Anxiety and Stress?

Many people ask me what the difference is between anxiety and stress, so it's worth discussing that briefly here given that much of this book concerns the effects of our modern society on anxiety as a psychological and psychiatric disorder and on stress as a physical and emotional reaction. First, let's be clear, both anxiety and stress have their origins in the threats and challenges we experience in our everyday lives, and many people use the terms anxiety and stress interchangeably[15]. In everyday use, stress does tend to be associated more with physical and physiological reactions to life's threats and challenges, including constant feelings of arousal, high blood pressure, muscle tension, rapid breathing, chest pains, hot flushes and panic attacks.

14 Kozlowska, K., Walker, P., McLean, L. & Carrive, P. (2015) 'Fear and the defense cascade: Clinical implications and management.' *Harvard Review of Psychiatry*, 23, 263–287.

15 https://www.psychologytoday.com/blog/the-dance-connection/200910/fear-vs-anxiety

In contrast, anxiety is a term associated with both physiological and cognitive elements as we've already described. Much of what we experience as stress is 'acute stress' in that it's short term and goes away quickly, like when we have an impending deadline at work or a fierce argument with our partner. It reflects that immediate physiological element that we associate with anxiety and helps us to manage difficult and dangerous situations.

Anxiety has a much broader remit. It can be viewed as an adaptive and helpful emotion (see below), but in its more chronic form it can develop into complex and disabling 'anxiety disorders' – disorders that take many different forms (see Chapter 4). I prefer to view stress as an immediate reaction to an existing stressor that primarily reflects the intense physiological elements of the anxiety schema. In contrast, anxiety can be both short term and long term, and can persist even after the initial threats and challenges that triggered the anxiety have gone.

Why Be Anxious?

In our discussion of the waiting room we've seen the many faces of anxiety – and none of these manifestations seem to be ones that these patients are enjoying. In fact, quite the contrary, all of our cases find some if not all of the experience distressing. I've talked of the 'manifestations of anxiety' as if anxiety were a vampire that had been accidentally released from the cellars to stalk the community and seek out its prey – a no-good monster consuming the lifeblood of any unfortunate victim it encounters. But we've seen that simply isn't what happens. Those people sitting in the waiting room may look like victims, and they all appear distressed by their circumstances and their reactions – but anxiety is not entirely a 'baddie'. Just as the evil Darth Vader was once the heroic Jedi Knight Anakin Skywalker before being seduced by the dark side of the Force, anxiety too has a past as a well-intentioned, benevolent hero.

What's That Over There?

So what advantages does anxiety bring? First, anxiety is associated with some important shifts in attention to events and the way you process information. When you feel anxious, you'll automatically preferentially allocate attention to things you find potentially threatening (such as someone frowning who is crossing the road and walking towards you), or to information that's threatening (for example, details on a TV programme describing increases in crime in your area). This shift in attention to things that may be threatening occurs automatically and pre-consciously – that is, when you're anxious your attention will have shifted to focus on the threat before you realise it's happened.[16] This is one of anxiety's many double-edged swords. This attention shift has the advantage of keeping you alert and focused on potential threats, and this increases the opportunity for you to nullify or avoid the threat. But it can also get you into a vicious cycle because attending automatically to things that might be threats will also increase your anxiety! For many people, the effect of this vicious cycle can be difficult to manage and for some is one source of chronic anxiety.

Another consequence of this attentional bias to threat is that it also affects how you interpret events around you. Much of what we encounter in our everyday lives is ambiguous. By that, I mean many things are not obviously positive or negative, benign or threatening – we have to make some additional judgements to decide whether something is good or bad for us. Let's imagine you overhear a friend saying that your speech at a recent wedding reception had made her giggle. Good thing or bad thing? Well, it's ambiguous. She may have loved your speech because it made her laugh, or

16 Mogg, K. & Bradley, B. P. (1998) 'A cognitive-motivational analysis of anxiety.' *Behaviour Research and Therapy*, 36, 809–848.

she may have giggled out of embarrassment because it was so bad. However, if you hear this remark while feeling anxious, you'll have a strong tendency automatically to accept the negative interpretation[17]. In an evolutionary or adaptive sense, anxiety is doing you a favour here. It's making you alert to potential threats and that will enable you to focus on dealing with them. But psychologically it can be pretty emotionally demanding, because this process will also make you interpret many things as threats that turn out not to be threats (i.e. you've interpreted them negatively when they are in fact benign).

These basic information-processing biases that are associated with anxiety are now recognised as a significant cause of prolonged, chronic anxiety states in many people, and clinical psychologists have recently been engaged in developing experimental procedures to neutralise these biases. This computer-based training is known as *attention bias modification (ABM)* and attempts to train anxious individuals to attend more rapidly to non-threatening words or stimuli than to threatening material[18].

Anxiety – What Is It Good For?

So, does anxiety actually work in practice? Does feeling anxious really bestow practical, adaptive advantages? Well, yes, it seems it does. William Lee, a psychiatrist at London's Institute of Psychiatry, looked at the lives of 5,362 people born in 1946. He discovered that those who exhibited high levels of anxiety (based on ratings by their teachers when they were thirteen years old) were significantly less

17 Eysenck, M. W., Mogg, K., May, J., Richards, A., & Mathews, A. (1991). 'Bias in interpretation of ambiguous sentences related to threat in anxiety.' *Journal of Abnormal Psychology*, 100, 144–150.

18 MacLeod, C. & Mathews, A. (2012). 'Cognitive bias modification approaches to anxiety.' *Annual Review of Clinical Psychology*, 8, 189–217.

likely to die an accidental death than those with low anxiety[19]. Only 0.1 per cent of the anxious individuals died accidentally compared with 0.72 per cent of the non-anxious individuals. There was no difference between the two groups on the number of non-accidental deaths. But here swings anxiety's double-edged sword again. After twenty-five years of age, the anxious individuals started to exhibit higher mortality rates due to illness-related deaths than their non-anxious counterparts. Lee and his colleagues concluded that their results 'suggest there are survival benefits of increased trait anxiety in early adult life, but these may be balanced by corresponding survival deficits in later life associated with medical problems'. What anxiety gives with one hand, it takes away with the other.

But there is a clear evolutionary benefit here. Anxiety helps people survive potential accidental deaths until they're well into early adulthood – a time when they're likely to be at their reproductive peak. This means they're more likely to survive to early adulthood to reproduce successfully than non-anxious individuals, and so their genes are more likely to survive into future generations. But once you've propagated your genes into future generations, anxiety then cares little for you and you're more likely to die of other medical ailments than the non-anxious individual.

In another series of studies, psychologists Tsachi Ein-Dor and Orgad Tal from the Interdisciplinary Center Herzliya in Israel conducted a number of imaginative experiments on worriers and highly anxious individuals. First, they found that worriers sense threats – such as detecting the smell of smoke – much faster than their

19 Lee, W. E., Wadsworth, M. E. J. & Hotopf, M. (2006) 'The protective role of trait anxiety: A longitudinal cohort study.' *Psychological Medicine*, 36, 345–351.

non-anxious counterparts[20]. In a second experiment, they found that highly anxious individuals are also much less likely to get distracted when attempting to deal with a potential threat or problem[21]. In this latter experiment, participants were asked to complete a computer assignment but the program developed a virus, which the participant was told they had activated (they actually hadn't, it was automatically activated as part of the experiment!), they were then told they should seek technical support urgently. As they tried to do this they were presented with a number of additional 'obstacles' such as a student dropping a stack of papers at their feet, and another asking them to complete a survey. Anxious participants were the least likely to be distracted by these challenges, and were more likely to get the required technical support quickest.

Just as we found with anxiety, worry too has two quite different sides to its character. While worry maintains your awareness of forthcoming dangers and helps you to think through possible solutions to deal with the danger, it too has negative longer-term effects. In a study entitled 'Is Worrying Bad for Your Heart?', Laura Kubzansky and colleagues asked 1,759 men free of chronic heart disease in 1975 to complete a questionnaire asking the extent to which they worried about each of five worry domains: social conditions, health, financial, self-definition and ageing[22]. Over the following twenty years they recorded the incidence of heart disease. They found a

20 Ein-Dor, T., Mikulincer, M. & Shaver, P. R. (2011) 'Effective reaction to danger: Attachment insecurities predict behavioural reactions to an experimentally induced threat above and beyond general personality traits.' *Social Psychology & Personality Science*, 2, 467–473.

21 Ein-Dor, T. & Tal, O. (2012) 'Scared saviors: Evidence that people high in attachment anxiety are more effective in alerting others to threat.' *European Journal of Social Psychology*, 42, 667–671.

22 Kubzansky, L. D., Kawachi, I., Spiro, A., Weiss, S. T., Vokonas, P. S. & Sparrow, D. (1997) 'Is worrying bad for your heart?' *Circulation*, 95, doi. org/10.1161/01.CIR.95.4.818.

significant relationship between worry severity and the subsequent risk of chronic heart disease, and in elderly men worrying predicted the risk of a second heart attack after having already experienced a first attack. A further study investigating the psychological effects of the 9/11 terror attacks in New York found that in those US citizens exhibiting extreme stress after the attacks, ongoing worries about terrorism predicted cardiovascular health problems up to two and three years after the attack[23].

And it's not just a heightened risk of cardiovascular problems that's associated with anxiety. A study that recently tracked 15,938 Britons over forty years of age found that men who had a lifelong diagnosis of Generalised Anxiety Disorder were 2.15 times more likely to die of cancer than those without the anxiety diagnosis – even when factors that are likely to cause cancer, such as age, alcohol consumption, smoking, and chronic disease were accounted for[24]. It's not clear from the study what the exact link is between anxiety and cancer, but it's clear that we need to consider anxiety as a warning signal for poor health in later life.

The story seems to be a consistent one. Yes, anxiety and its associated features such as worry do appear to have real, measurable adaptive benefits. They help you keep future dangers in mind; they give you the ability to process information automatically in a way that will maintain your focus on these dangers – often in a single-minded way; and productive worry may even help you find solutions to deal with the dangers and threats. To bolster these positive aspects of anxiety, there's evidence of real, practical benefits to these processes

23 Holman, E. A., Silver, R. C., Poulin, M., Andersen, J., Gil-Rivas, V., & McIntosh, D. N. (2008) 'Terrorism, acute stress, and cardiovascular health: A 3-year national study following the September 11th attacks.' *Archives of General Psychiatry*, 65, 73–80.
24 http://medicalxpress.com/news/2016-09-men-anxiety-die-cancer.html

in the form of fewer accidental deaths amongst anxious individuals in young adulthood. But anxiety cares little about you as you get older. There is an increased health-related mortality in older anxious individuals as well as a higher risk of specific illnesses such as cardiovascular disease. My suspicion is that, once you're older, anxiety will have assumed it's already done its job, so cares rather less about you than when you were a young adult. In evolutionary terms, the selective impact of anxiety is likely to be highest when it comes to ensuring that each individual can propagate his or her genes successfully. So anxiety will keep you alive until an age where you're most likely to have produced offspring[25]. Then its job is done! It's as if a lifetime of high anxiety shifts most of the positive effects of your life energy into the early half of your life, only to leave you to burn out prematurely in the latter half.

To the Point

In this chapter we've reviewed some of the complexities of the anxiety emotion. I've described many of the ways in which anxiety can manifest itself, and then I've tried to pin down exactly what anxiety is. Well, a simple description of the anxiety emotion is elusive because at least part of what we each understand as anxiety is something we learn during our lifetime – and we each learn this differently, and so we each experience anxiety slightly differently. Anxiety is an evolved emotion, which means it has a purpose. It makes us more attentive to challenges and dangers, and it makes us more cautious in our decisions. One concrete outcome of this is that the anxious person is less

---

25 The age of first-time parents has risen significantly in the past few decades. In the UK in 2014 the average age of a first-time mother was twenty-eight years of age, and a first-time father was thirty-two years of age. But these are still ages where the heightened risk of anxiety-related mortality is likely to be very low.

likely to die an accidental death – at least before the age of twenty-five! But lifelong anxiety has no pity, and it predicts increased mortality from a range of illnesses, including cardiovascular disease and cancer, and in our modern-day society we need to be aware of anxiety as a warning signal for poor health in later life.

CHAPTER TWO

The New Anxieties of the Modern Age

'Today, gone are the obvious sources of anxiety – the wild beasts, famines, uncontrollable diseases and (since 1945, at least) the global wars that once scythed us down on an industrial scale.'

— Jonathan Gornall (2015)

A century ago there were no nuclear weapons, and so no anxieties about nuclear annihilation. But in 1945 a new anxiety was created by the destruction of two Japanese cities by nuclear bombs as World War II drew to a close. This was only the beginning. After the end of the war came the Cold War – a state of tension between the Soviet Union and its satellite states and the Western Bloc consisting of the United States and its NATO allies. These two superpowers never actually engaged directly in full-scale hostilities but stockpiled huge arsenals of nuclear weapons and conducted thousands of nuclear tests between 1945 and 1992. For almost fifty years the world lived in the shadow of the doctrine of 'mutually assured destruction' – the belief that an all-out nuclear war would lead to the total destruction of both attacker and attacked, lay to waste much of the civilised world, and leave little hope of survival for those living in the regions that were likely targets for such attacks.

But even though countries still possess nuclear weapons today, fears of nuclear annihilation began to dissipate after the collapse of the Soviet Union in 1991, and a poll of Americans in 2010 found that only one in three feared that nuclear war would put an end to humanity – the remainder believed that humanity's demise would be the result of such things as a deadly virus, global warming, an asteroid hitting the earth, or even the second coming of Jesus Christ![1] So even a nuclear apocalypse is not the pervasive anxiety it used to be. But what's the 'nuclear bomb' of the twenty-first century, the invention or the 'new thing' that captures and propagates our anxieties?

Traditional sources of anxiety are things like health, relationships, unemployment, poverty and disadvantage, loneliness, and exposure to violence, trauma and conflict. But has our modern world created its own demons that fuel our worries and pump the cortisol around our bodies – demons that our ancestors would never have encountered because those demons have never existed before?

It's tempting just to look for specific examples of modern fears, and in a multidisciplinary collection of papers presented at the grandiosely named 2nd Global Fears & Anxieties Conference in 2015, the conveners noted that 'gun crime, gender equality, terrorism, technology, black holes, Ebola virus and the return of the dead can all be seen to produce fear and anxiety in the contemporary Western world'![2] You're probably a little bemused – black holes and return of the dead as typical modern-day anxieties? We'll come to that later! But there is one development in the twenty-first century that connects the realities of gun crime and terrorism with the improbable threats of black holes and the walking dead, and this is the ultra-connectivity

1 https://ropercenter.cornell.edu/public-opinion-using-nuclear-weapons/
2 http://www.interdisciplinarypress.net/product/theres-more-to-fear-than-fear-itself-fears-and-anxieties-in-the-21st-century/

provided by the Internet and other instantaneous forms of com-munication. Thanks to the Internet and our smartphones we are all instantaneously connected to almost everything. We avidly subscribe to news alerts, lest we miss out on something that our friends, family and colleagues know about before us – this is the new twenty-first century angst state called FOMO – fear of missing out. We check our phones before we go to sleep and it's also the first thing we do when we wake – it's 24/7 compulsive connectivity. Many of us have an addiction to the Internet and what it can access to the point where this behaviour bears all the hallmarks of a clinical addiction – we can't control it, it controls us, and we experience symptoms such as mood modification, the need for more tolerance, with-drawal, and relapse – just like we would to a drug we're dependent on[3]. Perpetual connectivity of this kind has a number of important consequences.

First, we're bombarded by so-called 'breaking news'. We're aware of things happening in the world often before they've happened. As Carolyn Gregoire wrote in the *Huffington Post*, 'Thanks to the 24-hour news cycle, alerts of shootings, plane crashes, ISIS behead-ings, crime, war and human rights violations are constant – and this incessant news of violence and destruction may be messing with our head. The world isn't falling apart, but it can sure feel like it.'[4] This is in part because the media have evolved ways of bringing the news directly into our kitchens and bedrooms, and then sensationally elab-orating on the dearth of real facts that often accompanies breaking news, being over-ready to create doomsday plots and hypothetical

3 Kuss, D. J., Lopez-Fernandez, O. (2016) 'Internet addiction and prob-lematic Internet use: A systematic review of clinical research.' *World Journal of Psychiatry*, 6, 1, 143–176.

4 http://www.huffingtonpost.com/2015/02/19/violent-media-anxiety_n_6671732.html

'what if . . . ?' scenarios that can ruthlessly expand our anxieties into fears of global, catastrophic proportions.

Second, the Internet is not an encyclopaedia conveniently providing all the neat facts of the known universe when we open up our web browser. It's a place that's bulging with emotive comments, bigotry, simplistic opinions, and – in today's modern parlance – fake news and fake facts. As the Roman Emperor Marcus Aurelius is supposed to have commented two millennia ago, 'Everything we hear is an opinion, not a fact, and everything we see is a perspective and not a truth.' That's certainly how we should treat the Internet. If you're searching for a 'truth' on the Internet, like many people often are, you're likely to end up stymied, frazzled, despondent and stressed by a plethora of inconsistent, contradictory and incomplete views, many of which will be actively peddling either fear or fads. As BBC columnist Nick Bryant rather succinctly pointed out, the Internet and social media were initially trumpeted as the ultimate tool for bringing people together. But they've actually become 'a forum for cynicism, division and a variety of outlandish conspiracy theories'[5] – devices for dividing more than uniting.

Third, the Internet provides a false escape from the challenges of contemporary living and offers a proxy for real life in the form of solitary pastimes such as Internet gaming and pornography, and in doing so, this escape creates its own problems. For example, as we're told in many TV adverts, winning money through convenient online betting is now as easy as clicking on the 'cash out' icon of the betting app on your smartphone. But this form of gambling is known to cause addiction problems for some Internet gamblers, and is predicted to cause even more related psychological problems in

5 https://www.bbc.co.uk/news/amp/world-us-canada-41826022

the future, especially as young gamblers take up online gambling[6]. Despite this, the Internet can undoubtedly be a distraction from the stresses and strains of everyday life, and adolescents and many teenagers in particular play computer games and surf the Internet to cope with everyday stressors and regulate their emotions. But as a consequence, excessive Internet use in adolescents may affect their ability to learn other ways of coping with stress – especially more active methods of coping that involve directly tackling a problem[7]. I'd certainly advocate that learning how to cope actively with stress is arguably a more important life skill than learning how to avoid it.

Fourth, the Internet provides a wealth of opportunities, but with that wealth of opportunities comes a web of complexities that add to our stresses. We can open up our browser and shop for almost anything we desire – and get it delivered the same day if we're desperate enough. We can access our utilities accounts, download our telecommunications bills and transfer funds across our bank accounts, all very simply and immediately. But these transactions can begin to seem strangely distant, and this cyber-distance turns into light years of frustration and stress when we try to do something outside of the system. As Nitsuh Abebe pointed out in the *New York Times*, 'You can argue with a store owner; you can't argue with the call-centre representative of the company contracted to maintain the point-of-sale machine owned by the other company contracted by the multinational conglomerate that owns the store'[8]! How often

6 Gainsbury, S. M. (2015) 'Online gambling addiction: The relationship between Internet gambling and disordered gambling.' *Current Addiction Reports*, 2, 185–193.

7 Kuss, D. J., Dunn, T. J., Wolfling, K., Muller, K. W. et al. (2017) 'Excessive internet use and psychopathology: The role of coping.' *Clinical Neuropsychiatry*, 14, 73–81.

8 https://www.nytimes.com/2017/04/18/magazine/americas-new-anxiety-disorder.html

have we been sucked into that particular black hole and longed for the simple opportunity to release our stress by marching down to the store and shouting at a real live sales representative? In this modern world, it's the unfortunate cat sitting next to you and your laptop that are likely to get the stick!

The perpetual connectivity of the Internet isn't a physical threat in the same way as a nuclear bomb, gun crime, terrorism, a black hole – or even the walking dead. It's worse than that. It's a communication conduit to and from everything. To things you wanted to know about, and things you didn't know you wanted to know about but have been seduced into believing you do. What's worse, it's a communication conduit that allows every pernicious element that has access to a computer or smartphone to spam you, phish you, hack you, stalk you, defraud you, groom you and troll you. The Internet demands that you have to know what's going on; the Internet also demands that you beware of it – that sounds like a traditional approach-avoidance conflict ripe for inducing stress. But what is arguably worse than that is that it demands our attention the moment we wake and throughout the day until we decide it's going to allow us to sleep. In addition, the complexities of our new cyber world also require us to multitask – switching from email, to Twitter, to Facebook, to Instagram, an occasional Google search, and then a WhatsApp discussion – and all this within the context of our necessary daily interactions with the so-called real world. We're not a part of the Matrix – we are the Matrix!

The Stresses of Perpetual Connectivity

When I got my first lecturing job, students would sit in lectures with a pen and a notebook, writing down every fact I uttered and copying the badly drawn figures displayed on my scrappy acetates. Nowadays they sit in lectures with tablets and laptops accessing the

PowerPoint presentation that's already been loaded onto the module's virtual learning environment and tapping notes directly onto their hard drives.

Or at least I thought that's what they did. It was only when I sat at the back of a lecture theatre when I was peer-reviewing a colleague's teaching that I saw what the row of students in front of me was actually doing. Two were online shopping, two were posting on Facebook, and one was emailing a friend. One even left the lecture midway through to answer a call on her smartphone! Connectivity is all pervading, and it's demanding – we have to do it right now, and that requires multitasking. In particular, media multitasking in younger people is dramatically on the increase with almost half of young people between the ages of eight and eighteen saying they multitask either 'some of the time' or 'most of the time'[9]. This may sound familiar to most of us – surfing the web, while listening to music, with the TV on, while sending a text, when we're doing work[10]!

In his book, *Cybercognition*, Lee Hadlington points out that such frequent media multitasking is associated with poorer capacity to ignore information, distraction proneness, and attentional failures. He also highlights the rise of the 'Zombie Smartphone User' – you encounter them every day – the young person walking while texting or listening to music on their smartphone, or probably both. So distracting are these multitasking activities that they significantly increase the likelihood of accidents, and many towns and cities throughout the world have passed laws to make texting while walking illegal, implemented pathway segregation to prevent collisions

9 Rideout, V. J., Foehr, U. G. & Roberts, D. F. (2010) Generation M2: Media in the Lives of 8–18 Year Olds. Retrieved from Kaiser Family Foundation website: http://www.kff.org/entmedia/mh012010pkg.cfm
10 Hadlington, L. (2017) *Cybercognition*. Sage.

between smartphone users, walkers and cyclists, and erected signs to warn car drivers of the dangers of zombie smartphone users. In one study, only 25 per cent of those youngsters walking and talking on their mobile phones reported noticing a unicycling clown pass close by![11]

The relevant point here is that multitasking and the constant, immediate switching from one task to another creates a sequence of biological events that makes us anxious, and it's the technology-enabled multitasking that's responsible for this. Daniel Levitin is an award-winning scientist and musician, and in his book *The Organized Mind* he describes the neuroscience behind technology-enabled multitasking. Frantically switching from one task to another causes the prefrontal cortex to burn up oxygenated glucose – a substance required for efficient cognitive performance, whose depletion makes us begin to feel exhausted and disoriented. These effects then boost production of the stress hormone cortisol, which in turn makes us feel anxious.

To add to this, Russ Poldrack and colleagues at Stanford University discovered that multitasking can have detrimental effects on learning. If we're multitasking while trying to learn something new (like the students in the lecture mentioned above), the newly learnt information can be misdirected and stored in the wrong part of the brain – areas of the brain that deal with new procedures and skills rather than organising new facts and ideas[12]. This kind of information suggests that one of the possible causes of the epidemic levels of anxiety amongst our younger generation of students is the constant

11 Hyman, I. E., Boss, S. M., Wise, B. W. et al. (2010) 'Did you see the unicycling clown? Inattentional blindness while walking and talking on a cell phone.' *Journal of Applied Cognitive Psychology*, 24, 597–607.
12 Foerde, K., Knowlton, B. J., Poldrack, R. A. (2006) 'Modulation of competing memory systems by distraction.' *Proceedings of the National Academy of Sciences*, 103(31):11778–83.

switching of attention to the demands of a smartphone while trying to learn – the multitasking generates anxiety, and the switching disrupts learning, and there is already some evidence consistent with this in that time spent on Facebook can be strongly negatively related to a student's overall grade point average (GPA)[13].

I'll talk in more detail about the way in which regular social media use can generate social media addictions in Chapter 3, but it's worth considering a couple of other effects that perpetual connectivity can have. In the UK in 2015 to 2016, more than ten thousand patients under the age of eighteen were admitted to hospital with a diagnosis of anxiety, and in 2017 the National Society for the Prevention of Cruelty to Children (NSPCC) warned that their ChildLine service had seen a 35 per cent rise in calls about anxiety in the preceding twelve months. The charity claimed that teenagers and children as young as four or five years old were becoming increasingly distressed by disturbing events and images they'd viewed on social media sites, and children were increasingly expressing anxieties about world events depicted on twenty-four-hour news outlets, including Brexit, the US election of 2016, and troubles in the Middle East. The chief policy adviser for the charity YoungMinds, Dr Marc Bush, has claimed that the sharp rise in the number of children being treated in hospital for anxiety is deeply alarming, and he added that 'We know from our research that children and young people face a huge range of pressures, including stress at school, body image issues, bullying on and offline, around the clock social media, and uncertain job prospects.' John Cameron, head of NSPCC helplines, has explicitly implicated perpetual connectivity as one important cause of the increase in childhood anxiety, with these problems being 'impacted

13 Junco, R. (2012) 'Too much face and not enough books: The relationship between multiple indices of Facebook use and academic performance.' Computers in Human Behavior, 28, 187–198.

by a need to keep up with friends and to have the perfect life; and the 24/7 nature of technology means that young people can never escape the pressure', an epidemic that the *Daily Telegraph* has seen as a consequence of the modern world's 'selfie culture'[14]. The ease with which Internet events can go viral and create ephemeral fads that each individual child and adolescent needs to be aware of simply add to the pressures to be continually connected (e.g. the Ice Bucket and Mannequin challenges of 2015 and 2016).

To the anxiety-provoking potential of multitasking, perpetual connectivity and Internet addiction, we can also add 'data-hacking anxiety', where an increasing number of people have concerns about privacy on social network sites and smartphones, keystroke loggers (covert recording of the keys struck on a keyboard), and the safety of exercise health data, video-surveillance, and geo-location data. Some initial studies of this phenomenon suggest that women are significantly more likely to be anxious about data hacking than men, and individuals in eastern cultures (where greater emphasis is placed on information privacy) more anxious than those in western cultures[15].

But if data hacking is not a big enough cause for concern, then what about that catastrophic moment when it dawns on you that your hard drive has not just crashed, but also corrupted all your precious files? You lose all those photos you'd lovingly collected over the years, the financial spreadsheet that documents your wealth, and that essay you have to hand in at 9 a.m. tomorrow! If that's not enough, this is inevitably followed by the stigma heaped on you when you tell

14 http://www.telegraph.co.uk/wellbeing/mood-and-mind/mental-health-crisis-among-children-selfie-culture-sees-cases/

15 Elhai, J. D., Chai, S., Amialchuk, A. & Hall, B. J. (2017) 'Cross-cultural and gender associations with anxiety about electronic data hacking.' *Computers in Human Behavior*, doi: 10.1016/j.chb.2017.01.002

friends and family that you'd forgotten to back everything up – the eleventh commandment of the modern world: 'Thou shalt always back up thy data files'! You're made to feel like a negligent techno-imbecile – 'You mean you didn't back up your files? I do mine at least twice a day!' Crashing hard drives are like flashbulb memory moments – they're so catastrophic that everyone can remember that searing moment of realisation when your heart stops beating and your throat plunges into the pit of your stomach – your computer is dead!

And one final point on perpetual connectivity – the Internet is a global network that we feed with our seemingly insignificant tweets, our banal Facebook posts, and our everyday email messages. But the beast is significantly more than the petty morsels that we feed it. It's a vibrant, changing index of global attitudes and feelings. In 2009 computer scientists Eric Gilbert and Karrie Karahalios at the University of Illinois at Urbana-Champaign constructed a metric of anxiety, worry and fear from over twenty million LiveJournal posts on the Internet – this effectively created a measure of global anxiety from weblogs.

What was surprising was that this index of global anxiety gleaned from a single journaling site, where people record their personal thoughts and discuss their daily lives, predicted future changes in an entirely unrelated system – movements on the Standard & Poor 500 stock market index[16]. A similar study by Brendan O'Connor and colleagues at Carnegie Mellon University in 2010 found that an index measuring either positive or negative sentiments in Twitter messages over a number of years correlated highly with surveys of consumer confidence and political opinion (e.g. approval of President Barack

16 Gilbert, E. & Karahalios, K. (2009) 'Widespread worry and the stock market.' *Association for the Advancement of Artificial Intelligence.* http://social. cs.uiuc.edu/people/gilbert/pub/icwsm10.worry.gilbert.pdf

Obama) over the same period[17]. In fact, a more recent study of Twitter by Emily Cody and colleagues at the University of Vermont showed that Twitter sentiment predicted President Obama's job approval three months in advance[18]. It seems that sentiments expressed in the most mundane Internet posts, about the weather, sports events, popular music, the activities of friends – and even posts about cute dogs and missing cats – can create a holistic, global 'mood' that predicts other forms of related and unrelated activity. Figure 2.1 opposite shows how average happiness ratings for Twitter sentiments have fluctuated between 2009 and 2017[19]. If each of us as individuals are able to sense this global mood or 'atmosphere' through our own contacts with the Internet and social media, then it's likely to predict our own moods and activities just as it predicts global systems such as stock market movements or political opinions.

However, it's a big step from these studies to say that the Internet creates its own global atmosphere that can *influence* our own moods – but it's not entirely improbable. For example, a sentiment analysis of all tweets published on Twitter in the second half of 2008 predicted future public mood along a range of mood dimensions[20], and we know from studies of twenty-four-hour news bulletins that other forms of media can directly influence personal mood, and as a consequence, our daily activities (see next section). Natural things

17 O'Connor, B., Balasubramanyan, R., Routledge, B. R. & Smith, N. A. (2010) 'From tweets to polls: Linking text sentiment to public opinion time series.' *Proceedings of the Fourth International AAAI Conference on Weblogs and Social Media*. http://www.aaai.org/ocs/index.php/ICWSM/ICWSM10/paper/viewFile/1536/1842

18 Cody, E. M., Reagan, A. J., Dodds, P. S. & Danforth, C. M. (2016) 'Public opinion polling with Twitter.' https://arxiv.org/pdf/1608.02024.pdf

19 http://hedonometer.org/index.html?from=2008-09-10&to=2017-10-05

20 Bollen, J., Mao, H. & Pepe, A. (2011) 'Modelling public mood and emotion: Twitter sentiment and socio-economic phenomena.' *Proceedings of the Fifth International AAAI Conference on Weblogs and Social Media*. http://www.aaai.org/ocs/index.php/ICWSM/ICWSM11/paper/viewFile/2826/3237

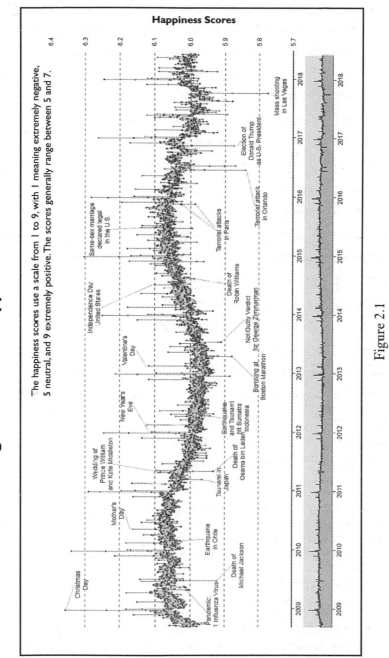

Figure 2.1

as simple as the weather influenced the moods of our parents and grandparents, but that global beast called the Internet that we feed with our petty morsels could easily become the monster of the future that determines our own daily diet of fears and anxieties.

Negative News and the Twenty-Four-Hour News Cycle

The news is just another form of connectivity, but I've deliberately included a separate section on the role of contemporary news in feeding the modern anxiety epidemic. The way that news is reported has changed significantly over the last ten to twenty years. Nowadays we can hardly avoid it, many of us actively feel the need to seek it out, and its modern-day tone is increasingly emotive, its medium increasingly visual and shocking, and its commentaries increasingly negative and fear-laden.

Journalists today consider it their job to use every modern media and technological innovation at their disposal to bring remote events into the here and now experience of the consumer, no matter how harrowing the content – but that's not something that everyone has the mental resources to cope with. It's an agenda that reminds me of the annual UK Christmas drink-driving campaigns in the 1980s and 1990s – each year attempting to invent ever more visually horrific and harrowing anti-drink-driving commercials. But year on year drink-driving convictions hardly ever fell – it was a campaign that failed to touch the hardened drink-drivers and instead scared the life out of many people who neither drank nor drove but watched a lot of TV commercials and grew anxious at the prospect of being the next mutilated victim of a drunk driver!

News is no longer simply about conveying facts of recent happenings. There are a lot of bad things that happen in the world, and it's probably right that people should know about these things through their reporting in news bulletins. These 'bad things' include crime, famine, war, terrorism, violence, political unrest and injustice, to name but a few. But there is also an increasing tendency for news broadcasters to 'emotionalise' their news and to do so by emphasising any potential negative outcomes of a story no matter how low the risks of those negative outcomes might be. Because we now have twenty-four-hour news coverage, gone are the days when a correspondent or journalist's role was simply to describe impartially what was happening in the world – because of satellite TV and social media we have an almost immediate visual record of what's happening anywhere in the world, and this is transmitted into every home as 'breaking news'. Through this process we become aware of events within moments of them happening, and certainly before a full understanding of the event is available. The demands of twenty-four-hour news coverage mean that journalists and commentators must fill the time before facts emerge with speculation and innuendo, and there is only a small step from 'evaluating' a story to 'sensationalising' it.

Professor of Journalism Studies at Cardiff University, Bob Franklin, wrote some years ago that 'entertainment has superseded the provision of information; human interest has supplanted the public interest; measured judgement has succumbed to sensationalism.[21]' In addition, news bulletins nowadays also have to compete with entertainment programmes for their audience and for their prime-time TV slots, and seem to do this by emphasising emotionally relevant material such as crime, war, famine, etc., at the expense of more positive material. The basic fear of all reporters and journalists is of being boring, and the best news is that which demands attention. As a result, news is not just news, but information that is increasingly harnessed for the purposes of spectacle and entertainment[22].

21 Franklin, B., (1997) *Newszak and News Media*, 4.
22 Kavka, M. (2008) *Reality Television, Affect and Intimacy*. London: Palgrave MacMillan.

The role of the digital age has also been significant in shifting the nature of news reporting. Alerts on our mobile phones keep us in direct contact with world events regardless of what we're doing. As Mark Deuze writes in his book *Media Life*, the modern world has become one in which the media are ubiquitous, pervasive and cannot be switched off – and this is also true of news, where immediate daily information about world events has become an accepted reality of everyday existence. But a more significant impact of the digital age on news reporting has been the dramatic shift to visual imagery in news items – especially visual imagery contributed by the audience and garnered by journalists from social media. User-generated images of important world events are now regularly captured on the smartphones of those close to or even directly involved in these events, and this new form of 'news reality' began to appear during the Asian tsunami, the 7/7 London underground bombings, and the Boston Marathon bombings – developments that effectively allowed the audience to witness such events in what was virtually real-time[23].

Because of developments such as this, media writers such as David Altheide have argued that news has become increasingly visual, with images taken from multiple sources, and presented especially to convey fear, danger, excitement and risk[24]. Such user-generated images permit news broadcasters to present ever more dramatic and shocking images that were either not available or not permissible in earlier times. For example, in news coverage of the 2015 terrorist attack on the *Charlie Hebdo* offices in Paris, images were made available worldwide of one of the gunmen shooting dead a

23 Allan, S. (2014) 'Witnessing in crisis: Photo-reportage of terror attacks in Boston and London.' *Media, War & Conflict*, 7, No.2.
24 Altheide, D. (2014) *Media Edge: Media Logic and Social Reality*. New York: Peter Lang.

policeman at point blank range[25]. By 2017, television news coverage of the terrorist attack on Westminster Bridge and the Houses of Parliament did not flinch at showing graphic smartphone-generated images of the dying, the injured and the dead. The news audience is now effectively being transported to the site of a news event by real-time graphic images so that those watching these images become directly connected to the events that are happening and the effect these events generate – 'the media does not merely report the scene but is part of the scene and action'[26].

Given the dramatic virtual proximity the modern viewer has to news events like a terrorist attack, a natural disaster, the suffering caused by wars and famine, it's not surprising that many people viewing these events will develop emotional and affective conditions as if they were physically present. For example, exposure to media coverage of the Boston Marathon bombings in 2013 generated acute stress symptoms in many viewing this news coverage[27], and exposure to images of the 9/11 terrorist attacks on TV also generated post-traumatic stress symptoms in some viewers[28].

It's not just the broadcasting of graphic visual imagery associated with news events that can generate fears and anxieties; the news media are also guilty of creating Doomsday scenarios and failing to convey the realities of the immeasurably low risk that most of these scenarios pose. One example of this was during the Ebola outbreak

25 Jukes, S. (2016) 'News in the digital age: What does it mean for media literacy?' http://eprints.bournemouth.ac.uk/23307/

26 Butler, J. (2015) *Notes Toward a Performative Theory of Assembly*. Cambridge, MA: Harvard University Press.

27 Holman, E. A. et al. (2013) 'Media's role in broadcasting acute stress following the Boston Marathon bombings.' *Proceedings of the National Academy of Sciences*, doi: 10.1073/pnas.1316265110

28 Piotrowski, C. S. & Brannen, S. J. (2002) 'Exposure, threat appraisal, and lost confidence as predictors of PTSD symptoms following September 11, 2001.' *American Journal of Orthopsychiatry*, 72, 476–485.

in the summer of 2014. While the world media reported the spread of the outbreak in Africa, those news media outside of Africa would invariably speculate on the possibility of Ebola spreading beyond that continent. Magdalena Hodalska, a specialist in the language and anthropology of the media, provides a particular example from the BBC who encouraged its viewers to 'look at how Ebola might come here: everyday around twenty-five people arrive at Heathrow from the countries in Africa affected by the virus. We know they will be screened. But let's imagine someone slipped through the net. One of them could be carrying the virus in their blood, without anyone knowing it. It's a scary thought. So could I or any of us get Ebola from a stranger?'[29] The speculation has already instilled a 'scary thought', and it ends with a slight reassurance that its quite hard to catch Ebola, but then immediately afterwards ratchets up the fear once more with 'the real fear is that it could mutate into a smarter virus. Turning airborne. It could infect with a single sneeze'[30]. No mention of the probability of these scenarios achieving the heady heights of reality – merely a mélange of scary language!

That brings me to more improbable Doomsday scenarios. The powering up of the Large Hadron Collider at CERN in 2008 resulted in claims that it would create a 'black hole' that would suck, eat or devour planet Earth, leading one newspaper to ask 'Who's afraid of black holes?' I suspect that more than a few people were after that headline! Thomas Kronschläger and Eva Sommer have argued that even articles about trivial or improbable threats can serve to fuel public fear about what apocalyptic dangers might be lurking. The

29 BBC, *Ebola*: BBC Documentary.
30 Hodalska, M. (2016) 'Ebola virus kills the other, but anytime it may land here: Media coverage of an African plague', in Selina E. M. Doran, Bethan Michael & Izabela Dixon (Eds.) *There's More to Fear than Fear Itself: Fears and Anxieties in the 21st Century*, Oxford: Inter-Disciplinary Press, s. 123–135.

reason for this is that articles and programmes about improbable dangers, such as being swallowed by a black hole, often give most credence to those supporting the Doomsday scenario, and significantly less exposure to the experts who critique these scenarios[31]. Most people wouldn't know what a black hole was even if it came straight up the toilet pan, dragged them screaming towards the singularity at the speed of light and ultimately spaghettified them. But the chances of that are quite remote! And that is the ultimate problem – most news consumers have extremely poor risk-assessment skills, as it also seems do journalists, because the latter rarely give an accurate appraisal of the chances of a particular danger happening, but instead wallow in the joy of seeing how many fearful adjectives they can cram into a single paragraph.

A typical example of fear-generating statistics from the media is when a newspaper headline claims a study shows that eating a particular type of food (say, bacon) increases the chances of you dying from a specific type of illness by 50 per cent. Sounds like you'd better stop eating that food pretty soon! But the article doesn't tell you the average risk of dying from that specific illness anyway, which may be as low as 1 per cent. If that's the case, then, eating bacon increases your risk of dying of that illness from 1 per cent to a mere 1.5 per cent! At those odds, I think I'll still carry on having the occasional bacon sandwich.

Given that modern-day news media have evolved a number of features that will facilitate your fears and anxieties, how does this anxiety manifest itself in the ordinary news consumer? First, I've already noted that exposure to vivid images of disasters or terrorist

---

31 Kronschläger, T. & Sommer, E. (2016) 'ConCERNs: An interdisciplinary analysis of the fear discourse connected with the implementation of the LHC at CERN', in Selina E. M. Doran, Bethan Michael & Izabela Dixon (Eds.) *There's More to Fear than Fear Itself: Fears and Anxieties in the 21st Century*, Oxford: Inter-Disciplinary Press.

attacks on television can induce acute stress symptoms or even conditions commonly displayed by sufferers of post-traumatic stress disorder. But negative news items can have a much more subtle psychological effect. In the knowledge that the proportion of negatively inclined emotional material in news bulletins was increasing, in 1997 we conducted a study looking at the psychological effects of viewing negative news items[32]. We constructed three different fourteen-minute news bulletins. One was made entirely of negative news items, one was made of entirely positive news items (e.g. people winning the lottery, recovering from illness, etc.), and one was made up of items that were emotionally neutral. We then showed these bulletins to three different groups of people. As we predicted, those who watched the negative news bulletin all reported being significantly more anxious and sadder after watching this bulletin than those people who watched either the positive or neutral news bulletin.

But what was more interesting was the effect that watching negative news had on peoples' own worries. We asked each participant to tell us what their main worry was at the time, and we then asked them to think about this worry during a structured interview. We found that those people who had watched the negative news bulletin spent more time thinking and talking about their worry and were more likely to catastrophise their worry than people in the other two groups. Catastrophising is when you think about a worry so persistently that you begin to make it seem much worse than it was at the outset and much worse than it is in reality – a tendency to make 'mountains out of molehills'.

So not only are negatively inclined news broadcasts likely to make you sadder and more anxious, they're also likely to exacerbate your

32 Johnston, W. M. & Davey, G. C. L. (1997) 'The psychological impact of negative TV news bulletins: The catastrophizing of personal worries.' *British Journal of Psychology*, 88, 85–91.

own personal worries and anxieties. We would intuitively expect that news items reflecting war, famine and poverty might induce viewers to ruminate on such topics. But the effect of negatively valenced news is much broader than that – it can potentially exacerbate a range of personal concerns not specifically relevant to the content of the programme itself. So, bombarding people with 'sensationalised' negativity does have genuine and real psychological effects.

All of this and we still have to throw the growing phenomenon of 'fake news' into the mix. Fake news is not a new thing and it's been part of journalism for a long time, but it has certainly become more prominent during the US Presidential election campaign and the Brexit referendum of 2016[33]. We're only just beginning to research the psychological effects of fake news, but clearly any effects will depend much on the believability of fake news and its attempt to target core emotions such as fear or anxiety.

For example, during the Ebola virus outbreak in Africa, fake news sites posted scary stories about whole towns in the United States being quarantined after families were diagnosed with Ebola – a scary story that reached many hundreds of thousands of readers after being shared on social media[34]. But what makes people believe these fake news stories? Well, one factor is anxiety. A study by researchers at the University of Michigan found that people who were anxious were likely to be more open-minded to views outside of their existing beliefs and so more likely to believe fake news – a process that is likely to exacerbate their anxiety if the fake news itself is fear- or anxiety-provoking[35].

33 Allcott, H. & Gentzkow, M. (2017) 'Social media and fake news in the 2016 election.' https://web.stanford.edu/~gentzkow/research/fakenews.pdf

34 http://www.theverge.com/2014/10/22/7028983/fake-news-sites-are-using-facebook-to-spread-ebola-panic

35 Weeks, B. E. (2015) 'Emotions, partisanship, and misperceptions: How anger and anxiety moderate the effect of partisan bias on susceptibility to political misinformation.' *Journal of Communication*, 65, 699–719.

In addition, the politics of the modern world have polarised significantly in the past decade, and this may also have indirectly increased the willingness to believe so-called fake news. Political views are more divided than they've been in a generation, with the divisive build up to the Trump presidency in the USA, the Brexit vote in the UK, and the rise of extreme right-wing political groups in major European countries such as Germany and France. The greater the gulf in political beliefs, the more that people will seek information that confirms their beliefs and condemns the beliefs of their opponents – whether that information is true or false. As columnist Roy Greenslade has argued, in today's media there is often a lack of distinction between news and comment, especially when news outlets are cynically attempting to broadcast their own heavily angled political views, and news-as-comment is just one step away from fake news[36]. Winning the political argument is all that matters – it's not important whether the information you garner to support your argument is heavily angled or even sheer fakery. This is because, by our very nature, human beings cannot allow their ingrained political or ideological beliefs to be destroyed by 'facts' because for many people those beliefs define them and are a central component of their self-identity. To destroy those beliefs is effectively to destroy the person, so any information that protects these beliefs is valuable – even if it's fake.

Finally, in a world where many people source their news on the Internet, those generating fake news often do so to bring more readers to their websites, which generates advertising revenue, and they post false stories and trick people into using them widely by decontextualising Facebook's news feeds – it may well generate advertising income, but it can also genuinely scare people!

36 https://www.theguardian.com/media/commentisfree/2017/oct/09/how-a-blurring-of-fact-and-comment-kicked-open-the-door-to-fake-news-roy-greenslade

The Modern Anxiety Ethos

No matter who you are, there will always be something that makes you anxious. Your parents experienced anxiety, so too did your distant ancestors. According to the Office for National Statistics, one in five of us in the UK is currently 'highly anxious' (see Chapter 3). There is no getting away from it – anxiety has always been around, and is still around.

In previous eras anxiety was often defined by how people were taught to deal with it (see Chapter 5). Today it's rather different. Rob Fisher, a philosopher and founder of Inter-Disciplinary.Net argues that modern-day anxiety is 'an atmosphere which has been largely manufactured for us and we have come to live it, breathe it, absorb it'. Somehow, anxiety has now become an accepted part of modern-day life. We're told it's a legitimate response to the stresses of modern-day living, we can even boast about our anxiety as an index of the importance of our lives and the significance of the demands placed on us – anxiety is not just an emotion, it's a modern-day status symbol. The new technologies of the Internet open up a wealth of opportunities that coldly persuade us to do more things in less time. They even paste these events into our electronic diaries without us having to raise a finger to the keyboard – whereas we only used to have events in our paper diaries for a couple of weeks ahead, we now have electronic diaries often full of commitments for a couple of years.

But today, the most successful people are perceived as the busiest, and the busier you are the more important you are deemed to be by others[37]. A full diary can signify a high social and economic standing, but a full diary can certainly make you anxious or stressed, ergo your anxiety or stress is a signal of your status and importance.

37 Bellezza, S., Paharia, N. & Keinan, A. (2016) 'Conspicuous consumption of time: When busyness and lack of leisure time become a status symbol.' *Journal of Consumer Research*, DOI: https://doi.org/10.1093/jcr/ucw076.

This contemporary acceptance of anxiety as a legitimate response to a demanding modern world has allowed people to talk more freely about anxiety and stress, to raise awareness of mental health problems generally, and has led to more and more people seeking treatment for their stress and anxiety-related problems. Anxiety is an integral part of the modern world.

But there are some other factors that have raised the profile of anxiety over the past decades, and which – rightly or wrongly – have established anxiety as an emotion in need of treatment.

My mother tells me she suffers from 'nerves' – at least that's what her GP told her in the 1950s. In those days there were few, if any, diagnostic categories into which anxiety problems could be slotted, and so the term 'nerves' became a common description of chronic anxiety and 'nervous breakdown' was the phrase used to describe more severe episodes. It wasn't until the American Psychiatric Association published its first Diagnostic and Statistical Manual (DSM) in 1952 that diagnostic categories for different anxiety-based problems became available. Well, I can hear you asking, that's a good thing isn't it? It's certainly good to have some clear, evidence-based criteria by which to diagnose problematic anxiety, but what many people have objected to is the way in which subsequent developments of the diagnostic manual have led to what many would call a 'proliferation' of anxiety disorders which run the risk of medicalising most people's conception of anxiety.

Allen Frances is an American psychiatrist who chaired the task force that produced the fourth revision of the DSM in 1994, but he is sheriff-turned-outlaw, and he's become one of the biggest critics of the most recent revision, the DSM-5 published in 2013[38]. He warned

---

38 Frances, A. (2013) 'The new crisis of confidence in psychiatric diagnosis.' *Annals of Internal Medicine*, 159, 221–222.

that the ever-increasing number of mental health diagnostic categories included in each revision of the DSM was causing 'diagnostic
inflation' that was 'swallowing up' normality, and causing the unnecessary diagnosis and treatment of many people who were merely
experiencing emotions such as anxiety in a normal everyday way.

Since 1952 there has been an exponential growth in the number of anxiety disorders included in the DSM. One reason for this
is that the experts involved in developing the DSM are primarily
worried about false negatives – that is, they're worried about the
missed diagnosis or patient who doesn't fit neatly into the existing
categorisations. This leads to more inclusive diagnostic criteria or
even more diagnostic categories in each new revision of the manual.
The result of this increased inclusiveness is a growing number of
people who receive an unnecessary diagnosis, and as a consequence,
unnecessary treatment. The outcome for those of us on the receiving end of diagnosis and treatment is the increasing perception that
all experienced anxiety is a medical problem in need of a medical
solution – when arguably it should not be.

This modern-day medicalisation of anxiety is also being reinforced from another source – the seemingly legitimate desire within
our society to quantify and pathologise anxiety and then sell you a
solution for it. In 2015 the revenue earned by the pharmaceutical
industry worldwide was over $1,072bn[39], and maintaining the pro-
fitability of drugs such as the anxiolytics used to treat anxiety will
depend on the public's conception of anxiety as a medical condition
that implies a medical solution – 'If you're anxious take a pill!' – and
a diagnostic system that will err towards over-diagnosis rather than
under-diagnosis. Brian Pilecki and colleagues at Fordham University

39 https://www.statista.com/statistics/263102/pharmaceutical-market-
worldwide-revenue-since-2001/

have written an insightful review of the corporate and political interests that either directly or indirectly may help pharmaceutical companies to maximise their sales in the mental health sphere[40], and how the medicalisation of anxiety as a condition in need of medical treatment continues. However, to be fair, there are institutions within our modern society that require mental health-related conditions such as anxiety to be clearly defined and categorised. For example, we might want to know whether someone is psychologically fit to stand trial for a criminal offence, whether a child has disabilities that will require special educational needs, whether financial compensation or damages should be awarded to an individual because of psychological symptoms caused by the actions of others, and – in countries where health insurance is the primary means of funding treatment – whether an individual qualifies for health services as a result of having a clearly defined mental health 'disease' or 'illness'. In order to ensure that these legal and financial decisions can be made, distinctive categories of mental illness were preferable to the existing conceptualisations such as those rather loosely framed within approaches such as traditional psychoanalytic theory – hence the significance of diagnostic manuals such as DSM.

And who invented these new distinctive, clearly defined diagnostic categories? Well, it was the medical profession, in the guise of the psychiatrists who designed the DSM for the American Psychiatric Association! This has had a number of consequences for our conceptualisation of emotions related to psychopathology, such as anxiety. It has effectively medicalised all forms of anxiety – even everyday anxiety that is a natural response to the threats and challenges we face during normal daily living. It has implied a biological cause for

40 Pilecki, B. C., Clegg, J. W. & McKay, D. (2011) 'The influence of corporate and political interests on models of illness in the evolution of DSM.' *European Psychiatry*, 26, 194–200.

anxiety, when there is just as much evidence that anxiety has psycho-logical or sociological origins[41]. And its conception of anxiety as a medical 'disease' category implies a biological solution that suits the pharmaceutical industry's mass production of anxiolytics – even when the evidence suggests that psychological treatments for anxiety, such as cognitive-behavioural therapy (CBT) are superior to medication alone[42]. Factors such as this have raised the profile of anxiety – not as an adaptive everyday emotion, but as a medical condition that requires treatment, and this manufactured status of anxiety as a biological disease condition must shoulder some of the blame for fuelling the modern-day anxiety epidemic that sees significant increases in the number of people of all ages seeking treatment for it.

Short and Sweet

If you're alive you'll experience anxiety. But what makes us anxious will change as the pressures and challenges of our evolving soci-ety changes. In this chapter I've described just a few of the things that have evolved to fuel our modern-day anxieties. They're new, but they only trigger a response that was probably the same as the anxiety response experienced by our parents, our grandparents, and our recent and ancient ancestors (see Chapter 5). What may have changed significantly in today's world is that anxiety is now seen as an emotion in need of treatment, and modern era innovations intro-duced to make living more convenient and the outside world more accessible have paradoxically evolved to become the new triggers for our anxieties.

41 Davey, G. C. L. (2015) 'The funding of mental health research in the UK – A biased and flawed system?' http://www.papersfromsidcup.com/graham-daveys-blog/-the-funding-of-mental-health-research-in-the-uk-a-biased-and-flawed-system
42 Barlow, D. H. (2002) *Anxiety and Its Disorders*. 2nd Edition. New York: Guilford.

CHAPTER THREE

The Anxiety Epidemic

'Anxiety is the Trash of Modern Life – It Will Pile Up
and Overtake You.'

Let's begin by getting a handle on just how anxious we are today.
Do we all feel anxious, or is it just some of us? Arguably, an anxiety
epidemic can be caused by either or both of two things – an increase in
the traditional social causes of anxiety that have been with us for many
generations (even many centuries), or by the emergence of entirely
new sources of anxiety that define our modern age. In this chapter we'll
have a detailed look at the former possibility – the traditional social
causes of anxiety and stress and their prevalence in present times, such
things as unemployment, marital status, loneliness, poverty, inequality
and poor health. We'll take a look at some of the information we have
available that gives us an insight into how anxiety is experienced today,
and the findings are more than just a little bit surprising.

We're still dogged by those traditional factors associated with
stress and anxiety, but how subtly these factors have changed to make
us anxious in much more selective ways. You can have hundreds of
friends on Facebook, but still feel lonely and anxious and disconnected. Your résumé is bulging with qualifications and experience,
but the process of applying for jobs is a trial of monumental proportions. Your monthly salary cheque is fatter than almost everyone

else's, yet you wake each morning anxious to maintain your status in this unequal society. You thank medical science for extending your lifespan beyond all your expectations, but curse them instead for condemning you to a longer life of stressful chronic disability surrounded by inadequate care facilities. How the beast is changing!

How Anxious Do You Feel?

Let's start by generally testing the temperature of the water – how anxious are most people? Think back to yesterday, how anxious were you yesterday on a scale of 0 to 10 where 0 is 'not at all anxious' and 10 is 'completely anxious'?

Most of you reading this book will understand this question and be able to provide a number between 0 and 10, so it's a simple way of seeing how relatively anxious different people are. This is a basic self-report method. It may not correlate with any underlying physiological measures such as blood pressure, heart rate, cortisol levels, etc., but that's not unexpected – what is important about anxiety is the personal distress that it inflicts on the individual, and only the whole person can tell us that. You can't really get this measure of personal suffering from an electrode taped to the skin or a saliva sample being analysed for cortisol levels in a lab. How someone reacts to anxiety depends less on their biological state and more on how they cope with the feelings of anxiety they experience.

The Office for National Statistics collects and publishes data as part of the Annual Population Survey in the UK[1], and in recent years this has included a measure of anxiety. Over three-year periods, the survey asks a sample of around a quarter of a million UK inhabitants 'Overall, how anxious did you feel yesterday?' using the 0 to 10 scale I've just described.

1 https://www.nomisweb.co.uk/articles/932.aspx

In data collected between April 2012 and March 2015, one in five people reported experiencing anxiety in the 'high' range (a rating of 6–10). On average that's one person in a string quintet, a five-a-side football team, or even, statistically speaking, one of the Rolling Stones! However, because the Office for National Statistics only started collecting data on anxiety in 2011, it's not possible to make any meaningful comparisons across time to see if the national levels of anxiety have been increasing significantly over recent decades or whether the number of people who rate their anxiety as 'high' has increased. Nevertheless, the current one-in-five figure for individuals suffering high levels of anxiety does correspond well with statistics from other countries such as the USA where 18 per cent of the US adult population (roughly one in five) is likely to suffer an anxiety disorder in any twelve-month period[2].

But while high levels of anxiety are experienced by one in five, anxiety isn't endemic across the whole population of the UK. The average rating across all respondents was just under 3 – an average rating that was classified as 'low'. But, nearly two out of every five respondents recorded a rating of 0 or 1 out of 10, which is classified as 'very low'. So, to provide a very simplified summary, one in five people suffer high anxiety regularly, two in five people suffer little or no anxiety, and the remaining two in five suffer 'some' anxiety probably 'some of the time' (which may on some occasions during an individual lifetime become severe).

The UK Office for National Statistics data show that men are only marginally less anxious than women. Men have an average rating of 2.8 and women 3.0; 18.2 per cent of men claim to be highly anxious and 21.7 per cent of women (a rating between 6 and 10). This

2 https://www.nimh.nih.gov/health/statistics/prevalence/any-anxiety-disorder-among-adults.shtml

comparison of male and female anxiety is rather different to the sex differences in recorded levels of anxiety disorders in a 2012 study by Amanda Baxter and colleagues at the University of Queensland. They found that females were more than *twice* as likely as men to have an anxiety *disorder*[3]. This suggests that women may be significantly more vulnerable to more severe anxiety-based problems, but this vulnerability is not simply the result of sex differences across the whole spectrum of anxiety severity – this sex difference occurs only at the level of the most disabling diagnosable anxiety problems such as panic disorder, Generalised Anxiety Disorder (GAD) and obsessive-compulsive disorder (OCD). We can only speculate why women are significantly more vulnerable to the more severe forms of anxiety when this difference doesn't show up in population surveys of general anxiety levels. Some factors might include (1) a greater willingness of women to seek help and treatment for more severe forms of anxiety than men and so be more likely to end up with an anxiety disorder diagnosis; (2) a greater likelihood in women to exacerbate their anxiety through worry about the things that cause their anxiety, whereas men tend to try to distract themselves or express their anxiety as anger[4]; (3) a greater willingness in women to report physical and emotional symptoms of anxiety and stress than men; and (4) women experiencing more life stressors than men after puberty[5] – a factor that may push high levels of anxiety into more severe and disabling forms of anxiety such as GAD, panic disorder and OCD.

3 Baxter, A. J., Scott, K. M., Vos, T. & Whiteford, H. A. (2012) 'Global prevalence of anxiety disorders: A systematic review and meta-regression.' *Psychological Medicine*, 43, 897–910.

4 Robichaud, M., Dugas, M. J. & Conway, M. (2003) 'Gender differences in worry and associated cognitive-behavioral variables.' *Journal of Anxiety Disorders*, 17, 501–516.

5 American Psychological Association (2010) 'Stress in America', http://www.apa.org/news/press/releases/stress/2010/gender-stress.pdf

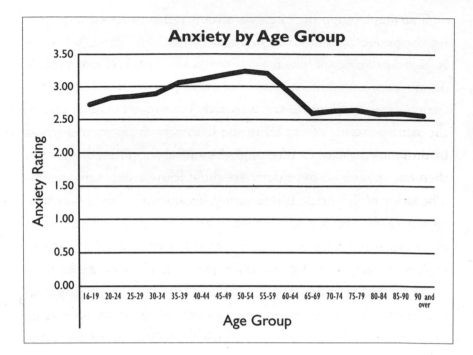

Anxiety by Age Group

Figure 3.1

How do anxiety levels map out across the lifespan? Are adolescents more anxious than adults, and do we become more anxious the older we get? Modern educational pressures are often seen as an important source of anxiety and stress for our children, and economic unpredictability following the financial crisis of 2007–08 will have increased stress levels through rising prices, the threat of unemployment, and a general economic squeeze on families generally. Even the elderly are not insulated against modern stressors, with more elderly people living alone than ever before, and in many countries they experience deteriorating care facilities[6].

6 http://www.telegraph.co.uk/news/health/elder/11299527/10-per-cent-rise-in-number-of-people-living-alone.html

The graph in Figure 3.1 shows anxiety ratings across the lifespan for the period 2012–2015 (UK Annual Population Survey). Anxiety is highest during middle age when a peak in experienced anxiety occurs between roughly thirty-five to fifty-five years of age, and anxiety is at its lifetime lowest after sixty years of age. This is exactly the same pattern as reported in the USA, where anxiety is highest in those aged thirty to fifty-nine years of age[7]. If this is the case, then the young and the elderly are those least troubled by anxiety. The shape of this graph is interesting, because news items regularly appear in the media arguing that modern living has given rise to increased anxiety in groups such as the young and the elderly. In the elderly, anxieties can often be quite specific to old age, and be triggered by health problems, the difficulties of living alone, anxieties caused by body image changes (especially in women)[8], relocation anxieties in the institutionalised elderly[9], and sleep problems[10]. But these age-specific anxieties don't appear to contribute to unusually high anxiety ratings in the elderly, with only 16–18 per cent of people between the ages of seventy and ninety years exhibiting high anxiety levels (compared to a national mean of 20 per cent). But what about the young?

In April 2015 the *Daily Telegraph* headlined an article 'ANXIETY: THE EPIDEMIC SWEEPING THROUGH GENERATION Y' (those born between 1980 and 2000) – an epidemic reportedly fuelled by the rise of technology, overly-protective parenting, exam-factory schooling,

7 https://www.nimh.nih.gov/health/statistics/prevalence/any-anxiety-disorder-among-adults.shtml

8 https://www.theguardian.com/society/2012/jun/10/body-image-elderly-hidden-illness

9 Thomasma, M., Yeaworth, R. C. & McCabe, B. W. (1990) 'Moving day: Relocation and anxiety in institutionalized elderly.' *Journal of Gerontological Nursing*, 16, 18–25.

10 Stranges, S., Tigbe, W., Góez-Olivé, F. X., Thorogood, M. & Kandala, N. (2012) 'Sleep problems: An emerging global epidemic?' *Sleep*, 35, 1173–1181.

too much choice, and the rise of social media which fosters FOMO, 'fear of missing out'. In 2013, the American College Health Association (ACHA) reported that one in every two college students in their survey (with an average age of around twenty-two years) had experienced overwhelming anxiety in the previous twelve months, with 12 per cent having been diagnosed or treated for anxiety by a professional over that same period[11]. These high anxiety statistics tend to be the ones that get reported in the media, but the statistics at the lower end of the anxiety continuum are equally interesting. In the ACHA study, almost half the respondents reported having felt no anxiety at all in the last twelve months, so anxiety isn't inevitable but appears to be highly selective in college age youngsters, and this corresponds well with what we see in the UK Annual Population survey, where around 40 per cent of people report very low anxiety, but at the other end of the scale, 20 per cent (one in five) report very high levels of anxiety.

Are Youngsters More Anxious Than Ever?

In 1966 a poll of college freshmen in the United States showed that 'developing a meaningful philosophy of life' was more important to them than 'being well off financially'. But forty years later, in 2006, this preference had been completely turned on its head, and youngsters were being driven by external goals that included high income, status and good looks[12]. This shift in cultural priorities was reflected in research by psychologist Jean Twenge, the author of *Generation Me*. She found that in the years between 1960 and 2002, youngsters' sense of control over their own futures had declined significantly. Whereas

11 http://www.acha-ncha.org/docs/acha-ncha-ii_referencegroup_executivesummary_spring2013.pdf

12 Pryor, J. H., et al. (2007). *The American Freshman: Forty-Year Trends, 1966–2006*. Los Angeles: Higher Education Research Institute.

in 1960 most youngsters aged from nine to twenty-one had a relatively strong sense of internal control over their destiny ('I am in control of the events that will happen in my life'), in 2002 this had switched dramatically in this age group to them feeling that events in their life were controlled by factors other than themselves ('The things that will happen in my life are dependent on the judgements and actions of others'). This shift in attribution was so great that the average young person in 2002 was more focused on external factors affecting their lives than were 80 per cent of young people in the 1960s[13]. Twenge points out that it's this shift away from internal and towards external locus of control in youngsters that appears to map on very closely to increases in childhood and adolescent anxiety over this same forty-year time period, and we know that measures of anxiety correlate quite highly with a person's sense of lack of control over their life.

Some detailed evidence on increases in young people's anxiety can be found in research sponsored by the Nuffield Foundation looking at changing social trends and mental health in adolescents over the past thirty years[14]. A study by Stephan Collishaw and colleagues funded by the Nuffield Foundation compared representative community samples of sixteen- to seventeen-year-olds living in England in 1986 and in 2006[15]. They found significantly higher levels in the reporting of anxiety-related symptoms such as irritable mood, sleep disturbance, and being worn-out/under strain in both boys and girls in the 2006 cohort. In addition, girls also reported significantly higher levels of

13 Twenge, J. et al. (2004). 'It's beyond my control: A cross-temporal meta-analysis of increasing externality in locus of control, 1960-2002.' *Personality and Social Psychology Review*, 8, 308–319.

14 http://www.nuffieldfoundation.org/sites/default/files/files/ Changing%20Adolescence_Social%20trends%20and%20mental%20health_ introducing%20the%20main%20findings.pdf

15 Collishaw, S., Maughan, B., Natarajan, L. & Pickles, A. (2010) 'Trends in adolescent emotional problems in England: A comparison of two national cohorts twenty years apart.' *Journal of Child Psychology & Psychiatry*, 51, 885–894.

general worry and fatigue in the 2006 cohort than the 1986 cohort. There were no changes over the twenty years in other anxiety-related symptoms such as loss of enjoyment, concentration difficulties, being keyed up or on edge, specific fears and difficulty coping. So, there is some evidence there of a modest increase in anxiety-related symptoms in the twenty years between 1986 and 2006.

An independent report commissioned by the National Union of Teachers in 2015 looked specifically at how tests, exams, Ofsted inspections and other 'accountability measures' were affecting today's schoolchildren. The report found that children as young as ten or eleven years were 'in complete meltdown', in tears, feeling sick during tests, and being driven by competitive parents. Self-harming is 'rife' and increased pressure from exams caused children to become significantly more aware at a younger age of their own 'failure'[16].

Collishaw and his colleagues were also able to compare anxiety symptoms in the parents of the students in the two cohorts. Interestingly, parents seemed to be getting more anxious, just like their children. The parents of the 2006 cohort showed significantly higher levels of sleep disturbance and general worry than the 1986 parents – which Collishaw says may raise the prospect of a 'vicious cycle' in which increases in youth emotional problems in one generation could further increase the risk for anxiety in future generations of youth. This is certainly consistent with much of the recent evidence that anxious parents create anxious children (see Chapter 4), and we'll discuss this phenomenon in more detail later.

So what might account for these increases in some anxiety-related symptoms between 1986 and 2006? There is good evidence that the increased systematic testing of schoolchildren across most age

---

16 https://www.theguardian.com/education/2015/jul/04/children-exams-teachers-school-anxiety-nut

ranges has introduced greater awareness of failure in students and the anxiety that's experienced with that. Being introduced at an early age to the idea that your future is dependent on you passing an exam is likely to raise the spectre of failure in the young, underdeveloped mind, and plant the seed of external control of one's destiny. If this focus on external control and away from internal control of events is reinforced during early development, then this feeling of lack of control will inevitably be accompanied by anxiety during childhood and into adolescence.

But there is also the possibility that today's schoolchildren have become more familiar with mental health problems and how to report them, and the apparent rise in youth mental health problems may merely reflect better access to medical and psychological help for these problems as well as an increasing demand from adolescents for such help, and there is some evidence to support this view[17].

The Traditional Social Harbingers of Anxiety

Anxiety is caused by the way you think about things; it's also caused by the various and complex biochemical reactions in your brain and your body. But none of these psychological and biological reactions would be of the slightest significance if there weren't threats and challenges out there in the real world that triggered these cognitive and organic reactions. So, a slightly different strategy to simply conducting surveys that measure levels of anxiety and its symptoms is to look at some of the traditional demographic factors that are related to higher levels of anxiety and see if these factors have increased in prominence over recent years. Here again, the UK Annual Population Survey data are helpful, and pinpoint three factors – marital

17 Smith, R. P., Larkin, G. L. & Southwick S. M. (2008) 'Trends in US emergency department visits for anxiety-related mental health conditions, 1992–2001.' *Journal of Clinical Psychiatry*, 69, 286–294.

status, unemployment and health status – that are associated with anxiety levels.

Anxiety and Marital Status

'A man doesn't know what happiness is until he's married – and by then it's too late!' Many Northern comedians doing the rounds of the working men's clubs during the latter half of the twentieth century had this very withering view of marriage which often formed the core of their stage shows – marriage was bad for you they preached, especially if you were a man. But research by the World Health Organization indicates something quite contrary to this pessimistic view – their research found that marriage appears to have a protective effect against many mental health problems, including anxiety and anxiety disorders, and that this protective effect might be stronger for men than for women[18]. Les Dawson, you were so wrong!

In addition, this same WHO study also suggested that being previously married but now divorced represented an *increased* risk for anxiety disorders in both genders, as did never being married – evidence that is consistent with anxiety data from the Annual Population Survey (see Figure 3.2).

There are a number of possible ways of explaining this relationship between marital status and anxiety levels. The first is an explanation based on selection. That is, married people may not have better mental health and lower anxiety because they are married, but people with better mental health are the ones who get married! For example, anxious individuals – especially those who are socially anxious – may not possess the social skills or have sufficient

18 Scott, K. M., Wells, J. E., Angermeyer, M., Brugha, T. S. et al. (2010) 'Gender and the relationship between marital status and first inset of mood, anxiety and substance use disorders'. *Psychological Medicine*, 40, 1495–1505.

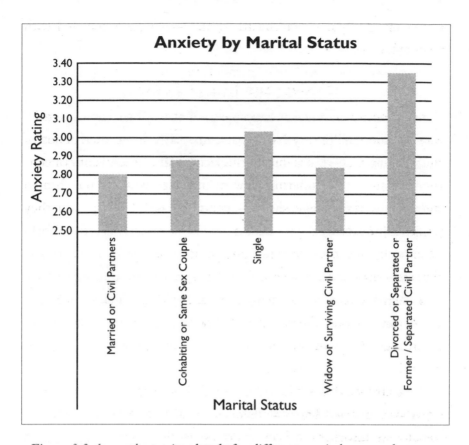

Figure 3.2 shows the anxiety levels for different marital statuses between 2012 and 2015. The statuses with the highest levels of associated anxiety are 'single' and 'divorced or separated', while all others show mean anxiety ratings below the national average of 2.9 out of 10 (from the UK Annual Population Survey).

social interactions to allow them to find a compatible marital partner easily. This would mean that those with less anxiety and better mental health would be the ones who married, and those with greater anxiety and poorer mental health would be more likely to remain unmarried. But what about people who get married very young – does this same selection argument still apply? Probably not, because early marriers may marry early in order to escape difficult or distressing life circumstances (such as a distressing home life), and this view is supported by the fact that psychiatric problems are in fact positively associated with marriage before nineteen years of age[19].

Alternatively, if the association between marriage and lower levels of anxiety is not simply a selection issue, then marriage may have a direct ameliorative effect on anxiety in a number of ways. First, marriage may reduce stress and anxiety by increasing economic resources (including economies of scale when two people live together, and the assurance of an able-bodied partner to help build a mutual future together). Second, marriage may reduce stress and anxiety by generating a sense of relationship permanence, and this is consistent with the fact that marriages are much more likely to last than other relationships such as cohabitations. Third, marriage may have a general psychological benefit by providing enhanced feelings of purpose, improved sense of self, and by generating social approval of the relationship.

Given that marriage seems to have such a protective effect against anxiety, then a potential contributor to any modern-day 'anxiety epidemic' might be a decrease in people getting married contrasted with an increase in individuals getting divorced or living a single life alone. The former could decrease protection against anxiety, and the latter two could exacerbate anxiety levels. Figure 3.3 shows the number of adults marrying and divorcing in England and Wales from 1933 to 2013[20].

19 Forthofer, M. S., Kessler, R. C., Story, A. L., Gotlib, I. H. (1996) 'The Effects of Psychiatric Disorders on the Probability and Timing of First Marriage.' *Journal of Health and Social Behavior*, 37, 121–132.

20 http://www.ons.gov.uk/peoplepopulationandcommunity/birthsdeath-sandmarriages/divorce/bulletins/divorcesinenglandandwales/2013

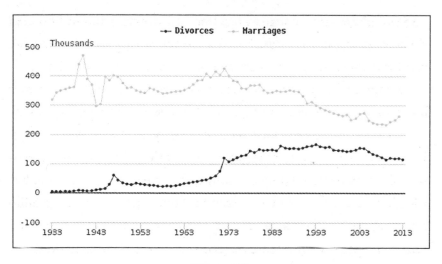

Figure 3.3

This shows a regular and steady decline in the number of marriages between the beginning of the 1970s and recent years, together with a contrasting increase in divorces during the same period. Given that marriage is associated with decreased anxiety and divorce associated with higher levels of anxiety, we would expect these figures to have contributed to an increase in the nation's experience of anxiety between 1970 and the present day. A similar trend can be found in other Western cultures such as the USA, where 50 per cent of marriages end in divorce and marriage rates per annum are down from 8.2 per cent in 2000 to 6.9 per cent in 2014[21]. However, this trend has been tempered in the last few years with news that the UK divorce rate in 2016 is the lowest in forty years, and one explanation for this is the growing acceptance of couples living together before eventually getting married, with the assumption that this prior cohabitation will strengthen the subsequent marriage and protect it

21 https://www.cdc.gov/nchs/nvss/marriage_divorce_tables.htm

against separation and divorce[22]. However, despite these very recent changes in marriage and divorce trends, the larger picture over the past forty years very clearly indicates a decline in marriage and an increase in the rate of divorce over this time. If there is a causal relationship between these events and anxiety – and that's still a big 'if' – these factors will have increased population anxiety levels through a reduction in the protective effect of marriage and the increased stress generated by divorce.

Apart from the obvious disruptive effects of divorce and separation, one of the consequences of a failed marriage is that members of the couple will often end up single and possibly living alone. So how does being single and living alone contribute to anxiety levels?

Living Alone, Loneliness and Anxiety

One implication of being single is that in many cases the single person may live alone, and we know that living alone is a source of anxiety for many people[23]. So has there been an increase in the number of people living alone? In England and Wales, those living alone aged forty-five to sixty-four years increased by a massive 51 per cent over the twenty years to 2016. This was partly due to the increasing population in this age range resulting from the 1960s baby boom, and also as a result of the rise in the proportion of forty-five to sixty-four-year-olds who were becoming divorced in the last twenty years[24] – the latter being a totally new phenomenon

22 http://www.telegraph.co.uk/news/uknews/12011714/Divorce-rate-at-lowest-level-in-40-years-after-cohabitation-revolution.html

23 Chang, E. C., Sanna, L. J., Chang, R. & Bodem, M. R. (2008) 'A preliminary look at loneliness as a moderator of the link between perfectionism and depressive and anxious symptoms in college students: Does being lonely make perfectionist strivings more distressing?' *Behaviour Research and Therapy*, 46, 877–886.

24 http://www.ons.gov.uk/peoplepopulationandcommunity/population andmigration/populationestimates/bulletins/populationestimatesbymarital statusandlivingarrangements/2002to2015

as social mobility allowed middle-aged people to be more aware of new opportunities in their lives. Those living alone aged sixty-five or over also significantly increased by around 16 per cent since 1996, and by 2010 it was acknowledged that over half of all people aged seventy-five and over in the UK lived alone[25]. But, in contrast, the surprise is that those in the much younger twenty-five to forty-four-year-old group living alone has fallen by 12 per cent since 1996, and this seems to be a result of young adults now being more likely to live with their parents or share living accommodation with others outside the family[26]. So, in some older age groups there is certainly some significant evidence that the incidence of living alone has increased over the last twenty years – but living alone may actually have decreased slightly in relatively younger age groups.

However, at least some people enjoy living alone, and loneliness is not the same as living alone. Loneliness is defined by feelings and thoughts of being isolated and disconnected from others[27] – it's an emotional experience, and you don't necessarily have to live alone to feel lonely. A 2012 survey of over two thousand people across all age ranges in the UK by Christina Victor and Keming Yang found that feelings of loneliness were most prevalent in those aged over sixty-five years and those aged under twenty-five years, with around one in ten of all respondents reporting that they always felt lonely – that extrapolates to around six million people in the UK who 'always feel lonely', which is an enormous figure. Data from the Victor and Yang survey identified a number of risk factors for loneliness. As

25 Office of National Statistics, 2010.

26 Stone, J., Berrington, A. & Falkingham, J. (2011) 'The changing determinants of UK young adults' living arrangements.' *Demographic Research, 125*, 629–666

27 Russell, D., Peplau, L. A., & Cutrona, C. E. (1980). 'The revised UCLA Loneliness Scale: Concurrent and discriminant validity evidence.' *Journal of Personality and Social Psychology*, 39, 471–480.

we might expect from what's already been discussed, risk factors included: household size (with those living alone most likely to be at risk of feeling lonely); marital status (those who were divorced, widowed or single were more likely to feel lonely); gender (females were more likely to feel lonely than males); and less education, bad or very bad physical health, fewer social activities, and fewer social contacts made up the remaining risk factors.

But what's interesting is that many of these risk factors didn't apply significantly to those younger than thirty years of age. For this young age group, marital status, household size, and education simply didn't predict loneliness, but instead risk factors were poor physical health, frequency of feeling depressed, and lack of social contacts and social relationships. Many young people may feel lonely regardless of whether they live alone or not, and the causes of loneliness in this age group may be very different to those in older age. For instance, younger people appear to be focused on friendship networks (i.e. the number of relationships they have) and experience loneliness as a function of the fewer friends they have. In contrast, older adults will feel lonely based on the 'quality' rather than 'quantity' of their relationships, and so value marital relationships and confiding relationships as factors that protect them from loneliness.

A simple way of summarising this age difference in loneliness is that loneliness is more likely to be experienced in older adults if they live alone, are not married, are less educated or lack quality relationships, but more likely to be experienced by young people the smaller their network of friends.

In some Westernised countries such as the United States, loneliness is already considered to be at an unprecedented level, with increases in social isolation, significant decreases in social connection to close friends and family, and an increased risk of early mortality. In a US National Science Foundation survey consisting of 1,500 face-to-face interviews, the number of people saying they did not have a confidant with whom they could discuss important matters increased by a third between 1985 and 2004[28].

The biggest increase in living alone has come for the middle-aged and elderly, and for the oldest of these age groups (over seventy-five years) living alone is a particularly distinct experience. Their age means they've lived with experiences that many younger people have not – they've fought wars, raised families and witnessed the death of loved ones, and these experiences bring with them a particular perspective on loneliness. Times have changed. Once upon a time the postman came, the baker delivered bread, the milkman delivered the milk – you knew them all. But nowadays you may not even know your neighbour[29]. This fosters feelings of disconnection and more often a feeling that you contributed usefully to life but now 'you're no longer needed', and this is especially the case if the older person has raised a family or had a productive working life. This loneliness can be compounded by the health anxieties that often accompany old age, including anxieties associated with difficulties in accessing help and treatment, and with mobility problems – especially in social situations.

While we tend to associate depression most often with loneliness, we've described how the state of loneliness is also stressful and anx-iety provoking. Human beings have evolved to be social animals, so a lack of social contact on its own will be a source of stress from a biological and evolutionary point of view. For instance, chronically lonely people have higher blood pressure, are more vulnerable to infection, and are also more likely to develop neurological disorders

28 McPherson, M., Smith-Lovin, L. & Brashears, M. E. (2006) 'Social isolation in America: Changes in core discussion networks over two decades.' *American Sociological Review*, 71, 353–375.
29 Stanley, M., Moyle, W., Ballantyne, A., Jaworski, K. et al. (2010) '"Now-adays you don't even see your neighbours": Loneliness in the everyday lives of older Australians'. *Health & Social Care in the Community*, 18, 407–414.

such as dementia and Alzheimer's disease. In her book *Lonely*, Emily White writes about the frustration and anger caused by being a young person feeling isolated and disconnected[30]. She writes how her intense loneliness drove her to spend afternoons at the local shops in order to seek companionship. While speaking to shop assistants cheered her up a little, she became stressed and angry when she returned home, wondering why she'd had to resort to shopping to find companionship – an example of the anxieties associated with how to go about becoming connected. Loneliness also has stigma associated with it – few people want to admit they're lonely, as if it's something that sets the lonely person apart from the rest of society. It's a term that often seems reserved for the 'unwelcome, the unwanted, and the marginalised', and with this stigma comes the anxiety of how the lonely person feels they should behave when asked about their loneliness, how they should go about seeking companionship, and how they should consider their role in society.

We also know that social isolation causes immune system reactions and inflammation – factors that may have helped our ancient ancestors cope with the many physical risks of being alone. Feelings of illness caused by inflammation and immune system reactions would restrict activity generally and help to keep the individual quietly in a safe place away from survival threats and predators, something that would probably have little benefit in today's modern society.

However, in addition to the many physical risks of loneliness, many of the important effects of lonely isolation are cognitive ones. In a famous study published in 1956, the psychologist Donald Hebb asked volunteers to spend days or weeks by themselves without any other human contact. Most of them soon became very anxious or highly emotional; they struggled to perform simple cognitive tests, but also

30 White, E. (2010) *Lonely*. Harper.

began to suffer hallucinations and paranoia. In modern times, people rarely spend their time in complete isolation experiencing sensory isolation as Hebb's participants did, but loneliness itself can harbour many significant physical and psychological dangers. John Cacioppo at the University of Chicago has spent many years researching how loneliness can compromise psychological and physical well-being[31]. Amongst his findings are that loneliness increases risk of suicide, increases levels of perceived stress – even when the lonely person is exposed to the same stressors as non-lonely people or when they are trying to relax. Lonely people wake up more at night and have less restorative sleep than non-lonely people and spend less time in bed. Some of the physical consequences of loneliness include raised cortisol levels and higher blood pressure, and psychologically the social interactions that lonely people have are less positive than those of other people. These increased health risks of loneliness come with an increased risk of mortality, and this increased mortality risk is comparable to smoking fifteen cigarettes a day!

Finally, social support is psychologically powerful, and if people don't feel socially supported they are more at risk for anxiety and anxiety problems. Because anxiety causes negative thoughts and thought processes may become internalised and self-defeating, anxiety then makes it harder to get out and meet others and make friends – another of the vicious cycles that allows anxiety to breed in those who are lonely.

Is Social Media to Blame?

Is there a role for social media in perpetuating anxiety through feelings of disconnection and loneliness? At first glance, social

31 https://www.theguardian.com/science/2016/feb/28/loneliness-is-like-an-iceberg-john-cacioppo-social-neuroscience-interview

networking sites such as Facebook and Twitter seem to be a modern means of facilitating our connectedness with others, sharing activities and news, and keeping in touch with friends both old and new. But new technologies are usually a mixture of both good and bad, and modern social media are no different.

First, loneliness appears to have a reciprocal relationship with social anxiety. Social anxiety is an anxiety problem where a person has an excessive and unreasonable fear of social situations (see Chapter 10). This may involve a self-consciousness arising from a fear of being closely watched, judged and criticised by others, and will often result in the individual avoiding social or performance situations. Social anxiety disorder is one of the most common of the anxiety disorders and affects 7–13 per cent of individuals in Western countries in their lifetime. In particular, it's highly prevalent in the young, with an age of onset around sixteen years[32]. Social anxiety is known to facilitate loneliness; but loneliness also increases social anxiety and feelings of paranoia, and this may represent a cyclical process that is especially active in the young and in our modern times may be mediated by the use of social media[33].

So how might social media be involved? We've already seen that loneliness in the young is largely a function of perceived friendship networks. Effectively, feelings of loneliness increase the fewer friends that an individual has. In the modern day, social media such as Facebook and Twitter are a significant contributor to the friendship networks of young people, so whether you perceive yourself to be a

32 Magee W. J., Eaton, W. W., Wittchen, H. U., McGonagle, K. A. & Kessler, R. C. (1996) 'Agoraphobia, simple phobia and social phobia in the National Comorbidity Survey.' *Archives of General Psychiatry*, 53, 159–168.

33 Lim, M. H., Rodebaugh, T. L., Zyphur, M. J. & Gleeson, J. F. M. (2016) 'Loneliness over time: The crucial role of social anxiety.' *Journal of Abnormal Psychology*, 125, 620–630.

successful user of social media is likely to have an impact on feelings of loneliness, anxiety, paranoia and mental health generally. In her book *The Happiness Effect*, Donna Freitas draws on survey material from thirteen college campuses across the United States to describe the effects of social media on contemporary adolescents. She concludes that they face continual pressure to project themselves as being perfect online – yes, perfect, not just happy and contented, but ecstatic and successful. This is inevitably a thankless task, doomed to failure, and most young people become anxious lest they portray themselves as being less than perfect or unwittingly post something online that they'll come to regret[34]. There is also growing evidence that this link between social media and the need to be perfect has given rise to significant increases in cosmetic procedures such as Botox and dermal fillers as a result of the pressures exerted by social media on young people[35].

In addition, the relatively modern phenomenon of social media and its associated technology adds a new dimension to loneliness and anxiety by offering the young person a way of directly quantifying friendships, viewing the friendship networks of others for comparison, and providing immediate information about social events. You can compare your own popularity with that of your peers, and manage that adolescent 'fear of missing out' (FOMO) by continually monitoring what's going on socially. So it's easy to see how technology use can take the place of more traditional social interaction and provide a yardstick for one's popularity – or more significantly, one's feelings of loneliness and alienation.

There's no shortage of evidence that loneliness, social anxiety and social isolation can cause excessive use of social networking sites in

34 Freitas, D (2017) *The Happiness Effect*. Oxford University Press.
35 http://www.bbc.co.uk/news/health-40358138

young people. For example, a study of university students in the UK found that real-life social interaction was negatively associated with excessive use of Twitter, and loneliness was a significant factor that mediated this relationship[36], so it's clear that many people use social networking sites in general to relieve themselves of their loneliness. Social anxiety and the need for social assurance are also associated with problematic use of Facebook to the point where Facebook use can become an addiction[37], and has even been shown to activate the same brain areas as addictive drugs such as cocaine[38]. This addiction poses a threat to physical and psychological well-being, interferes with performance at school or work, and staying away from Facebook is viewed by users as an act of 'self-sacrifice' or a 'detoxification'. So the vicious cycle is that loneliness and social anxiety generate use of social networking sites, but then problematic addiction to these sites itself causes further forms of anxiety and stress.

For instance, a study of 1,839 college students by Reynol Junco at Lock Haven University in the US found that time spent on Facebook was strongly and significantly negatively related to an overall grade point average (GPA), but it was only time spent socialising on Facebook that had this negative relationship with school performance[39]. Using Facebook for collecting and sharing information was

36 Ndasauka, Y., Hou, J., Wang, Y., Yang, L. et al. (2016) 'Excessive use of Twitter among college students in the UK: Validation of the Microblog Excessive Use Scale and relationship to social interaction and loneliness.' *Computers in Human Behavior*, 55, 963–971.

37 Lee-Won, R. J., Herzog, L. & Park, S. G. (2015) 'Hooked on Facebook: The role of social anxiety and need for social assurance in problematic use of Facebook.' *Cyberpsychology, Behavior, and Social Networking*, 18, 567–574.

38 Turel, O., He, Q., Xue, G. & Bechara, A. (2014) 'Examination of neural systems sub-serving Facebook "addiction".' *Psychological Reports: Disability & Trauma*, 115, 675–695.

39 Junco, R. (2012) 'Too much face and not enough books: The relationship between multiple indices of Facebook use and academic performance.' *Computers in Human Behavior*, 28, 187–198.

positively predictive of GPA – suggesting that, like most technologies, Facebook use can have some good as well as negative impacts. This study provides no real insight into the direction of cause here – do low grades cause more Facebook use or does more Facebook use cause low grades? However, if Facebook use is a genuine addiction that the user cannot easily control, it takes little imagination to see that Facebook use when it has become uncontrollable may be detrimental to academic performance.

Second, a study of college student Facebook use by Jay Campisi and colleagues at Regis University in Colorado found that almost all respondents experienced some form of Facebook-induced stress and that this stress was directly associated with physical health problems such as upper respiratory infections[40]. But what was interesting was that this stress wasn't a function of how small a respondent's social network was, but how large it was – the larger the Facebook social network, the greater the stress – so a large network of friends on social networking sites is also an added source of stress to today's young people. The added stress and anxiety that large cyber social networks bring has been well illustrated in a study by Julie Morin-Major and colleagues at Harvard[41]. They found that after controlling for other relevant factors such as sex, age, time of awakening, perceived stress and perceived social support, the larger your Facebook network, the greater your diurnal cortisol production – and higher awakening cortisol levels are associated with chronic stress and worry, burnout, and are a vulnerability factor for depression. The authors of this study speculated that the number of Facebook friends

40 Campisi, J., Bynog, P., McGehee, H., Oakland, J. C. et al. (2012) 'Facebook, stress, and incidence of upper respiratory infection in undergraduate college students.' *Cyberpsychology, Behavior, and Social Networking*, 15, 675–681.
41 Morin-Major, J. K., Marin, M.-F., Durand, N., Wan, N. et al. (2016) 'Facebook behaviors associated with diurnal cortisol in adolescents: Is befriending stressful? *Psychoneuroendocrinology*, 63, 238–246.

you have might be positive up to a point, and offer social reassurance and social support, but after this optimum level is passed, this may switch social support into social pressure and lead to increased stress and higher cortisol levels.

We've already seen that use of social media can affect physical health and college or work performance, but just as with any other forms of addiction, fear of not being able to use or access social networking sites causes added distress – in this case caused by feelings of social exclusion that would result from being unable to access these sites[42]. This is a significant sign of addiction – for many of us, our social media is often the first thing we check in the morning and the last thing we check before going to sleep. Social media such as Facebook and Twitter provide constant updates which can turn a mere interest in social networks into an unhealthy, stressful compulsion that not only affects stress levels, but leads to feelings of inadequacy and low self-esteem. As empowering as our modern culture is, it's also dangerous. Young people can talk readily about their addiction to social media, but how candidly can they talk about the anxieties that it generates?

So what exactly are the overarching dynamics of the relationship between social media and loneliness? A study of social isolation in the United States by Miller McPherson and colleagues found that over the twenty years between 1984 and 2005 a person's network of confidants decreased significantly from a mean of 2.94 to 2.08 – a significant drop in what we would call 'real friends'[43]. This is important, because as the sociologist Eric Klinenberg pointed out, it's the

42 Chiou, W. B., Lee, C. C. & Liao, D. C. (2015) 'Facebook effects on social distress: Priming with online social networking thoughts can alter the perceived distress due to social exclusion.' *Computers in Human Behavior*, 49, 230–236.

43 McPherson, M., Smith-Lovin, L. & Brashears, M. E. (2006) 'Social isolation in America: Changes in core discussion networks over two decades.' *American Sociological Review*, 7, 353–375.

quality of your social interactions, not the quantity that defines loneliness[44]. As we saw earlier, this is something that older people are aware of, and life seems to have taught them that a few quality friends are more important than the quantity of connections in your friendship network. Yet although connectedness has fallen significantly over the past forty to fifty years, we still have the compelling evolutionary need to connect with other human beings.

As John Cacioppo has pointed out 'forming connections with pets, or online friends, or even with God, is a noble attempt by an obligatory gregarious creature to satisfy a compelling need', and this continuing need in the face of creeping social isolation has coincided with the Internet providing us with an 'army of replacement confidants' – none of whom are confidants in the original meaning of the term. In this sense, social media such as Facebook have become surrogates for seeking connectedness, and as a consequence our connections grow broader but shallower[45].

But our use of social media to chase connectedness may merely make us feel more disconnected and lonelier. For example, feelings of disconnectedness are associated with passive interactions with Facebook such as using Facebook only to update your own activities or merely scanning the activities of friends. If you log on to Facebook every day like more than half of all Facebook users in the world do, and you use it in this passive way, there is evidence it may well reinforce any feelings you have of loneliness or disconnectedness.[46]

44 Klinenberg, E. (2013) *Going Solo: The extraordinary Rise and Surprising Appeal of Living Alone*. Penguin Books.

45 Marche, S. (2012) 'Is Facebook making us lonely?' http://www.theatlantic.com/magazine/archive/2012/05/is-facebook-making-us-lonely/308930/

46 Ryan T & Xenos S (2011) Who uses Facebook? An investigation into the relationship between the Big Five, shyness, narcissism, loneliness, and Facebook usage. *Computers in Human Behavior*, 27, 1658–1664.

What comes out of these findings about the use of social networking sites is that loneliness and social anxiety do indeed appear to facilitate use of these sites – often to the point of an addiction, when there is an unhealthy desire to spend hours each day checking them. However, even with a good sized social network on sites such as Facebook and Twitter comes added stressors and feelings of disconnectedness – anxieties that can cause physical health problems and negatively affect academic performance in the young. It's fair to say that use of social media by young people is not just a consequence of their social anxieties, but causes additional anxieties and stresses that are all grist to the modern-day anxiety epidemic.

Anxiety and Employment Status

In a 2014 study by the Prince's Trust in the UK, nearly six out of ten unemployed young people said anxiety had prevented them from sleeping well and had even stopped them from asking for help. Four out of ten said that anxiety had caused them to avoid meeting new people, and even stopped them from leaving their home. One in three felt they were simply 'falling apart'. Kirsty Drew, a twenty-one-year-old sales assistant from Birmingham, told interviewers, 'When I left school I just didn't believe in myself. If I went to a job interview I wouldn't be able to make eye contact with the interviewer and I would just think that there is no way I am going to get the job.' She added, 'Every time I thought I was getting somewhere, I would face another barrier.'[47]

The UK Annual Population Survey provides us with evidence of another source of modern-day anxiety – unemployment. The bars in Figure 3.4 show the anxiety ratings provided by those who are in

47 https://www.theguardian.com/society/2015/jan/14/more-than-half-unemployed-young-people-anxious-about-life-report

employment, those jobless people who want to work, are available to work and are actively seeking employment (known as the International Labour Organization, ILO, measure of unemployment), and those who are economically inactive. As we might expect, anxiety levels are highest in those jobless people actively seeking work – an average rating of 3.41 compared with a national mean of only 2.90 – and 20 per cent higher than for those in employment or inactive but not seeking employment.

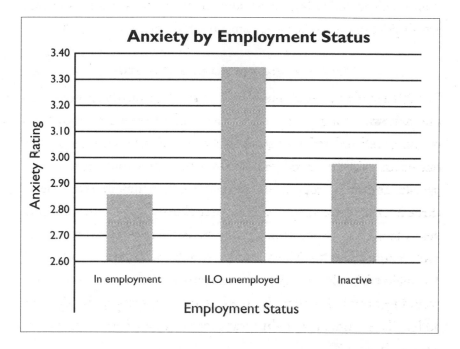

Figure 3.4

If unemployment is a significant source of anxiety and depression, then the recent worldwide economic recession dating back to 2007 should have been one factor in any increase in anxiety and related mental health problems since that time. One study of the impact of this recession demonstrated a significant 3.8 per cent increase in the suicide rate in fifty US states since 2007 – that's 4,750 more suicide deaths between 2007 and 2010 than would have been predicted prior to 2007[48]. Some countries experienced a significant change in mental health behaviours after the beginning of the recession in 2007. For example, a country such as Spain that was significantly affected by the economic recession reported increases in anxiety-based mental health problems and significant increases in the consumption of anti-anxiety medications and sleeping pills after 2007[49]. Other studies suggested that much of this increase in national levels of anxiety and stress in Spain over this period was probably mediated by the negative impact of unemployment[50]. So, it's no surprise to anyone that unemployment is associated with anxiety and stress, and unemployment is an unequivocal *cause* of anxiety because it is known to pre-date symptoms of anxiety in young men who have recently become unemployed[51].

Most people unemployed for six months or more often show signs of depression and this is associated with increased risk of domestic violence and alcohol abuse according to Robert L. Leahy, the author of *The Worry Cure*. Being unemployed is in itself a devastating experience, both financially and in terms of the blows to self-esteem and productivity caused by failing to find work. But it's

48 Reeves, A., Stuckler, D., McKee, M., Gunnell, D. et al. (2012) 'Increase in state suicide rates in the USA during economic recession.' *Lancet*, 380, 1813–1814.

49 Perez-Romero, S., Gascon-Canovas, J. J., de la Cruz-Sanchez, E., Sanchez-Ruiz, J. F. et al. (2016) 'Economic recession (2006–2012) and changes in the health status of the Spanish population.' *Salud Publica de Mexico*, 58, 41–48.

50 Urbanos-Garrido, R. M. & Lopez-Valcarcel, B. G. (2015) 'The influence of the economic crisis on the association between unemployment and health: An empirical analysis of Spain.' *European Journal of Health Economics*, 16, 175–184.

51 Montgomery, S. M., Cook, D. G., Bartley, M. J. & Wadsworth, M. E. J. (1999) 'Unemployment pre-dates symptoms of depression and anxiety resulting in medical consultation in young men.' *International Journal of Epidemiology*, 28, 95–100.

not just the economic consequences of being unemployed that give rise to anxieties; the modern-day job search itself creates anxiety, as does the anticipation of rejection. Only five days after losing her job as a creative director in New York, Kate Kemp wrote about how anxiety began to rule her life as she searched for another job:

> 'Anxiety tells me I need to have every single answer to every single question figured out before anyone even asks. So, I put together a web-based spreadsheet that tracked every job lead along with the primary contact's info, our last date of communication and all the notes on what we'd talked about so far. I also kept folders for every lead containing all the homework I'd done on the company, every email I'd sent/received and any notable industry news stories that might add to interview conversations.
>
> 'When I was tossing, turning and not sleeping in the middle of the night, I'd grab my phone, pull up my spreadsheet and see who I needed to contact next. I'd use my nervous energy to write emails to people I hadn't talked to in a few weeks, then save them as drafts to re-read the next morning with a clear head before sending them out. If writing felt like too much work, I'd search job boards and my favourite agency sites for new job postings. If I found a good one, I'd email it to myself so I could dig a little deeper the next day.'[52]

Just as new forms of Internet social networking may have unexpectedly increased feelings of disconnectedness for many people, modern technology may also have contributed significantly to the factors that make unemployment and job-seeking an even more

52 https://www.monster.com/career-advice/article/life-after-layoffs-anxiety-depression-unemployed

anxious and stressful process. In our earlier quote, Kate Kemp reported using web-based technology to find and track job-opportunities, and there's no doubt that the Internet has made it significantly easier for people to search out and apply for job opportunities to the point where four out of every five job-seekers in the United States report having researched and applied for jobs online[53]. But these technological developments also have huge downsides. It means more and more people end up applying for each vacancy, and leads to many people applying for jobs they're simply not qualified for. This increases the rejection rates, with each individual job opportunity being associated with a growing mountain of rejections – to the point where employers no longer even bother to respond to failed applications. What can make you feel less worthy than a rejection letter? Well, how about not even getting a response at all! In these circumstances you receive no feedback on why you didn't get the job, or even why you didn't get an interview – you're kept in the dark, events begin to seem uncontrollable and irredeemable, and stress is an inevitable consequence of this kind of lack of confidence and lack of control. Because of the ease with which applicants can source job vacancies and apply for them on the Internet, often as many as 75 per cent of applicants are not qualified for the jobs they apply for, and as many as one in three employers claim they will simply blacklist such candidates from other jobs as well[54].

Gone are the days when the unemployed person heard about a local job opportunity from a friend or relative, and was one of only a handful of potential applicants for it. Work organisations have created their own selection headache by massively increasing the

53 http://www.pewinternet.org/2015/11/19/1-the-internet-and-job-seeking/

54 http://careers.workopolis.com/advice/the-dark-side-of-hiring-five-things-employers-would-probably-rather-you-didnt-know/

breadth of advertising for job vacancies with the aid of social media and other Internet technologies to spread their search for the best applicants. In 2014 there were thirty-nine applicants for every graduate employment vacancy in the UK[55], and between 2011 and 2016 these applications were increasing at the rate of around 10 per cent each year[56]. Just do the sums. If an organisation selects only five applicants to interview, that's potential selection odds of eight to one just to get an interview – and once you have the interview, a one-in-five chance of the job itself. Some employment agencies reckon that someone seeking work should expect to attend around fourteen interviews before finally being offered the job they would accept.

The effect of these expanding job selection procedures on applicant stress and anxiety will be significant. First, most job-seekers simply aren't aware of the sums – that jobs are advertised so broadly, and that applying is now so simple and instantaneous that even those who are not desperate for the job are tempted to apply – just to see what happens. You no longer have to take a drive in the rain to the employers' premises and turn up at reception asking if there are any vacancies – you can simply click 'send' on your laptop in the warmth of your own home, just like hundreds of other people nationwide with the same employment desire in mind. The application failure rate is thus colossal and still growing, and if the applicant's expectations aren't properly managed (which they usually aren't), the slowly seeping psychological damage of serial rejections can be significant. Furthermore, the sheer volume of rejections means most organisations don't even send rejection letters that would allow the applicant to seek feedback and at least contemplate the possibility of improving their future applications. Finally, just as Kate Kemp's experience

55 http://www.telegraph.co.uk/finance/jobs/10949825/Employers-receive-39-applications-for-every-graduate-job.html
56 http://www.agcas.org.uk

testifies, the presence of new technology enables the job applicant to relentlessly seek ways of refining their applications, evolve better interview techniques, seek and collate relevant job information, and – sadly – wake regularly throughout the night worrying about the next steps in the relentless search for employment. The modern job-seeker's lot is not just the depression associated with the loss of a job, but the anxiety-provoking challenge of refining the résumé, cramming for the interviews, and handling the growing volume of rejections. Without doubt, the requirements of modern-day job-seeking have added anxiety to the list of negative emotions felt by those who are unemployed.

Anxiety, Poverty and Economic Status

Anxiety is an emotion elicited by life's threats and challenges, and there can be few greater threats and challenges in life than those posed by poverty. It's long been known that there's a significant association between poverty and mental health problems – particularly anxiety and depression – although it's never been quite clear what the direction of this relationship is. Does poverty cause mental health problems, or do mental health problems cause people to drift into poverty? In all probability, it's a bit of both, because we certainly see those with some of the more severe mental health problems, such as psychoses, being unable to maintain employment and so drifting downwards into conditions of poverty and even homelessness. Whereas, alternatively, the conditions of poverty, such as stress, negative life experiences, poor physical health, reduced access to health care and education are likely causes of mental health problems related to both anxiety and depression[57].

57 Weich, S., & Lewis, G. (1998). 'Poverty, unemployment, and common mental disorders: Population based cohort study.' *British Medical Journal*, 317, 115–119.

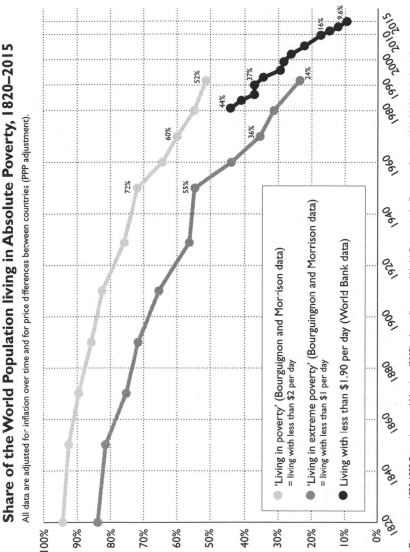

Share of the World Population living in Absolute Poverty, 1820–2015

All data are adjusted for inflation over time and for price differences between countries (PPP adjustment).

'Living in poverty' (Bourguignon and Morrison data)
= living with less than $2 per day

'Living in extreme poverty' (Bourguignon and Morrison data)
= living with less than $1 per day

Living with less than $1.90 per day (World Bank data)

Data sources: 1820-1992 Bourguignon and Morrison (2002) – Inequality among World Citizens, in the Economic Review; 1981-2015 World Bank (PovcalNet)
The interactive data visualisation is available at OurWorldinData.org. There you find the raw data and more visualisations on this topic.
Licensed under CC-BY-SA by the author Max Roser

Figure 3.5

As we've already noted, anxiety is an emotional experience prompted by life's adversities, so is poverty on the increase and contributing to the anxiety epidemic? Contrary to this view, there is no doubt that there have been significant reductions in extreme poverty worldwide – even in the last twenty years or so. Figure 3.5 shows the decline in the share of the world population living in poverty[58] and extreme poverty over the past two hundred years, so we can thankfully say that poverty on a global scale is on the decline – but even twenty years ago around half the world's population were defined as 'living in poverty' earning less than $2 a day[59].

Judith Baer and colleagues at the State University of New Jersey have explored the relationship between anxiety and poverty in a study of 4,898 poor mothers and their children in the USA[60]. They found that the poorest mothers had a significantly higher chance of being diagnosed with Generalised Anxiety Disorder – one of the most common of the anxiety disorders (see Chapter 7). But their interpretation of this finding was rather different to the traditional view that poverty is more likely to cause psychiatric problems. They argued that anxiety in poor mothers was not psychiatric, but a very natural reaction to their severe environmental challenges caused by living in poverty. That is, in the context of poverty, anxiety was a perfectly normal reaction and not a psychiatric dysfunction. Baer and colleagues pointed out that this anxiety was not caused by the malfunction of some internal mechanism, but by physical needs in

58 Poverty is defined as not having enough income to cover the amount of money necessary to meet basic needs such as food, clothing and shelter, and extreme poverty is a condition characterised by severe deprivation of basic human needs, including food, safe drinking water, sanitation facilities, health, shelter, education and information.

59 https://ourworldindata.org/world-poverty/

60 Baer, J. C., Kim, M. & Wilkenfeld, B. (2012) 'Is it generalized anxiety disorder or poverty? An examination of poor mothers and their children.' *Child & Adolescent Social Work Journal*, 29, 345–355.

the real world that were being unmet, and that this anxiety did not prevent the mothers from providing positive parenting for their children. To be sure, the anxiety and stress experienced by these mothers was probably distressing and in need of some palliative treatment – but it was a perfectly natural emotional reaction, where anxiety becomes activated as an adaptive emotion to help these mothers negotiate the many threats and challenges that daily life presents to those in poverty.

Nevertheless, despite a gradual fall in poverty worldwide, we know that the recent worldwide economic recession has resulted in greater income inequalities – even in many wealthy countries the gap between the rich and the poor appears to be widening. Figure 3.6 shows what proportion of all income in five English-speaking countries has gone to the richest 1 per cent[61].

It's clear to see that this income inequality has been continually increasing since the 1980s. In the UK, the accumulated wealth of Britain's richest 1 per cent is more than twenty times the total of the poorest fifth, making the country one of the most unequal in the developed world according to Oxfam[62]. This increasing income inequality has given rise to a relatively new form of anxiety, known as 'status anxiety'. In a report for the Growing Inequalities Impact (GINI) project, Marii Paskov and colleagues from the University of Amsterdam assessed the effects of income inequalities across a range of European countries[63]. They found that income inequality was associated with higher levels of status-seeking, suggesting that people are more anxious about their position in the social and

61 OurWorldinData.org.
62 https://www.theguardian.com/business/2016/sep/13/oxfam-calls-on-theresa-may-to-tackle-rising-uk-inequality
63 Paskov, M., Gerxhani, K., van de Werfhorst, H. G. (2013) 'Income inequality and status.' GINI Discussion Paper 90.

The evolution of inequality in English-speaking countries

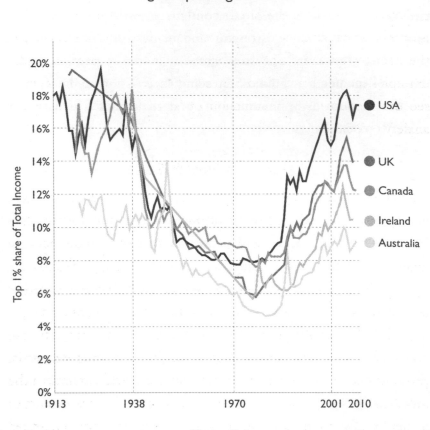

Figure 3.6

The share of total income going to the richest 1 per cent
in five English-speaking countries.

economic hierarchy where income inequalities are high. What is interesting is that these concerns about status and striving to increase status are not just restricted to the poor, but both the poor and the rich feel more anxious about their status in unequal societies. In effect, while anxiety associated directly with poverty may be on the decrease, 'status anxiety' associated with income inequalities is burgeoning across all income groups.

But not all countries have shown this increase in economic inequality since the 1980s (countries like Germany, Japan, France and the Netherlands have exhibited economic growth without a rise in economic inequality), so economic inequality is not universally on the rise. But in those countries where it is on the rise (particular examples include the United States and the UK), we can expect to see the modern-day phenomenon of 'status anxiety' fuelling the anxiety epidemic.

Anxiety and Health Status

People with significant illnesses such as cancer, cardiac disease and dementia are simply not dying as early as they used to. Just to illustrate the effect of this, an interesting fact that used to be found in many medical textbooks was that cigarette smoking appeared to have a protective effect against dementia – fewer regular smokers died of dementia than non-smokers. But, of course, this was because smokers regularly died of other causes such as cancer and heart disease long before they grew old enough to begin developing dementia, and so smoking – in its rather dramatic fashion – actually limited the number of people who went on to develop later-life diseases such as dementia! This tongue-in-cheek example illustrates how increased survival rates (in this case by reducing smoking prevalence) extends the lifespan of individuals which makes them vulnerable to contracting other, later-life chronic illnesses such as dementia.

Now, we've known for a long time that chronic illnesses such as heart disease, stroke, cancer, diabetes, obesity and arthritis put people at greater risk of developing anxiety and depression[64], and experiencing anxiety during illness can also increase the risk of

64 Deloitte Access Economics (2013), 'The Economic Impact of Stroke in Australia', Melbourne: National Stroke Foundation.

other forms of somatic ill-health such as pain awareness, increased medical complications, poor adherence to self-care regimes, and increased susceptibility to additional illnesses such as cancer, cardiac diseases and diabetes[65]. So without doubt, anxiety has always been a companion of chronic illness, and a companion that exacerbates the negative aspects of physical illness. But is illness on the increase and contributing to the modern-day anxiety epidemic? Our first reaction is to suspect it's not on the increase – especially with medical science making exponential strides in the treatment and care of many common illnesses over the past quarter century. However, is the advance of modern medical science promoting longevity but in so doing creating a larger pool of people who live longer with chronic illness and disability?

The 2011 UK Office for National Statistics report on Health makes interesting reading. In 2009 around 79 per cent of adults in the UK reported they were in good health, compared to 75 per cent in 2005. However, in 2009 around one in three adults reported that they had a long-standing illness or disability, compared to just one in four people in 1972 – an increase of almost 10 per cent in thirty-seven years![66] So while there is prima facie reason to believe that more people today are feeling in good health than in previous years, there is also a growing increase in people who report having a chronic or long-lasting illness or disability, and it is chronic illness that we know is linked to experiencing anxiety.

This state of affairs is also apparent in figures published in the US in 2013[67]. Life expectancy in the US increased from 75.2 years

65 Katon, W. K., Lin, E. H. B. & Kroenke, K. (2007) 'The association of depression and anxiety with medical symptom burden in patients with chronic medical illness.' *General Hospital Psychiatry*, 29, 147–155.

66 Office for National Statistics (2011) Health. ISSN 2040-1620

67 'The State of US Health, 1990–2010.' JAMA 2013; 310(6): 591-608. doi:10.1001/jama.2013.13805

in 1990 to 78.2 years in 2010, and death rates at all ages had decreased – leading the report to conclude that 'the United States made substantial progress in improving health'. However, ten of the main diseases and injuries contributing to the number of years that people live with disability increased by over 30 per cent from 1990 to 2010, and chronic illness and disability now accounted for half of the health burden in the United States.

What is clear from these reports is that significant progress has been made in improving health and in improving life expectancy. But a major consequence of the fall in mortality rates in many developed countries is that more people are living longer – and living longer with chronic illness and disability.

But increased survival rates that extend the lifespan of individuals with chronic illnesses not only affect the frequency of anxiety experienced by those who suffer these illnesses, it also has another impact on national anxiety levels – through the mental health of those whose job it has become to care for people with these chronic illnesses. In 2011 there were approximately 5.8 million people providing unpaid care for chronic illness sufferers in England and Wales – just over one in ten of the population were unpaid carers. This number had grown by over 10 per cent in the ten years since 2001[68], and was expected to grow to over nine million unpaid carers in the UK by 2037[69] – largely because of the significant increase anticipated in care for dementia over the next thirty years or so. Families and individuals bear the biggest burden of caring for this increase in people living with chronic illness, and about 40 per cent of carers of family members with dementia have clinically significant

68 Office for National Statistics (2013) '2011 Census Analysis: Unpaid care in England and Wales, 2011 and comparison with 2001.'
69 CarersUK (2015) Facts about carers. https://www.carersuk.org/images/Facts_about_Carers_2015.pdf

anxiety or depression[70]. This inevitably leads to the conclusion that, unless structured coping programmes are made available for unpaid carers in the future, the number of carers suffering anxiety-based problems will increase significantly over the next thirty years.

Despite the fact that medical science makes significant advances year on year, health status will still remain an important contributor to the anxiety epidemic for the foreseeable future. This will fuel the anxieties felt by those with chronic illnesses whose life expectancy is being continually extended by improvements in medical treatment and care, and this significant pool of anxieties will be combined with the high levels of chronic stress experienced by those families and individuals required to act as unpaid carers for them.

The Facts

So have those demographic factors traditionally associated with stress and anxiety increased in our modern times? The answer on balance is probably 'yes', but they've done so in a very selective and interesting way. Community surveys seem to suggest that one in five of us are highly anxious on a regular basis – a figure that's close to what we've come to expect over the years and one that's also consistent with current levels of diagnosis of anxiety disorders and referrals to mental-health services for anxiety-related problems. On the flip side, two in five of us regularly report only very low levels of anxiety – so distressing anxiety hasn't yet extended to everyone.

What else do we know? Well, current anxiety levels are highest in middle age, with the young and the elderly relatively less troubled by anxiety. The significant decline in marriages and increase in divorces since 1970 has almost certainly fuelled anxiety levels given that

70 Cooper, C., Balamurali, T. B. & Livingstone, G. (2007) 'A systematic review of the prevalence and covarites of anxiety in caregivers of people with dementia.' *International Psychogeriatrics*, 19, 175–195.

marriage is a known 'protective' factor against anxiety. Loneliness and living alone are also causes of anxiety, and in the UK today the equivalent of six million people report 'always feeling lonely', and between 1996 and 2016 there was a staggering 51 per cent increase in older people (forty-five to sixty-four years) living alone in the UK. This was partly a result of those in the 'baby boom' of the 1960s becoming older, and also a result of a significant increase in divorce rates among older married couples in the last twenty years. But loneliness is not necessarily the prerogative of the elderly, and many young people suffer the anxieties of loneliness and social anxiety. Paradoxically, the use of social media such as Facebook and Twitter doesn't necessarily offset this loneliness, but can often fuel anxieties by increasing feelings of disconnectedness, facilitating social media 'addictions', and focusing misplaced significance on shallow 'friend' networks rather than encouraging traditional social interaction and the development of genuine 'confidants'.

The financial crisis of 2007–2008 also had its impact on anxiety levels through unemployment and economic recession, with some studies directly linking increased levels of anxiety and stress since 2007 to this crisis. Modern-day unemployment also brings its own brand of anxieties through the complexities of the contemporary online job search and application – the challenges of refining the résumé, cramming for the endless interviews, and handling the growing volume of rejections. On the positive side, one cause of anxiety – poverty – is certainly on the decline globally, but has been replaced by a new and related source of anxiety called 'status anxiety'. Income inequalities are on the rise in many countries, including the UK and USA, and where income inequalities have grown, both rich and poor have become more anxious about their own status.

Poor health is also a source of chronic anxiety, but just as poverty may be on the decline globally, we can also conclude that more people than ever are in better health than was the case twenty to thirty years ago. However, health status is contributing to modern-day anxiety levels in an indirect and probably unsuspected way. With increases in life expectancy has come an increase in the number of people living with chronic illness and disability, and chronic illness is a known associate of anxiety. Just to compound this issue, people with chronic illness (such as dementia) often need personal care on a daily basis, and this is usually dispensed by unpaid carers (often family members or close friends). A consequence of this is that by 2037 there are likely to be around nine million unpaid carers in the UK, of which we can expect around 40 per cent to have debilitating levels of stress and anxiety.

As long as there's a world for human beings to live in, anxiety will never go away. An evolving world will simply change and redefine the challenges that demand us to be anxious. This is the case with traditional sources of anxiety, where our attempts to eliminate global causes of inequality and stress merely create more sophisticated, focused and undeniably modern anxieties – their modernity defined by new technology, modern fashion, contemporary social change, and in some cases by the careless loss of traditional ideas and knowledge – such as our failure to understand that the number of friends we have on a social network is no substitute for just one or two true confidants.

But as we discovered in Chapter 2 we do have genuinely new anxieties – not anxieties shaped by changes in traditional sources of anxiety, but anxieties uniquely created by our modern world. Bring on the zombies and the vampires, and unleash the swarms of rats!

CHAPTER FOUR

Anxiety & Anxiety Disorders

The Origins of Individual Differences in Anxiety

'What does your anxiety do? It does not empty tomorrow of its sorrow, but it empties today of its strength. It does not make you escape the evil; it makes you unfit to cope with it if it comes.'

— A. W. Pink

'My name is Millie. I'm forty-two and I've worked as a hospital radiographer since 1998. This is when my washing problems started and I became aware of the obsessive compulsive disorder that was to rule my life for the next thirteen years.

'The first time it happened was in the operating theatres. Going for my break I went to the scrub room, washed my hands and opened the door. In the kitchen I washed my hands again because I'd touched the door. I made my tea and washed again because I'd touched the fridge and kettle.

'It felt like something was hanging off my thumb and forefinger. Until I'd wet "it" (whatever "it" was) I couldn't use them because I felt like everything I touched would be contaminated. I never had to scrub: simply touching something wet and rubbing them together would remove the "thing". Getting a parking ticket from the machine at work was an issue . . . I was happy if it had rained as I could wipe my finger and thumb on the machine to wet them. One day I used snow.

It wasn't the wiping but more the thought processes involved and the time wasted trying to avoid touching things. Working in a busy department was tricky, watching colleagues touching everyday objects that had dropped on the floor and not cleaning their fingers. Eventually I wasn't comfortable touching patients' beds, or door handles – I would kick the doors open to save touching them! The rituals became relentless.'[1]

Millie has a diagnosis of obsessive-compulsive disorder. She differs from most of those people we described in the Waiting Room in Chapter 3 because anxiety has crept into almost every waking moment of her life. In her case, anxiety rears its head in the most mundane of daily activities, such as opening a door, switching on a kettle, or getting a ticket from a parking machine. Then, each time these regular anxieties are encountered, the fear has to be 'neutralised' through ritualised behaviours that take time and effort. Anxiety is a charming manipulator. It spins you an elaborate story of a world that's frightening, threatening, dangerous and unpredictable. Our good-intentioned hero can then turn villain and we're likely to realise this only when it's too late.

Take the example of the child who believes there's a monster in the bedroom closet. The child is too afraid ever to open the closet door, and the consequence is that each night the child's belief in the monster becomes more and more entrenched and elaborate. What's more, this belief in the closet monster will never be disconfirmed

1 Moulton-Perkins, A., Whittington, A. & Chinery, M. (2015). 'Working with people with anxiety.' In G. Davey, N. Lake & A. Whittington (Eds.) *Clinical Psychology*. Routledge.

while the closet door remains firmly shut. This is how our everyday anxiety gets transformed into a debilitating disorder that's distressing and disabling. In the case of anxiety disorders, not only do we end up creating anxieties for ourselves, we also become disabled by the need to control what happens in the future. The Lebanese poet and artist Kahlil Gibran got it about right when it comes to anxiety disorders: 'Our anxiety doesn't come from thinking about the future, but from wanting to control it.'

Have another look at those clients in the Waiting Room. Thinking about the future – the dentist's drill, the possible pain, the need to distract – it's making them all behave in the very different ways they do. In these cases each of them is only reacting naturally with their own brand of anxiety to their thoughts of what is to come. But what happens if you try to impose a further layer of control on this anxiety – just as Millie the radiographer has done?

Even when it's working for us, anxiety is not a particularly pleasant experience. But when it turns into an anxiety disorder it's distressing, disabling and difficult to shake off. We're still unsure about how normal anxiety turns into an anxiety disorder, and even less clear about how we develop one particular anxiety disorder rather than a different one. I'll be taking a detailed look at the main anxiety disorders in the next few chapters, but in this chapter I'll briefly describe these disorders, have a look at some of the psychological processes that lead many of us from experiencing normal levels of anxiety to developing an anxiety disorder, and look at the impact of anxiety disorders on the modern world. But first, where does our individual sensitivity to anxiety come from?

Individual Differences in Anxiety

What influences individual differences in anxiety – why are some people more anxious than others? We each have an anxiety level that seems to stay with us for most of our lives. For some this means that many aspects of daily life make them feel anxious, but for others literally nothing seems to faze them at all. This indigenous anxiety level is commonly called *trait anxiety* because it's a lifelong 'trait' that we each carry around with us. But what instils this personal baseline level of anxiety in each of us?

First, do you simply inherit your level of anxiety from your parents? There's certainly an inherited component to anxiety, but it's not as large as we might have expected. Studies of the heritability of individual traits are often carried out on twins, and these studies compare the probability with which monozygotic twins (MZ, identical twins) and dizygotic twins (DZ, non-identical twins) exhibit a trait such as anxiety. MZ twins share 100 per cent of their genetic material, whereas DZ twins share only 50 per cent of their genes, so if there's a direct effect of inheritance on trait anxiety, we'd expect greater concordance in anxiety measures between MZ twins than between DZ twins. From these comparisons a heritability estimate can be calculated, and most twin studies of anxiety in children and adults come up with a heritability estimate of around 30 per cent[2]. The heritability measure is an attempt to establish the influence of genes versus environment on the *variability* in levels of anxiety in the population. In this case, genetics is responsible for around 30 per cent of the variability in anxiety levels between individuals, and while measurement error is likely to account for at least some of the unexplained variance, much of the remaining 70 per cent of variance will probably be due to the experiences that people have during their lifetime.

We've already discussed what a complex psychological and biological phenomenon anxiety is. It has physiological components,

2 Eley, T. C. & Gregory, A. M. (2004) *Behavioral Genetics*. New York: Worth Publishers.

cognitive components and behavioural components, all of which might be influenced by many different genes, and this seems to be the story told by genome-wide association studies of anxiety. When genes can be identified that influence anxiety, the findings are that anxiety is influenced by very many genes each of which exerts only a relatively small effect[3]. This leads us to suspect that a greater influence on the variability of levels of anxiety between individuals will be the experiences that those individuals have during their lifetime, and there are certain types of experiences that appear to be risk factors for greater anxiety levels and even the development of anxiety disorders later in life.

One of these risk factors for subsequent anxiety is childhood adversity. Childhood adversity is a broad category of negative events that can impact on a child during early life. Many of these experiences may represent extreme experiences for any individual (such as childhood physical and sexual abuse), and there are clear links between such experiences and childhood anxiety generally[4]. But there are a whole range of more normative types of childhood adversity within the family that can generate anxiety in the child across the course of their lifetime, and these include such things as maternal depression, family financial stress, parental conflict, family anger, maternal role overload, and negative parenting. The last factor includes disciplining strategies such as threatening a child – 'You stop crying or I'll give you something to cry about' – or attending to the child only

3 Trzaskowski, M., Eley, T. C., Davis, O. S. P., Doherty, S. J. et al. (2013) 'First genome-wide association study on anxiety-related behaviours in childhood.' PLOS One. doi.org/10.1371/journal.pone.0058676.

4 Whiffen, V. E. & MacIntosh, H. B. (2005). 'Mediators of the link between childhood sexual abuse and emotional distress. A critical review.' Trauma, Violence & Abuse, 6, 24–39.

when they're doing something wrong[5]. Quite strikingly, childhood adversity such as parental mental health problems and household dysfunction have affected as many as two out of every three children by the age of eighteen[6].

In addition, during childhood, even many experiences that seem relatively unexceptional may seem stressful to a child who is relatively inexperienced in the world, and these can provide significant events that trigger bouts of stress and anxiety[7]. For example, living with illnesses such as asthma and eczema increases childhood anxiety, and the death of a pet – to whom a child may have been significantly attached – can cause prolonged anxiety and depression[8].

So how does childhood adversity facilitate trait anxiety? There are probably a number of psychological and biological mechanisms that mediate the link between adversity and anxiety, but neuroimaging studies by Ryan Herringa and colleagues at the University of Wisconsin suggest that childhood adversity has some significant long-lasting effects on brain wiring. In particular, childhood adversity can often lead to altered connectivity in the brain's fear circuitry and cause internalising symptoms typical of childhood anxiety and depression. In a study of sixty-four adolescents, childhood adversity predicted increased amygdala-hippocampus connectivity, and increased connectivity between these centres facilitates fear

5 Essex, M. J., Klein, M. H., Cho, E., & Kalin, N. H. (2002) 'Maternal stress beginning in infancy may sensitize children to later stress exposure: Effects on cortisol and behavior.' *Biological Psychiatry*, 52, 776–784.

6 Anda, R. F., Felitti, V. J., Bremner, J. D., Walker, J. D. et al. (2006) 'The enduring effects of abuse and related adverse experiences of childhood. A convergence of evidence from neurobiology and epidemiology.' *European Archives in Psychiatry and Clinical Neuroscience*, 256, 174–186.

7 Lewis-Jones, S. (2006) 'Quality of life and childhood atopic dermatitis: The misery of living with childhood eczema.' *International Journal of Clinical Practice*, 60, 984–992.

8 Kaufman, K. R. & Kaufman, N. D. (2006) 'And then the dog died.' *Death Studies*, 30, 61–76.

and anxiety to negative events and negative stimuli[9]. Subsequent studies indicated that even experiences of childhood adversity that are relatively common, such as family financial stress or maternal depression, can bias the amygdala towards reactivity to negative content, potentially tipping the brain's emotion regulatory circuits towards vulnerability to anxiety by late adolescence[10]. But while childhood adversity is a risk factor for anxiety, Ryan Herringa has discovered that some children who suffer adversity have also developed greater connectivity between the amygdala and the pre-frontal cortex – an area of the brain involved in complex behaviours such as decision-making, planning and emotion regulation. These children did not exhibit internalising symptoms and may have developed a way of dealing with anxiety by engaging deliberate forms of emotion regulation that dampen down amygdala reactivity and inhibit experienced anxiety.

Are examples of childhood adversity on the increase, and as a consequence helping to contribute to the modern anxiety epidemic? It's hard to estimate, but the Crime Survey for England and Wales in 2016 notes that police forces in England and Wales had been dealing with a growing number of reports of child abuse in recent years, although many of these have been historical cases reported by adults many years after the event[11]. Figures compiled by the National

9 Herringa, R. J., Birn, R. M., Ruttle, P. L., Burghy, C. A. et al. (2013) 'Childhood maltreatment is associated with altered fear circuitry and increased internalizing symptoms by late adolescence.' *Proceedings of the National Academy of Sciences*, 110, 19119–19124.

10 Herringa, R. J., Burghy, C. A., Stodola, D. E., Fox, M. E. et al. (2016) 'Enhanced prefrontal-amygdala connectivity following childhood adversity as a protective mechanism against internalizing in adolescence.' *Biological Psychiatry*, 1, 326–334.

11 https://www.ons.gov.uk/peoplepopulationandcommunity/crimean djustice/articles/abuseduringchildhood/findingsfromtheyearendingmarch 2016crimesurveyforenglandandwales#main-points

Society for the Prevention of Cruelty to Children (NSPCC) showed that sexual offences against children under eighteen in the UK had increased by some 50 per cent between 2008 and 2014, quite possibly as a result of more people finding the confidence to report childhood abuse rather than a direct increase in the level of abuse itself[12]. However, this increase in reported abuse still raises questions about the level of support for victims when budgets for criminal justice, welfare and health are all under strain, raising doubts about the ability of services to identify victims and provide suitable care and treatment for resultant mental health problems such as anxiety.

Some of the other forms of normative adversity in childhood are also at disturbingly high levels. For instance, maternal depression has been identified as a major public health problem in the United States, with an estimated one in ten children experiencing a depressed mother in any given year[13]. Similarly, in 2017, a report by Nationwide set out to discover what the average British family was like, and found that just under half of all families surveyed were deeply worried about finances[14]. These were not families on the poverty line, but families with an average of two children and two working parents. But bringing up a family in the current times of financial austerity is an alarmingly expensive business, and involves the stress of 'just about coping' – a stress that we know can influence a child's vulnerability to anxiety.

The conclusion seems to be that it's not just severe forms of childhood adversity that are on the increase, but more 'normative' forms of stress within the family are also at unacceptably high levels

12 http://www.bbc.co.uk/news/uk-33160361
13 Ertel, K. A., Rich-Edwards, J. W. & Koenen, K. C. (2011) 'Maternal depression in the United States: Nationally Representative Rates & Risks.' Journal of Women's Health, 20, 1609–1617.
14 http://www.aol.co.uk/money/2017/02/06/report-reveals-families-on-a-financial-knife-edge/

– all grist to the anxiety mill in the form of family stressors that can have a lifelong influence on a child's vulnerability to anxiety.

Helicopter, Snowplough and Bubble-Wrap Parenting

It's hard to deny that parents are more involved in their children's lives and education than ever before. Parents micromanage their offspring in almost every way – often in the form of contradictions, such as limiting TV time and iPhone activity but providing them with the latest X-Box and every new gadget that'll make them the envy of their peer group. Then there's the after-school geography club and taekwondo lessons, the Saturday morning dance class and junior football league, the meticulously selected sleepovers, and the fastidious monitoring of daily sugar and chocolate intake. The modern Internet era allows even more forms of elaborate child monitoring, from ensuring that location services are constantly active on little Noah's smartphone, to employing drones to watch Olivia walk to school.[15]

These micromanaging mums and dads are known as *helicopter parents*, and are a modern-world phenomenon – constantly searching the Internet for 'better' ways of parenting, using modern communications technology to monitor their offspring's every move, and paying particularly close and cosseting attention to their child's educational progress – who else could have designed eight-year-old Liam's elaborate school science fair project depicting perfectly scale-sized models of craters on the moon? In addition, there are also the *snowplough parents* – the overprotective ones who 'plough' onwards before their child, removing everything in life that might be a potential obstacle before their child encounters it.

15 http://whnt.com/2015/04/22/helicopter-parenting-dad-uses-drone-to-walk-daughter-to-school/

What's all this got to do with anxiety? Well, maybe parents who swathe their children in protective bubble-wrap do have a lot to answer for when it comes to their offspring's anxieties. We've known for decades that anxiety seems to run in families, with over 80 per cent of parents of children with anxiety problems exhibiting significant levels of anxiety themselves[16]. Given that genetic inheritance is not an overwhelming contributor to the variance in our anxiety levels, this strongly suggests that anxiety may somehow be socially 'transmitted' within the family. We would automatically assume this is a parent influencing their children, but we also know that children can quite regularly influence the behaviour of their parents – so this transmission might easily be bidirectional.

To begin with, there are a number of ways in which parents might transmit anxiety to their children – both direct and indirect. In an important early study, Peter Muris, Professor of Child Psychology at the University of Maastricht, asked mothers the extent to which they generally expressed their fears in the presence of their children. He found that mothers who always reported expressing their fears in their children's presence had children with the highest levels of self-reported fears. Interestingly, this effect of the mother's expressed anxieties on their offspring's fears was not found for fathers – it was an effect entirely specific to mothers.

Another direct way in which anxiety can be transmitted from parents to their children is through the modelling of avoidance – it's likely to be the case that extremely avoidant parents model avoidance as a coping strategy when confronted with potential threats and challenges. This has been shown to be the case with the transmission of social anxiety between parents and offspring. For example,

16 Ginsburg, G. S. & Schlossberg, M. C. (2002) 'Family-based treatment of childhood anxiety disorders.' *International Review of Psychiatry*, 14, 143–154.

parents who tend to be socially isolated (who rarely go out except on special occasions), or express concern with other people's opinions (by placing importance on how it would look to other people if, for example, their child didn't do well at school), or show avoidance to socially relevant stimuli (by avoiding some social gatherings because of shyness) tend to have children who also show high levels of social anxiety during their development[17]. And this too is an effect that's found much more reliably with anxious mothers than with anxious fathers. In fact, it's not just older children who are affected by the anxiety cues transmitted by their parents – infants and toddlers as young as ten-months old have been shown to be influenced by their mother's behaviour, including responding with fear to fearful gestures and expressions[18], and – in a research article intriguingly titled 'Mother knows best' – showing avoidance to toys to which their mother has reacted negatively[19].

Now we come to the helicopter and snowplough parents. Parents can bring many different characteristics to their parenting, and one of the characteristics that appears to facilitate child anxiety is over-protectiveness. Overanxious or overprotective parenting generates a lack of confidence and feelings of inadequacy in a child. Studies carried out by psychologist Ron Rapee and colleagues at Macquarie University in Australia cleverly demonstrated that when mother and child are jointly engaged in a puzzle task, overprotective or anxious mothers are significantly more likely to be intrusive and become

17 Bruch, M. A. & Heimberg, R. G. (1994) 'Differences in perceptions of parental and personal characteristics between generalized and nongeneralized social phobics.' *Journal of Anxiety Disorders*, 8, 155–168.

18 Feinman, S. (Ed.) (1992) *Social Referencing and the Social Construction of Reality in Infants*. New York: Plenum Press.

19 Gerull, F. C. & Rapee, R. M. (2002) 'Mother knows best: Effects of maternal modeling on the acquisition of fear and avoidance behavior in toddlers.' *Behaviour Research and Therapy*, 40, 279–287.

overly involved with the child in order to reduce the child's distress. This over-involvement increases the child's vulnerability to anxiety by increasing the child's perception of threat, reducing their perceived control over threat, and increasing their avoidance of threat[20]. Being a mother and doing the right thing for your child is clearly a thankless task!

Ron Rapee has argued that overprotective parents may regularly – but inadvertently – support, assist in, or reward their children's anxious or avoidant behaviour. Allowing a child to stay home from a social event or school when they're feeling anxious or fearful, reducing a child's distress with special treatment, bringing toys in from the garden if there's a feared dog present – such acts may well encourage children to continue to be anxious in order to receive comfort from their parents or avoid situations that make them fearful. Just to exacerbate these kinds of effects, it's also clear from many early studies that once a child begins to react anxiously, their mother will often begin to behave more negatively towards them, creating a potential vicious cycle of anxiety and negativity between mother and child[21].

You'll have noticed that this section has very much focused on mothers as being the agents of the transmission of anxiety within families. This is because studies have often failed to find similar effects with fathers. So, what's the role of the father in all this? This is far from clear, although Susan Bögels and colleagues from the University of Amsterdam have argued that the evolved basis of sex differences in parenting means that mothers and fathers will convey quite different aspects of anxiety to their offspring. Mothers will

20 Hudson, J. L. & Rapee, R. M. (2002) 'Parent-child interactions in clinically anxious children and their siblings.' *Journal of Clinical Child & Adolescent Psychology*, 31, 548–555.
21 Dumas, J. E. & LaFreniere, P. J. (1993) 'Mother-child relationships as sources of support or stress: A comparison of competent, average, aggressive, and anxious dyads.' *Child Development*, 64, 1732–1754.

tend to transmit caution and information about threat (with overly anxious mothers transmitting more anxiety to their offspring), whereas fathers may be more likely to teach their offspring how to explore the environment and compete with others (and in so doing, reduce anxiety)[22]. One implication of this argument is that it may be more difficult for anxious fathers to alleviate their children's anxiety, because a father's anxiety will hinder their own role in exploring the external world and interacting with others – behaviours that would be important in demonstrating to their offspring what is safe in the world.

'They f**k you up, your mum and dad.
They may not mean to, but they do.
They fill you with the faults they had
And add some extra, just for you.'

That's the first verse of Philip Larkin's famous – but harsh – poem *This Be the Verse*. So, good luck, kids! Every year around 130 million children are born to parents who know relatively little about parenting, and probably even less about protecting the mental health of their offspring. The Internet provides a confusing manual, and to be safe and sure parents often end up protecting their children from the bad things out there rather than teaching them how to cope with them. You didn't come with a manual, so you've only got a lifetime to live with the anxieties your poor, struggling parents bestowed on you! What's the best you could expect? Well, think yourself lucky if you have a non-anxious mother who is not overprotective and

22 Möller, E. L., Majdandžić, M., de Vente, W., & Bögels, S. M. (2013) 'The evolutionary basis of sex differences in parenting and its relationship with child anxiety in western societies.' *Journal of Experimental Psychopathology*, 4, 88–117.

has a good set of positive coping strategies to model for you. And then there's Dad – make sure he's also non-anxious, outgoing and sociable, and ready and willing to show you what's safe and fun in the modern world. Have you got them both? Then you're very, very lucky!

How to be a parent in 2018:

Make sure your children's academic, emotional, psychological, mental, spiritual, physical, nutritional and social needs are met while being careful not to over-stimulate, under-stimulate, improperly medicate, helicopter, or neglect them in a screen-free, processed foods-free, GMO-free, negative energy-free, plastic-free, body-positive, socially conscious, egalitarian but also authoritative, nurturing but fostering of independence, gentle but not overly permissive, pesticide-free, two-storey, multilingual home, preferably in a cul-de-sac with a backyard and 1.5 siblings spaced at least two years apart for proper development . . . also don't forget the coconut oil.

How to be a parent in every generation before the present one:

Feed them sometimes.[23]

---

23 Laditan, B. https://www.facebook.com/BunmiKLaditan/posts/1899244 270322560:0

Turn Off the TV or Hide Behind the Sofa

There are many types of specific experiences that can affect individual differences in anxiety levels, and I'll be describing many of these in subsequent chapters. Some of these individual experiences can be very salient and not only raise anxiety levels generally but lead to the development of more severe and disabling anxiety disorders. But in this modern world, many experiences often come in a vicarious form – through the TV, newspapers, media broadcasts and the Internet. What's significant is that the information these forms of media can transmit can often have an impact on anxiety levels that are equivalent to first-hand experience.

One of the defining memories for me as a youngster was hiding behind the sofa while my parents watched those monstrous metallic aliens called Daleks screeching 'Exterminate!' at everything on the TV screen during one of the first episodes of the *Doctor Who* science-fiction series. Not only did it stick in my memory, I also made sure I stayed in my bedroom when the next few weeks' episodes were being shown. To the best of my knowledge, I've never been attacked by a real-life Dalek, but just watching them on black-and-white TV was enough to instil anxiety for quite some time (in case you're concerned, I'm over it now!).

Much of the information that young people get about the world (real or fictional) comes in a vicarious form. For example, whether it's in school, at home, or through the media, youngsters are regularly exposed to information about potential threats and dangers. They're bombarded with violent, threatening and scary images on television and are being constantly warned about the dangers of the Internet, sexual grooming, drugs, or even abduction. So what effect does this information have on levels of anxiety?

Research pioneered by Andy Field at the University of Sussex suggests that mere information about potential fears may be a significant source of childhood anxiety. In Professor Field's experimental procedures children aged seven to nine years were shown pictures of animals they were unfamiliar with (such as the rare Australian marsupial known as a quoll – see Figure 4.1). They were then given some information about the animal. Some were told the animal was benign and friendly, while others were told it was scary and dangerous. The researchers found that fear beliefs about the animal increased significantly if the children had been given negative information about the quoll (e.g. 'I would be scared if I found a quoll in my garden') – but only if the information had been provided by an adult and not by a peer[24]. Subsequent studies showed that fear of the quoll instilled merely by an adult providing negative information about it resulted in active avoidance of the animal (children wouldn't go near a box in which they were told there was a quoll), the fear of quolls could still be detected six months later, and this fear learning was facilitated if the child had high levels of trait anxiety[25].

As parents, we already know that our children can periodically pick up intense fears and anxieties that seem to come 'out of the blue'. But studies such as these strongly suggest that young children can acquire quite resilient fears vicariously through even just snippets of negative information provided by an authority figure – and they're fears and anxieties that can be relatively long lasting.

It's significant that these vicariously acquired fears occur primarily as a result of information from authority figures such as parents

24 Field, A. P., Argyris, N. G. & Knowles, K. A. (2001) 'Who's afraid of the big bad wolf: A prospective paradigm to test Rachman's indirect pathways in children.' *Behaviour Research and Therapy*, 39, 1259–1276.

25 Field, A. P. (2006) 'Watch out for the beast: Fear information and attentional bias in children.' *Journal of Clinical Child and Adolescent Psychology*, 35, 337–345.

Figure 4.1 Are you frightened of this animal? Professor Andy Field has developed a procedure for investigating how exposure to information about potential threats affects fear acquisition in children. This photo shows an Australian quoll – an animal not well known to most children in the northern hemisphere. Some children are then told the quoll is potentially dangerous and others told that they are harmless and benign. Children told they are dangerous subsequently fear them more and avoid possible contact with them in experimental approach tasks, and this fear can often last up to six months. Just in case you need to know the truth, despite a sometimes fierce appearance, quolls are typically calm. The right combination of calm quoll and tolerant human could be a good match!

or teachers, but in each of our homes there's a potential source of authoritative negative information lurking in the corner of the sitting room – the television! It's not surprising then that children's fears and anxieties are significantly influenced by what they see on the TV screen. Juliette van der Molen and Brad Bushman from the University of Amsterdam studied the effects of violence on TV in

572 children aged between eight and twelve years old[26]. They found that violent threats viewed on TV increased both fear and anxieties (the latter in the form of increased worrying). When violent content was described as news, it produced more fear than when it was described as fiction. Fright and worry were greater in girls than boys and in younger children than older children. Furthermore, these effects of TV on childhood anxiety can be relatively long lasting. A study of undergraduate students found that over 90 per cent of them recalled enduring fears and anxieties caused by viewing frightening media during childhood or adolescence[27], and many children retain vivid memories of disturbing TV content – especially on news programmes showing items about natural disasters, war, kidnappings, and burglaries[28].

It's not just the TV that's the culprit in this modern world, children and adolescents can easily access negative emotional material on digital devices such as smartphones, tablets and laptops – allowing them to view material that may have a long-lasting effect on anxieties and worries. As a consequence, managing a child's access to media these days can be a 24/7 problem for parents, and many modern guidelines for parents emphasise the need to limit daily screen time for their children. Families can do this creatively by designating media-free times together, agreeing rules such as banning TV and smartphones from the dinner table, or keeping media devices out of bedrooms[29]. But we must remember that media such as TVs

26 Van der Molen, J. H. W. & Bushman, B. J. (2008) 'Children's direct fright and worry reactions to violence in fiction and news television programs.' *Journal of Pediatrics*, 153, 420–424.

27 Harrison, K. & Cantor, J. (1999) 'Tales from the screen: Enduring fright reactions to scary media.' *Media Psychology*, 1, 97–116.

28 Riddle, K., Cantor, J., Byrne, S. & Moyer-Guse, E. (2012) '"People killing people on the news": Young children's descriptions of frightening television news content.' *Communication Quarterly*, 60, 278–294.

29 http://edition.cnn.com/2016/10/21/health/screen-time-media-rules-children-aap/

and digital devices are not just purveyors of negativity and fear, they also contribute positively to our modern society, facilitating communication and creativity, and promoting education and learning. Parents shouldn't just be the strict guardians of the children's access to the digital media, they should be their media mentors and tutors – teaching them about both the negatives and the positives of the modern digital era, and being an appropriate digital media role model themselves.

Many of these developmental experiences will contribute to any one individual's level of anxiety, and will often determine those levels throughout a lifetime. These effects of parenting are often moderated by other factors (such as the child's existing level of trait anxiety), and generalisations about the effects of parenting on offspring anxiety are difficult to make because of the significant methodological differences between studies[30]. However, parenting is important and clearly has some effect on children's anxiety, but as yet we don't quite know how much.

The Seduction by the Dark Side –
The Development of Anxiety Disorders

Anxiety disorders are the baddies of the anxiety world. They each come with a clinically diagnosable list of symptoms, and by definition they cause significant distress to the sufferer and extensively impair occupational, educational, social and family functioning (that's pretty much everything!). There are a number of important anxiety-based or anxiety-related clinical disorders. I'll cover these in greater depth in subsequent chapters, but let's just give you the flavour of what each of these disorders entails.

30 Percy, R., Creswell, C., Garner, M., O'Brien, D. & Murray, L. (2016) 'Parents' verbal communication and childhood anxiety: A systematic review.' *Clinical Child & Family Psychology Review*, 19, 55–75.

The most basic of these disorders are *specific phobias*. These are defined as a 'marked fear or anxiety about a specific object or situation' (e.g. flying, heights, animals, etc.). As many as 60 per cent of the population will hold unreasonable fears about something or other[31], but this would only be diagnosed as a clinical disorder if the fear was distressing to the sufferer and interfered significantly with normal daily living. Chapter 6 looks in depth at the mysterious origins of specific phobias.

Next is *social anxiety disorder*. This is a form of phobia, but is specific to social situations such as eating or drinking in front of others, or performing in front of others (e.g. giving a speech or presentation). The individual with symptoms of social anxiety disorder tries to avoid any kind of social situation in which they believe they may behave in an embarrassing way or be negatively evaluated by others – which for the social phobic is almost all social situations and interactions. Social anxiety disorder is one of the most common of the anxiety disorders with up to 13 per cent of people in Western societies having diagnosable symptoms within their lifetime[32]. More of this anxiety problem in Chapter 10.

As the name suggests, *panic disorder* is characterised by repeated panic attacks. These attacks can be associated with a range of physical symptoms such as heart palpitations, perspiring, dizziness, hyperventilating, nausea and trembling. The sufferer may also experience severe apprehension that something bad is going to happen to them (they may feel they're going crazy, or that the attacks indicate an underlying serious medical condition, such as a heart

31 Chapman, T. F. (1997) 'The epidemiology of fears and phobias.' In G. C. L. Davey (Ed.) *Phobias: A Handbook of Theory, Research and Treatment.* Chichester: Wiley.
32 Memik, N., Yildiz, O., Tural, U. & Agaoglu, B. (2011) 'The prevalence of social phobia: A review.' *Journal of Archives of Neuropsychiatry*, 48, 4–10.

attack). They may also experience feelings of depersonalisation. In the overwhelming majority of panic attacks, the symptoms are not signs of serious illness, but are associated with anxious arousal. For those diagnosed with panic disorder, panic attacks can seem uncontrollable, can happen with regular frequency, and may last in some cases for many years. Concerns about future attacks often result in the development of avoidant behaviour, when sufferers may find it hard to leave the 'safety' of their own home, in which case panic disorder with agoraphobia is a common diagnosis. See Chapter 9 for a more detailed discussion of panic disorder.

We've all occasionally gone back to check whether we locked a door or switched off the gas stove, or had an intrusive thought that we find disturbing or out of place. However, for people such as Millie at the beginning of this chapter, a diagnosis of *obsessive-compulsive disorder* (OCD) means that such thoughts and actions are repeated often and can result in a distressing and disabling way of life. Obsessions are intrusive and recurring thoughts that the individual finds disturbing and uncontrollable (such as the person having uncontrollable thoughts about killing their own child), whereas compulsions represent repetitive or ritualised behaviours that the individual feels driven to perform in order to prevent some negative outcome. Compulsions can take the form of persistent checking of doors and windows, but can also be repetitive stereotyped behaviours such as ensuring the light switch in the bedroom is switched on and off a specific number of times before going to bed. OCD-related disorders also include body dysmorphic disorder (a preoccupation with assumed deficits in appearance) and hoarding disorder (collecting too many items that result in large piles of clutter that make living spaces impassable, and home utilities, such as toilets, unusable). Chapter 8 contains more on OCD and related disorders.

Generalised Anxiety Disorder (GAD) is another pervasive anxiety condition in which the individual experiences high levels of apprehension and anxiety about future events, and this leads to chronic, uncontrollable worry, which is the cardinal diagnostic feature of this disorder. This chronic worrying is distressing for the individual because it feels uncontrollable (once that person starts worrying they don't feel capable of stopping it), it's closely associated with catastrophising (worrying only seems to make the worry worse), and it's accompanied by physical symptoms such as tiredness, trembling, muscle tension, and sometimes headaches and nausea. I'll discuss more about how the worry monster develops in Chapter 7.

The final disorder we'll discuss in detail later in Chapter 11 is the trauma and stress-related disorder known as *post-traumatic stress disorder* (PTSD). PTSD is one of the few disorders in which the cause of the disorder is a defining factor in diagnosis (as we'll see in later chapters, the causes of the other anxiety-related disorders are not so easy to define). A diagnosis of PTSD is considered only if the individual has experienced an extreme trauma prior to the development of symptoms. Such traumas may often be life-threatening ones and include being caught up in natural disasters such as floods or earthquakes, experiencing physical or sexual abuse, or being the victim of a terrorist attack. Living in a war zone is another risk factor, as is being a combatant in a war zone or being a first responder to emergencies[33]. Symptoms of PTSD fall into four distinct categories: (1) intrusive symptoms such as vivid, uncontrollable flashbacks of the trauma; (2) active avoidance of thoughts, memories or reminders of the trauma; (3) negative changes in mood, such as persistent fear,

---

33 Berger, W., Coutinho, E.S.F., Figueira, I., Marques-Portella, C. et al. (2012) 'Rescuers at risk: A systematic review and meta-regression analysis of the worldwide current prevalence and correlates of PTSD in rescue workers.' *Social Psychiatry & Psychiatric Epidemiology*, 47, 1001–1011.

horror, anger, guilt or shame; and (4) increased arousal and hyper-reactivity, such as sharpened startle responses and hypervigilance for threat.

What's striking about these anxiety-related mental health disorders is that anxiety can generate such a variety of very different symptoms in these different disorders. Physical symptoms in panic disorder, pathological worrying in GAD, flashbacks and nightmares in PTSD, and elaborate rituals and compulsions in OCD. This can undoubtedly be perplexing if you don't understand two things. First, what causes adaptive or normal levels of anxiety to develop into distressing and disabling anxiety disorders? And second, how is it that an individual will develop one disorder rather than another? But initially, let's just say a little more about anxiety disorders generally, and in particular the alarming prevalence of anxiety disorders worldwide and the costs that come with these disorders.

The Physical and Economic Costs of Anxiety Disorders

In 2012 a thorough review of eighty-seven studies across forty-four different countries by Amanda Baxter and colleagues from the University of Queensland concluded that the global current prevalence of anxiety disorders is 7.3 per cent. This boils down to one in fourteen people around the world at any given time having a diagnosable anxiety disorder, and one in nine will experience an anxiety disorder in any one year[34]. These are startling statistics. Compare these figures for anxiety disorders with the figures for a prominent medical condition such as cancer. In 2014 the US National Cancer Institute reported there were 14.7 million people in the United States

34 Baxter, A. J., Scott, K. M., Vos, T. & Whiteford, H. A. (2012) 'Global prevalence of anxiety disorders: A systematic review and meta-regression.' *Psychological Medicine*, 43, 897–910.

living with cancer. That's a prevalence rate of 4.6 per cent or one person in every twenty-two. The Centers for Disease Control and Prevention estimate that every year about 735,000 Americans have a heart attack. That's a prevalence rate of around 0.23 per cent or one person in 434. Without doubt, heart disease and cancer are the leading causes of death for both men and women, but severe lifelong anxiety also has a significant effect on an individual's personal and social productivity, and also on their mortality. Yes – anxiety may kill.

Tom Russ and colleagues at the University of Edinburgh investigated the deaths of 68,222 people in England between the years 1994 to 2004[35]. They found that levels of anxiety and stress predicted the future probability of a person dying during that decade. Even individuals with sub-clinical levels of anxiety had a 20 per cent increased risk of mortality. This relationship between anxiety and mortality rate could not be accounted for by factors such as age, sex, social class, body mass index, systolic blood pressure, physical activity, smoking, alcohol consumption, or diabetes. But anxiety and stress was associated with an increased risk of death from cancer and cardiovascular disease. Even though this was a prospective study, we still cannot definitely infer causality, but Russ and colleagues speculated that anxiety and stress may have their own direct effect on the body that increases the risk of death by cancer and heart disease, contributing directly to the known leading causes of death worldwide.

But being diagnosed with an anxiety disorder is not just a risk factor for early mortality; anxiety disables the individual in a way not dissimilar to the major physical illnesses such as cancer and

35 Russ, T. C., Stamatakis, E., Hamer, M., Starr, J. M. et al. (2012) 'Association between psychological distress and mortality: Individual participant pooled analysis of 10 prospective cohort studies.' *British Journal of Medicine*, doi: 10.1136/bmj.e4933

heart disease. Effectively, the one in fourteen people worldwide with an anxiety disorder will be unable to work to their full potential, learn to their full potential, or even perform their social and family responsibilities to their full potential. In 2016 the UK Health & Safety Executive estimated that anxiety and stress accounted for over a third of all work-related ill health cases and almost half of all working days lost due to ill health[36]. The wider economic cost of mental health problems in the UK is immense, and it's been estimated at over £100 billion each year in England alone, including the costs of services, lost productivity at work, and reduced quality of life. The cost of poor mental health to businesses amounts to £1,000 per employee per year[37].

Ironically, in recent years it's not been the specific need to aid individual recovery from distress that's driven the increased provision of psychological treatments for these disorders, it's been the desire to reduce the economic burden of anxiety disorders and other mental health problems. It took an unlikely partnership between a clinical psychologist, David Clark, and an eminent economist, Richard Layard, to pioneer the UK's *Improving Access to Psychological Therapies* (IAPT) programme, which was launched in 2006 and provided funds for increased access to, and resources for, psychological treatments for common mental health problems such as anxiety. It was argued that this was a more cost-effective way of providing services by using evidence-based interventions that would return more people to work more quickly and reduce the costs to the economy caused by loss of productivity. Clark and Layard were canny enough to realise that the best way to get a Government to fund large increases in services for mental health problems was to make

36 http://www.hse.gov.uk/statistics/causdis/stress/
37 https://www.centreformentalhealth.org.uk/economic-and-social-costs

the economic argument, but we also shouldn't let this approach lead us to underestimate the importance of dealing directly with personal distress and poor quality of life. IAPT is an example of a 'global return on investment' approach to funding services for mental health problems such as anxiety disorders, but the initial investment required globally for such an approach is immense. Mental Health researchers at the World Health Organization have calculated that the investment needed over the period 2016–30 to scale up effective treatment coverage for depression and anxiety disorders is estimated at US$147 billion. But they estimate that this would lead to forty-three million extra years of healthy life, and a net economic benefit in terms of productivity gains of $169 billion for anxiety disorders alone[38].

It does seem that the modern way of arguing for more services and resources for treating mental health problems such as anxiety is by viewing it as a 'return on investment'. But, just think how this would look if we took the same approach to funding services for cancer and heart disease – it would undoubtedly be seen as putting economic benefits before the alleviation of suffering. I probably don't have to persuade many of you that provision of mental health services is inadequate in most countries of the world. In 2014, the mental health charity Mind reported that local authorities in England spent an average of 1.3 per cent of their public health budget on mental health. Neil Balmer, Head of Communications at the mental health research charity MQ, also drew my attention recently to some startling facts. The UK Government spends an average of £1,571 per year on cancer research per individual cancer patient. The equivalent for mental health is 150 times less – at

38 Chisholm, D., Sweeny, K., Sheehan, P., Rasmussen, B. et al. (2016) 'Scaling-up treatment of depression and anxiety: A global return on investment analysis.' *Lancet Psychiatry*, 3, 415–424.

£10 per mental health patient! In addition, for every £1 spent by the UK Government on cancer research the general public donates £2.75, but the equivalent donated for mental health research by the public is 30 pence per £1[39]. We have a lot of ground to make up if we're to ensure that services and care for mental health programmes are properly researched, funded and delivered. The anxiety epidemic has arrived but we're woefully unprepared to deal with it.

The Journey to the Dark Side – When Anxiety Becomes an Anxiety Disorder

I'll be quite candid at the outset here – there really is no current consensus amongst anxiety researchers about how normal levels of anxiety develop into individual disabling anxiety disorders. Those medical guardians of the diagnostic manual of psychiatric disorders – the American Psychiatric Association – would love to identify biomarkers for anxiety disorders[40], but there are few that even remotely fit the bill when it comes to consistently predicting and defining individual anxiety disorders[41]. More interestingly, in their large meta-review of the prevalence of anxiety disorders, Amanda Baxter and colleagues noted that a number of significant risk factors for anxiety disorders had already been identified. These included urbanicity, marital status, socio-economic disadvantage, relationship difficulties, and exposure to violence, trauma and conflict. Did you spot the significance here? These aren't biological factors, they're largely socio-economic factors. The development of an anxiety disorder appears to be predicted by lifestyle, life experiences, and

39 https://blog.wellcome.ac.uk/2015/04/21/mental-health-how-much-does-the-uk-spend-on-research/

40 http://jamanetwork.com/journals/jama/fullarticle/1656312

41 Martin, E. I., Ressler, K. J., Binder, E. & Nemeroff, C. B. (2013) 'The neurobiology of anxiety disorders: Brain imaging, genetics, and psychoneuro-endocrinology.' *Psychiatric Clinics of North America*, 32, 549–575.

life circumstances rather than the catastrophic dysfunction of your neurobiology.

But from our understanding of anxiety at a psychological level, we can identify a number of psychological processes that seem to be important in providing a pathway from normal acceptable levels of anxiety to severe anxiety problems. These processes don't necessarily help us understand how someone develops one particular disorder rather than another, but they do help to understand how severe anxiety problems develop over time.

First, it's certainly the case that some anxiety disorders have their origins during a period of stress in a person's life, and most of the socio-economic stress factors identified in the 2012 study by Amanda Baxter and colleagues look like significant life stressors. But these stressors don't have to be extreme experiences to cause anxiety-based problems – even normative stressors that most of us are likely to encounter at some point in our lives can be triggers for periods of severe anxiety.

In the 1960s, two psychiatrists, Thomas Holmes and Richard Rahe, developed a league table of stressful events that is still used today to assess how life events can affect health[42]. The top ten life stressors in order of severity were death of a spouse, divorce, marital separation, imprisonment, death of a close family member, personal injury or illness, marriage, dismissal from work, marital reconciliation (yes, really!) and retirement. Any one of us would be extremely lucky if we managed to avoid all ten of those during a single lifetime! Anxiety disorders such as specific phobias and panic disorder tend to develop during periods of life stress, and even a slow onset disorder such as obsessive-compulsive disorder can often be traced back to a

42 Holmes, T. H., Rahe, R. H. (1967). 'The Social Readjustment Rating Scale.' *Journal of Psychosomatic Research* 11(2): 213–218.

period of stressful life changes (such as starting high school or experiencing stressful health problems). So the socio-economic factors that cause us life stress are significant contributors to the origins of anxiety disorders.

Work Stress as a Risk for Anxiety Problems

Perpetual work stress in this modern age of performance indicators and competitive standards is one common and distinctive risk factor. In many countries in the world we've seen increases in weekly working hours over the past couple of decades. In the UK, a TUC report notes that the number of people working more than forty-eight hours a week has increased by 15 per cent between 2010 and 2015[43], and in the United States, there was a 10 per cent increase in working hours between 1979 and 2007. American economist Lawrence Mishel lets us know very clearly that this trend is not simply about greater wealth for workers when he writes, 'the vast majority of wage earners are working harder, and for not much more.'[44] Indeed, many managers and professionals working long hours are neither paid for their overtime nor given time off in lieu. Working longer hours is not just a case of wanting to earn more money, many people work long hours in anticipation of higher earnings or promotions in the future, but in a majority of cases working longer hours is a necessity to deal with the volume of work. Modern organisational practices are almost entirely responsible for this increase in volume of work, and these include having to deal with new organisational initiatives such as regular organisational restructuring, project-based working,

43 https://www.tuc.org.uk/international-issues/europe/workplace-issues/work-life-balance/15-cent-increase-people-working-more

44 Mishel, L. (2013) 'Vast majority of wage earners are working harder, and for not much more: Trends in US work hours and wages over 1979–2007.' *Issue Brief, Economic Policy Unit.*

greater customer focus, and a growing 'meetings' culture. Then there are staff shortages, an IT/email overload, and the increasing need for many workers to travel some distance to their place of work[45]. It's not rocket science to assume that an increase in working hours merely to cope with a growing volume of work will adversely affect mental health, and long working hours can almost double the risk of developing significant anxiety symptoms[46]. In 2017 the NHS issued a report that analysed twelve million sick notes and found that one in three sick notes issued by GPs in the UK were for mental health symptoms – that's a 14 per cent rise in notes relating to anxiety and stress in just one year between 2015–16 and 2016–17. This makes mental health problems such as anxiety the most common reason for people to take time off work, ahead of musculoskeletal diseases – and over 20 per cent of mental health sick notes were issued for longer than twelve weeks, compared with only 3 per cent for respiratory problems[47]. Anxiety and stress at work is very clearly on the rise – and rising with spectacular rapidity.

This growing expectation of longer hours to maintain higher performance standards is nowhere better demonstrated than in élite sport, where more and more of our finest sportsmen are becoming more willing to reveal the stresses of maintaining high performance standards during the relentless schedules of high-profile competitions, tours and tournaments. For example, one of English cricket's finest-ever opening batsmen, Marcus Trescothick, returned home suddenly from the England cricket team's 2006 tour of India suffering from a stress-related disorder. Even someone with the mental

45 http://www.employment-studies.co.uk/report-summaries/report-summary-working-long-hours-review-evidence-volume-1---main-report

46 Virtanen, M., Ferrie, J. E., Singh-Manoux, A., Shipley, M. J. et al. (2011) 'Long working hours and symptoms of anxiety and depression: A year follow-up of the Whitehall study.' *Psychological Medicine*, 41, 2485–2494.

47 http://www.bbc.co.uk/news/health-41124238

resilience required to face the most hostile bowlers in the world – and even score fourteen test centuries off them – can succumb to the symptoms of a diagnosable anxiety disorder. Another test cricketer who had to take a break from international and county cricket was England batsman Jonathan Trott. He describes how he'd become unable to deal with the stresses and strains of a demanding schedule: 'Just coming down to breakfast, I'd sit on my own away from the guys with my cap over my head because I didn't know how I was going to react to having to go to the cricket ground again. I was waking up looking at the clock hoping the clock had stopped, or that a pylon had fallen on the field and the game had been cancelled, or the stadium had collapsed – as long as there was no one in it, of course. You end up thinking all sorts of ways you wouldn't have to go to the ground.'[48]

But why do some of us come out of a period of life stress with an anxiety disorder, and others of us emerge unscathed? The previous quote by Jonathan Trott is instructive here. When stress becomes overwhelming, we have a fairly natural tendency to want to avoid it and also to avoid those things that create our stress. Jonathan Trott's fantasising about how he might be able to escape playing yet another day's cricket is just one form of this desire to avoid the sources of his stress. Yet anxiety feeds off avoidance like a glutton at a feast – it's arguably the most significant factor that enables anxiety to grow, and it's a key symptom of all the anxiety disorders. In specific phobias we stay away from feared objects, we overly prepare for social inter- actions in social anxiety, we avoid reminders of trauma in PTSD, and in Generalised Anxiety Disorder and OCD we're convinced that worrying helps us to avoid or prepare for possible future nega-

48 http://www.independent.co.uk/news/people/jonathan-trott-and-the-problems-of-describing-mental-illness-9275507.html

tive consequences. DSM-5 defines avoidance as 'the act of keeping away from stress-related circumstances: a tendency to circumvent cues, activities and situations that remind the individual of a stressful event experienced'[49]. During periods of stress and anxiety, avoidance becomes facilitated and will often become maladaptive. By maladaptive we mean that it's a process that impairs general functioning – it interferes with achieving important life goals and it interferes with normal daily living. Just take a look back at the avoidance behaviours of Millie on page one of this chapter. Her desire to avoid perceived contamination had escalated to such an extent that it makes even the most mundane of her everyday activities painfully more difficult and tedious. Individuals suffering stress or anxiety will also exhibit avoidance behaviours even if those behaviours are associated with significant costs or loss of gains. In a series of studies, Andre Pittig and colleagues at the University of Mannheim demonstrated that individuals at risk of developing anxiety disorders would press a button to avoid a signal warning them of an aversive event – even when this caused them financial loss[50]. Those high in anxiety also preferred to avoid immediate negative consequences, even if that meant receiving a greater number of negative consequences in the future[51].

Not only is avoidance maladaptive in this way, it also affects emotional regulation. When you actively attempt to avoid threats, you're not only trying to put both physical and psychological distance

49 American Psychiatric Association (2013) *Diagnostic and Statistical Manual of Mental Disorders* (5th edition). Washington, DC: American Psychiatric Association.

50 Pittig, A., Schulz, A. R., Craske, M. G. & Alpers, G. W. (2014) 'Acquisition of behavioral avoidance: Task-irrelevant conditioned stimuli trigger costly decisions.' *Journal of Abnormal Psychology*, 123, 314–329.

51 Pittig, A., Brand, M., Pawlikowski, M. & Alpers, G. W. (2014) 'The cost of fear: Avoidant decision making in a spider gambling task.' *Journal of Anxiety Disorders*, 28, 326–334.

between yourself and that perceived threat, you're also avoiding the emotional reaction that this threat would normally evoke. This is generally a bad thing. It means you become less emotionally reactive the more you avoid. This then has a number of negative knock-on consequences. You'll be less privy to a range of useful information conveyed by an emotional response (an emotion will tell you whether you should be frightened of something, angered by it, or merely surprised by it), you'll become less adaptive in your interactions with your environment (because your emotional reaction would normally signal which adaptive responses are most appropriate to deploy in those circumstances), you'll be more likely to make less effective actions in the future (and thereby likely to experience more emotional distress), the interpersonal value of the emotion is lost (your friends, family and colleagues will be less likely to understand your behaviour – or they may even entirely misinterpret it), and any input of the emotion into decision-making processes is lost (you'll never truly find out if you genuinely fear that thing you think is a threat)[52].

If all that's not bad enough, avoidance has one more devastating effect that contributes to anxiety surviving and breeding in the minds that host it. It creates a deluded worldview. There'll always be a monster in the closet until you open the door and discover there's nothing there. But avoidance makes sure that door is never opened! We all create our own representation of the world in our minds, but very often these representations can be at odds with what is out there in the real, physical world, and this is also the case with anxiety. All anxiety disorders are associated with highly exaggerated perceptions of threats. The spider phobic believes that every time they see a spider it intends to bite them or crawl into their clothes;

---

52 Salter-Pedneault, K., Tull, M. T. & Roemer, L. (2004) 'The role of avoidance of emotional material in the anxiety disorders.' *Applied & Preventive Psychology*, 11, 95–114.

the person with panic disorder believes that their racing heart during a panic attack means they're about to die of a heart attack; and the student with Generalised Anxiety Disorder worries so much about getting good grades in school that they catastrophise that a poor grade will effectively make them destitute and friendless! These are all consequences that don't match with the reality of what is likely to happen in each of these circumstances. Yet the person with the anxiety disorder will never have the opportunity to find this out, because avoidance of their fears means they'll never allow themselves to get into a situation that will disconfirm their fearful beliefs.

The failure to confront fear in this way and experience the reality of an anxiety merely allows the delusional beliefs about the fear to propagate and become even more embellished. A couple of studies have looked in detail at the belief systems of severely spider phobic individuals and they provide some fascinating examples of the bizarre and fantastic beliefs that develop to maintain anxiety and fear[53,54]. These beliefs extend from the possible: 'When I encounter a spider it will be very quick'; via the relatively improbable: 'When a spider is in my vicinity I believe that the spider will crawl towards my private parts'; to the fantastic: 'When spiders come near me I believe they'll do things on purpose to tease me.' The more bizarre and improbable that these beliefs become, the more difficult it becomes to unpick them and challenge them. This is because to the anxious person who holds these beliefs they are far from bizarre, and they represent a set of logical (if unreal) reasons for justifying their own fear.

53 Arntz, A., Lavy, E., van den Berg, G. & van Rijsoort, S. (1993) 'Negative beliefs of spider phobics: A psychometric evaluation of the Spider Phobia Beliefs Questionnaire.' *Advances in Behaviour Research and Therapy*, 15(4), 257–277.
54 Thorpe, S. J. & Salkovskis, P. M. (1995) 'Phobic beliefs: Do cognitive factors play a role in specific phobias?' *Behaviour Research and Therapy*, 33(7), 805–816.

This role of avoidance in developing delusional sets of beliefs about an anxiety is a significant process on the road from normal levels of anxiety to an anxiety disorder. It's also a reason why exposure therapies have been so successful in treating anxiety disorders (see Chapter 12). Allowing someone with an anxiety disorder to experience the fears they perceive in a controlled way does allow them to disconfirm many of the extreme beliefs avoidance has allowed them to build up around the fear – and it's these beliefs that ultimately drive the fear and anxiety and so need to be challenged.

The final twist in the seduction of anxiety to the dark side is that anxiety can teach you to fear it. The charming manipulator can turn full circle into the bully that controls through fear and threat. Even though it can act as an adaptive emotion, anxiety is not usually a pleasant emotion to experience, so it's easy to become fearful of it. This happened to me during the 1990s when I began to experience bouts of panic attacks. Family life with two small children had become demanding and I'd just taken over a new role as head of department at my university in London. Add to that a gruelling daily commute to and from my home on the south coast into London each day. It began with feelings of depersonalisation, a racing heart-beat and chest pains – I really thought I was going to die. Eventually, each morning I'd wake up with the first thought in my head being 'please don't let me feel like that again today!' But anxiety on the dark side is unforgiving – if you fear it, it'll embrace you. And that's what inevitably would happen within minutes of me waking up – a shot of adrenaline through my body before my head would fill with a welter of fearful thoughts about the panic I expected during that day. Lucky for me I was a research psychologist who had some knowledge of how panic disorder is caused and maintained, so I did possess some insight into my condition and was eventually able to convince myself I wasn't going to die and I wasn't going crazy. As a result the symptoms and attacks began to subside over time. But it wasn't an easy job even for someone with my knowledge of aetiology, and it's easy to see how anxiety can very quickly create more anxiety.

This is commonly known as 'fear of fear' or more formally as 'anxiety sensitivity'. Fear of anxiety in the form of anxiety sensitivity is significantly higher in individuals with a diagnosed anxiety disorder, suggesting that it may be implicated in the journey from normally experienced anxiety to an anxiety disorder[55]. Anxiety sensitivity is a known risk factor for subsequent anxiety symptoms, and has been shown to predict panic symptoms and anxious avoidance in children, adolescents and adults[56]. Anxiety sensitivity probably does its job indirectly by making us avoid things that are anxiety provoking[57]. This in turn leads to the development of unhelpful strategies for dealing with anxiety – strategies such as suppressing negative emotions and avoiding stressful situations. Avoidance once more rears its ugly head as a significant roadside culprit on the journey from anxiety to anxiety disorders.

Winding Up the Discussion

In this chapter I've covered some of the socio-economic and psychological processes that can determine our lifelong levels of anxiety and also turn normally experienced anxiety into an anxiety disorder. I've identified childhood adversity, negative parenting, overprotective

55 Olatunji, B. O. & Wolitzky-Taylor, K. B. (2009) 'Anxiety sensitivity and the anxiety disorders: A meta-analytic review and synthesis.' *Psychological Bulletin*, 135, 974–999.

56 Schmidt, N. B., Keough, M. E., Mitchell, M. A., Reynolds, E. K. et al. (2010) 'Anxiety sensitivity: Prospective prediction of anxiety among early adolescents.' *Journal of Anxiety Disorders*, 24, 503–508.

57 Manser, R., Cooper, M., & Trefusis, J. (2012) Beliefs about emotions as a metacognitive construct: Initial development of a self-report questionnaire measure and preliminary investigation in relation to emotion regulation. *Clinical Psychology & Psychotherapy*, 19, 235–246.

'helicopter and snowplough' parenting, and media and digitally based vicarious learning as modern-day contributors to our individual trait anxiety levels. In addition, life stress, avoidance and anxiety sensitivity are factors that have all been linked to the development of individual anxiety disorders. Some of these factors, such as avoidance and anxiety sensitivity, are psychological vulnerabilities that are likely to be culture neutral and so relatively unaffected by the changing demands and values of modern society. But some other predictors of anxiety and anxiety disorders are fundamental attributes of the social, economic and technological conditions in which we live, and their influence will fluctuate depending on changes in those conditions. Childhood adversity, parenting practices, media exposure and work stress are all examples of factors that can influence experienced anxiety, and modern society appears to be shifting these factors in directions that are likely to propagate rather than quell our anxieties.

CHAPTER FIVE

Anxiety Through the Ages

'Whoever has learned to be anxious in the right way has
learned the ultimate.'

— Søren Kierkegaard

*'The title I have chosen for this treatise, is a reproach
universally thrown on this island by foreigners, and all
our neighbours on the continent, by whom nervous distempers,
spleen, vapours, and lowness of spirits, are in derision, called the
English Malady. And I wish there were not good grounds for
this reflection. The moisture of our air, the variableness of our
weather (from our situation amid the ocean) the rankness and
fertility of our soil, the richness and heaviness of our food, the
wealth and abundance of the inhabitants (from their universal
trade) the inactivity and sedentary occupations of the better sort
(among whom this evil mostly rages) and the humour of living in
great, populous and consequently unhealthy towns, have brought
forth a class and set of distempers, with atrocious and frightful
symptoms, scarce known to our ancestors, and never rising to such
fatal heights, nor afflicting such numbers in any other known
nation. These nervous disorders being computed to make almost
one third of the complaints of the people of condition in England.'*[1]

1 Cheyne, G. (1733) *The English Malady*. London: Strahan.

Heard something like this before? No, it's nothing to do with Brexit! This is part of the Preface from George Cheyne's treatise *The English Malady* published in 1733. George Cheyne was one of the first writers to popularise the notion of nervous disorders, of which anxiety was a significant component. He viewed nervous conditions as not only originating within the body, but also as a consequence of the social, economic and cultural factors of the time. So here is George Cheyne in 1733 talking about an epidemic of nervous diseases that had scarcely been known before caused by the contemporary lifestyles of the wealthy living in modern unhealthy, large towns. He even saw nervousness as becoming a status symbol signalling the superiority of the wealthy classes. So talk of anxiety epidemics is not new, talk of anxiety as a status symbol is not new, and talk of modern changes in society as a cause of escalating anxieties is also not new. Many eras of history seem to have had what the contemporaries at the time called their own anxiety epidemics.

I won't spend too much time in this chapter describing how thinkers and physicians from previous eras attempted to explain anxiety – because their explanations were usually incomplete, conceptually naïve, or simply wrong. In addition, although there's evidence that Greco-Roman philosophers and physicians identified anxiety as a specific negative affect state, in times after the classical period right up to the nineteenth century anxiety was more usually lumped together with other negative emotions such as depression under the label 'melancholia'. But what is important is the social context of anxiety throughout the ages, because this defines what things triggered anxiety, how people living at different times perceived anxiety and its role within their society, and how they should cope with it. Did our ancestors experience OCD, social anxiety, PTSD, height phobia, and what did they worry about? Anxiety is the emotion that's evolved to help us human beings deal with threats and challenges, and there have been many of those during the evolution of human civilisation, so we might expect that anxiety was a prominent feature of life throughout history.

In all probability fear and anxiety were a normal way of life from classical times onwards, with regular violence and conflict, famine, epidemics of plague and disease, and poverty and starvation. Fear and anxiety were valued as sensible emotions, with the Dutch theologian Erasmus writing in the fifteenth century: 'I consider total absence of fear in situations such as mine [fleeing from a plague-ridden area], to be the mark not of a valiant fellow but of a dolt.' In the seventeenth century, the English physician and clergyman Richard Napier collected the worries and anxieties of hundreds of anxious individuals who attended his general practice. These included anxieties about debt and loss of money, and fear of poverty. Anxieties about death and disease were also prominent: 'Seventeenth-century Englishmen were death's familiars, for epidemics, consumption, parasites and dysentery, accidents, infections, and botched childbirths killed children and adults, family and friends, earlier and more suddenly than the diseases we dread today.'[2] The perpetual spectre of death in its various forms was a contributor to the more spiritual existential dread described by the Danish philosopher and theologian Sören Kierkegaard in the early nineteenth century, an unremitting dread in the form of anxieties about the inevitability of death, the spiritual consequences of death, the existence of God or the futility of a meaningless existence.

Anxieties about witches and witchcraft, and religious despair about sins that could lead to eternal damnation troubled Napier's villagers, and much of seventeenth-century anxiety also revolved

2 MacDonald, M. (2009) *Mystical Bedlam: Madness, Anxiety and Healing in Seventeenth-Century England*. Cambridge University Press.

around relationships – much like it still does in the present day. Napier's villagers expressed anxieties around courtship and married life, lover's quarrels, unrequited love, parental objections to relationships, and partners' unfaithfulness[3].

It wasn't until around the time of Napier in the seventeenth and eighteenth centuries that people began to expect a basic level of safety and certainty in their lives, and this is when anxiety came to be viewed more as a medical abnormality than a necessary way of life[4]. Prior to this time, anxiety was a pervasive and normal emotion in response to the trials and tribulations of a challenging world, and from an early age the individual was taught to accept anxiety and to cope with it in a way that was dictated by the moral virtues of the era.

Anxiety and Moral Virtues

Emotions can be dangerous things, and if allowed free reign can escalate even to the point of destabilising a society – or so it was thought in classical times. For example, an emotion such as fear can make the average person oblivious to logic and behave in a way that's self-serving rather than for the good of the social community. A real concern in ancient Greece and Rome was that negative emotions such as fear, anxiety and anger might destabilise the political and social status quo if they were left unchecked. Anger in particular was seen as a danger to the state because it could lead to political violence, tyrannical abuse by rulers, and family feuding. As a consequence, expressing anger was viewed as a personal moral failure and the essence of good behaviour was considered to be self-control[5].

3 Horwitz, A. V. (2013) *Anxiety: A Short History*. Johns Hopkins.
4 Clark, M. J. (1995) 'Anxiety disorders: Social section.' In Berrios, G. E., Porter, R. (Eds.) *A History of Clinical Psychiatry*. New York: University Press.
5 Harris, W. V. (2004) *Restraining Rage: The Ideology of Anger Control in Classical Antiquity*. Harvard University Press.

Anxiety about the many challenges life provided in classical times was also a serious matter. Anxieties caused by poverty, famine, disease and violent oppression or conflict might lead to rioting, insurrection and revolt, and needed to be managed. Similarly, fear itself was the enemy of courage – courage required in combat and conflict. Classical societies didn't try to eliminate fear and anxiety, they attempted to control such negative emotions by espousing the significance of moral virtues such as courage and labelling expressions of fear and anxiety as cowardice – 'an honourable man displayed his character and lived up to social standards by containing his anxious feelings'[6]. As a consequence, young Greeks and Romans from the classical era were trained to resist fear and anxiety in dangerous and challenging situations, bravery was viewed as a noble ideal, and courage was not considered an innate personality trait but a trait to be learnt as a valued moral virtue to combat fear and anxiety.

And Then God Took Over . . .

In 312 AD at the Battle of Milvian Bridge over the Tiber River, an event happened that changed the course of scientific and medical enquiry for the next thousand years or more. On the morning of the battle, Roman Emperor Constantine looked up towards the sun and saw a cross of light above it. As a result he ordered all his troops to adorn their shields with a Christian cross. Constantine subsequently won the battle, and it gave him undisputed control of the western half of the Roman Empire. After his victory, Constantine became a patron of the Christian faith and issued the Edict of Milan, which made Christianity the officially recognised religion of the Roman Empire and eventually the whole of Europe.

6 Horwitz, A. V. (2013) *Anxiety: A Short History*. Johns Hopkins.

This historical event introduced a new and more dominant worldview. Whereas the classical view of the world had been largely an empirical one, the new Christian religiosity supplanted this with attempts to explain the world in terms of spirituality, faith, sin and divine will – at least in those parts of Europe dominated by the Christian faith. In particular, the empirical conceptions of disease and emotion championed by the likes of Hippocrates and Galen were overshadowed by views in which the threats and challenges posed by the world in the form of famine, plagues, natural disasters and violent conflict were manifestations of God's wrath, and relief from these anxieties could only be found in faith in God and His Christian teachings. Religion had become the cause of anxieties and the source of relief from them. As Allan Horwitz points out in his excellent book *Anxiety: A Short History*, preoccupations with Christian doctrine began to generate new anxieties about how you could reserve your place in the kingdom of heaven, or whether your sins could be absolved or would merely condemn you to eternal damnation – fears and anxieties that persisted right through to the Reformation in the sixteenth century. Perhaps more significantly, the dominance of the Christian Church for more than a millennium after the Battle of Milvian Bridge meant that both science and medicine were closely subjected to ecclesiastical control. The Church was more interested in saving souls than healing bodies and, according to St Augustine, faith in God was assumed to be the best therapy for anxiety[7].

But even during the centuries when religion dominated the interpretation of people's anxieties and the way that medical science should consider those anxieties, there was still a thread of classical empiricism that persisted in medical writings. The Hippocratic

7 St. Augustine (2009) *Confessions*. Oxford: World Classics.

conception of *melancholy* as a mixture of modern-day depression and anxiety still survived and became prominent in writings and observations published from the fifteenth century onwards – the most prominent example being Robert Burton's *The Anatomy of Melancholy* in 1621 (more interesting examples from that treatise later). Burton described melancholy as something that could be either a disposition or a habit – very much like the distinction between modern-day state and trait anxiety – and, as a condition that anyone might suffer, it was a regular feature of everyday life: 'Melancholy . . . is either a disposition or a habit. In disposition, it is that transitory melancholy which goes and comes upon every small occasion of sorrow, need, sickness, trouble, fear, grief, passion, or perturbation of the mind, any manner of care, discontent, or thought, which causeth anguish, dullness, heaviness, and vexation of spirit . . . And from these melancholy dispositions, no man living free, no Stoic, none so wise, none so happy, none so patient, so generous, so godly, so divine, that can vindicate himself; so well composed, but more or less, some time or other, he feels the smart of it. Melancholy, in this sense is the character of mortality.[8]' Anxiety and depression are part of the very fabric of life itself, and so no one is spared from them.

The Scientific Revolution

By the middle of the seventeenth century, religious and spiritual explanations of emotions such as anxiety were being replaced by more objective, medical explanations as a consequence of the new empirical and observational scientific methods being pioneered across Europe by thinkers and scientists such as Isaac Newton, René Descartes and Galileo. For example, the body-mind dualism of René Descartes introduced some significant re-orientations in the explanation

8 Burton, R. (1621) *The Anatomy of Melancholy*. Vol 1. 170.

of mental health issues such as anxiety. According to Descartes, because minds could not be diseased, mental illnesses such as anxiety must be located in the body, and more specifically in the brain. It's at this point that conditions such as melancholia moved from being the concern of theology to being in the realm of medicine.

It was also a time when the traditional all-inclusive conception of anxiety and depression as melancholia was being unpicked. In 1739 the Scottish philosopher David Hume began to describe some of the basic distinctions between anxiety and depression in his book *A Treatise on Human Nature*. He differentiated between grief and fear (with the latter being highly correlated with states of anxiety). The actual experience of bad or evil things led to grief or sorrow, but fear and anxiety occurred when bad or evil things were anticipated but were uncertain. This distinction is almost identical to our modern-day association of depression with experienced losses and failures, and anxiety with future threats and challenges. What is more, Hume seems to have stumbled across another modern-day construct in 'intolerance of uncertainty' as a cause of worry and anxiety.[9]

By the middle of the eighteenth century medical perspectives on melancholia had largely superseded spiritual or ecclesiastical ones, and the search for the origins of melancholia were being sought in the brain and nervous system of the body. The author of the quote at the beginning of this chapter, George Cheyne, was one of the most influential originators of this approach. His book, *The English Malady* (1733), was widely read at the time, and it introduced the new term 'nervous distempers' – a term that encompassed hysteria, hypochondria and melancholy, and attempted to explain these

9 Carleton, R. N., Mulvogue, M. K., Thibodeau, M. A., McCabe, R. E., Antony, M. M., & Asmundson, G. J. G. (2012). 'Increasingly certain about uncertainty: Intolerance of uncertainty across anxiety and depression.' *Journal of Anxiety Disorders*, 26, 468–479.

symptoms as nervous conditions rooted in the nerve fibres and organs of the body. Melancholia had well and truly become the domain of medicine and the physician. But unlike many later attempts to formulate melancholia and other mental health problems solely in terms of medical conditions, Cheyne not only saw that nervous conditions were biological, but that they were also rooted in social and cultural factors. The epidemic in nervous disorders that he claims to have observed in eighteenth-century England he saw as being caused by changes in the social conditions of the time – such factors as increased prosperity and unhealthy lifestyles. Although it's not clear that these social conditions were causes of an anxiety epidemic in the eighteenth century, it's an approach that echoes that of modern-day psychopathologists who readily accept that social conditions can be risk factors for many mental health problems, including anxiety and its disorders (see Chapter 4).

Many medics and physicians gladly grasped the baton that writers such as George Cheyne had offered and refined the medical model of melancholia. Scottish Professor of Medicine, William Cullen (1710–90) emphasised how increases and decreases in brain activity could underlie mental disturbance, and he was arguably the first to coin the term 'neurosis' to describe ailments of the central nervous system for which no physical basis had yet been established. William Battie (1703–76) was the English physician who first differentiated anxiety from other forms of mental illness in his book *A Treatise on Madness* published in 1758. His Treatise was primarily a damning critique of the archaic custodial methods still used in asylums such as the Bethlem Hospital in London, and he espoused the view that mental disturbance was not the manifestation of disturbed animal passions that required restraint, but the result of the problematic joining together of ideas – surely a prophetic insight into modern-day cognitive approaches to anxiety and its treatment. He even argued that anxiety could be adaptive and was 'absolutely necessary to our preservation'.

During the nineteenth century, the medical model of anxiety became even more established. A rising wealthy middle class, with more time and more money than ever before, were willing patrons of the medical model – readily seeking medical attention for their nervous conditions, and very content to view their symptoms as a medical condition in need of treatment rather than a sign of insanity[10]. But there was still a disconcertingly large gap between the increasingly detailed definition of the symptoms of nervous conditions and an understanding of their causes in terms of physiology and the nervous system. The view was that symptoms of anxiety could not be manifestations of the mind and so they must be traceable either directly or indirectly to the physical activity of the brain or to its abnormalities.

By the 1840s, nervous disorders for which there was no known anatomical basis (and most anxiety symptoms were included in this category) were known as 'psychoneuroses', and the medical profession genuinely believed that it was only a matter of time before underlying organic causes for these conditions would be found. Interestingly, we're now over 175 years on from this and the medical profession still holds the same set of beliefs! After all this time (and effort) there are still very few if any reliable and valid biological markers for the diagnosis of anxiety disorders, and diagnostic manuals such as the DSM continue to offer diagnostic criteria almost solely in terms of the description of symptoms. Yet, just prior to the most recent revision of the DSM in 2013, those psychiatrists responsible for overseeing the revision were still unabashedly trying to align the diagnosis of mental health problems with the rest of

10 Horwitz, A. V. (2013) *Anxiety: A Short History*. Johns Hopkins.

medicine (despite the lack of biological markers for many individual disorders), and hoping against hope that future advances in the neuroscience and genetics of psychiatric illness would be incorporated into subsequent revisions (shall we wait and see what we have in a further 175 years?)[11]. Perhaps one answer here is to take the view that psychological science provides a much more valid and valuable way of understanding anxiety and its disorders than does medicine, and that's the position I've argued in the later chapters in this book. It's also a view that a certain Austrian neurologist by the name of Sigmund Freud took towards the end of the nineteenth century – rather than defaulting to the physical brain and its abnormalities, perhaps neuroses and anxieties could be better understood and explained in the context of the psychological processes that related our experiences to the neurotic symptoms that we subsequently develop.

'The Greatest Love Specialist in the World'

In 1925 Sigmund Freud had become so famous that Samuel Goldwyn, head of Metro-Goldwyn-Meyer film studios, offered him $100,000 to write a film script about love. Goldwyn called him 'the greatest love specialist in the world'. Perhaps the movie producer had got the wrong end of some kind of stick here, because Freud was not exactly the world's expert on love – but he was undisputedly the world's expert on neuroses and the role of unconscious sexual memories and drives. But the Nazis thought rather differently of Freud, ceremoniously burning his books after their seizure of power in Germany in 1933. If some people are offering you a king's ransom to work for them, and other people are simultaneously and publicly destroying your works, then you must be someone special.

11 Kupfer, D. J., Kuhl, E. A. & Regier, D. A. (2013) 'DSM-5 – The future arrived.' JAMA, 309, 1691–1692.

Freud was not just a neurologist who'd turned his hand to explaining some of the unexplained 'psychoneuroses' of his time, he also became the modern guru of the unconscious mind and a pin-up of contemporary bohemians, artists and writers who found in his writings new ways to express, describe and explain their own artistic angst. Freud had provided a non-medical way of explaining anxiety and neuroses in terms of unconscious processes, and it was one that could easily be adapted to speculate about the motives and desires behind almost any behaviour. Two topics that had previously been considered taboo – neuroses and sex – had been released from the box, and were avidly devoured and broadcast by a modern, liberal intelligentsia who saw the potential to explain the quirks and excesses of modern behaviour in ways that had never been possible before.

I remember as an undergraduate student attending a viewing of Luis Buñuel's surrealist classic *Un Chien Andalou*. The film lasts twenty-one minutes, but it was followed by a lecture of almost two hours by a film critic exploring the Freudian meanings in the succession of images that make up the film. I was stultifyingly bored by the stream of hypothetical speculations. Even Buñuel himself had admitted 'no idea or image that might lend itself to a rational explanation of any kind was accepted [in the film] – nothing in the film symbolises anything.' Yet so enticing and radical were Freud's theories that in the first half of the twentieth century they popularised anxious neuroses and spurred many to search for unconscious causes and repressed sexual impulses in the behaviours of characters both real and fictional. Both anxiety and angst became culturally fashionable.

In terms of his impact on conceptions of modern-day anxiety, Freud can be remembered for two important developments. First, he rejected the view that mental disorders and in particular neuroses emerged from physiological forces, and instead argued that they arose from psychic conflicts. These psychic conflicts were often unconscious and the result of processes that actively repressed some memories and experiences. At first he claimed that these conflicts were of a sexual nature, that sexual urges were often repressed, and that these conflicts gave rise to external symptoms of neurosis such as phobias or obsessions. Later, he maintained that people who experienced trauma of any kind could consequently develop neuroses, but only if they had deeper, unconscious factors contributing to their symptoms. Although the details of the theories and mechanisms are very different, this is a general approach that bears more than just a passing resemblance to modern-day cognitive accounts of anxiety – these modern-day cognitive accounts also emphasise the importance of thoughts and beliefs that have been shaped by experiences, many of which may have been traumatic, and many of which operate outside of conscious awareness. While cognitive therapists will often disagree with the details of Freud's models, they must thank him for freeing the study of mental health problems from the constraints of physiology and neurology and emphasising the significance of psychological processes.

Second, Freud was one of the main forces responsible for identifying anxiety as a specific entity with a number of different symptom sub-groups. Although therapists worldwide remember him mainly for his influential theory of psychoanalysis, his earlier work was responsible for identifying anxiety as a psychiatric diagnosis separate from neurasthenia (an ill-defined condition characterised by fatigue, irritability and emotional disturbance) and hysteria. He described a previously diverse set of conditions such as phobias, obsessions, panic and general anxiety, and considered them all to be related to one another under the general umbrella of anxiety symptoms. Not only are these anxiety conditions very closely related to their contemporary counterparts defined in modern-day diagnostic manuals,

Freud also described the role that pathological worrying would play in the diagnosis of free-floating anxiety or Generalised Anxiety Disorder: 'A woman who suffers from anxious expectation will imagine every time her husband coughs, when he has a cold, that he is going to have influenza pneumonia, and will at once see his funeral in her mind's eye. If when she is coming towards the house she sees two people standing by the front door, she cannot avoid the thought that one of her children has fallen out of the window; if the bell rings, then someone is bringing news of a death, and so on.'[12] Now there's a very vivid example of a threat interpretation bias of the kind that's found in most modern-day models of anxiety!

You may or may not be a fan of psychoanalysis, but aside from this, Freud's was a significant contribution in the history of anxiety. He was one of the first to move away from neurological and physiological explanations to psychic or psychological explanations of anxiety, and he helped to define anxiety and a number of its important disorders. During the twentieth century he also introduced a way of analysing neuroses to a world hungry to find ways of understanding the complexities and peculiarities of human behaviour. His impact was both scientific and cultural. Anxiety was now very significantly in both psychological and cultural domains.

Beyond Freud

As revolutionary as Freud's new ideas about anxiety were, many therapists and researchers with a scientific background found his theories too flighty for their liking. You couldn't directly observe many of Freud's hypothetical constructs such as the 'id', 'ego' and 'superego', and as a consequence you couldn't measure them. If you

---

12 Freud, S. (1894/1959) 'The justification for detaching from neurasthenia a particular syndrome: The anxiety-neurosis.' *Collected Papers*, Vol 1. Basic Books, New York.

couldn't measure them, then you couldn't conduct studies on them within the rules of contemporary scientific method. If you couldn't conduct scientific studies on them, then you could neither prove them nor disprove them. These criticisms of Freudian theory stem back to the 1920s and the days of the methodological behaviourists such as the American J. B. Watson, the one who conducted experiments on anxiety by conditioning an eight-month-old baby called Little Albert to fear his pet rat.[13] Then, during the 1950s, the surge in popularity of experimental psychology gave rise to behaviour therapy, one of the important predecessors of CBT. This school of psychologists emphasised that many mental health problems, such as anxiety, were learned, and probably learned through basic processes of conditioning. So if anxiety was learned, it could be effectively unlearnt if the right learning procedures were followed. This is behaviour therapy, and encompasses therapeutic techniques such as systematic desensitisation, counterconditioning, flooding, and most other exposure therapies[14].

The leaders of this movement were highly vocal and charismatic, people such as South African psychiatrist Joseph Wolpe, and Hans Eysenck, a German-born English psychologist. They not only vigorously supported the experimental method, they were also highly critical of earlier approaches such as psychoanalysis, with the controversial Eysenck deriding Freud's theories by claiming 'what is new in his theories is not true, and what is true in his theories is not new.[15]' Hans Eysenck was never someone to mince his words,

13 Watson, J. B. & Rayner, R. (1920) 'Conditioned emotional reactions.' *Journal of Experimental Psychology*, 3, 1–14.
14 Davey, G. C. L. (1998) 'Learning theory.' In C. E. Walker (Ed.) *Comprehensive Clinical Psychology: Foundations of Clinical Psychology*. Vol 1. Elsevier.
15 Eysenck, H. (1985) *Decline and Fall of the Freudian Empire*. Transaction Publishers.

nor did he lack self-confidence. While having lunch with him in the 1990s I asked him if he was working on any new projects. 'A book on intelligence', he replied, ' . . . but it's not all about me!' I delved no further.

While trying to explain anxiety and its disorders solely in terms of basic learning processes such as classical conditioning was in keeping with the experimental ethos of the 1950s and 1960s, it was not always a convincing explanation (see Chapter 6 as an example). By the 1980s behaviour therapy had almost seamlessly merged with cognitive approaches to create an empirical, scientific approach to the study of anxiety that could objectively allude to and examine the cognitive processes involved in anxiety and create evidence-based treatments such as CBT. That is pretty much where we are now, and there are numerous examples in the following chapters of how this cognitive-behavioural approach has contributed to our understanding of anxiety and its causes.

Anxiety Disorders Through the Ages

In the early chapters in this book I've attempted to look in detail at whether the causes of anxiety have changed in the modern era, and in this chapter I've already described some of the causes of anxiety that have been identified since Greek and Roman times. But what about the nature of anxiety disorders themselves? The major anxiety disorders summarised in Chapter 4 are each characterised by their distinctive symptoms, and in some cases their distinctive causes. Have the nature and symptoms of anxiety disorders changed over the centuries? Have they evolved to reflect new and more modern anxieties? Or is there evidence that the symptoms of anxiety disorders have remained pretty much the same for as far back as we can explore?

As early as 1621, English vicar Robert Burton described many of our modern anxiety disorders in his book *The Anatomy of Melancholy*.

In particular, he noted a specific form of anxiety very similar to panic attacks (see Chapter 9, p.256), and appeared to link it to agoraphobia, just as modern-day anxiety theorists have done. French psychiatrist Henri Legrand du Saulle also linked panic attacks with agoraphobia symptoms in 1878 saying, 'Although we can observe now and previously that these patients fear open places, they can feel fear of theatres, churches, high balconies in buildings or whenever they are found near wide windows, or buses, boats, or bridges.' Du Saulle even predicts the association between panic attacks and fear of heights, which was not established empirically until over a century later (see Chapter 6). In medical writings over the past five hundred years, panic attacks appear to be the most common form of anxiety symptoms, and many medical authors were regularly describing the symptoms of panic attacks as far back as the sixteenth and seventeenth centuries. They were diagnosed as melancholia or 'panic terrors caused by vapours.'[16]

While, we've already identified examples of a common modern-day phobia, height phobia, in the writings of Robert Burton and Henri Legrand du Saulle, there are examples of more exotic phobias in the ancient writings of Hippocrates and his disciples. These writings describe the case of a man called Nicanor: 'Nicanor's affliction, when he went to a drinking party, was fear of the flute girl. Whenever he heard the voice of the flute begin to play at a symposium, masses of terror rose up. He said that he could hardly bear it when it was night, but if he heard it in the daytime he was not affected. Such symptoms persisted over a long period of time.[17]' You might think

16 Coste, J. & Granger, B. (2014) 'Mental disorders in ancient medical writings: Methods of characterization and application to French consultations (16th–18th centuries).' *Annales Médico-Psychologiques*, 172, 625–633.

17 Hippocrates. Vol VII. *Epidemics 2, 4–7*. Trans: Smith, W. D. Loeb Classical Library. Cambridge, MA: Harvard University Press; 1994.

this is a very unusual phobia, but it's almost certainly not out of place with the unusual modern-day phobias I describe in Chapter 6! Even during Greco-Roman times, phobias were as exotic and unusual as many are today, but we also see examples of today's most common phobias, such as water phobia and height phobia, being described as early as the third century BC.[18]

The cardinal diagnostic feature of Generalised Anxiety Disorder (GAD) is excessive worrying (see Chapter 7), and there has certainly been plenty of that over the centuries. English writers such as George Cheyne and Robert Napier were already collecting details of the worries of common people in the seventeenth and eighteenth centuries, and many of these worries reflected the same themes as modern-day worrying, covering topics such as relationships, finances, health and death. But Generalised Anxiety Disorder is characterised by excessive worrying, and this was noted in the writings of Boissier de Sauvages (1706–67). He reported patients presenting with symptoms of grief or worries in a condition he called *panophobia phrontis* (from the Greek φροντις: care, worry, preoccupation). Such patients were constantly extremely worried, and complained of pain and bodily tension, a description closely resembling the excessive worrying, irritability and muscle tension diagnostic criteria for Generalised Anxiety Disorder in DSM-5.

Classical cultures tended to have very strong notions of social status and social norms that regularly gave rise to social anxieties. In ancient Greek society social anxiety was an attribute of one's social status – it was important not to make any faux pas, especially in front of your social superiors[19]. Even in Roman times, social situations were sources of anxiety that generated fears of social evaluation as

18 Caelius Aurelianus, quoted in Roccatagliata, G. (1986) *A History of Ancient Psychiatry*. Greenwood Press.
19 Aristotle (1991) *The Art of Rhetoric*. New York: Penguin.

the sufferer anticipated the judgements of others over the way they had behaved or performed – a fear of being negatively evaluated by others that is a central feature of modern-day social anxiety disorder (see Chapter 10). Epictetus (AD55–135) describes this form of social anxiety thus: 'A musician, for instance, feels no anxiety while he is singing by himself; but when he appears upon the stage he does, even if his voice be ever so good, or he plays ever so well. For what he wishes is not only to sing well but likewise to gain applause. But this is not in his own power.[20]'

Prior to its first appearance in the major diagnostic manuals in 1980, many of the symptoms of obsessive-compulsive disorder (OCD) were viewed as symptoms of other disorders such as phobias or panic, or were thought to be delusional disorders and labelled as 'impulsive insanity' (see Chapter 8). But even so, we can see examples of compulsive behaviours and obsessive thinking being recorded throughout history. The Greek philosopher Plutarch (AD50–120) writes about the mental anguish caused by religious fears – fears of not praying well enough, not confessing fully, or having impure thoughts – fears which lead to religious compulsions such as praying for many hours, restarting when this 'does not feel right', or performing acts that would 'neutralise' unacceptable thoughts[21]. This is a description of OCD compulsions and its associated fears that could have come directly from a modern-day clinical psychology textbook.

Examples of the intrusive obsessive thoughts that are also a common symptom of OCD are commonplace. In 1691, the Bishop of Norwich, John Moore, recorded that many individuals

20 Epictetus (1916) *The Discourses of Epictetus Including the Enchiridion.* New York: Oxford University Press.
21 Friedrich, P. (2015) *The Literary and Linguistic Construction of Obsessive-Compulsive Disorder: No Ordinary Doubt.* AIAA.

were obsessed by 'naughty and sometimes blasphemous thoughts [which] start in their minds, while they are exercised in the worship of God [despite] all their endeavours to stifle and suppress them … the more they struggle with them, the more they increase.'[22] What is intriguing about these historical examples is that religiosity plays a central role in generating these symptoms, and even in the present day, highly religious individuals appear to be at greater risk of developing symptoms of OCD because of the constraints imposed on their thinking and behaviour by their religious beliefs – but more of that in Chapter 8.

Finally, we know that the trauma-related condition now known as post-traumatic stress disorder (PTSD) has been around for some time, despite its current diagnostic definition not being established until 1980. American cardiologist Jacob Mendes Da Costa noted flashbacks and anxiety as a condition in some soldiers returning home after the American Civil War. Similar conditions were known as 'Shell Shock' in World War I veterans, and 'Combat Stress Reaction' during World War II. But wars are nothing new, and consequently neither are PTSD symptoms. Professor Jamie Hacker Hughes of Anglia Ruskin University found descriptions of traumatic symptoms closely resembling PTSD when he examined ancient manuscripts describing the outcomes of battles and combats occurring in ancient Mesopotamia during the Assyrian Dynasty between 1300 and 609 BC[23].

It seems that disorders of anxiety have been around for as long as there have been people able to write about them, and in the selection of cases I've described the symptoms have been favourably

22 http://ocd.stanford.edu/treatment/history.html
23 Abdul-Hamid, W. K. & Hacker Hughes, J. (2014) 'Nothing new under the sun: Post-traumatic stress disorders in the ancient world.' *Early Science & Medicine*, 19, 549–557.

comparable to those we see in modern-day sufferers. We can probably assume that the psychological and physiological mechanisms that generate these disorders were as relevant two to three thousand years ago as they are today (you can be the judge of that when you read the subsequent chapters of this book). But while the underlying mechanisms that generate these anxiety disorders may be the same across the centuries, we might expect details in these disorders to change with the social and cultural circumstances of different eras. What a GAD sufferer worries about will depend on the threats and challenges that beset daily living in that era; the nature of OCD obsessions and compulsions will depend on how the social, moral and religious rules of the time impose constraints on thoughts and actions; the prevalence of disease will determine phobias, hypochondriasis and cleanliness compulsions; and even contemporary conceptions of anxiety itself are likely to impact on how anxiety disorders are experienced – is it a medical condition in need of treatment, is it a status symbol signifying wealth, achievement and a busy life, or is it a sign of moral failure in a cultural climate that admires courage, bravery and self-control? Each era's conception of anxiety is different and likely to have its own impact on individual experiences of anxiety.

Signs of the Times

The modern-day concept of anxiety has developed out of historical conceptions of *melancholia* – a condition that embraced modern definitions of both anxiety and depression. In earlier times, anxiety was a natural response to violence and conflict, famine, epidemics of plague and disease, and poverty and starvation. In Greco-Roman times emotions such as fear and anxiety were viewed as socially destabilising and a sign of moral failure, and the young were trained to resist fear and anxiety and adopt the virtues of bravery and courage.

However, during the scientific revolution, views of anxiety became increasingly medicalised, but continued failure to find neurological causes for the 'psychoneuroses' (which included anxiety) eventually led to psychic or psychological interpretations of anxiety, of which Sigmund Freud was one of the principal proponents. From classical times onwards there have been many eras that believed they were experiencing an anxiety epidemic – often as a result of changes in contemporary lifestyles, the introduction of new technologies and practices, or, paradoxically, increased wealth or increased poverty. Anxiety is not a new emotion – it evolved to help human beings deal with the plethora of threats and challenges throughout evolution, and it seems – from the brief review above – anxiety disorders themselves are not new, and conditions with symptoms very similar to modern-day anxiety disorders can be found in writings dating back to the classical period.

CHAPTER SIX

The Mystery of the Origins of Phobias

'Fear makes the wolf bigger than he is.'

— German Proverb

When I begin to teach my undergraduate students about phobias, I always start with a slide showing a large pile of coloured buttons next to a pad of cotton wool. Everybody knows about the most common phobias – things like fear of heights, spiders, water, snakes, creepy crawlies, darkness, death, etc. But sometimes you get what I call 'common uncommon phobias' – phobias of everyday objects that people shouldn't have anxieties about but with a little probing you find that a lot of people do. Cotton wool is one in particular. There seem to be quite a few people who can't bear to touch cotton wool. If you blindfold someone with a cotton wool aversion and then unexpectedly get them to touch some cotton wool, their hands recoil from it like they've just touched a red-hot stove.

Aversion to buttons is another puzzling phobia. In my life alone, I've come across dozens of people who insist on having all the buttons cut off their clothes before they'll wear them. They are certainly uncomfortable enough with buttons to insist on this strange ritual. One particular example of button phobia reported in the psychological literature is of a nine-year-old Hispanic American boy who was unable to handle buttons. As a consequence he couldn't dress himself and had difficulties concentrating at school because of an excessive preoccupation with not touching his school uniform or touching anything that his buttoned shirt touched. Outside of school, he avoided wearing clothes with buttons and avoided contact with buttons that others wore[1].

Unlike many of the phobias we'll talk about later, there did seem to be an event that precipitated this specific fear of buttons. When he was five years old he was pasting buttons on to his poster board and ran out of them. He was asked by his teacher to come to the front of the class and fetch some more buttons from a bowl on the teacher's desk. On reaching for the bowl, his hand slipped and he accidentally tipped the whole bowl of buttons over himself – an event that he described as very distressing. I doubt very much whether all button phobias are caused in the same way as this, but this example does highlight some interesting features of phobias. First, after the precipitating event his fear of buttons simply got worse and worse – despite reassurances from his family and friends. This is known as 'incubation', in which – for no obvious reason – fear of the object or event simply escalates over time. Second, this boy's phobia significantly interfered with his normal daily living, affecting his ability to look after himself and affecting his educational development. Third, the fear develops into an intrusive and dominating cognitive preoccupation, in which he has to be continually hypervigilant that he doesn't accidentally come into contact with buttons. Finally, there's an interesting element of fear of contamination in this case history that is common to many phobias. Not only is he fearful of buttons,

1 Saavedra, L. M. & Silverman, W. K. (2002) 'Case Study: Disgust and a Specific Phobia of Buttons', *Journal of the American Academy of Child and Adolescent Psychiatry*, 41, 1376–1379.

he's also anxious about other things that may have come into contact with buttons.

While we're on the topic of unusual phobias, let me describe another interesting case history so that you can get a flavour of how severe specific phobias are experienced and how this experience develops. Many years ago, eminent clinical psychologist Jack Rachman described in detail a chocolate phobia exhibited by a patient known as Mrs V[2]. She complained of an extreme fear when confronted with chocolate or any object or place associated with chocolate, and even avoided anything that was brown (she would even refuse to sit on any brown furniture). This avoidance extended to avoiding shops that might stock chocolate, and she once walked up eight flights of stairs rather than use the lift because of a brown stain next to the lift buttons. As with our previous button phobia example, her phobia 'incubated' over time to the point where she'd ceased working because of her fear and was practically housebound.

As Rachman points out, fear of chocolate is extremely rare (for which chocolatiers are extremely grateful!) and it's difficult to argue that it has any obvious survival value. Unlike the Hispanic American boy with the button phobia, Mrs V. was relatively inarticulate about the history of her fear. But according to the accounts she was able to give, her anxieties began shortly after the death of her mother whom she was very close to. Her anxieties first became focused on fear of cemeteries and funeral parlours, and then she became aware of a mild distaste for chocolate some months later. Four years on from her mother's death and she'd become entirely chocolate phobic – avoiding chocolate and even becoming extremely frightened of it. This example illustrates the gradual onset of severe phobias

2 Rachman, S. & Seligman, M. E. P. (1976) 'Unprepared Phobias: "Be Prepared"', *Behaviour Research and Therapy*, 14, 333–338.

that eventually 'incubate' to become distressing and life disrupting. It also emphasises the lack of insight that the sufferer has into the processes that gave rise to the phobia. Mrs V. felt sure that she'd seen a bar of chocolate in the room containing her mother's coffin, but in all probability this was a fanciful reconstruction in her attempt to explain her irrational feelings, and in the next section we'll discuss the fact that a majority of phobia sufferers (even those suffering mild phobias) are usually at a loss to explain how their phobia started or how it developed.

'It's a Past-Life Thing'

Billy Bob Thornton is a famous actor, screenwriter, director and musician. As accomplished as that sounds, he once told chat-show host Oprah Winfrey that he had a fear of antique furniture – so much so that he simply couldn't eat anywhere in the vicinity of antiques. Thornton also admitted that he has a fear of certain types of silverware, and wrote this fear into his character Hank Godowsky in the film *Monster's Ball*, who insists on eating his food with a plastic spoon and fork. What does Thornton have to say about his fears? In an interview with the *Independent* newspaper, he explained, 'It's just that I can't use real silver. You know, like the big, old, heavy-ass forks and knives, I can't do that. It's the same thing as the antique furniture. I just don't like the old stuff. I'm creeped out by it, and I have no explanation why . . . I don't have a phobia about American antiques, it's mostly French – you know, like the big, old, gold-carved chairs with the velvet cushions. The Louis XIV type. That's what creeps me out. I can spot the imitation antiques a mile off. They have a different vibe. Not as much dust.'[3] How did he acquire this

3 Rose, T. (3 September 2004) 'Interview with Billy Bob Thornton: Acting very strange.' Independent.co.uk (London). Retrieved 30 May 2008.

very unusual fear? Well he says that 'maybe it's a past-life thing and I got beat to death with some old chair'! We'll discuss that possibility later.

It's been reported that other celebrities have more mundane phobias; film actress Megan Fox is said to be afraid of paper; country singing star Lyle Lovett is afraid of cows; Cameron Diaz is reported to have a fear of door handles; and former *Baywatch* star Pamela Anderson has a fear of mirrors. You may be thinking, 'Well, these are not as crazy as Billy Bob Thornton's fears.' But even so, how do people get fears of paper, cows, door handles and mirrors?

By comparison, my own fears seem by my own admission much more adaptive and sensible. As a child I was completely panicked by loud noises – especially pneumatic drills. Whenever we saw a worker in the street using a pneumatic drill my mother insisted on taking me by the arm and dragging me as near as she could to it until I completely freaked out. All I ever remember is struggling frantically so I could just run as far away as possible. Her intention was simply to 'get me used to the noise' and my fear would go away. How many parents have tried that? Well, no it didn't go away, it just got worse to the point where I became scared of noisy cars, barking dogs, large crowds and vacuum cleaners.

Perhaps more understandable was my fear of dentists that I described in Chapter 1. One day I was unexpectedly called out of class and taken across the school yard to a room where there were two people in white coats standing either side of what I thought was just an oversized, leather armchair. Without explanation they asked me to sit in it, lean back and open my mouth. I was only seven years old and no one had told me about dentists! It's bad enough having someone you don't know messing around in your mouth for reasons that are beyond you, but then when the loud whirring noise of the drill started up and they began to drill my teeth (without anaesthetic in those days) – in the words of Billy Bob Thornton, I completely freaked. I don't remember whether I felt any pain, but I remember the sheer terror of such an unexpected oral intrusion by complete strangers wielding a whining instrument that was suddenly pulled towards my face like a screaming animal in the act of pouncing. I really did think I was going to die. My terror appeared to serve its purpose because they were entirely unable to continue, and I was told not to be so childish and stop yelling for my mother (yes, the same mother that dragged me screaming towards pneumatic drills!). Decades later I still only go to the dentist's when I'm suffering the most unbearable toothache, I simply can't watch dentists on TV, and I become anxious when I read a copy of *Punch* magazine – traditionally the dentists' favourite waiting-room periodical.

I've described just a few examples of specific phobias that afflict famous people as well as myself. Strangely, as odd as some of these fears are, we seem quite happy to accept that people acquire them and suffer them, perhaps because specific fears and phobias are so prevalent in the population – almost everybody seems to have one. Large scale scientific surveys suggest that a clear majority of the population (over 60 per cent) report having symptoms of a specific fear or phobia at some time in their lives[4], and around one in ten people in their lifetime will report fears of a severity that make them clinically diagnosable and in need of treatment[5]. This makes specific fears and phobias one of the most widely experienced anxiety-based problems, and they can cause both distress to the sufferer and

4 Chapman, T. F. (1997)'The Epidemiology of Fears and Phobias.' In G. C. L. Davey (Ed.) *Phobias: A Handbook of Theory, Research and Treatment*, Chichester: John Wiley & Sons.

5 Stinson, F. S., Dawson, D. A., Chou, S. P., Smith, S., Goldstein, R. B., Ruan, W. J. & Grant, B. F. (2007) 'The Epidemiology of DSM-IV Specific Phobia in the USA: Results from the National Epidemiologic Survey on Alcohol and Related Conditions', *Psychological Science*, 37, 1047–1059.

disruption to that person's normal daily living. While we've so far discussed a few unusual fears, the vast majority of phobias that are experienced revolve around just a limited number of situations and objects. These include animals – especially bugs, rodents, spiders, snakes and invertebrates (such as snails and slugs) – then heights, water, enclosed places, social situations, and blood, injury and injections[6]. Most other phobias are much rarer, but no less scary or debilitating for their sufferers. Even so, the origins of these common phobias are no less puzzling than those of Billy Bob Thornton and his fellow celebrities.

The commonness of fears and phobias seems at least in part to explain why we appear to accept that people acquire and suffer specific fears and why it seems almost 'normal' in a strange way. But this does raise the matter of where specific fears come from and how they're acquired. For example, how can people acquire fears that are so very specific (e.g. antique furniture, door knobs, paper) and represent debilitating fears of things that the vast majority of people would say are absolutely – and without argument – harmless!

Well, why don't we just ask them how they acquired their fears? What's surprising is that most people simply won't be able to tell you. Their usual response is, 'Well, I always seem to have been frightened of mice.' Some years ago now, we conducted a survey of 120 people who claimed to have a fear of spiders (one of the commonest phobias in Western cultures), and we asked them all to try and recall an event that precipitated their fear. Only one person out of 120 was able to do this. She'd worked as a secretary and told us that her fear of spiders started on an occasion when she was being sexually harassed by her boss, and at that very moment she remembers seeing

---

6 The Latin names for phobias are merely the domain of pub quizmasters and film producers, and are rarely used in psychiatry or clinical psychology!

a spider scuttle across the floor in front of her. From that moment on she couldn't go near a spider, watch spiders on TV, or even stay in the same room as one[7]. In contrast, no other respondents could recall a specific event as the cause of their phobia – only that they seemed to have had the fear for as long as they could remember, or that it had developed so gradually that no one single event seems to have been responsible. These findings are not unusual. Snake phobics, for example, have hardly ever been bitten by snakes. In a study of thirty-five highly snake phobic individuals in the USA, only three had been bitten by a snake – yet most were still so fearful of snakes that they couldn't even bear to look at a picture of a snake[8].

It's the same with water phobia and height phobia. For example, Australians love their beaches and their water sports, so water phobia is a real problem if you're a red-blooded Australian youngster growing up on the coast. Not surprising, then, that much of the research on water phobia has been carried out in Australia. However, rather than being able to identify the causes of water phobia and develop interventions to prevent it, these studies merely added to the mystery. Are water phobic kids having bad experiences with water? Are they being thrown into the deep end of swimming pools by their older siblings? Seemingly not, over half the parents of children with water phobia believed their child's phobic concerns about water had been present from their first contact with water[9]. So their fear of water seemed to exist even before their first serious encounter with it.

Just one final example before we move on. I am severely height phobic – which doesn't help when I have to call in on the ever-

7 Davey, G. C. L. (1992) 'Characteristics of Individuals with Fear of Spiders'. *Anxiety Research*, 4, 299–314.

8 Murray, E. & Foote, F. (1979) 'The origins of Fear of Snakes', *Behaviour Research and Therapy*, 17, 489–493.

9 Menzies, R. G. & Clarke, J. C. (1993) 'The Aetiology of Childhood Water Phobia', *Behaviour Research and Therapy*, 31, 431–435.

growing number of University Psychology Departments with trendy glass atriums and visit monolithic shopping malls with glass-sided elevators. I even had to leave the Van Gogh museum in Amsterdam in panic a few years ago when I realised I'd have to walk up a glass stairway to the mezzanine floors to view my favourite Van Gogh paintings. Needless to say, my fear won out and I didn't view any of the exhibits and now have a strangely ambivalent reaction to any Van Gogh paintings. Height phobia is universal and also very common. But the number of height phobics who acquired their fear by falling off ladders or cliffs, falling down steep flights of stairs, or breaking their legs falling off mezzanine floors in Van Gogh museums is very small. Around one in five height phobics can recall some bad experience when their phobia began, but then again – paradoxically – these recalled events are rarely accidents. They are often just recollections of feeling very frightened or panicky while in a high place. Around six out of ten people with height phobia claim their fear has always been present[10] – just like water phobics.

We've now discussed a number of common phobias in which a large majority of sufferers can't recall a precipitating event or experience. This mystery is puzzling given how frequent specific fears and phobias are in the general population. Billy Bob Thornton's tongue-in-cheek view of his phobia of antiques is that 'it's a past-life thing and I got beat to death with some old chair'. Alternatively, he might have been abducted by aliens and taken to a room on their spaceship filled with dazzling white light where they implanted the fear of antique furniture in his brain and beamed him back down to earth to ponder his baffling complaint. But I doubt it.

10 Menzies, R. G. & Clarke, J. C. (1993) 'The Etiology of Fear of Heights and its Relationship to Severity and Individual Response Patterns', *Behaviour Research and Therapy*, 31, 355–365.

Figure 6.1 My height phobia meets my nemesis – The Van Gogh
Museum in Amsterdam. Note the architect's 'modernist vision stressing
geometric shapes, light and open spaces, this is particularly evident in
the staircase in the central hall'. My height phobia was also 'particularly
evident' on the glass stairways leading up to the galleries!

So, if phobia sufferers are at a loss to explain their condition,
and these fears seem to have been around for as long as they can
remember. Where do they come from? Are they a result of some
biological pre-wiring constructed by our evolutionary past? Many
psychologists think so. So much so that this is almost the explanation of choice for many people. But before you start warming to this
theory, let me tell you the story of the man-eating slugs.

Escape from the Man-Eating Slugs

Conjure up an image of your ancestors from fifteen thousand years
ago, tirelessly migrating across continents, discovering fire, invent-
ing the wheel, domesticating animals and building civilisations.
However, during this process of social and cultural evolution they

are continuously and mercilessly being hunted down by herds of giant, man-eating slugs. The sick and lame are picked off one-by-one and children are consumed as snacks as these rampant predators satisfy their appetite for food and carnage. During this particularly challenging time of pre-history, slugs occupied the ecological predatory niche later to be filled by wolves, bears, tigers and alligators. Their cunning and ruthlessness knew no bounds and those humans who survived were the ones who were the first to spot the looming shadows of the giant slug herd, the percussive shrill sound of their hunting cries, their erratic rapid movements across the savannah, and their staring eyes standing high on their eye-stalks as they fixated their human prey.

Unfortunately, we're unable to verify this historical scenario because giant slugs left no fossil remains, but did they leave a different legacy – our modern-day phobic dislike of slugs? Slug phobia is one of the commonest animal fears, and is often reported in the top ten animal fears worldwide[11]. Have you ever been gardening with bare hands and – before you're aware it's happened – you've recoiled and shaken a slug from your fingers? Interestingly, women also tend to be significantly more slug phobic than men[12] – presumably because females were tastier to those ancient predatory giant slugs and so had to develop stronger biologically wired avoidance responses.

The reason I've laboured this fictitious example (yes, it was fictitious!) is because it helps to caricature a process that is very easy to slip into when it comes to trying to explain phobias. We've

11 Davey, G. C. L., McDonald, A. S., Hirisave, U., Prabhu, G. G., Iwawaki, S., Im Jim, C., Merckelbach, H.,. de Jong, P.J, Leung, P. W. L. & Reimann, B. C. (1998) 'A Cross-Cultural Study of Animal Fears', *Behaviour Research and Therapy*, 36, 735–750.
12 Davey, G. C. L. (1994) 'Self-Reported Fears to Indigenous Animals in an Adult UK Population: The Role of Disgust Sensitivity', *British Journal of Psychology*, 85, 541–554.

already noted that most people lack an understanding of how they acquired their fears. There's also a tendency for people to believe that they've had their fear for as long as they can remember. This failure to identify both a cause and an event that precipitated the fear can lead to the assumption that it's biologically pre-wired – 'If I don't recall it starting, then it must have been part of me forever'. This certainly rings true if the fear appears to be an adaptive one that could prevent harm, and fear of heights, water, snakes, spiders, etc. could all be construed in this way. The argument here is that heights, water, snakes and spiders have all been around for many tens of thousands of years, and could all be harmful in some way. Therefore, the genes of our ancestors who actively avoided these things would be selected, and in this way a 'fear' or avoidance of them would be genetically handed down to us in the present day. This is certainly consistent with the fact that many people do exhibit fear of heights, water, snakes and spiders. But there is something disconcertingly easy about this type of explanation.

Our story about the giant slugs provides one example of how this type of explanation might be fallacious. It's easy to believe how snakes and spiders (which can often be fatally venomous) might have been genuine threats to the survival and well-being of our ancestors, but surely not slugs? And slugs are a very common object of phobic fears. It's also scientific bad practice to allocate a cause to an effect without providing any supportive evidence. For example, to my knowledge there's no substantial evidence that snakes and spiders ever represented a significant survival selection pressure to our ancestors, and this would be critical for the biological pre-wiring of any fears to these animals. We will certainly discuss the view that some aspects of phobic fear are biologically determined, but it's hard to substantiate this down to the level of individual specific phobias. For example, we have biologically pre-wired startle reflexes that react to rapid movement towards us, rapid unpredictable movement, looming shadows, loud noises and staring eyes. This should be quite enough to help us detect most types of predator with some urgency. So why would evolution also want to equip us with what would be redundant pre-wired detailed templates to detect and avoid very specific predators such as snakes and spiders?

It is probably useful at this point to introduce you to a character called Pangloss from Voltaire's satirical novel *Candide*. Pangloss was someone who exhibited universal optimism best captured in the phrase 'all is best in the best of all possible worlds', and American biologists Stephen Jay Gould and Richard Lewontin coined the term 'Panglossian' to refer to the misguided view that everything present in the world today exists because it has a specific beneficial purpose. So, according to the Panglossian view, the task for scientists is not to discover whether a given characteristic (such as a phobia) has an adaptive function, but to clarify *how* the characteristic has served an adaptive function. This Panglossian view (that everything that exists must be adaptive) generates what is known as the 'adaptive fallacy', and this fallacy is that if you're trying to generate reasons why something might be adaptive you can do that quite easily no matter what it is you're thinking about, and this appears to be how some psychologists have considered phobias. That is, it's assumed that those phobias that are most common (e.g. heights, water, spiders, snakes, blood, injury, etc.) *must* be so common because they have an adaptive function – that is, they enable people to successfully avoid potentially harmful and threatening things.

I have argued many times in the past against these types of Panglossian views that claim that phobias are evolutionary pre-wired adaptations – it smacks of a scientific 'cop out'. In 1971, the famous American psychologist Martin Seligman wrote a short but very influential paper entitled 'Phobias and Preparedness', arguing that we hardly ever have phobias of things like pyjamas, guns, electricity outlets and hammers, even though these things are likely to be associated with trauma in our world[13]. Instead, we tend to have phobias of spiders, snakes, insects, heights, fire, deep water, etc. – things that have been around for a long time in evolutionary terms and were potentially harmful to our pre-technological ancestors. Seligman left us with the implication that most phobias are exaggerations of evolutionary adaptations that are pre-wired and that we are biologically prepared to acquire very rapidly given the appropriate learning conditions. This paper spawned a good twenty-five years of research on the view that phobias were 'biologically prepared', and – even today – a glance at most introductory psychology text books shows that they still consider this evolutionary view to be an important potential theory of phobias.

There was not a lot of solid evidence in Martin Seligman's seminal paper to support the view that common phobias exist because of their adaptive evolutionary function, and as I recall, he only authored a couple of other tangential papers on this topic before moving on to other things, leaving us all to thrash around in the void trying to put some evidential flesh on these very speculative bones. While adaptation through natural selection is one possible mechanism by which common modern-day phobias could exist, Gould and Lewontin also point out that some modern-day characteristics arise from random genetic sampling, and others may exist because they're associated with other structures and behaviours that do confer a selective advantage, and not because they directly increase survival themselves.

But all these arguments assume that phobias are biologically pre-wired and merely contest the mechanism by which this has occurred.

13 Seligman, M. E. P. (1971) 'Phobias and Preparedness', *Behavior Therapy*, 2, 307–320.

There are equally good arguments that phobias are *not* biologically pre-wired.

To add a further element of scepticism to this adaptionist view of phobias, it doesn't provide a genuinely balanced picture of how phobias might be caused. If you look at the top ten list of predatory animals that kill human beings each year you won't find the spider amongst them. But you will find animals such as lions, elephants, tigers and bears[14] – all are animals that people rarely acquire a clinical phobia to. It's true, if you were confronted by one of these animals in a confined space you would be right to be very scared, and would be well advised to run like the wind at the first opportunity. But this adaptive fear is not the same as phobic fear. Very few people attend phobia clinics with debilitating fears of tigers or bears, hardly anyone gets a rush of fear-laden adrenaline when they hear the word 'lion' in a conversation, and people just do not turn away in panic when shown a picture of an elephant. All of these reactions are certainly true of people with severe snake or spider phobia (and even in many cases, slug phobia!). Indeed, most of us happily send our children to bed with cuddly replicas of bears and make them watch TV programmes depicting tigers, lions and elephants as good-natured cartoon characters – hardly the stuff that would be expected if evolution was constantly telling us to beware of them.

To put this discussion into perspective, the adaptionist or evolutionary view of phobias might seem compelling because it appears to explain why common phobias focus on things that have been around for a long time (in evolutionary terms), why it might be adaptive to avoid or fear these things, and why sufferers can only rarely recall when and how their phobia started. However, it's still a highly

14 'Animal Danger', available at http://www.animaldanger.com/most-dangerous-animals.php.

speculative approach, and I'll argue that it's almost certainly wrong, and that people acquire phobias during their lifetime through one of a number of very different psychological mechanisms and not because their phobias are biologically pre-wired.

Finally, if we go back to our celebrity phobias, it's hard to claim that phobias of more unusual things such as antique furniture, silverware, paper, door handles and mirrors are a direct result of evolutionary pre-wiring – mainly because these things have not been around for long enough for fear of them to become encoded in the gene pool. So they've probably been acquired during the sufferer's lifetime. What is even more intriguing is that in most cases these fears have been acquired without the sufferer noticing how they were caused, without any awareness of the conditions critical to their learning, and without any insight into how their thoughts and beliefs about the world have been manipulated and shaped. In 1950s speak, there is something akin to 'brainwashing' going on here but who or what is doing the brainwashing, and why should we want to become so fearful of things that, by any objective logic, we shouldn't be frightened of at all?

Pathways Through the Maze

Whenever the causes of a phenomenon are concealed or difficult to identify we are often seduced into seeking magical or mystical explanations for them. Historically, phobias have been variously described as 'manifestations of evil spirits and evidence of an imbalance in the hierarchical order of the universe', an excess of black bile, emotional delirium, lucid insanity, a poor upbringing, or stomach ailments[15]. In addition, Hippocrates believed that phobias were due

15 Thorpe, S. J. & Salkovskis, P. M. (1997) 'Animal Phobias.' In G. C. L. Davey (Ed.) *Phobias: A Handbook of Theory, Research and Treatment*, Chichester: John Wiley & Sons.

to an overheating of the brain caused by a build-up of bile. But it's easy to see how explaining the causes of phobias becomes difficult when even the sufferer is unable to provide significant insight into the acquisition process. Nevertheless, it's the purpose of science to provide rational and objective insight into nature and its causes, and the scientific path is the one we will steer in detail here.

Perhaps the first mistake when trying to understand phobias is to assume they are all the same thing, and so must have one single underlying cause. This homogeneous view is probably reinforced by the fact that the most important psychiatric diagnostic manual in the world – the Diagnostic & Statistical Manual of Mental Disorders (DSM) – defines specific phobias as a single diagnostic category 'characterised by clinically significant anxiety provoked by exposure to a specific feared object or situation, often leading to avoidance behaviour'[16]. So for diagnostic purposes chocolate phobia and button phobia are lumped together with height phobia, spider phobia, slug phobia, and even phobia of antique furniture. Mrs V., Billy Bob Thornton and I are all burdened with the same descriptive diagnostic label for our very different anxiety-based problems.

Yet everyone is different. Everyone's experience of the world is different – including the route we steer through our lives and the way we perceive and interpret the world, and these individual differences will give rise to phobic experiences that are personal and unique. Nevertheless, scientific enquiry would have no value if it were unable to pluck some common routes from the multitude of footpaths that define individual experience, and these pathways are often unusual and unexpected, but on reflection make psychological sense and fit with psychological fact. The subtlety of some of these

16 American Psychiatric Association (2013), *Diagnostic and Statistical Manual of Mental Disorders* (5th edition). Washington, DC: American Psychiatric Association.

processes explains precisely why many phobia sufferers are unable to understand how their fears were acquired, their thoughts were brainwashed, and their lives disrupted to such degree by fear and avoidance.

Being Chased by Pavlov's Dogs

In the world of anxieties, phobias are relatively simple things. They're anxiety that's focused on one very specific event or situation while the phobic's life appears to go on quite normally around this single irrational fear. The focused nature of this fear almost begs for a simple explanation, and one simple explanation is that form of classical conditioning originally demonstrated by Russian physiologist Ivan Pavlov and his 'slobbering' dogs in the early 1900s. Pavlov's dogs learned to associate a bell with the delivery of food to the point where they began to salivate in anticipation of food when they heard the bell. Now consider what happens if you replace food with a nasty, frightening event like an electric shock (don't try this at home on the family dog!). To be sure, the dog will come to react fearfully to the sound of the bell. Bells aren't intrinsically frightening, but can become so if they predict something nasty is about to happen. The same might be true of specific phobias. Maybe the phobia sufferer had their phobic stimulus paired with something nasty or frightening at some time, and this is what's generated a seemingly irrational fear to something that shouldn't normally be frightening. Simple, isn't it?

Well, no, it's not. You might expect people with phobias to remember a really scary event that occurred in conjunction with their current phobia, but a majority of phobia sufferers recall nothing of the kind at the point when their phobia started. More to the point, they can only rarely tell you exactly when their phobia started in the first place. As much as we'd all love classical conditioning to be the nice simple process by which we acquire phobias, it just isn't.

If it were as simple as that we'd all be getting phobias of ovens when we regularly burn ourselves taking out the Sunday roast, or phobias of those pesky little kittens that keep playfully tearing our flesh with their very sharp claws! However, perhaps phobias are acquired only after very traumatic experiences are paired with the phobic stimulus. This was certainly the case with my own dental phobia. The trauma was very intense, but because it was intense it left an indelible memory that I've never forgotten. This suggests that at least some phobias are acquired through this simple associative learning process, and examples of these include accident phobia[17] (a fear of riding in cars following an automobile accident), many forms of dental phobia[18] (following painful or traumatic dental surgery), choking phobia[19] (fear of choking when eating after having a frightening choking experience), and most forms of dog phobia[20].

Dog phobia is an interesting example because kids don't have to be bitten by dogs to become fearful of them. As human beings, one of our biologically pre-wired startle reactions is to very rapid movement of an object towards us (just as a pouncing predator would appear to us), and many dog phobias are acquired when a dog runs towards a child, with the rapid movement towards eliciting reflexive fear reactions. Apologetic dog owners will often try to calm the situation by saying 'It's okay, he's only playing', but by then the damage is done. Here's a typical example: 'When she was three, we were

17 Kuch, K. (1997) 'Accident phobia.' In G. C. L. Davey (Ed.) *Phobias: A Handbook of Theory, Research and Treatment*. Chichester: Wiley.

18 Davey, G. C. L. (1988) 'Dental phobias and anxieties: Evidence for conditioning processes in the acquisition and modulation of a learned fear.' *Behaviour Research and Therapy*, 27, 51–58.

19 Greenberg, D. B., Stern, T. A. & Weilburg, J. B. (1988) 'The fear of choking: Three successfully treated cases.' *Psychosomatics*, 29, 3–17.

20 Doogan, S. & Thomas, G. V. (1992) 'Origins of fear of dogs in adults and children: The role of conditioning processes and prior familiarity with dogs.' *Behaviour Research and Therapy*, 30, 387–394.

walking along on our way to nursery and a dog ran out of a garden straight up to her. It didn't jump up or bark or anything, just stopped dead in front of her. She screamed and ran into the road before I could grab her, (luckily a cul-de-sac and no cars about) where she fell over and cut her knee. Ever since this incident she has been scared of dogs.'[21] I suspect the bloody knee had very little to do with this fear, it was the dog running towards the child and triggering an innate defensive startle reflex in typical classical conditioning style.

Dogs, cars, dentists, choking! Classical conditioning only offers a comprehensive explanation for just a very small proportion of the phobias in the world, but what about the bulk of our day-to-day phobias, including snakes, spiders, bugs, water, heights, blood and claustrophobia, to name just the major ones?

'Don't Panic!' – Just Step Away from the Edge

Looks like I'm not the only one scared of heights – there are a lot of us out there, including singer Nik Kershaw and football pundits Alan Hansen and Michael Owen[22]. As anyone who has a fear of heights will tell you, the experience of height phobia is an unusually frightening one. As Adventure Blogger Zabdiel Scoon explains, 'As we go through our everyday lives we naturally avoid our fears to the point that it becomes an unconscious action. It's only when you're faced with those fears that you really start to consciously consider how they impede what it is you wish to do. In my case, I didn't realise how debilitating a fear of heights could be when coupled with long-term travel. In La Boca, Buenos Aires, I had another confrontation with my fear of heights. After looking around this stunning museum

21 'Daughter has a dog phobia, can anyone help?' http://forums.money savingexpert.com/showthread.php?t=175934

22 http://www.dailymail.co.uk/health/article-3523436/Why-develop-fear-heights-age.html

we were asked if we would like to view the sculptures on the roof terraces and take in the views of the harbour from the balcony on the top roof. This all sounded terrific and was indeed impressive until I had to climb a very tall, open spiral staircase to the top balcony. Looking up I thought "this doesn't look particularly solid". My hands felt incredibly clammy and my heart beat faster as I began to climb the staircase.'[23]

There's a compelling mix of catastrophic thoughts and physiological manifestations of anxiety here, but as I said earlier, height phobics aren't people who've suffered trauma by falling off a ladder or such like and are now frightened of heights because of it – they would never have gone up a ladder in the first place! The only trauma that height phobics have ever experienced is being on a height, so we need a radically different kind of theory to explain how some people develop height phobia and other people don't.

One key to understanding height phobia is its link to panic and to panic attacks (see Chapter 9), and many of the physical manifestations of height phobia are very similar to panic symptoms – trembling, sweaty palms, nausea, dizziness, for example. Another important fact is that phobias of situations (such as heights or enclosed spaces) often share many characteristics in common with panic symptoms. For instance, height phobia appears to have a preponderance of spontaneous onsets typical of panic disorder[24], and if someone is height phobic they're significantly more likely than a non-height phobic individual to also have a diagnosis of panic disorder[25]. The

23 http://www.indefiniteadventure.com/acrophobia-personal-story/
24 Himle, J. A., Crystal, D., Curtis, G. C. & Fluent, T. E. (1991) 'Mode of onset of simple phobia subtypes: Further evidence of heterogeneity.' *Psychiatry Research*, 36, 37–43.
25 Starcevic, V. & Bogojevic, G. (1997) 'Comorbidity of panic disorder with agoraphobia and specific phobia: Relationship with the subtypes of specific phobia.' *Comprehensive Psychiatry*, 38, 315–320.

link between panic symptoms and situational phobias such as height phobia and claustrophobia also extends to cognitive factors – height phobics also think like people who have panic attacks. Certain types of cognitive predispositions can often precipitate panic attacks, and two of the most important predispositions are a tendency to be acutely aware of one's bodily sensations, and a bias towards inter- preting ambiguous bodily sensations as threatening. Just think about what it means to hold these two types of cognitive biases. It means you're much more likely to be tuning into your various bodily sen- sations, are more likely than the average person to notice changes in bodily sensations, and even when you notice one that's ambiguous, you're more likely to think it means something bad is happening to you – there's a catastrophe waiting to happen in your mind! It's quite likely that this style of thinking triggers a vicious cycle that increases anxiety that in turn increases bodily sensations that are interpreted as threatening. Final outcome – panic!

In the case of the height phobic this process has become specific to heights, and detection of bodily sensations and interpretation of them as threatening is channelled into negative thoughts related to heights such as 'I will lose my balance', 'If I stand on the edge I'll be tempted to jump', or 'I will get dizzy or have a heart attack and fall.' As a height phobic, each of those thoughts is familiar to me – but how odd these thoughts are. How odd it is to think 'I'll be tempted to jump' when on a height, but you wouldn't dream of thinking that or any other related self-destructive thought anywhere else. Yet it's a thought that's been created out of two very simple cognitive biases and is a thought shared by many millions of otherwise sane height phobics worldwide. That's how the mind can play some devious tricks on you when anxiety's involved.

The link between situational phobias such as height phobia and panic is important. We now know that height phobia itself is associated with a bias towards interpreting ambiguous bodily sensations as threatening[26], and also that height phobia in early adolescence is a vulnerability factor for panic disorder later in life. I've argued that height phobia and claustrophobia probably have their origins in this link to panic and to the cognitions associated with panic, and I wouldn't be at all surprised if most cases of water phobia weren't also developed in a similar way.

The process that creates people with height phobia is primarily cognitive and shaped by ways of thinking that rarely enter into conscious awareness – so it's not surprising that most height phobics can't articulate how their phobia began. But this is anxiety in its most devious form – creating delusional fears with the most basic of tweaks to our thought processes. Now that's genuine brainwashing for you!

The 'Disgusting' Spider

Arguably the most common group of phobias are animal phobias – the most well-known is fear of spiders, but we also have fears of bugs and creepy-crawlies, insects generally such as cockroaches and daddy long-legs (crane flies), invertebrates such as the slugs we discussed earlier, rodents such as rats and mice, bats (do they really get tangled in your hair?), and reptiles such as frogs and snakes. What's perplexing is that we're significantly more likely to have phobias of these types of animals than genuinely predatory animals such as lions, tigers, alligators, sharks etc. Many people can't even bear to look at a photograph of a rat or a maggot or a snake, let alone go near a real one. And just like height phobia, most people fearful of these types of animals can only rarely recall how their phobia started.

26 Davey, G. C. L., Menzies, R. G. & Gallardo, B. (1997) 'Height phobia and biases in the interpretation of bodily sensations: Some links between acrophobia and agoraphobia.' *Behaviour Research and Therapy*, 35, 997–1001.

To try to understand animal phobias we need to go back to basic emotions. Throughout this book I've emphasised that anxiety is the emotion that's evolved to help us deal with anticipated threats and challenges, but there's one particular threat out there in the world that is so significant and such an important threat to our survival that we developed a separate emotion to deal specifically with it. That threat is disease and illness, and the emotion designed specifically to help us combat this threat is the disgust emotion.

Disgust is an interesting emotion. It's basically that 'Yuk!' response we reflexively emit when we encounter vomit, poo, mucus and the like. We feel slightly nauseous, and disgust has a very distinctive facial expression that is universal – crinkling of the nose (to prevent bad odours being inhaled) and a down-turning of the corners of the mouth (enabling anything disgusting in your mouth the opportunity to dribble out!). We avoid things that disgust us, but in particular we avoid 'oral incorporation' of disgusting objects – we just don't put them near our mouths, let alone into our mouths. Disgust has evolved primarily as a food-rejection response whose main function is to prevent the transmission of disease and illness, especially through the oral incorporation of items and products that may transmit disease[27].

What's all this got to do with animal phobias? Well, let's begin with some interesting facts about animal phobias. In a study of spider-fearful individuals that we conducted some years ago, we asked spider phobics to describe what it was about spiders that made them fearful[28]. Interestingly, we found absolutely no consensus amongst spider phobics about what was frightening about them (some people said their hairiness, some their staring eyes, some their legs, and

---

27 Davey, G. C. L. (1994) 'Disgust.' In V. S. Ramachandran (Ed.) *Encyclopedia of Human Behavior*, Vol 2, 135–141, San Diego, CA: Academic Press.
28 Davey, G. C. L. (1992) 'Characteristics of individuals with fear of spiders.' *Anxiety Research*, 4, 299–314.

so on). This strongly suggests that it's not a single physical feature of spiders that necessarily makes them frightening but something else – something that's hidden from the conscious awareness of our spider phobics.

A second interesting point was that everyone who was fearful of spiders also showed an increased fear to all other animals in our animal phobia category (creepy-crawlies, rodents, reptiles, invertebrates, etc.), but didn't show increased fear to other animals such as lions, tigers, bears and sharks. There's something common to the animals in our animal phobia category that makes people fear them, and, yes – you guessed it – that factor is 'disgust'. For example, fear of spiders correlates highly with measures of disgust sensitivity (a measure of the strength of your disgust reaction when you encounter disgusting objects like vomit, poo, etc.), and disgust sensitivity appears to be the hidden factor that drives the fear of spider phobics. This is consistent with the fact that the disgust emotion has a specific relationship with animals. We know that primary disgust is only elicited by animals, animal products, parts of animals, animal body products, or objects that have had contact with animals or animal products[29] – for instance, we rarely, if ever, get disgusted by the vegetables we have for dinner (even Brussels sprouts), only the meat!

All of this begs two very specific questions. First, what makes some of us more disgust-sensitive than others? And second, how have certain animals acquired a disgust-relevance? That is, what's their association with disease and illness that makes us disgusted by them? In answer to the first question, well, we don't really know yet! In all probability disgust sensitivity is acquired through various forms of

29 Angyal, A. (1941) 'Disgust and related aversions.' *Journal of Abnormal & Social Psychology*, 36, 393–412.

social learning – especially within families, where parents will pass on their sensitivity to disgust-relevant objects to their children in very subtle and indirect ways. If your parents don't like handling poo, then in all probability neither will you! It's relevant here that spider phobia also seems to run in families, and the assumption has always been that parents (especially mothers) will model their fear of spiders for their offspring to learn (usually their daughters). However, a study I conducted on spider phobics with Lorna Forster and George Mayhew suggested that intra-familial spider fear may not be determined by the direct transmission of spider fear from parents to offspring.[30] We found that the only significant predictor of an offspring's spider fear was the disgust sensitivity level of the parents (not their level of spider fear) – no wonder spider phobics don't know where their spider fear comes from!

But disgust is an emotion evolved to help us avoid illness and disease, so how did some quite specific animals get involved in this disease-avoidance process? If we look closely at the individual animals in this animal phobia category we can see that they've acquired disgust relevance in a number of different ways. First, some of these animals have a history of directly spreading disease or being a source of contamination (such as rats or cockroaches). Second, others possess features that mimic primary disgust stimuli that act as vehicles for the spread of disease such as faeces or mucus. For example, slugs can resemble faeces or feel like mucus when touched, and animals that are perceived as slimy such as snakes, snails or lizards, also resemble mucus. Third, some animals have acquired disgust relevance by being contingently associated with dirt, disease or contagion, or acting as signals for infection or diseased food (such

30 Davey G.C.L., Forster L. & Mayhew G. (1993) 'Familial resemblances in disgust sensitivity and animal phobias?' *Behaviour Research & Therapy*, 31, 41–50.

as maggots and mice that have become associated with rotting food and the contamination of food stores).

At first sight, the spider doesn't appear to fit easily into any of these three categories. However, some historical detective work reveals that there's a historical association between spiders and disease and infection that dates at least from the Middle Ages and probably even earlier. For instance, in most of Europe during the Middle Ages spiders were considered a source of contamination, that they absorbed poisons in their environment (e.g. from plants), and any food that had come into contact with them was considered to be infected[31]. Physician H. F. Gloyne has argued that the spider's bite was one way for the people of the time to explain the causes of the many terrible epidemics of plague and disease that swept across Europe from the Middle Ages onwards. While not fatally venomous, many European spiders do possess bites that cause a painful systemic reaction, and these bites are known to have become opportunistically associated with causally unrelated illnesses and diseases[32].

Probably as a result of this spurious association, in Central Europe during the Great Plagues, spiders were seen as harbingers of the plague and death, and this association was subsequently used as the basis for Jeremias Gotthelf's famous story *The Black Spider*. This association between spiders and disease, and subsequently between spiders and fear may be something that has significance only for Europeans because of the spider's historic role as a harbinger of the Great Plagues of Europe.

Indeed, if we look to other parts of the world, spiders are not the scary creatures that we love to hate in Western cultures. In many

---

31 Renner, F. (1990) Spinnen: Ungeheuer – sympathisch. Kaiserslautern: Verlag.
32 Gloyne, H. F. (1950) 'Tarantism: Mass hysterical reaction to the spider bite in the Middle Ages.' *American Image*, 7, 29–42.

areas of Africa the spider is revered as a wise creature and its dwelling places are cleaned and protected by the local people. Native American children often keep spiders as pets, and many cultures consider spiders to be symbols of good fortune rather than fear. For example, Hindus in eastern Bengal collect spiders to release at weddings as a symbol of good luck, and in Egypt it's common practice to place a spider in the bed of a newly married couple![33] When we carried out a large-scale cross-cultural study of animal phobias, it was interesting to see that it was only in those countries populated by Europeans and their descendants that spiders came near the top of the list of animals people feared – a fact that's consistent with spiders becoming associated with disgust and disease, and consequently fear, during the course of European history[34].

So the disgust emotion is quite important in our understanding of the causes of phobias. Disgust not only plays a central role in the acquisition of many animal phobias, but it's also been linked to other common phobias, such as blood-injury-inoculation phobia – here again the importance of body parts and body products are central to triggering disgust reactions[35]. I've no additional evidence on which to base this, but I wouldn't be at all surprised if the unusual phobias we described earlier – Mrs V's phobia of chocolate and Billy Bob Thornton's phobia of antique furniture – weren't underpinned by disgust rather than spine-chilling fear. Billy Bob describes antique furniture as 'dusty' – well, there's a sense of contamination fear there; and in our lab studies of disgust we used chocolate to mould into the shape of dog poo to disgust our participants – no need to explain that

33 Bristowe, W. S. (1958) *The World of Spiders*. London: Collins.

34 Davey, G. C. L., McDonald, A. S., Hirisave, U., Prabhu, G. G. et al. (1998) 'A cross-cultural study of animal fears.' *Behaviour Research and Therapy*, 36, 735–750.

35 Page, A. C. (1994) 'Blood–injury phobia.' *Clinical Psychology Review*, 14, 443–461.

one! There's no doubt that disgust as a disease-avoidance emotion has a bigger part to play in our anxieties than we might immediately imagine.

Phobias and the Anxiety Epidemic

So, are we likely to get a sudden rash of new, modern-day phobias contributing to the anxiety epidemic? It's very hard to tell, but our growing knowledge of the origins of phobias does allow us to make some interesting inferences. First, there's good reason to believe that there may not be radical change in the *types* of phobic fears we experience in the new modern age. For instance, spider phobia is currently one of our most prevalent fears and seems to have been around for centuries in Western societies. But it would be very difficult to argue that spider phobia was a consequence of modern-day stresses and strains. Spider fear is still with us today despite the fact that the poor creature's link to disease and illness was originally spurious, and we no longer suffer the plague epidemics for which it was believed to be the harbinger!

There's a similar story with height phobia and agoraphobia. In 1878 the French psychiatrist Henri Legrand du Saulle wrote about 'fear of spaces' saying 'although we can observe now and previously that these patients fear open places, they can feel fear of theatres, churches, high balconies in buildings or whenever they are found near wide windows, or buses, boats or bridges.'[36] In this insightful quote, du Saulle recognises that agoraphobia is not simply a fear of open spaces, it's a fear of public spaces generally – and he also makes the interesting link between panic attacks and height phobia. We could possibly attribute the predominance of height phobia today to

36 Berrios, G. E. (1996) 'Anxiety and cognate disorders.' In G. E. Berrios *The History of Mental Symptoms. Describing Psychopathology since the Nineteenth Century*. Cambridge University Press.

increased high-rise living in the modern era (or to the preponderance of atriums in buildings and shopping malls!), but there it was, just as noticeable well over a century ago – its prevalence is not new (see also Chapter 9, p.257).

These types of phobia have been around for centuries because the factors that cause them are fundamental to human survival. Spider phobias are a response to our desire to avoid disease and are mediated by our disgust sensitivity; height phobias are a response to our desire to protect the self and are mediated by an increased tendency to monitor bodily sensations and interpret any ambiguous sensations as a potential threat – better safe than sorry! Any stresses and strains that the modern world throws at us are likely to trigger these basic survival processes but may not necessarily create new phobias. They may merely activate and strengthen the existing culturally predominant forms of phobia that are linked to these basic survival processes.

For example, in 2014 the Ebola epidemic in Africa became one of the biggest news stories of the year, and two-thirds of all Americans were worried about an Ebola epidemic in the United States[37]. However, news of a new deadly virus may not create a new 'Ebola Phobia', but would almost certainly activate general psychological processes and emotions that protect against disease and illness by, for example, raising levels of disgust sensitivity. A knock-on consequence of this is a corresponding facilitation of all existing responses linked to disgust sensitivity, including spider phobia, and indeed any other phobia supported by disgust[38]. Contemporary fears and

37 https://www.washingtonpost.com/business/economy/an-epidemic-of-fear-and-anxiety-hits-americans-amid-ebola-outbreak/2014/10/15/0760fb96-54a8-11e4-ba4b-f6333e2c0453_story.html?utm_term=.e66911b055f6

38 Webb, K. & Davey, G. C. L. (1992) 'Disgust sensitivity and fear of animals: Effect of exposure to violent or revulsive material.' *Anxiety, Stress & Coping*, 5, 329–335.

stresses may not create their own new category of clinical anxieties but could facilitate existing ones.

But what about new technologies – can they contribute their own very specific, modern-day fears and phobias? Computers and social media immediately come to mind, but they're already so integrated into our everyday lives that it's almost impossible to fear them to the point of totally avoiding them. But when people do become anxious of new technologies, can this fear reach levels where the anxiety they generate meets diagnostic criteria for a clinical phobia? Apparently they can. Sue Thorpe from the University of Surrey found that computer anxiety could reach clinical levels that conformed to official diagnostic criteria for a specific phobia, and the levels of anxiety and the phobic beliefs of computer-anxious individuals compared well with the anxiety levels and beliefs of spider phobics[39]. But what was different about computer phobics was that their concerns were not so much about their reaction to computers ('I would panic' or 'I would go hysterical') but more about social anxieties associated with using a computer (e.g. 'I would make a fool of myself'). To this extent, this is rather more like social anxiety than a brand-new clinical category called 'technophobia', so even modern technophobias may be nothing more than a contemporaneous manifestation of a good old-fashioned phobia such as social phobia.

In conclusion, the phobias we live with today still appear to be the phobias our ancestors lived with a century ago, or even a millennium ago. But while new technologies and the stresses and strains of our modern world may not create any radically new clinical phobias, they can still contribute to the anxiety epidemic by influencing the intensity and frequency of our traditional phobias.

39 Thorpe, S. J. & Brosnan, M. J. (2007) 'Does computer anxiety reach levels which conform to DSM IV criteria for specific phobia?' *Computers in Human Behavior*, 23, 1258–1272.

CHAPTER SEVEN

The Worry Monster

'I'm a born worrier. Fear is my best friend and worst enemy. I worry if I have nothing to worry about.'

— Black Sabbath rocker Ozzy Osbourne[1]

'One day in the early months of pregnancy, I sat at my work computer crying my eyes out. Why? In my eagerness to learn and search everything pregnancy, I somehow happened upon a mother's account of a terrible (extremely rare) defect found *in utero*. I understood that statistically, the chances my baby would ever have this same defect were close to zero but there I sat, feeling the worry monster sharpening its claws. Since that day, my worry monster can overtake my brain in mere seconds. My worries often keep my thoughts whirling, and the Internet has officially made me lose my mind.'[2]

When worry kicks in, it literally knows no bounds. Every single niggle hides an anxiety that spawns a worry, and every worry feeds an even greater worry. For many people, worrying is a highly skilled

1 http://www.contactmusic.com/ozzy-osbourne/news/worried-rocker-ozzy-osbourne_1117753
2 http://albuquerque.citymomsblog.com/health/worry-modern-age-internet-mind-loss/

process, honed over a lifetime of regular practice, but for others, like the mother in the opening quote, it just creeps up on you unexpectedly and then you can't shake it off. That quote at the beginning of the chapter was from a blog post with the title *Worry in the Modern Age – Or How the Internet Makes Me Lose My Mind*! Once again, we can point to the Internet as a contemporary source of information to fuel worries and stoke anxiety. Worry is a close ally of anxiety. But worry and anxiety are not the same thing because you can be anxious without worrying, and worry without being anxious[3]. Anxiety is that gut feeling you get when you're confronted with threats and challenges – a gut feeling associated with a cascade of psychological and physiological processes to help you react to those threats and challenges. In contrast, worry is just one of the cognitive processes that we deploy to try and help us understand these threats and challenges and evolve solutions for them.

But worry can often go wrong. How often have I woken up at 3 a.m. worrying about some up-coming life issue? I then try desperately to work this issue out while lying in the dark silence of the bedroom without any means of enacting solutions to the problem in a world that is currently asleep and inactive – I tirelessly think through potential scenarios and mentally rehearse possible solutions. The usual outcome of this nocturnal activity is that I end up feeling very tired and out of control of my worry – I can't stop it, and it's making me feel more anxious and more stressed the more I try to solve it. This is worry going wrong and simply creating more anxiety.

Yet, like the mother in our opening example, worriers still go on worrying as if they were habitual gamblers addicted to losing every

3 Davey, G. C. L., Hampton, J., Farrell, J., & Davidson, S. (1992) 'Some characteristics of worrying: Evidence for worrying and anxiety as separate constructs.' *Journal of Personality and Individual Differences*, 13(2), 133–147.

penny on the blackjack tables. Just as the pathological gambler will often explain their addiction by claiming, 'I'm a born gambler', so too do chronic worriers – how often have we heard our worrisome friends and family members claim that they're 'born worriers'? But that may be just an excuse to justify a behaviour that they simply can't control. No one is born a worrier, we each develop our own style of worrying during our lifetime, but for some of us, the style we develop is dysfunctional, uncontrollable, overwhelming and distressing.

To try and understand how worry can go wrong, let's continue this chapter with a rather unusual example. The Statue of Liberty is a 150-feet-high neoclassical sculpture on Liberty Island in New York Harbor. It's a robed female figure representing the Roman goddess Libertas. She's holding a torch above her head, is made of copper, and was a gift from the people of France to the United States. The Statue of Liberty has stood in New York Harbor since its dedication in 1886, and over the ensuing decades had been a welcoming sight for immigrants to the USA arriving from abroad. Now, what must it be like being the Statue of Liberty, having stood there season after season in New York Harbor for over a hundred and thirty years? Holding a torch above your head 24/7 can be pretty tiring.

Well, in one of our early studies of worrying, we asked participants to imagine they were the Statue of Liberty standing in New York Harbor. Then we asked them to imagine that they were 'worried' about being the Statue of Liberty. Finally, we then engaged them in an interview to discuss their worries about being the Statue of Liberty. We didn't do this entirely out of a sense of perverse surrealism! We wanted to see what happened when we asked groups of high and low worriers to worry about something they'd never ever worried about before. Almost everyone we tested had never worried about this before (but we did have one participant we had to eliminate from the study because they claimed they'd previously worried about being the Statue of Liberty. But I expect that was the result of an entirely different psychopathology to anxiety!). At the time, the *London Evening Standard* picked up on the study and ran an article describing the research next to a cartoon of the Statue of Liberty anxiously claiming she was 'Worried about people walking around in her head'!

The interview we conducted with participants in our Statue of Liberty study is called a catastrophising interview. This interview allows us to see how long people will continue to worry about a topic and also reveals the kinds of 'what if . . . ?' scenarios they're willing to create. We start by asking them, 'What is it about your worry that worries you?' So, for example, if someone says they're worried about their finances, we ask, 'What is it that worries you about your finances?' If the person then replies, 'I may have to leave my home if I can't pay the mortgage,' we then ask, 'What is it that worries you about leaving your home if you can't pay the mortgage?' We keep throwing the last reply back at the interviewee until the person can think of no more responses. Interestingly, chronic worriers will continue with this process for much longer than people who worry much less – thinking up many more responses in the chain and elaborating their initial worry with more worries in the process. Low-frequency worriers tend to stop very quickly, and so don't elaborate their worries in such a viral fashion.

So what happens when we ask high and low worriers to worry about being the Statue of Liberty? We get exactly the same pattern as if we'd asked them to fret about a real worry. People who score high on measures of pathological worrying continue the catastrophising interview for much longer than people who worry much less. This suggests that it's not the worry topic *per se*, nor the degree to which people have already rehearsed that worry that causes these differences in catastrophising – it's more like an iterative worrying style that chronic worriers bring to *any* worry, whether the worry is real to them or not. Figure 7.1 shows the responses given in the catastrophising interview to the Statue of Liberty worry by a high worrier and a low worrier respectively. The obvious difference here is that the high worrier goes through many more iterative steps than the low worrier. But that's not the only interesting feature of these worry streams. If you look closely at the responses in the various steps given by the high worrier, we begin to see issues of personal inadequacy ('I would not be able to cope'), low self-esteem ('It would cause a loss of self-esteem'), and lack of control over events ('Eventually my problems would have more control over me than I had over them') creeping into the worry stream[4]. Again, this is a typical finding with those who worry a lot. Their catastrophising of an individual worry tends to bring out feelings of inadequacy, inability to cope, and lack of confidence in their own ability to deal with life's challenges and threats – even if it's a completely hypothetical worry such as imagining they're the Statue of Liberty!

This tells us two very distinctive things about chronic worriers. They bring an iterative style to any worry topic that makes their worrying perseverative – that style is one of the main reasons why they worry for longer than non-worriers. And second, worrying seems to bring out the worst in them. This catastrophising style allows worriers to drag all kinds of lurking inadequacies into their stream of consciousness – something which ends up making the chronic worrier feel more and more inadequate, depressed and anxious as the worry bout continues.

4 Davey, G. C. L. & Levy, S. (1998) 'Catastrophic worrying: personal inadequacy and a perseverative iterative style as features of the catastrophising process.' *Journal of Abnormal Psychology*, 107, 576–586.

Catastrophising sequences from the 'Statue of Liberty' worry*

High worrier

1. I'm worried about not being able to move
2. That I would be attacked in some way
3. That I would not be able to fight back
4. That I would not be able to control what other people did to me
5. That I would feel inadequate
6. That other people would begin to think I was inadequate
7. That in my relationship with those people I would not be respected
8. That I would not have any influence over others
9. That other people would not listen to me
10. That this would cause a loss of self-esteem
11. That this loss of self-esteem would have a negative effect on my relationships with others
12. That I would lose friends
13. That I would be alone
14. That I would have no one to talk to
15. Because it would mean that I would not be able to share any thoughts/problems with other people
16. That I would not get advice from others
17. That none of my problems would be adequately sorted out
18. That they would remain and get worse
19. That eventually I would not be able to cope with them
20. That eventually my problems would have more control over me than I had over them
21. That they would prevent me from doing other things
22. That I would be unable to meet new people and make friends
23. That I would be lonely

Low worrier

1. I can't move
2. I enjoy being free

*Numbers indicate sequential steps in the catastrophising interview

Figure 7.1

Why Worry at All?

Michel de Montaigne was a sixteenth-century French philosopher best known for his sceptical remark '*Que sais-je?*' – 'What do I know?' He may have thought he knew nothing, but he was a prolific source of aphorisms, many of which are highly relevant to today's modern world. The one that's pertinent here is '*My life has been filled with terrible misfortune – most of which has never happened!*' Perfect – what statement could better describe the conundrum that is the chronic worrier! If you Google the question 'What percentage of what we worry about *never* happens?' the figure 85 per cent regularly crops up. But no one is quite sure where this figure comes from. It's often attributed to Robert Leahy's influential book *The Worry Cure*, but it's difficult to find an exact empirical study on which this figure is based. But perhaps the actual percentage figure is not what matters. What does matter is that chronic worriers do spend a disproportionate amount of their time creating future scenarios that exist only in their heads and not in the cold reality of the outside world.

So is worrying worth it – especially if we spend so much time worrying about things that are never likely to happen? Well maybe us chronic worriers hoodwink ourselves into believing that worrying really is useful, and that's why we do it. Adrian Wells, a good friend of mine, and a prominent worry researcher, is Professor of Clinical and Experimental Psychopathology at the University of Manchester. I remember him beginning his conference presentations by admitting in a serious voice, 'I wake up every morning worrying about being trampled to death by a herd of elephants.' The audience would look bemused – a herd of elephants in Manchester? After a pause he'd then continue ' . . . but I haven't been trampled to death yet – so my worry must be working!' It was a facetious example, but with a very good point. If around 85 per cent of what we worry about is never likely to happen then it might appear to us that our worrying about these things is actually helping us deal with these bad things – if we didn't worry about them, then maybe they'd creep up on us and catch us out unawares! In the terminology of the famous behaviourist B. F. Skinner, this is a form of superstitious reinforcement – we worry about something, and then it doesn't happen (in fact it was never likely to happen anyway), so our worry has been rewarded. In this sense, it's the mental equivalent of using Greek worry beads to superstitiously 'guard against bad luck'.

In ways such as this, worriers come to believe that worry is a very useful and important thing to do – otherwise bad things will happen – and over the course of their lifetime, worriers build up a very ingrained set of beliefs about how worry is useful. In the studies we've conducted, we've found that chronic worriers hold a wide range of positive beliefs about the utility of worrying including 'in order to get something done I have to worry about it', 'worrying allows me to work through the worst that can happen, so when it does happen things are better', 'worrying starts off as a process of preparing me to meet new situations', and so on[5]. Once these beliefs are firmly established the chronic worrier begins to come out with the ubiquitous assertion that 'I'm a born worrier'. This is not so much a comment on their inherited attributes as on their inability to stop worrying – they're basically saying 'I worry . . . I worry a lot . . . but don't try to stop me or change me, because I need to do it!' It's a compulsion. That's all fine and well, but for many people who are perpetual worriers, this process is not a happy one, and it causes a lifetime of distress and anxiety, and we'll look in more detail at how a supposedly positive process goes bad later in this chapter.

5 Davey, G. C. L., Tallis, F. & Capuzzo, N. (1996) 'Beliefs about the consequences of worrying.' *Cognitive Therapy & Research*, 20, 499–520.

What Is There to Worry About?

If there's an anxiety epidemic, then there's plenty to worry about! *The Hunger Games* star Jennifer Lawrence is said to worry about constant scrutiny in the media and her private details being made public, it's claimed that actress and singer-songwriter Amanda Seyfried worries about her dog, and will picture him opening the apartment window and falling out, while singing star Adele is said to get so worried about going on stage that she's physically sick before performances.[6] I worry about the health of my mother, the future of my daughters, and whether my flimsy garden fence will be blown down in the next gale (not necessarily in that order). Professor Wells worries about being trampled to death by a herd of elephants. What does this all tell us? Well, we basically worry about anything and everything!

But the chief domains of worrying are ones that certainly won't surprise us, and we've come across these worry topics earlier in this book. Major worries tend to group around domains such as relationships, finances, work and health[7], and these reflect anxieties triggered by factors related to love and marital status, loneliness, poverty, unemployment, economic status and disability, to name just a few of the factors we discussed in Chapter 3. These are worries that are driven by traditional sources of anxiety, and as such would have been worries experienced by previous generations, and even our more ancient ancestors.

But what about modern-day worries – the typical daily worries of Generations Y and Z? We can conveniently divide worries into two

6 https://www.buzzfeed.com/maggyvaneijk/it-aint-about-the-ass-its-about-the-brain?utm_term=.oiZ1dYX84#.di2a8BwZOhttps://archive.org/details/englishmaladyort00chey

7 Craske, M., Rapee, R., Jackel, L. & Barlow, D. (1989) 'Qualitative dimensions of worry in DSM III-R generalized anxiety disorder subjects and non-anxious controls.' *Behaviour Research and Therapy*, 27, 397–402.

basic types: the first are worries about life events (such as that job interview, relationship difficulties, or our annual health check); and the second type is what are known as 'daily hassles'. Daily hassles are the little things that can occur on an almost daily basis and cause us acute bouts of stress, and it's with these daily hassles that we begin to see how the modern world has created entirely new worries for our Generations Y and Z.

In 2015 the insurance provider Direct Line published a survey of 2,025 adults in the UK after asking them about the stressors that worried them on a daily basis[8]. Here's the top ten daily worries: (1) Not being able to sleep; (2) losing your keys; (3) being stuck in a traffic jam when already late; (4) losing an important paper or document; (5) having nowhere to park; (6) printer not working when you need to print something; (7) running out of battery on your mobile phone while out; (8) discovering you're out of toilet paper while you're on the loo; (9) dealing with computerised customer service; and (10) finding you've forgotten your bank card when paying for an item.

What's striking about this list is that at least half of these daily hassles would have meant nothing a generation ago and they're the product of technologies and lifestyles that have become central features of our lives only in the twenty-first century. As Professor Jonathan Freeman of Goldsmith's College London puts it, 'We weren't expecting to find that one of the major triggers (for stress) is the way in which people mentally process the spiralling effects of an everyday emergency . . . you may be sat in traffic on your way to the train station – and the worry about having to pay for a new ticket after missing the train can cause a feeling of hysteria!'[9]

But these events aren't just stressors that we simply react stress-

8 http://www.dailymail.co.uk/femail/article-3030649/Top-10-everyday-things-stress-Brits-revealed.html

9 http://www.gold.ac.uk/news/fearcasting---i2-media-direct-line-study/

fully to only when encountered. Professor Freeman has coined the term 'fearcasting' to describe the way we now forward-plan for eventualities such as those in our list of top ten daily hassles. We're not just worrying about future life event scenarios, our lives are so busy that our brain is continuously planning how to deal with a whole range of daily hassles – missed trains, parking problems, dead phones, lost keys and traffic jams – many of which, of course, may simply never happen.

In addition to this list of modern daily hassles, there's one particular personality characteristic that appears to foster worrying and is especially implicated in worrying about current affairs. This characteristic is known as 'intolerance of uncertainty', and it's a feature that is likely to generate many modern-day worries that are associated with uncertainty in the world. People who have this characteristic believe that any form of uncertainty is a bad thing and it gives rise to anxiety, stress and worrying. Intolerance of uncertainty is on a continuum – we all experience some intolerance of uncertainty, but some more than others, and at the high ends of this continuum, intolerance of uncertainty is associated with a number of anxiety disorders and with the pathological worrying that's experienced in Generalised Anxiety Disorder[10]. Dan Grupe at the University of Wisconsin-Madison compared intolerance of uncertainty to an allergic reaction: 'If you're allergic to nuts, and you have a piece of birthday cake that has a drop of almonds in it, you have a violent physical reaction to it. A small amount of a substance that's not harmful to most people provokes a violent reaction in you. Intolerance of uncertainty is like a psychological allergy'[11].

10 Boswell, J. F., Thompson-Hollands, J., Farchione, T. J. & Barlow, D. H. (2013) 'Intolerance of uncertainty: A common factor in the treatment of emotional disorders.' *Journal of Clinical Psychology*, 69, doi: 10.1002/jclp.21965
11 https://www.theatlantic.com/health/archive/2015/03/how-uncertainty-fuels-anxiety/388066/

But here lies the problem – as my grandmother used to say, 'There's only one thing in life that's certain, and that's uncertainty!' So those individuals with an intolerance of uncertainty will spend much of their time fruitlessly worrying about how to acquire that unobtainable state of certainty. Given that we all have at least some intolerance of uncertainty, growing political uncertainty over recent years appears to have contributed to the modern list of worries. A survey conducted on 1,700 people by the British Mental Health Foundation found that two in five people in the UK have felt anxiety in relation to Brexit, and almost half reported a 'fair or great deal' of anxiety in relation to the US election in which Donald Trump was elected president – both represent ongoing international uncertainties giving rise to what some psychologists have labelled 'Brexit anxiety' and 'Trump anxiety'[12]! I expect, though, that these new anxieties will be relatively fleeting, and you certainly shouldn't expect to see them in future editions of psychiatric diagnostic manuals.

If modern life's so busy, then when do we find time to do all this worrying? As part of our initial research into worrying in the 1990s we published a study on the phenomenology of worrying – it was basically a description of the ways in which people experienced their worries[13], and the bedroom has a lot to answer for. Two out of three people said they mainly worried at home, and 57 per cent of those said their worrying took place in the bedroom when they were lying in bed. The most common worry times during the day were between nine at night and three in the morning. More recent research by home insurance provider Privilege adds some more detail to this

12 http://www.express.co.uk/news/uk/829442/brexit-anxiety-negotia tions-theresa-may-donald-trump-eu-referendum-talks-michel-barnier

13 Tallis, F., Davey, G. C. L. & Capuzzo, N. (1994) 'The phenomenology of non-pathological worry: A preliminary investigation.' In G. Davey & F. Tallis (Eds.) *Worrying: Perspectives on Theory, Assessment and Treatment*. Wiley.

evolving picture of a nation of night-time worriers[14]. Their 2016 survey of 2,005 adults in the UK found that we spend on average eighty-one minutes per night worrying – the study concluded that this added up to a staggering fifteen months or 10,920 hours of our lives lying awake at night worrying. They found that the prime time for night-time worrying was 2–3 a.m., with an estimated 12.4 million Britons awake at this time. Two in every five of these night-time worriers were worrying about their finances, and one in three worried about their health. So, what's the impact of all this sleep lost through nocturnal worrying? Just look back to what was number 1 in our list of top ten daily hassles – yes, that's right, not being able to sleep! It seems the modern-day human being spends the daytime worrying about how they're going to deal with the sleep they've lost at night because of their nocturnal worrying! How did we get ourselves into such a perfect vicious cycle?

What Exactly Is Worrying?

Worrying is an internal process with a narrative style – that is, you think to yourself about your problems. People rarely worry in images; they worry in words. The subjective function of worry is generally twofold – first, it's your attempt to identify future threats and challenges; and second, you also try to find solutions to these problems. But one person's problem-solving is another person's stress, and while some people view worrying as stressful, many others view it as a perfectly natural process of 'thinking through' a problem and derive no stress at from it at all.

To put this into a context, prior to 1990 it was almost as if worrying as a psychological process didn't exist. We began to consider running some studies on worry around that time, and an extensive

---

14 http://www.directlinegroup.com/media/news/brand/2016/11a-01-16.aspx

search of the psychological and psychiatric literature only revealed around half a dozen scientific articles with the word 'worry' in the title. So we began by trying to find out what psychological processes were associated with what people understood by the terms 'worry' and 'anxiety'. The results were surprising. Measures of worrying were associated largely with very positive traits such as use of adaptive problem-focused coping (dealing with a problem by trying to find a solution to it) and an information-seeking cognitive style (seeking out information to help inform you about a problem). In contrast, measures of trait anxiety were associated largely with processes considered to result in poor psychological outcomes, including poor problem-solving confidence, poor perceived personal control, taking responsibility only for negative but not positive outcomes, an increased tendency to define events as threats, and the deployment of avoidance or emotion-focused coping strategies[15].

Interestingly, this study also indicated that worry and anxiety were independent processes, whereas prior to this time, many psychopathology researchers had considered worrying merely as just another characteristic of anxiety. What jumps out at you when you consider these findings is that worry appears to be 'good' and anxiety is 'bad'! So where does it all go wrong? Why is worrying such a distressing and unproductive process for some people, and not the positive, productive activity that our study seemed to imply?

The Birth of the Worry Monster

An initial way to consider how worrying might become dysfunctional is to consider worrying in anxious versus non-anxious people. If worrying is an attempt to problem-solve by thinking through

15 Davey, G. C. L., Hampton, J., Farrell, J. & Davidson, S. (1992) 'Some characteristics of worrying: Evidence for worrying and anxiety as separate constructs.' *Journal of Personality and Individual Differences*, 13(2), 133–147.

possible scenarios and how you would deal with them, then if you're an anxious person, your anxiety might easily 'thwart' this process through the negative thinking that we've found is associated with anxiety[16]. As I mentioned earlier, trait anxiety is associated with 'poor problem-solving confidence, poor perceived personal control, taking responsibility only for negative but not positive outcomes, an increased tendency to define events as threats, and the deployment of avoidance or emotion-focused coping strategies'. Quite a list! So, imagine trying to create constructive ways of coping with a future challenge when you have poor confidence in your ability to solve problems, a tendency to interpret even benign events as threatening, you don't have confidence in your ability to change events, you have a tendency to believe that you're responsible for negative things happening, and you feel you can only cope with life's problems by avoiding them. This is the anxious worrier – someone who's creating more problems rather than solving existing ones, and murdering their self-esteem in the process!

Because we all get anxious sometimes, anxiety will often steer our worrying down a negative path by setting in action those negative cognitive processes I've described above – processes that thwart successful problem-solving. This is why we may often feel even more distressed and anxious at the end of a worry bout than when we began – our anxious brain has successfully steered our thoughts down a 'better safe than sorry' route, identifying even more potential threats for us to be wary of, and failing to solve any of our problems to our own satisfaction.

But anxiety doesn't suddenly make us bad problem-solvers – it simply takes away our confidence. We asked eighty-two undergraduate

16 Davey, G. C. L. (1994) 'Pathological worrying as exacerbated problem-solving.' In G. C. L. Davey & F. Tallis (Eds.) *Worrying: Perspectives on Theory, Assessment and Treatment*. Wiley.

students to complete measures of worrying and problem-solving confidence, and then we asked them to provide their own solutions to some real-life problems[17]. We would present them with the beginning and the end of a scenario, and then ask them to make up a brief story that connects the beginning with the end. An example situation is: 'Mr A. was listening to the people speak at a meeting about how to make things better in his neighbourhood. He wanted to say something important and have a chance to be a leader too. The story ends with him being elected leader and presenting a speech.' The students were asked to write the middle of the story about how Mr A. achieved his goal. These responses were then independently assessed for relevant means and effectiveness. We found that scores on the measure of pathological worrying were directly related to measures of poor problem-solving confidence and poor perceived control over the problem-solving process, but worry was unrelated to problem-solving ability *per se*. That is, chronic worriers were just as good as non-worriers at thinking up good solutions for personal problems, but their deficit occurred at the level of solution implementation rather than solution generation. Chronic worriers can think up good solutions, but lack the skills or confidence to implement those solutions. If you go back and take a look at the catastrophising steps to the Statue of Liberty worry in Figure 7.1, you'll see these themes of low self-confidence coming out in the worry stream in a number of different ways.

But poor self-confidence is only the beginning of the road to chronic and pathological worrying. A number of other psychological processes become involved along the way that turn worrying from a simple daily problem-solving exercise into a distressing,

17 Davey, G. C. L. (1994) 'Worrying, social problem-solving abilities, and social problem-solving confidence.' *Behaviour Research and Therapy*, 32, 327–330.

uncontrollable and perseverative activity that can establish itself as a life-long anxiety condition known as Generalised Anxiety Disorder.

Generalised Anxiety Disorder

Generalised Anxiety Disorder (or GAD for short) is the diagnostic category that defines the worry monster. It's one of the most common of the anxiety disorders, and is a pervasive condition in which the sufferer feels continual apprehension and anxiety about future events and experiences intense, uncontrollable worrying. It's accompanied by symptoms of restlessness, agitation and muscle tension, and a consequence of these symptoms is disruption in a number of areas of daily functioning, including impairment in family, social and occupational functioning, and a poor health-related quality of life[18]. GAD is twice as common in women as in men (as are most of the anxicty disorders). Over 5 per cent of the population will be diagnosed with GAD at some point in their lifetime, and 3 per cent of the adult population will be suffering from GAD in any twelve-month period[19]. That's just under two million diagnosable sufferers in the UK and 9.6 million sufferers in the USA in any one year period. That's a lot of worrying going on and a lot of distressing pathological worrying requiring treatment. Here's an example.

Jim is a fifty-four-year-old man who went to see his GP about feeling anxious and depressed. He was unable to shake off worries about many topics, including family relationships, housing and health issues. He believed he'd 'always been a worrier' but things had got worse as a result of a series of negative life events. He'd had

18 Revicki, D. A., Travers, K., Wyrwich, K. W., Svedsater, H. et al. (2012) 'Humanistic and economic burden of generalized anxiety disorder in North America and Europe.' *Journal of Affective Disorders*, 140, 103–112.
19 https://www.nimh.nih.gov/health/statistics/prevalence/generalized-anxiety-disorder-among-adults.shtml

a stressful time in his job as a senior accountant, he injured his back and was retired on medical grounds, his wife left him and his teenage daughter began avoiding school work. He now began to find decision-making difficult and worried over every eventuality. Should he move to a bungalow to help his mobility problems, how could he repair the relationship with his wife, how should he occupy his time now he was retired, how could he encourage his daughter to pursue her school work? He began to feel that these worries would drive him mad, seriously damage his health, or send him into deep depressions. Jim's childhood and adolescence included an unaffectionate father who praised him only on achieving perfect school performances, and an anxious mother who saw potential disaster everywhere. Jim gradually developed beliefs about himself as unlovable, other people as generally critical of him, and the world as a dangerous place. Subsequent psychological assessment confirmed Jim with a diagnosis of GAD[20].

Looking at these descriptions of Jim's life in the light of some of our earlier discussions, we can see a possible chain of events that will have led to him becoming a pathological worrier. An anxious mother alerts him to the dangers that lurk in the world; an unaffectionate father's behaviour leads Jim to believe he is unlovable and that others are generally critical of him. Soon he's ready to admit that he's 'always been a worrier'. A series of negative life events then reinforce his view of the world as a dangerous and unpredictable place, and his beliefs in his own inadequacies prevent his worrying from providing him with helpful solutions or ways of coping. There is plenty to worry about but no solutions, and paradoxically, worry is seen as a necessary activity but is distressingly uncontrollable and unproductive.

20 Moulton-Perkins, A., Whittington, A. & Chinery, M. (2015) 'Working with people with anxiety disorders.' In G. Davey, N. Lake & A. Whittington (Eds.) *Clinical Psychology*. Routledge.

The Origins of GAD

There is relatively little detailed research on the developmental origins of GAD, but we can probably paste together a realistic story of what's happening from the study of risk factors for GAD and our current understanding of the cognitive processes that underlie pathological worrying.

Risk factors for GAD fall into three distinct categories – attachment and parenting style, environmental factors, and temperament[21]. Children are relatively new travellers on that bumpy road we call life and are programmed to learn hard and fast about how to negotiate the world – survival and success are demanding teachers! So what's the message about worrying that our children take from their parenting? The early life of a famous child developmentalist is highly relevant here.

John Bowlby was a British psychologist famous for his interest in childhood development and for his pioneering work on attachment theory. He firmly believed that childhood anxiety stemmed from concerns about parental availability, and his own early life is brimming with examples of parental absence and neglect. Bowlby was born in 1907 and as a young child he saw his mother only one hour a day after teatime (lest young Bowlby should be spoilt – it was a common view of the British upper classes at the time that too much parental contact would spoil a child). In 1914 his father left to fight in World War I, coming home briefly only once or twice a year. Even Bowlby's beloved nanny, Minnie, left the family when he was four; he described it later as the tragic loss of a mother figure. Then at the age of ten he was sent off to boarding school, a period

21 Newman, M. G., Llera, S. J., Erickson, T. M., Przeworski, A. & Castonguay, L. G. (2013) 'Worry and generalized anxiety disorder: A review of theoretical synthesis of evidence on nature, etiology, mechanisms, and treatment.' *Annual Review of Psychology*, 9, 275–297.

of his life that he described as a 'terrible time' in his 1973 book *Seperation: Anxiety & Anger*[22]. 'I wouldn't send a dog away to boarding school at age seven,' he was later to claim. Bowlby's own childhood experiences led to his interest in attachment and emotions, and studies soon began to identify insecure attachment styles that nurture anxiety and worrying.

Two particular types of insecure attachment style are anxious-avoidant and ambivalent/resistant styles. Anxious-avoidant children are rejected by their mothers and avoid relationships because of the anxiety that was experienced with the rejecting mother. In the case of ambivalent/resistant attachment style, children tend to react with fluctuating emotions such as anger and anxiety as a result of inconsistent or intrusive parenting. They learn to react with anxiety and worry in order to prepare for unpredictable behaviour from their parents. Subsequent studies have shown that both avoidant and ambivalent attachment are associated with worry severity in children and with GAD symptoms[23,24].

Children who receive parenting that is highly controlling and negative (characterised by harsh discipline), and are subjected to strict rules and high expectations from their parents also exhibit increased symptoms of pathological worrying in general and GAD in particular[25]. The messages that children may take into adulthood from

22 Bowlby, J. (1973) *Separation: Anxiety & Anger. Attachment and Loss* (vol. 2) (international psycho-analytical library no. 95). London: Hogarth Press.

23 Brown, A. M. & Whiteside, S. P. (2008) 'Relations among perceived parental rearing behaviors, attachment style, and worry in anxious children.' *Journal of Anxiety Disorders*, 22, 263–272.

24 Muris, P., Mayer, B. & Meesters, C. (2000) 'Self-reported attachment style, anxiety, and depression in children.' *Social Behavior & Personality*, 28, 157–162.

25 Shanahan, L., Copeland, W., Costello, E. J. & Angold, A. (2008) 'Specificity of putative psychosocial risk factors for psychiatric disorders in children and adolescents.' *Journal of Child Psychology & Psychiatry*, 49, 34–42.

these experiences are likely to be that they're incapable of handling challenges and threats on their own, that they're unable to cope with negative events and the emotional reactions these elicit, and overprotective or overcontrolling parenting is also likely to undermine the child's emotional development leading to emotion regulation difficulties and subsequent anxiety[26]. All grist to the worry mill in later life.

There is one final set of parenting experiences that have been associated with later adult GAD symptoms, and they are maternal role-reversal and enmeshment[27]. Role-reversal puts the child in the position of being the adult in the parent–child relationship (sometimes known as 'parentification'). This may involve the child looking after a sick relative, paying bills, or providing assistance to young siblings. In contrast, enmeshment describes a style of parenting where the parent's life and worth is defined in terms of the child's own happiness or pain, success or failure – the child is the centre of the parent's life and the sole purpose of the parent's life. With both maternal role-reversal and enmeshment the child is likely to grow up feeling responsible for the feelings of others, have problems in their adult relationships, and continually seek to ensure that they themselves are prepared for threats and challenges that may adversely affect the physical and emotional needs of others. That's quite a significant worry workload!

Some of these parenting styles will give rise to anxiety, some to worry, and some to both worry and anxiety, but the detailed effects of these different styles are still unclear. If they generate both worry and anxiety, then that's a toxic mix, because I've already described

26 Wijsbroek, S. A., Hale, W. W., Raaijmakers, Q. A. & Meeus, W. H. (2011) 'The direction of effects between perceived parental behavioral control and psychological control and adolescents' self-reported GAD and SAD symptoms.' *European Child & Adolescent Psychiatry*, 20, 361–371.

27 Cassidy, J., Lichtenstein-Phelps, J., Sibrava, N. J., Thomas, C. L. & Borkovec, T. D. (2009) 'Generalized anxiety disorder: Connections with self-reported attachment.' *Behavior Therapy*, 40, 23–38.

how high levels of anxiety will often act to thwart effective problem-solving and give rise to dysfunctional forms of perseverative and distressing worry. In this respect, the most damaging forms of parenting will be those that generate lifelong anxiety, instil low self-esteem and a perceived inability to cope, and foster beliefs that worrying is necessary to prepare for future threats, challenges and uncertainties.

Apart from parenting style, the second known risk factor for developing GAD is experiencing unexpected negative life events[28]. If we look back at the example of Jim earlier in this chapter, it's clear that the severity of his GAD symptoms and his pathological worrying become worse following a period of negative life events, including health problems, job loss, a broken marriage, and the need to manage a difficult teenage daughter. Such events will lead to worry becoming a means of preparing for an unpredictable future, and a string of negative life events can often radically change a person's whole worldview – from the world being a predictable, safe place, to it seeming like an unpredictable and dangerous one. Indeed, many individuals who develop GAD have a chronic history of negative life events[29], including physical and psychological abuse, and parental neglect, and for their whole lifetime they will only have held the view that the world is a dangerous, threatening and unpredictable place that they need to be constantly wary of.

Finally, there's not a great deal of evidence that genetics or brain dysfunction play a major defining role in the development of GAD.

28 Nordahl, H. M., Wells, A., Olsson, C. A. & Bjerkeset, O. (2010) 'Association between abnormal psychosocial situations in childhood, generalized anxiety disorder and oppositional defiant disorder.' *Australian & New Zealand Journal of Psychiatry*, 44, 852–858.
29 Cougle, J. R., Timpano, K. R., Sachs-Ericsson, H., Keough, M. E. & Riccardi, C. J. (2010) 'Examining the unique relationships between anxiety disorders and childhood physical and sexual abuse in the National Comorbidity Survey-Replication.' *Psychiatry Research*, 177, 150–155.

Twin studies estimate the inherited component of GAD at around 30 per cent, exactly the same as for anxiety generally, but what appears to be inherited more than anything else is a vulnerability to anxiety disorders generally, rather than vulnerability to a specific disorder such as GAD[30]. If one of your parents has been diagnosed with GAD, then there's a slightly higher probablity that you'll be diagnosed with an anxiety problem – but that could be any of the anxiety disorders, and not necessarily GAD. Brain imaging studies have also been relatively unsuccessful in clarifying the origins of GAD or the mechanisms involved. For instance, brain scan studies show that activity in the prefontal brain regions are associated with GAD[31]. But this is not a surprising finding because these brain areas are associated with a range of complex cognitive processes, including planning and decision-making, all of which would be important components of worrisome thought. While this may be where worrying takes place in the brain, brain imaging studies have not yet provided any convincing reasons why worrying in GAD sufferers should be so extreme and distressing. However, other neuroimaging studies have focused on possible abnormalities in emotional regulation in GAD, and such studies do suggest that individuals with a diagnosis of GAD do have a reduced capacity for emotional regulation[32] – a characteristic that may contribute to difficulties in coping

30 Tambs, K., Czajkowsky, N., Roysamb, E., Neale, M. C., Reichborn-Kjennerud, T., Aggen, S. H. et al. (2009) 'Structure of genetic and environmental risk factors for dimensional representations of DSM-IV anxiety disorders.' *British Journal of Psychiatry*, 195, 301–307.

31 Paulesu, E., Sambugaro, E., Torti, T., Danelli, L., Ferri, F., Scialfa, G., et al. (2010) 'Neural correlates of worry in generalized anxiety disorder and in normal controls: A functional MRI study.' *Psychological Medicine*, 40(1), 117–124.

32 Etkin, A., Prater, K., Hoeft, F., Menon, V. & Schatzberg, A. (2010) 'Failure of anterior cingulate activation and connectivity with the amygdala during implicit regulation of emotional processing in generalized anxiety disorder.' *American Journal of Psychiatry*, 167(5), 545–554.

with threats and challenges, and which may also contribute to worry being a distressful activity in GAD.

Clearly, the origins of a disorder of worrying such as GAD are in our experiences and not significantly in our genes. We are not 'born worriers', we are 'contrived worriers' shaped by our experiences to view the world as challenging, threatening and unpredictable. A world where the future cannot be contemplated without significant torment and detailed planning.

But there's still one thing that we haven't yet quite been able to explain. Why is it that when worrying goes wrong it seems uncontrollable? If it's a process that can be productive and useful – even when we feel that the world is generally a threatening and unpredictable place – why is it that we lose control of it, why does it take us over, and why can't we simply switch it off once it's started?

Why Doesn't Worry Have an 'Off' Switch?

Who would you most trust to do an important task properly that requires a lot of attention to detail? Someone in a happy, positive mood, or someone in a negative mood who's stressed, sad, or just plain angry?

Well, it depends on the nature of the task. People in a positive mood are better at creative tasks, while people in negative moods perform better on analytical tasks. For example, psychologist Jeffrey Melton at Indiana University gave a group of sixty undergraduate students a series of logistical syllogisms to solve (puzzles of the kind: 'If all A are B, and some B are C, how many of A are C?'). Before tackling these puzzles, half the participants were made happy and amused by reading Far Side cartoons or listening to a tape of comedian Rodney Dangerfield; the other half acted as a control condition and read only a boring set of adjectives. Positive mood participants performed significantly worse on the syllogisms than the control participants, they took less time on the task, used fewer diagrams to help them solve the problems, and gave riskier 'all' or 'none' answers[33].

This isn't simply about positive mood impairing analytical performance. Negative mood itself actually *facilitates* performance on tasks with an analytical element that requires systematic processing of individual elements in order to solve the problem. Joseph Forgas and Rebekah East from the University of New South Wales divided 117 student participants into three groups. Those in the positive mood group watched an excerpt from a British comedy series, those in the neutral mood group watched a nature documentary, and those in the negative mood group watched an edited excerpt from a film about dying of cancer. They were then asked to watch deceptive or truthful interviews with individuals who denied committing a theft. Those in the negative mood group were the most accurate in detecting deceptive communications, and those in the positive group were most trusting and gullible[34].

The general view seems to be that this kind of effect occurs because negative mood makes us process information in a more detailed, systematic way, whereas positive mood tends to make us take shortcuts in our analytical thinking by using 'heuristics' and stereotypes. A heuristic is a mental shortcut that allows us to solve problems and make judgements quickly. For example, imagine you've just met a little old lady in the street who's asked you to lend her some money. If you're in a negative mood, you're more likely to analyse systematically as much information about her

33 Melton, R. J. (1995) 'The role of positive affect in syllogism performance.' *Personality & Social Psychology Bulletin*, 21, 788–794.

34 Forgas, J. P. & East, R. (2008) 'On being happy and gullible: Mood effects on skepticism and the detection of deception.' *Journal of Experimental Social Psychology*, 44, 1362–1367.

as you can before deciding to trust her. However, if you're in a positive mood, you're more likely to use a heuristic. For instance, she may remind you of your grandmother, so you might immediately assume she's kind, gentle and trustworthy. The heuristic allows you to take an analytical shortcut and make a decision quickly – but it may be the wrong decision!

What's all this got to do with worry? Well, quite a lot actually. Most chronic or pathological worrying occurs while we're in a negative mood. We may be stressed, anxious, sad, tired, in pain . . . or even hung-over! That negative mood has a lot to answer for. It contributes to perseverative worrying in a number of different ways and helps to make our worry seem uncontrollable. First, as we've already noted, negative mood activates a systematic form of information processing which simply isn't going to allow you to use shortcuts to come to conclusions about your worry. You're going to have to go through everything – fact by fact, scenario by scenario, catastrophic outcome by catastrophic outcome! To support this view of worrying as a form of systematic information processing, the two appear to share similar functional brain characteristics. Systematic processing appears to be supported by functionally distinct brain processes located in the left frontal lobes, and studies have reported evidence that increases in worrying are also associated with increased left-hemisphere activation. This is consistent with systematic processing and worrisome thought both being predominantly left-hemisphere activities involved in the systematic, verbal processing of information[35].

Second, negative mood states are associated with increased performance standards – they make you more determined to achieve your goals successfully. Walter Scott and Daniel Cervone from the

35 Dash, S. R., Meeten, F. & Davey, G. C. L. (2013) 'Systematic information processing style and perseverative worry.' *Clinical Psychology Review*, 33, 1041–1056.

University of Wyoming divided undergraduate students into either a negative or a neutral mood condition by asking them to listen to an audiotape – in the negative condition they were instructed to imagine a scenario in which their best friend was dying of cancer; in the neutral scenario they were instructed to imagine visualising their room at home. After this, all participants were asked to complete an irrelevant task in which they had to rate the meanings of presented words. But the real purpose of the study was contained in a questionnaire consisting of four items that had participants rate the minimum standard of performance with which they would be satisfied across a range of tasks (e.g. 'given your GPA for this semester, what is the minimal level of performance you'd have to get this semester to be satisfied with how you'd done?'). As expected, the negative mood group had a higher minimal standard of performance than the neutral group.

This has a number of consequences for worriers who are in a negative mood. Once your criteria for successful worrying have been raised by your negative mood, this will extend the length of the worry bout until you feel satisfied that those more stringent criteria have been met. Sadly, these more stringent criteria for successful worrying are often never met, leading to ever more lengthy bouts of worrying in order to try and reach the unreachable. This is negative mood instilling the worry process with a hefty dose of perfectionism by raising minimum standards for successful worrying – and we know that perfectionism is very closely linked to both chronic worrying and GAD symptoms[36].

All of these effects of negative mood, of course, occur out of conscious awareness – otherwise we might be able simply to tell ourselves to stop worrying and that would be the end of it! But

36 Pratt, P., Tallis, F., Eysenck, M. (1997) 'Information-processing, storage characteristics and worry.' *Behaviour Research and Therapy*, 35(11), 1015–1023.

chronic worriers practise their art a lot. So much so that most of the cognitive processes involved in worrying occur automatically, and once a threat or challenge is identified, these prime well-rehearsed and habitual goal-directed worrying in an automatic fashion[37].

Finally, negative mood has one last and unexpected card to play in generating perseverative worry that feels uncontrollable. The aim of most worrying is to cover all eventualities and find solutions that will deal with our upcoming problems. But how do we decide if we've achieved this goal? This can be the real killer because chronic worriers tend to have poor problem-solving confidence, so this makes it hard to find objective, evidence-based reasons to believe we've achieved our problem-solving goals. So what happens when people find it hard to find objective reasons to make a decision? Yes, you guessed it, they default to their current mood! Positive mood suggests we've achieved our goals; negative mood suggests we haven't (even if the reasons for us experiencing those moods have nothing to do with our worry). Since chronic worriers regularly undertake their worrying in negative mood, this mood state is effectively telling them, 'No you haven't achieved your worry goals yet – so keep on worrying!'

Be clear – this is not a conscious process. We regularly make decisions about the success of an activity based on our current mood, and we do it automatically, and worrying is no exception to this. We all worry in a negative mood – often with the purpose of alleviating those negative feelings of anxiety and stress – but our negative mood keeps insisting we haven't achieved that goal so we need to keep fretting away. It's a vicious cycle that's difficult to break out of, it perpetuates our worrying, and it takes the whole process out of our conscious control.

37 Davey, G. C. L. & Meeten, F. (2016) 'The perseverative worry bout: A review of cognitive, affective and motivational factors that contribute to worry perseveration.' *Biological Psychology*, 121, 233–243.

The Worry Machine

It's a complex piece of machinery that churns out our worrisome thoughts. It makes us think about our worries in considerably more detail than we would about any other set of thoughts, and worries can readily and simply push other thoughts out of the way and take over our conscious experience. We can quite easily stop thinking about how pleasant our garden is looking today, but we find it almost impossible deliberately to stop thinking about that bank balance that's in the red.

So let me quickly review the elements that make up the cogs in this machine. The first element is our anxiety or stress. As I described in Chapter 1, these negative emotions cause our brains automatically to bias attention towards threatening or challenging stimuli, they also bias us towards interpreting ambiguous information as threatening. This is the start of the process where our brain begins to process potential worries before we've even become consciously aware of them. Once we've identified a potential worry, then the chronic worrier usually has a set of beliefs that worry is the necessary thing to do to avoid bad things happening, and as a consequence of these beliefs the worrier automatically deploys a set of strict goals that the worrying must achieve – it must identify all other possible outcomes and scenarios (the worrier's perpetual 'What if ... ?' question), and begin to develop solutions for dealing with these problems. Our negative mood during worrying ensures that we use a very effortful systematic form of thinking that prevents us from taking any short-cuts when considering the problem.

Negative mood also raises our standards – we simply must ensure that we complete our worrying fully and properly. But then, with a sudden act of sabotage, the worrier's poor problem-solving confidence prevents him/her from believing that workable solutions have been found or that all potential scenarios have been reviewed. Our negative mood then delivers the final *coup de grâce* by informing us that the whole process so far has been unsuccessful and we must continue worrying. It's like running a marathon, but as you near the end the finishing line keeps being moved further away!

With continued use, this worry machine becomes well oiled, reliable and starts automatically, but some psychologists believe that worry also has some other unintended effects that reinforce its use and make worry a chronic condition. This relates to one particularly perplexing fact about people with a diagnosis of GAD. Rather than having high heart rate variability – which we might expect if someone has regular feelings of anxiety and fear that may trigger activation of the sympathetic nervous system – people suffering GAD instead have high muscle tension and very *low* heart rate variability. Professor Tom Borkovec and colleagues at Penn State University have argued that this is pathological worriers entering a physiological state of 'freezing' which is one of the traditional fight-fright-flight responses we see in animals when confronted with a threat. This view claims that the autonomic inflexibility and inhibition of sympathetic nervous system activation seen in relation to GAD is a result of constant worrying. The narrative style of worrying has come to act as an avoidance response that suppresses the ability of aversive images to enter consciousness, and thereby prevents somatic activation and emotional processing – with heart rate variability being an index of emotional processing. Thus, apart from its attempts to help deal with impending threats and challenges, worry also becomes a negatively reinforced avoidance behaviour that reduces somatic or physiological reactions to emotional material that would otherwise be experienced in a neutral or relaxed state[38].

38 Sibrava, N. J. & Borkovec, T. D. (2006) 'The cognitive avoidance theory of worry.' In G. C. L. Davey & A. Wells (Eds.) *Worry and Its Psychological Disorders*. Wiley.

However, Professor Michelle Newman, also at Penn State University, has a slightly different take on the low heart rate variability in GAD sufferers. She claims that pathological worriers are highly anxious people who continually feel emotionally vulnerable to unexpected negative events[39]. Because of this, they worry chronically in order to maintain a negative emotional state that allows them to be constantly alert to any unexpected threats. It is this constantly maintained negative emotional state that Professor Newman argues maintains stress that is associated with a high heart rate, but low heart rate variability[40] – the chronic worrier is attempting to maintain a constant state of arousal so as not to be caught out by unexpected threats and challenges.

In this way, while worrying may initially be utilised as a means of thinking through life's threats and challenges, it also has other effects which reinforce its use and make it a chronic condition for many people. Worry becomes a complex piece of machinery that serves a number of different psychological functions for the pathological worrier – but usually at the cost of much stress and distress.

Boiling it Down

Worry is an internal cognitive process with a narrative style in which we try to think through possible problems posed by upcoming life events. Worry and anxiety are not the same thing, but worry will often accompany anxiety, and excessive worry is a common feature of almost all of the anxiety disorders. For many people worry is a

39 Newman, M. G. & Llera, S. J. (2011) 'A novel theory of experiential avoidance in generalized anxiety disorder: A review and synthesis of research supporting a contrast avoidance model of worry.' *Clinical Psychology Review*, 31, 371–382.

40 Brosschot, J. F., Van Dijk, E. & Thayer, J. F. (2007) 'Daily worry is related to low heart rate variability during waking and the subsequent nocturnal sleep period.' *International Journal of Psychophysiology*, 63, 39–47.

helpful process, but for others it can become a compulsive activity that brings only more anxiety and distress. In this chapter I've tried to describe some of the complex processes that lead to worry becoming a chronic and distressing aspect of life, and there isn't just one route to pathological worrying, there are many. For some, anxiety and personal inadequacies can thwart the problem-solving process for which worrying is often deployed. For others, the negative mood in which worrying occurs can have a variety of effects which make the worrying perseverative and seemingly uncontrollable. For still others, worrying can be reinforced by a range of effects that the worrier finds rewarding. These can include the fact that many worries actually never happen, and the worrier views this as a result of worrying being successful (even though around 85 per cent of worries are never likely to happen anyway!), others believe that worrying prevents the worrier from experiencing fearful imagery or maintains them in a state of arousal in readiness for those unexpected threats. These reinforcing effects of worry will often generate a set of beliefs in the worrier that worrying is a necessary thing to do in order to avoid bad things happening.

No one is a 'born worrier'; worriers are manufactured by early experiences or exposure to trauma at certain times in their lives. However, while the processes that generate chronic worrying are unlikely to have changed significantly over time, there are certainly new topics of worry that engage the active worrier, including missed trains, parking problems, dead phones, lost keys, traffic jams and forgotten credit cards – all daily hassles that are a product of twenty-first century technologies and lifestyles. Basically, it doesn't matter what it is, but if it's a threat or a challenge, then it's a legitimate source for worry, and that includes the uncertainties of Brexit and the presidency of a certain Donald John Trump!

CHAPTER EIGHT

The 'Perfect' Modern Malaise

Obsessive-Compulsive Disorder

'Officially, it is no more possible to be a little bit OCD
than it is to be a little bit pregnant or a little bit dead.'

— David Adam, *The Man Who Couldn't Stop*

Imagine, if you can, the unlikely scenario of controversial US
President Donald Trump, actor Leonardo DiCaprio, and ex-
England footballer David Beckham together entering the art deco
splendour of Claridge's iconic foyer in Mayfair. If their well-managed
profiles on the Internet are anything to go by, Leonardo DiCaprio
would fall behind the other two as he focused hard on trying to
tread only on the black tiles of the highly polished chequered marble
floor. Donald Trump reaches the reception desk first, but refuses
to shake hands with the receptionist claiming 'receptionists have
17,000 germs per square inch on their desks'. On the way to their
rooms Leonardo DiCaprio is then delayed as he retraces his steps
to the front door, just to make sure he'd stepped on every black tile
between the main entrance and the reception desk, and Donald
Trump waits nervously at the elevator door unable to press the call
button for the lift for fear it may be contaminated. In the meantime,

David Beckham has reached his penthouse suite, let himself in and immediately begun to rearrange all the ornaments in the room so they're in pairs. He then goes to the mini-bar and finds three cans of Diet Coke in there. He takes the odd one out and immediately throws it away so there's an even number of cans left.

If the Internet is to be believed these are some of the obsessive-compulsive afflictions suffered by celebrities. Just as our anxiety and stress levels have become a measure of our status and importance in the bustling and competitive world of career achievement and business success, although no doubt in many cases genuine and professionally established, claiming 'self-diagnosed' OCD seems to have become a status symbol in its own right for many celebrities and their publicists. The media of the modern world have dissociated OCD from its illness roots, sanitised it, and projected it as a desirable quality – and all of this at a time when the casual use of mental health labels is increasingly frowned upon. Cultural psychologist Yulia Chentsova Dutton from Georgetown University argues that common usage of the term OCD has created a 'cultural script' where the term has become synonymous with words like 'clean' or 'organised' – qualities that most people would perceive as being 'good'[1]. Perhaps there's an assumption that obsessiveness means perfection. But being a perfectionist is not the same as being perfect, and being obsessive is not the same as being diligent. Let's be clear that our modern-day willingness to use the term OCD to denote positive qualities is light years distant from the distressing reality of obsessive-compulsive disorder, and the modern world's 'perfect' malaise bears little resemblance to the eccentric behaviours of celebrities in the iconic luxury of Claridge's foyer.

1 https://www.theatlantic.com/health/archive/2015/02/ocd-is-a-disorder-not-a-quirk/385562/

We've all done something in the past that we've felt is a little obsessive or even compulsive – like returning to check whether a door is locked, or a window is shut, or we really did turn the gas off on the cooker. It's also quite common for us to experience intrusive thoughts that seem to enter our heads spontaneously – usually these are quite mundane thoughts, such as a craving for chocolate or a random thought about a friend or relative. However, for the individual with a diagnosis of obsessive-compulsive disorder (OCD) these thoughts and actions become distressing and disabling and are driven by intense feelings of anxiety. From being something of a psychiatric oddity a hundred years ago, OCD is now in the top five of the most common mental health problems in most parts of the world. It afflicts men, women and children alike, and without regard to race, nationality or socio-economic group.

In 2010, using a sample from the US National Comorbidity Survey, Ayelet Ruscio and colleagues from Pennsylvania State University found a twelve-month prevalence rate for DSM-diagnosed OCD of 1.2 per cent[2]. They also asked respondents whether they had any OCD symptoms at the time (whether these met diagnostic criteria or not), and one in four claimed they did – the most common being checking and hoarding. In the UK around 1.2 per cent of the population are diagnosable with OCD, which means that around 780,000 people will be currently suffering those symptoms[3].

OCD has two important and sometimes independent characteristics. These are known as *obsessions* and *compulsions*, and it may be that some sufferers only experience obsessive thoughts, but others may

2 Ruscio, A. M., Stein, D. J., Chiu, W. T. & Kessler, R. C. (2010) 'The epidemiology of obsessive-compulsive disorder in the National Comorbidity Survey Replication.' *Molecular Psychiatry*, 15, 53–63.

3 https://www.ocduk.org/ocd

experience both obsessive thoughts and compulsive actions – such as checking and washing – that are triggered by the obsessive thoughts.

Obsessions are intrusive and recurring thoughts that the person finds disturbing and uncontrollable. These thoughts frequently take the form of causing some harm or distress to oneself or to some important other person (such as your partner or your child). Common obsessions also take the form of fear of contamination (i.e. contaminating oneself or important others – see the example of Millie in Chapter 4) – thoughts about harm, accidents and unacceptable sex are also prominent[45]. Obsessive thoughts can also take the form of pathological doubting and indecision, and this may lead to sufferers developing repetitive behaviour patterns such as compulsive checking or washing. Very often, obsessive thoughts can be *'autogenous'* – that is, they seem uncontrollable and 'come out of the blue', and it's this autogenous characteristic that helps to make obsessive thoughts distressing.

Compulsions represent repetitive or ritualised behaviour patterns that the individual feels driven to perform in order to prevent some negative outcome happening. This can take the form of ritualised and persistent checking of doors and windows (to ensure that the house is safe), or ritualised washing activities designed to prevent infection and contamination. Ritualised compulsions such as these also act to reduce the stress and anxiety caused by the sufferer's obsessive fears. Whilst the main compulsions are usually related to checking or washing, compulsions can also manifest less regularly as compulsive hoarding[6], compulsive hair-pulling (known as trichotillomania)

---

4 Rowa, K. & Purdon, C. (2005) 'Why are certain intrusive thoughts more upsetting than others?' *Behavioural and Cognitive Psychotherapy*, 31, 1–11.

5 Berry, L. M., & Laskey, B. (2012) 'A review of obsessive intrusive thoughts in the general population.' *Journal of Obsessive-Compulsive and Related Disorders*, 1, 125–132.

6 Steketee, G., Frost, R. O. & Kyrios, M. (2003) 'Cognitive aspects of compulsive hoarding.' *Cognitive Therapy & Research*, 27, 463–479.

or skin picking (known as excoriation), the systematic arranging of objects[7] (à la David Beckham!), or superstitious ritualised movements. In most cases, compulsions are clearly excessive, and are often recognised as so by the sufferer. *Compulsive rituals* can become rigid, stereotyped sequences of behaviours which the individual is driven to perform as a result of intrusive thoughts related to their specific fears and anxieties.

The label 'obsessive-compulsive disorder' came about almost by accident. Freud believed these symptoms were a form of neurosis and called it '*Zwangsneurose*', and in London '*Zwang*' became 'obsession' and in New York it became 'compulsion', and by way of international compromise the condition became known as obsessive-compulsive disorder. Freud was also instrumental in providing OCD with many of its stereotypic modern character traits, and traits such as perfectionism and anal retentiveness stem from his seminal work on obsessive neurosis. In previous times, the symptoms that we now know as OCD have been subjected to various forms of social and medical interpretation.

In the seventeenth century obsessions and compulsions were seen as symptoms of religious melancholy. For example, in 1691, the Bishop of Norwich, John Moore, noted that some individuals were obsessed by 'naughty, and sometimes blasphemous thoughts [which] start in their minds, while they are exercised in the worship of God [despite] all their endeavours to stifle and suppress them ... the more they struggle with them, the more they increase.'[8] These appear to be simple examples of intrusive unwanted thoughts occurring in inappropriate circumstances, and obsessive thoughts of a blasphemous nature were experienced by many famous religious

7 Radomsky, A. S. & Rachman, S. (2004) 'Symmetry, ordering and arranging compulsive behaviour.' *Behaviour Research and Therapy*, 42, 893–913.
8 http://ocd.stanford.edu/treatment/history.html

figures such as Martin Luther and John Bunyan. Even today, very strictly religious individuals appear to be at high risk of developing symptoms of OCD because of the constraints imposed on their thinking and behaviour by their religious beliefs – constraints that cause anxiety when obsessions and compulsions make the individual feel as if they are about to do something blasphemous or ungodly. But more of that later.

During much of the nineteenth century OCD symptoms were viewed as either 'impulsive insanity' or a disorder of intellect, and the symptoms were either considered as examples of other anxiety-based problems such as phobias, panic, agoraphobia or hypochondriasis, or as delusions that were indicative of psychosis. For instance, the eminent French psychiatrist Valentin Magnan thought OCD symptoms were a *'folie des dégénérés'* – a psychosis of degeneration indicative of an inherited brain pathology. But by 1980, OCD symptoms had appeared under the label 'obsessive-compulsive disorder' in the American Psychiatric Association diagnostic manual DSM-III as an anxiety-related disorder – a categorisation that most clinicians, researchers and sufferers felt was appropriate (although some confusion about the anxiety-related status of OCD was caused when, in the fifth edition of DSM published in 2013, OCD was moved out of the chapter on anxiety disorders and given the distinction of its very own chapter).

Prior to the inclusion of OCD as a diagnostic category in DSM-III, a significant National Institute of Mental Health (NIMH) study published in the 1970s revealed how underestimated OCD symptoms had been. The study claimed that dysfunctional compulsive behaviours such as counting, washing, and checking were up to fifty to one hundred times more common than had been previously believed – largely because sufferers were either able to conceal their symptoms successfully or were so embarrassed by their compulsions that they were reluctant to seek help[9]. In this way, OCD is very much a modern condition in the sense that its complexity and relationship to anxiety has been identified only in the last few decades, and OCD has certainly been one of the hot psychiatric and psychological research topics of the 1990s and 2000s.

Living with OCD

I must admit, I've never really had a problem with compulsions – or 'over-perfectionism' come to that (but I have agonised for years over whether there should be a hyphen between obsessive and compulsive in the phrase obsessive-compulsive disorder – or is it obsessive compulsive disorder?).

In contrast, Rosa is forty years old. She remembers her obsessions and compulsions starting around the age of ten, soon after the death of her mother. After her mother died, Rosa's father moved the family from a quiet country town to the city of Manchester, and Rosa immediately found it an anxious struggle to adapt to living in a big city. She soon acquired a number of anxieties, including a fear of being run over by a car in the busy streets of this new home city. She was also frightened of the relative lawlessness of the big city, and came to develop a fear that criminals would kidnap her new friends. These fears led to the development of detailed rituals that Rosa hoped would keep her and her friends safe and quell her fears. These rituals included an elaborate lengthy prayer routine with many rules that she enacted every single night. She believed she needed to repeat each family member's name up to twenty times in her prayers to keep them safe. She also had to kneel down and stand up eight times during this whole process. Like many individuals

9 Tallis, F. (1995) *Obsessive Compulsive Disorder: A Cognitive and Neuro-Psychological Perspective*. Wiley.

suffering OCD she would have to begin the routine again from the very beginning if she made even the slightest mistake[10].

Obsessions and compulsions regularly begin in late childhood or early adolescence, and at twelve years old Jason began exhibiting a significant number of ritualistic and avoidance behaviours. In particular he developed a fear of contamination which involved the excessive use of a hand sanitiser, and avoidance of doorknobs, library books and the bathroom for fear that they'd contaminate him. His checking behaviours extended to checking food expiry dates, and he avoided sitting on chairs, or public benches, or using sheets or pillows for fear they were dirty. These fears and rituals began to interfere significantly with his social and school life, and his teachers became aware that he couldn't turn pages with his hands, touch papers that other students had touched, or sit comfortably on his chair during lessons[11]. It's important to note here that Jason was also diagnosed with high-functioning autism, a condition that's a specific risk factor for developing OCD, and a number of researchers have suggested there may be a symptoms overlap between autistic spectrum disorder and OCD[12].

From twelve-year-olds to eighty-seven-year-olds, OCD knows no age boundaries. Mr Rossi is an eighty-seven-year-old retired businessman whose obsession was remembering names (who hasn't suffered that problem?). His core obsession was remembering the names of past acquaintances, including celebrities he'd met

10 Davey, G. C. L., Dash, S. & Meeten, F. (2014) *Obsessive Compulsive Disorder*. Palgrave.

11 Lehmkuhl, H. D., Storch, E. A., Bodfish, J. W. & Geffken, G. R. (2008) 'Brief report: Exposure and response prevention for obsessive-compulsive disorder in a 12-year-old with autism.' *Journal of Autism Development Disorders*, 38, 977–981.

12 Wakabayashi, A., Baron-Cohen, S. & Ashwin, C. (2012) 'Do the traits of autism-spectrum overlap with those of schizophrenia or obsessive-compulsive disorder in the general population?' *Research in Autism Spectrum Disorders*, 6, 717–725.

in relation to his work, professional baseball players, and current associates at his business. His obsession with names led to a series of compulsive activities that he found impossible to control, including checking how accurate his recall of names was, asking friends and relatives to help him recall names, and contacting the employees at his business at all times of the day and night to help him remember names. Mr Rossi's OCD began just months after a heart attack, and many instances of late-onset OCD are known to be associated with cardiac-related neurological abnormalities in old age[13].

But let's express genuine sympathy for the wife of Mr E. who lived in the Netherlands. She contacted mental health services in Amsterdam in utter desperation at having spent sixteen years listening to her husband whistling the same carnival song for between five to eight hours every day – a carnival song that she recalls was one he'd enjoyed singing in his role as head of his local carnival association. When healthcare psychologist Rosaura Polak and colleagues from the University of Amsterdam visited Mr E. they were immediately confronted with the clear and perfectly tuneful whistling of the same song. This occurred without interruption, and Mr E. forcefully expressed his annoyance if he was asked to stop. While Mr E.'s whistling is a form of compulsion, it's more typical of the kinds of repetitive behaviour that can occur in autism spectrum disorder and tic disorders, but it's unlikely to be a simple repetitive behaviour because Mr E. clearly felt anxious when asked to stop, and the whistling may well serve some form of calming function, helping to keep Mr E.'s anxieties at bay. His wife recalls that the repetitive whistling began after her husband was found unconscious in his car after suffering a heart attack, and immediately after this

---

13 Calamari, J. E., Pontarelli, N. K. & Armstrong, K. M. (2012) 'Obsessive-compulsive disorder in late life.' *Cognitive & Behavioral Practice*, 19, 136–150.

incident close relatives noticed a deterioration in his social behaviour, including regular sexual inferences, spitting and continuous whistling. Thankfully for Mr E.'s wife, the spitting and sexual inferences disappeared after a short time – but the whistling persisted.

Dr. Polak and colleagues suggest that Mr E.'s repetitive whistling may have been caused by frontal lobe brain damage incidentally caused by his heart attack, with damage resulting in the inability to inhibit repetitive, irresistible urges to perform particular behaviours. However, several aspects of Mr E.'s behaviour show similarities with what is known as *punding* – purposeless, repetitive behaviours such as collecting or arranging things, and these are often related to the sufferer's previous behaviours and hobbies (compulsive singing is a particularly common example[14]). Punding behaviours have a repetitive but comforting character (for the sufferer that is – but not necessarily for friends and family!), and are often related to dysregulation of the brain's mesolimbic reward pathway that makes the activity rewarding and which gives rise to addictive-like behaviours.

We get a clear indication from the wife of Mr E. that living with OCD is not just a matter for the sufferer, it also has a significant impact on immediate family, friends and colleagues. This can be the sheer irritation of intrusive, repetitive behaviours, or the stifling, laborious monotony of complex and lengthy rituals that those living or working with people suffering OCD not only endure but are frequently dragged unceremoniously into colluding with.

Here's an example of the complex and rigid anti-contamination rituals that the famous American billionaire Howard Hughes was believed to have insisted on during his declining years: 'For the most part he successfully avoided touching any person or object

---

14 Bonvin, C., Horvath, J., Christe, B., Landis, T. & Burkhard, P. R. (2007) 'Compulsive singing: Another aspect of punding in Parkinson's disease.' *Annals of Neurology*, 62, 525–528.

directly – instead he covered himself with paper tissues and other protective materials. His barber was required to repeatedly sterilise all of his instruments by immersing them in alcohol. There was a complicated ritual for handling objects. Before handing Hughes a spoon, his attendants had to wrap the handle in tissue paper and seal it with cellophane tape. A second piece of tissue was wrapped around the first protective wrapping to ensure that it would be protected from contamination. Hughes would use it only with the handle covered. The spoon itself had to be carefully cleaned after use. On one occasion he observed that a bottle had been broken on the steps of his range. He wrote out a series of instructions that involved marking out a grid of one-inch squares on each step and then meticulously cleaning one square at a time to ensure that every splinter of glass had been removed.'[15]

These examples give some sense of the diversity of compulsions and obsessions, their incessant intensity, and the consuming nature of their impact on the daily lives of those who suffer the condition or live their lives around the condition. As a diagnosable anxiety-based disorder, OCD is usually associated with a high degree of impairment. When compared with individuals with other types of anxiety disorder, OCD sufferers are less likely to be married, more likely to be unemployed, more likely to have low income levels, and more likely to have low occupational status – all of which is consistent with the severe disabling effects that OCD symptoms can have[16]. OCD is a slow-onset disorder where symptoms increase only gradually over a number of years, and having lived with sub-clinical symptoms for

15 Rachman, S. & Hodgson, R. J. (1980) *Obsessions and Compulsions.* *Prentice-Hall.*

16 Torres, A. R., Prince, M. J., Bebbington, P. E., Bhugra, D. et al. (2006) 'Obsessive-compulsive disorder: Prevalence, comorbidity, impact, and help-seeking in the British National Psychiatric Morbidity Survey of 2000.' *American Journal of Psychiatry*, 163, 1978–1985.

many years may be one reason why many sufferers fail to seek help when the symptoms become well established. There is typically an astonishing average interval of eleven years between a sufferer meeting the diagnostic criteria for OCD and receiving treatment[17]. This can be attributed to the slow onset, and also to the stigma associated with unusual and excessive compulsive behaviour preventing people seeking professional help.

However, OCD sufferers can find it difficult to contemplate the loss of their compulsions and many view their symptoms as a way of life. As a consequence they either resist seeking help, or frequently fail to complete the therapies they've entered. OCD is undoubtedly a very resilient disorder. Without treatment, remission rates are low, and only 20 per cent of those with diagnosable OCD symptoms have fully recovered from the disorder up to twenty years later[18]. Indeed, in an age when we're studiously attempting to develop more effective talking therapies for anxiety-based problems, the outcomes for OCD do not look encouraging in this age of modern evidence-based treatments.

Even when those suffering from OCD do seek help, at the end of treatments such as CBT only around half have recovered to a point where they no longer meet diagnostic criteria[19]. The reasons for this seemingly high failure rate are complex. At least some sufferers who are offered therapy decline to take part even before the treatment

17 Pinto, A., Mancebo, M. C., Eisen, J. L., Pagano, M. E. & Rasmussen, S. A. (2006) 'Brown Longitudinal Obsessive-Compulsive Study – Clinical features and symptoms of the sample at intake.' *Journal of Clinical Psychiatry*, 67, 703–711.

18 Bloch, M. H., Green, C., Kichuk, S. A., Dombrowski, P. A. et al. (2013) 'Long-term outcome in adults with obsessive-compulsive disorder.' *Depression & Anxiety*, 30, 716–722.

19 Öst, L. G., Havnen, A., Hansen, B. & Kvale, G. (2015) 'Cognitive behavioural treatments of obsessive-compulsive disorder. A systematic review and meta-analysis of studies published 1993–2014.' *Clinical Psychology Review*, 40, 156–169.

has begun, others drop out during treatment or fail to attend sessions regularly, and many others fail to complete the behavioural tasks their treatment requires of them. If this says anything about people with a diagnosis of OCD it probably testifies to the significant role that their obsessions, compulsions and rituals play in their lives. Giving up established compulsions is contemplated with a fear and distress that even overshadows the anxiety and disability of the disorder itself, and a common plea of the OCD sufferer seeking treatment is something along the lines of 'Can you make everything all right without me having to stop doing my compulsive behaviours?' – well, no actually, we can't, because it's the compulsions that are the major part of the problem. It's hard to explain to someone that the compulsive behaviours that they believe quell their anxiety are also paradoxically maintaining it. A compulsion is basically an avoidance response, and we know that avoidance responses act to maintain anxiety by never allowing the sufferer to get close enough to the threat to disconfirm their fears (see Chapter 4).

The Twenty-First Century OCD Brand

When he received three different cats on separate occasions, a local vet in Manitoba, Canada, was alerted to animal welfare problems at a small house on the outskirts of town. In each case, the cats required front limb amputations. The vet reported treating many cats from the house, but seldom was the same cat presented more than once. The house belonged to a middle-aged woman and her elderly mother. On visiting the house, animal welfare officers found the house cluttered with boxes of belongings, and the kitchen was the only practical living space that the women could occupy. There were also many, many cats. The woman couldn't say how many cats there were, but she was unable to give any of them up because she felt others simply wouldn't be able to care for them as well as she could. The cats were not in a good condition. Some were found in confined areas that didn't allow any exercise or ventilation, while many were kept locked in crates. Others lived in semi-feral conditions in a cellar that was littered with debris and cat excrement. Four cats were found in a bedroom living in darkness at all times. Neighbours even reported that the woman had been seen actively trapping free roaming cats in the community. At the end of the day, the officers removed sixty-one cats from the premises, and three days later returned to remove a further seventeen that had since emerged from the clutter and refuse stored in the house[20].

This is animal hoarding. It was first reported in the medical literature in 1981[21], and thirty-five years later it's now considered to be a symptom of Hoarding Disorder, which is itself considered to be an OCD sub-category diagnosis. How the OCD brand has taken off! From being effectively underestimated and hardly acknowledged in the 1970s, it now has its own chapter in the most recent American Psychiatric Association diagnostic manual along with its own clutch of 'related' disorders. This is a brand awareness success story and product range expansion that any company CEO would be immensely proud of. Newly incorporated 'products' into the OCD brand include Body Dysmorphic Disorder (a preoccupation with assumed defects in appearance), Hoarding Disorder (compulsive collecting of items – including animals – and general problems with organising possessions), Trichotillomania (compulsive hair-pulling, resulting in hair loss), and Excoriation (recurrent skin picking resulting in skin lesions). Even Onychophagia (compulsive nail biting) crops up in some books under OCD (OK – I'll hold my hand up – one of those

20 Reinisch, A. I. (2009) 'Characteristics of six recent animal hoarding cases in Manitoba.' *Canadian Veterinary Journal*, 50, 1069–1073.
21 Worth, D. & Beck, A. M. (1981) 'Multiple ownership of animals in New York City.' *Transactions and Studies of the College of Physicians of Philadelphia*, 3–4, 280–300.

books is co-authored by me!). Nail biting seems like an unnecessary medicalisation of one of the most common responses to anxiety.

But what are the inclusion criteria for these new products? Are they really OCD? We could argue that they've been sucked into the OCD domain because OCD has been a trending brand for a number of years now – and that may be one of the salient reasons. But most of these conditions that have been subsumed under OCD do share one characteristic in common with OCD, which is compulsivity – a drive to perform behaviours that seems to be out of the performer's voluntary control. But just because compulsive behaviours share one feature in common doesn't mean they have the same causes. Psychiatric diagnostic categories are still very primitive compared to other medical diagnostic criteria. We still don't have a good enough understanding of most mental health problems to create a diagnostic system based on the *causes* of these problems, so we can only categorise them on the basis of what they look like. This raises a number of problems. If two different disorders only 'look' similar but don't have the same causes, then they may not respond to the same treatments – whether those treatments be either psychological or pharmaceutical – so trying to rationalise treatment services on the basis of a diagnostic category such as 'OCD and related disorders' will probably be a difficult task.

Many OCD sufferers and relevant health professionals have been unhappy with the fact that OCD has been diagnostically isolated from the anxiety disorders in DSM-5. Most sufferers with insight into their obsessions and compulsions view their underlying problem as an anxiety-based one, and it's well known from the psychiatric literature that OCD and other anxiety disorders respond to similar treatments and tend to co-occur. For instance, a study by Joe Bienvenu and colleagues at Johns Hopkins University looked at case family data from the OCD Collaborative Genetics Study and compared this with control family data from the Johns Hopkins OCD

Family Study[22]. These data provided family histories and comorbidity information on more than 450 individuals over ten years. They found that anxiety disorders generally were significantly more common in those with a diagnosis of OCD or had an immediate family member with OCD, suggesting that anxiety is a significant feature of OCD, adding, 'Our preliminary recommendation is that OCD be retained in the category of anxiety disorders.' OCD-UK chief executive Ashley Fulwood concurred, saying, 'I'm surprised that any specialist in OCD would consider moving OCD from outside an anxiety category … Surely anxiety is the key component that drives the OCD cycle of the obsessions and compulsions for people with OCD? The increased anxiety from the preceding obsessional thought creates the main problem for a person, that leads to the compulsive behaviours, so categorising OCD within an anxiety category makes sense.'[23] I agree wholeheartedly!

None of this is to doubt that the new disorders found in the OCD-related disorders category are not significant problems in their own right, and both Body Dysmorphic Disorder and Hoarding Disorder have prevalence rates in the general population that may even be higher than OCD itself![24] But it's a testimony to our fascination with OCD and the notions of obsessions and compulsions that OCD has become a modern-day household term that's culturally imbued with qualities that perversely we even perceive as positive. Perhaps it was this obsession with obsessions that prompted psychiatrists working on the fifth revision of the DSM to reify the OCD brand into an overarching diagnostic category – a diagnostic

22 Bienvenu, O. J., Samuels, J. F., Wuyek, L. A., Liang, K. Y. et al. (2011) 'Is obsessive-compulsive disorder an anxiety disorder, and what, if any, are spectrum conditions? A family study perspective.' *Psychological Medicine*, 42, 1–13.

23 https://www.ocduk.org/should-ocd-be-removed-from-dsm5

24 Davey, G. C. L., Dash, S. & Meeten, F. (2014) *Obsessive Compulsive Disorder*. Palgrave.

change that many sufferers and professional mental health workers have their doubts about.

What Puts You at Risk for Developing OCD?

Between two to three people in a hundred will suffer distressing and disabling symptoms of OCD during their lifetime, so what are the factors that put this small percentage of people at risk for developing OCD? Well, because everything we do, we do with our biological bodies, there will inevitably be a genetic element. But in the case of OCD this is not overwhelming. Large-scale community twin studies suggest that the heritability estimate for OCD is 'moderate'[25] – and it's well known that OCD tends to run in families, which may reflect this heritable component. Some types of OCD, such as skin-picking disorder and trichotillomania, have a higher inherited component than others, and there are also some inherited conditions that can increase your risk of OCD (more of those later). But there are clearly many other non-shared environmental determinants of OCD, which means that it's likely to be your experiences that put you most at risk for developing OCD.

Psychologist Jessica Grisham and colleagues in Australia, Spain, New Zealand and the UK conducted a prospective study of risk factors for OCD using participants in the Dunedin Study birth cohort in New Zealand[26]. This is a cohort born in 1972–73 that was assessed on a range of psychological and physical measures at regular

25 Monzani, B., Rijsdijk, F., Harris, J. & Mataix-Cols, D. (2014) 'The structure of genetic and environmental risk factors for dimensional representations of DSM-5 obsessive-compulsive spectrum disorders.' *JAMA Psychiatry*, 71, 182–189.

26 Grisham, J. R., Fullana, M. A., Mataix-Cols, D., Moffit, T. E., Caspi, A. & Poulton, R. (2011) 'Risk factors prospectively associated with adult obsessive-compulsive symptom dimensions and obsessive-compulsive disorder.' *Psychological Medicine*, 41, 2495–2506.

intervals throughout their life. This allows the researchers to see how factors that have been measured earlier in an individual's life predict symptoms or behaviours that occur later in their life.

Their study identified a number of risk factors for OCD in adulthood. These included childhood isolation and poor peer relationships during childhood, negative emotionality in adolescence (this is a measure of interpersonal alienation, irritable-aggressive attitudes, and reactivity to stress), a history of childhood physical and sexual abuse (those who reported physical abuse had a specific risk for OCD), experiencing problems at birth such as haemorrhaging or respiratory distress, poor motor skills, and lower IQ measures during childhood. This is a motley crew of risk factors! But let me make it clear what it means. It simply means that if you possess one of these characteristics or experiences, you have a slightly increased probability of experiencing OCD in adulthood. It doesn't mean you will *certainly* develop OCD, and you can also develop OCD without possessing any of these characteristics at all. In fact, many of these risks for OCD are also risks for other mental health problems, such as other anxiety-based problems or depression, so they are not even specific to OCD.

But there are some cultural and ethnic practices that also seem to increase the risk of developing OCD symptoms specifically. Ana is an Orthodox Jew, and as early as aged seven she remembers being uncertain about adhering to many of the religious rituals normally associated with her community's religious beliefs. For example, Orthodox Jewish religion requires a waiting period of six hours between eating meat and dairy foods. Ana would carefully count the hours between eating meat and eating dairy, but began doubting whether she'd waited the required time. Ana met her husband in an arranged meeting, and her obsessions and compulsions began to trouble her more than ever. After marriage, Orthodox Jewish men are prohibited from touching their wives during menstruation or for seven days thereafter. According to ritual, Orthodox Jewish wives are responsible for ensuring that they no longer exhibit vaginal bleeding by swabbing themselves with a linen cloth for seven days following the end of menstruation. It is only then, after a ritual bath (the Mikvah), that wife and husband are allowed to touch each other. Ana obsessed about whether there was even a hint of blood on her linen cloths, and checked them repetitively, but was unable to decide definitively that the menstrual flow had ceased. Finally, she consulted with her rabbi, who agreed to check the linen on a regular basis and make her decisions for her[27].

Many cultural, ethnic and religious practices possess two factors that are likely to promote OCD symptoms. They define taboos that explicitly prohibit certain behaviours or thoughts, and they often ritualise many basic aspects of daily life. This is a toxic combination for an anxious individual like Ana. She becomes uncertain about whether she's completed ritualistic activities fully and properly, and whether she's avoided the damning consequences of violating her religious taboos – especially when non-adherence may lead to spreading sin throughout the world or even being condemned in the world to come! We find that strictly religious OCD sufferers often have religious themes to their obsessional thoughts and compulsions. For example, there are very high levels of symptoms related to contamination and washing in Hindus with OCD – a finding consistent with the emphasis in Indian culture on purity and cleanliness[28]. Psychologist Jonathan Huppert at the University of Pennsylvania School of

27 Burt, V. K. & Rudolph, M. (2000) 'Treating an Orthodox Jewish woman with obsessive-compulsive disorder: Maintaining reproductive and psychologic stability in the context of normative religious rituals.' *American Journal of Psychiatry*, 157, 620–624.

28 Khanna, S. & Channabasavanna, S. M. (1988) 'Phenomenology of obsessions in obsessive-compulsive neurosis.' *Psychopathology*, 20, 23–28.

Medicine has also pointed out that religions such as ultra-Orthodox Judaism scrupulously espouse many everyday customs and rituals that represent risk factors for compulsive behaviours or obsessive thoughts, including cleanliness related to dietary restrictions, family purity, praying correctly, studying correctly, and rituals that apply to washing, checking, cancelling vows, consulting rabbis, mentally reassuring oneself, washing hands, checking for blood and praying.[29]

In her book *Devil in the Details: Scenes from an Obsessive Girlhood*, author Jennifer Traig recalls how her childhood experiences with religious scrupulosity affected her every interaction with modern life: 'Scrupulosity is sometimes called the doubting disease, because it forces you to question everything. Anything you do or say or wear or hear or eat or think, you examine in excruciatingly minute detail. Will I go to hell if I watch HBO? Is it sacrilegious to shop whole-sale? What is the biblical position on organic produce?'[30] Religious scrupulosity is not just a process directed at religious customs, but it's also a process that leads the individual to raise doubts about every aspect of modern life and the modern world.

However, this relationship between religiosity and OCD doesn't necessarily mean that religiosity causes these types of OCD symptoms, it could equally be the case that certain personality characteristics (such as perfectionism) may cause a person to be both religious and develop OCD symptoms, but we can be reasonably sure that religious, cultural and ethnicity factors can often determine the form that OCD obsessions and compulsions take once the symptoms have developed, and can also independently lead to detailed questioning of many facets of modern life.

29 Huppert, J. D., Siev, J. & Kushner, E. S. (2007) 'When religion and obsessive-compulsive disorder collide: Treating scrupulosity in ultra-Orthodox Jews.' *Journal of Clinical Psychology*, 63, 925–941.

30 Traig, J. (2006) *Devil in the Details: Scenes from an Obsessive Girlhood*. Back Bay Books.

The Psychology of OCD

On one occasion during the 1970s, when psychologists had just begun detailed research on obsessions and compulsions, a decision was made to hospitalise a participant with severe obsessive checking problems so that the researchers could measure and assess his multiple checking rituals in a controlled environment. To their surprise, once he'd been admitted to hospital most of his checking behaviours disappeared and he readily and without anxiety began to involve himself quite normally in the daily life of the ward. At first it wasn't obvious what had caused this sudden and dramatic loss of symptoms – perhaps it was a miraculous spontaneous recovery. But as soon as he returned home, all of the old rituals reappeared as severely as ever.

Quite soon it became apparent what was happening, and this insight cast light on one of the most significant psychological factors that causes and maintains behaviours such as compulsive checking and compulsive washing. Many compulsions are enacted because the sufferer believes this will prevent something bad happening. Checking the stove is off prevents a potential gas explosion; checking the doors and windows are locked prevents the house being burgled; washing hands until they are raw prevents contamination and the possible spread of diseases to others. These activities confer on the checker and the washer a significant *responsibility* for ensuring that these bad things don't happen. Not only do individuals with OCD tend to feel responsible for ensuring bad things don't happen, they have a highly inflated sense of responsibility that evokes guilt and shame at the possibility of bad things happening if their compulsive rituals are not completed properly and thoroughly[31].

31 Salkovskis, P. M. (1985) 'Obsessional-compulsive problems: A cognitive-behavioural analysis.' *Behaviour Research and Therapy*, 23, 571–583.

OCD is a slow-onset disorder, but we can often trace the beginnings of obsessions and compulsions to either a stressful life event or a life change that bestows greater responsibilities on the individual, such things as a new job, the birth of a child, or even puberty. Many people take their new responsibilities very seriously and develop *inflated responsibility* that generates anxiety and a driving desire to ensure that they don't let themselves and others down by allowing bad things to happen. Early studies of OCD often failed to get sufferers to indulge in their compulsions and rituals in the lab in the same way they would in other situations. It eventually became clear that while they were in the lab, these participants had transferred responsibility for any misfortunes happening to the experimenter so there was significantly less need to indulge in their checking and washing behaviours[32]. This also appears to explain the behaviour of our hospitalised patient in the opening paragraph – hospitalisation had led to the transfer of responsibility for any unfortunate outcomes to the hospital staff.

Inflated responsibility is one of the most significant cognitive characteristics underlying OCD. It's why checkers check and why washers wash. But it's also why those with obsessive thoughts find those thoughts aversive – because if they have intrusive thoughts about bad things (e.g. blasphemous behaviours if they're religious, or thoughts about killing their own child) they believe they are fully responsible for having those thoughts (even though they probably have no voluntary control over intrusive thoughts such as these), and this evokes high levels of anxiety, guilt and shame. CBT that targets inflated levels of responsibility and attempts to reduce feelings of responsibility results in significant therapeutic gains often with a

32 Röper, G. & Rachman, S. (1976) 'Obsessional-compulsive checking: Experimental replication and development.' *Behaviour Research and Therapy*, 14, 25–32.

50–100 per cent reduction in OCD symptoms over a significant post-treatment period[33].

Now for something rather different. What gives a person the urge to murder another human being – a psychopathic personality, a grudge, an angry, impulsive action? Maybe, but Adam Shaw believed he'd kill someone with a thought. One day he was passing through reception at an airport in Arizona, and noticed the young receptionist at the desk. 'I'm going to strangle her,' he thought, 'it must mean I'm going to do this, therefore I'm dangerous, they'll arrest me and put me in a mental hospital or prison. I can't get the thought out of my head. It's such an awful thought, it must mean I'm going to do it.'[34]

No, Adam didn't murder the receptionist; he'd come to believe that if he had a thought about something it was the same as doing it. Adam is founder of the mental health charity *The Shaw Mind Foundation* and co-author of *Pulling the Trigger* that describes Adam's lifelong struggle with OCD[35]. Adam's belief that he would kill by just having a thought is known as *thought-action fusion*, and it's a common characteristic of individuals who have developed OCD symptoms. It's a belief that thoughts and actions are linked and that having an unacceptable thought can also influence the real world – effectively it means that having a thought about an action is like doing the action. Thought-action fusion is just another way in which appraising unwanted and intrusive thoughts as meaningful not only increases distress and feelings of responsibility, it also increases the urge to neutralise and suppress the unwanted thoughts. As you can imagine,

33 Ladouceur, R., Léger, E., Rheaume, J. & Dubé, D. (1996) 'Correction of inflated responsibility in the treatment of obsessive-compulsive disorder.' *Behaviour Research and Therapy*, 34, 767–774.

34 http://www.ocduk.org/pulling-the-trigger-air-crash

35 Shaw, A. & Callaghan, L. (2016) *Pulling the Trigger: OCD, Anxiety, Panic Attacks and Related Depression – the Definitive Survival and Recovery Approach.* Trigger Press.

thought-action fusion is found at significantly higher levels in individuals with OCD than in non-clinical samples[36]. It's still not clear why some people exhibit thought-action fusion and others don't, but some studies suggest it may be related to personality traits such as magical thinking in which people hold strong beliefs in psychic phenomena (such as feeling that they can communicate telepathically with other people), and believe that some things can affect other things in ways as yet unknown to science[37]. But when it generates distressing OCD symptoms, thought-action fusion is a characteristic that can be successfully addressed by cognitive restructuring therapies. This helps sufferers to learn to recognise the irrationality of thought-action fusion, and to respond to an irrational thought ('I may wander out into the road and cause an accident') with a more rational and evidence-based thought ('I have had this thought many times, and never once have I wandered out into the road and caused an accident').

For the next example I want you to spend a few seconds imagining there's a translucent green rabbit sitting on your head. Done it? . . . Can you feel it sitting there? . . . Can you visualise its greenness? . . . Now focus on its fluffy, green translucent ears. Right, next count to five, and when you've done that I want you to spend the next sixty seconds *not* thinking in any way, shape or form about a translucent green rabbit that's just been sitting on your head.

Did you find it difficult to suppress thoughts about the imaginary rabbit deliberately, and did you experience images of the rabbit spontaneously hopping into your stream of consciousness? That's what

36 Rassin, E., Merckelbach, H., Muris, P. & Schmidt, H. (2001) 'The thought action fusion scale: Further evidence for its reliability and validity.' *Behaviour Research and Therapy*, 39, 537–544.

37 Lee, H.-J. & Telch, M. J. (2005) 'Autogenous/reactive obsessions and their relationship with OCD symptoms and schizotypal personality features.' *Anxiety Disorders*, 19, 793–805.

research psychologist Dan Wegner has found. He asked participants in his experiments to try not to think of a white bear, but found that after being given this instruction they were unable to stop thinking of white bears[38]. It seems that attempted thought suppression has paradoxical effects as a self-control strategy, often producing the very obsession or preoccupation that it was directed against. This finding has a particular relevance for OCD when individuals deliberately attempt to control their aversive intrusive thoughts by ignoring, neutralising or suppressing them. Clinical Psychologist Paul Salkovskis has argued that unwanted distressing thoughts may be converted into obsessions when active thought suppression ironically increases their frequency or causes their frequency to 'rebound' after a period of suppression[39]. The perceived failure to suppress particular thoughts after a period of active attempts at suppression also has the effect of causing increased distress and anxiety[40]. It's a process that has a significant effect on OCD symptoms for many people.

Finally, OCD is frequently known as the 'doubting disease'. People with OCD often claim that when they're checking, washing or systematically ordering objects in their environment, they'll need to continue doing this because things feel 'not quite right'. This is a doubting feeling that appears to drive their ritualistic compulsions to be completed fully and properly. For many years it was assumed that this doubting might be underpinned by some memory problems

38 Wegner, D. M., Schneider, D. J., Carter, S. R. III & White, T. L. (1987) 'Paradoxical effects of thought suppression.' *Journal of Personality and Social Psychology*, 53, 5–13.

39 Salkovskis, P. M. (1996) 'Cognitive-behavioral approaches to understanding obsessional problems.' In R. M. Rapee (Ed.) *Current Controversies in the Anxiety Disorders*. Guilford.

40 Purdon, C., Rowa, K. & Antony, M. M. (2005) 'Thought suppression and its effects on thought frequency, appraisal and mood state in individuals with obsessive-compulsive disorder.' *Behaviour Research and Therapy*, 43, 93–108.

in OCD sufferers. But ironically, rather than memory deficits causing repeated checking, it's repeated checking that appears to cause memory doubts. For example, individuals with OCD symptoms will spend a lot of time checking both relevant and irrelevant things on a daily basis, and this overloads executive processes in the brain and results in poor encoding of information and poor attention to relevant information – both of which together will cause memory deficits[41]. In effect, the more that someone checks, the less confident they'll be about what they've checked! So paradoxically, one of the symptoms of OCD has become a cause of it, creating what may well be a toxic vicious cycle of doubting and ensuing checking[42].

These are some of the important psychological processes that give rise to OCD symptoms and frequently have to be addressed during treatment. Once again we see that anxiety-based problems regularly revolve around distorted thinking and the way we each interpret our own thoughts. It also illustrates the way that thoughts influence actions (such as feelings of responsibility generating complex compulsions), and actions also influence thoughts (the compulsions themselves can also generate doubting), and these relationships can often become cast in a vicious cycle that maintains our compulsive behaviours and obsessive thoughts.

OCD and the Brain

Obviously the brain is involved in everything to do with anxiety because it mediates the relationship between our environment and how we think, feel and behave. But in the case of OCD, does the

41 Harkin, B. & Kessler, K. (2011) 'The role of working memory in compulsive checking and OCD: A systematic classification of 58 experimental findings.' *Clinical Psychology Review*, 31, 1004–1021.

42 Van den Hout, M. & Kindt, M. (2003) 'Phenomenological validity of an OCD-memory model and the remember/know distinction.' *Behaviour Research and Therapy*, 41(3), 369–378.

brain simply mediate the effects of our learned experiences to create our OCD symptoms, or is there some dodgy wiring in the brain that plays a direct role in creating symptoms? There is evidence that, in some people, small but significant deficits in brain functioning may be associated with generating repetitive and compulsive responding.

But before we investigate specific brain areas, let's look at some of the cognitive deficits that have been identified in individuals with OCD and linked to their symptoms. These cognitive deficits may not necessarily give rise to OCD symptoms on their own, but in combination with life experiences that give rise to anxiety (e.g. periods of stress or increased responsibility) they may help to establish compulsions and rituals as a way of dealing with that anxiety. They may also make it difficult to inhibit or control the obsessive aversive thoughts that often generate anxiety during OCD.

Cognitive problems identified in those with a diagnosis of OCD include: difficulties in shifting attention (which will make it difficult to shake off obsessive thoughts or to move away from ritualised trains of behaviour); difficulties in suppressing tendencies to behave in old, no-longer relevant ways (this deficit would help to maintain dysfunctional, lengthy rituals once they've been established); problems with working memory updating (meaning that more time is required to collect sufficient information to inform actions and decision-making, leading to uncertainty and doubting); poor working memory capacity (making it hard to keep in mind relevant information for decision-making resulting in doubting caused by reduced memory confidence); and deficits in what are known as *executive functioning skills*, such as strategic planning, organised searching, goal-oriented behaviour, and ability to suppress responding when required (all of which give rise to impaired cognitive flexibility and poor abstraction skills, and may lead to the development of very explicit and well-defined sequences of behaviour that the individual finds difficult to inhibit)[43]. But all of this begs one big question that we've yet to answer. Because all of the studies that have identified these cognitive deficits were carried out on individuals already exhibiting OCD symptoms, are these deficits a *cause* of the symptoms or are these deficits simply an *outcome* of having already developed the symptoms. For example, temporary deficits in executive functioning and working memory capacity are known to be *consequences* of high anxiety – when we're anxious we find it more difficult to switch attention, make decisions, keep in mind relevant information, and this in turn creates doubting and lack of confidence in memory[44].

However, a case can be made for these neurocognitive deficits being a precursor to OCD symptoms in patient groups known to have these deficits as a result of neurodevelopmental abnormalities. One such group is those individuals with an autism spectrum disorder (ASD). Apart from being associated with social and communication deficits, repetitive behaviours are a significant diagnostic feature of autism spectrum disorder, and around one in three children with ASD also suffer diagnosable OCD symptoms (which is significantly higher than the one-in-eighty rate found in the general population)[45]. However, there are differences between the types of symptoms exhibited by individuals with autism and those with a single diagnosis of OCD. Individuals with ASD tend to exhibit higher levels of touching/tapping/rubbing, repetitive self-injury, hoarding, ordering, and repeated compulsions, and significantly lower levels of

43 Aydin, P. C., Koybasi, G. P., Sert, E., Mete, L. & Oyekcin, D. G. (2014) 'Executive functions and memory in autogenous and reactive subtype of obsessive-compulsive disorder patients.' *Comprehensive Psychiatry*, 55, 904–911.

44 Hayes, S., Hirsch, C. & Mathews, A. (2008) 'Restriction of working memory capacity during worry.' *Journal of Abnormal Psychology*, 117, 712–717.

45 Leyfer, O. T., Folstein, S. E., Bacalman, S., Davis, N. O. et al. (2006) 'Comorbid psychiatric disorders in children with autism: Interview development and rates of disorders.' *Journal of Autism & Developmental Disorders*, 36, 849–861.

checking and counting[46]. Interestingly, individuals with ASD regularly exhibit deficits in executive functioning and working memory capacity that may represent a significant risk factor for OCD in this group, and suggests that certain cognitive deficits may play a genuine causal role in many cases of OCD.

Despite difficulties in interpreting many of the studies that have linked cognitive and brain deficits with OCD, there is one brain area that has been regularly associated with OCD. This is the *basal ganglia*. The basal ganglia is made up of a series of structures deep in the brain, including the striatum, the globus pallidus, the substantia nigra, the nucleus accumbens and the subthalamic nucleus. When all the structures in the basal ganglia are functioning properly, they are believed to contribute to voluntary planning of actions, and habit formation. Attention was first drawn to the basal ganglia when it was found that individuals with a condition known to affect the basal ganglia (such a Huntington's Disease and Parkinson's Disease) were shown to be at significant risk for OCD. In addition, lesions to that area of the basal ganglia called the striatum resulted in behaviours similar to those seen in OCD sufferers, such as stereotyped activities with highly patterned compulsive and obsessive behaviour[47]. However, rather than this being the result of a localised abnormality in the basal ganglia, it is possible that it's the cortico-basal ganglia neurocircuitry itself that's dysfunctioning. This pathway links the basal ganglia with cortical brain regions that are involved in decision-making, and may be responsible for developing

46 Ruta, L., Mugno, D., D'Arrigo, V. G., Vitiello, B. & Mazzone, L. (2010) 'Obsessive-compulsive traits in children and adolescents with Asperger syndrome.' *European Child & Adolescent Psychiatry*, 19, 17–24.

47 Laplane, D., Levasseur, M., Pillon, B., Dubois, B. et al. (1989) 'Obsessive-compulsive and other behavioural changes with bilateral basal ganglia lesions. A neuropsychological, magnetic resonance imaging and positron tomography study.' *Brain*, 112, 699–725.

smooth sequences of behaviour. A problem in this pathway would therefore lead to disjointed sequences of behaviours very much like the over-controlled and ritualised chains of behaviour seen in many OCD sufferers.

My guess is that there will definitely be some cognitive deficits and brain abnormalities that directly contribute to OCD symptoms in some people, and so are responsible for OCD in some people. But as yet we've not seen the definitive studies that confirm this. It's also highly probable that cognitive deficits (such as executive functioning and working memory deficits) combine with periods of increased anxiety, stress and responsibility to facilitate compulsions and rituals as a way of combatting doubting and uncertainty and quelling anxiety.

But compulsions are not just a clinical phenomenon confined to OCD sufferers. Nonclinical compulsions are common in everyday life and take many forms – and they're not just purposeless eccentricities, they serve an important function in helping to manage anxiety and instilling us with a sense of agency.

Are We Becoming a Population Addicted to Our Compulsions?

There's something about compulsions that seems to both drive us and calm us down. We use the word 'compulsive' to describe almost everyone in some way or another. These days there are compulsive joggers, gamblers, liars, tweeters, dieters, cleaners, gossipers, smartphone users, shoppers, and so on. We even boast about many of our compulsions. We're proud that we struggle out of bed every morning to run that circuit of the park come rain or shine. We're delighted that the agony of sticking with our non-fat diet every day for the past few months has lost us a couple of pounds in weight. We stay up into the early hours playing *Football Manager* so we can tell our college friends about the joy of winning the Premiership title. And then we go back and do it all again tomorrow.

In her book *Can't Just Stop*, Sharon Begley argues that compulsions are the safety valve that allow us to diffuse the stress generated by the anxieties that plague us as we negotiate the demands of our modern world[48]. She claims that, overwhelmed by these anxieties, we grasp at anything that provides relief by offering an illusion of control and agency. We compulsively clean or compulsively check, we hoard or shop, or surf the web, or 'wear out our thumbs with video games. We cling to compulsions as if to a lifeline, for it's only by engaging in compulsions that we can drain enough of our anxiety to function.' It's as if our compulsive addictions serve to convince us of our ability to manage events by exerting excessive control over those aspects of our lives that we know we – and only we – can influence. We compulsively exercise, we compulsively diet, we compulsively consume alcohol, we compulsively gamble – all are activities prominent in the modern era through which we try to lift our mood and regain our sense of agency and control.

The biology and psychology of compulsions are complex. Some compulsive activities come with their own indigenous rewards, and continuous exercise is one example. When you start to exercise, your brain interprets this as a reaction to threat. As your heart rate increases, your brain believes you're fighting an enemy or fleeing from a threat, so the brain releases endorphins, a chemical that minimises the discomfort of exercise, blocks feelings of pain, and even creates a feeling of euphoria. This is known colloquially as 'runner's high' in distance running or a 'rower's high' in rowing. The rewarding effect of this euphoria is stored in the brain and

48 Begley, S. (2017) *Can't Just Stop: An Investigation of Compulsions*. Simon & Schuster.

these memories help to create a conditioned response – a desire to perform those behaviours again. In this way a compulsion begins – a compulsion that may even turn into an involuntary addiction.

But apart from creating feelings of euphoria that counter our existential stress, exercise plays another role in helping to quell our anxiety. Exercise generates physical reactions such as sweating, dizziness and a racing heart, all of which are associated with our fight and flight responses in reaction to threat, but are also sensations experienced during panic attacks. Bearing this in mind, Jasper Smits, co-director of the Anxiety Research & Treatment Program at Southern Methodist University in Dallas has argued that regular workouts might help people prone to anxiety become less likely to have panic attacks when they experience these fight or flight sensations[49]. Indeed, when they tested their theory on sixty volunteers with heightened sensitivity to anxiety, participants who exercised for two weeks showed significant improvements in anxiety sensitivity compared with a group who did not exercise[50].

However, the point at which a behaviour we find rewarding becomes a compulsion is an interesting one. The brain tends to register all pleasures in the same way, with a release of the neurotransmitter dopamine in that area of the brain known as the nucleus accumbens. This process occurs whether the reward is a drug, a sexual pleasure, a tasty meal, a gambling win, buying a new dress, or achieving yet another level on Candy Crush! Yet as we continue to repeat the behaviours that generate these rewards the pleasurable outcome associated with the behaviour begins to subside – but the

---

49 Otto, M. & Smits, J. A. (2011) *Exercise for Mood and Anxiety: Proven Strategies for Overcoming Depression and Enhancing Well-Being*. Oxford University Press.

50 Smits, J. A., Berry, A. C., Rosenfield, D., Powers, M. B. et al. (2008) 'Reducing anxiety sensitivity with exercise.' *Depression & Anxiety*, 25, 689–699.

memory of the original desired effect is retained together with the need to recreate it, so we feel compelled to keep trying in anticipation of achieving that original high again. This is why we persist at a computer game into the depths of the night – just to try and achieve that high we felt when we last won.

Sharon Begley believes this is a process that helps to explain many of the puzzling features of our compulsions. Such as why we compulsively check our phone when it pings or buzzes – no matter whether we're in the street, about to fall asleep in bed, or even in an important meeting with the bank manager. Answering most of our texts or emails is not that pleasurable at all, but we're driven to see if that next text or email is the one that's going to live up to our expectations and bring us the pleasure that we know some messages can do – a pleasure that will replace the drudgery of our daily stresses and anxieties. Even President Trump's compulsive tweeting may be explained in this way, says Begley – being the smartest guy in the room is something that gives him a lot of pleasure, so whenever he's feeling inferior for whatever reason (perhaps because he's just compared his inauguration crowds to the Women's March crowds), he tries to regain that feeling of 'being the smartest guy' by tweeting[51]. His tweeting alleviates his anxiety, and that tweet may just be the one that 'wins the game' and makes him the 'smartest guy in the room' again.

Many of us develop compulsions as a tool to manage the anxieties, demands and stresses of the modern world. They provide us with a sense of control over our lives; some repetitive activities such as exercise provide us with an indigenous high that consigns our daily stresses and anxieties to the back of our mind; and still other activities remind us of the highs they can bestow and instil us with

51 http://www.independent.co.uk/life-style/why-keep-checking-phone-psychology-smartphone-notifications-social-media-a7572916.html

a compulsive urge to try and re-achieve that high. The more the modern world makes us anxious and stressed, the more compulsive behaviours will wheedle their way into our daily routines offering a distraction, a sense of control where none seemed to exist before, and that hope of a brief dopamine rush if we can only persevere long enough to get it right and 'win the game'!

In a Nutshell

The modern world has taken the term OCD, sanitised it, and created a cultural script that perversely imbues the term with positive qualities – but this is in stark contrast to the distress and disability that OCD confers on those who suffer from it. A diagnosis of OCD is associated with a high degree of impairment. It's an insidious, slow onset disorder that's highly resilient – 80 per cent of those with a diagnosis of OCD still haven't recovered twenty years later. Some cultural and personality traits are likely to put an individual at risk of developing OCD, and these include religiosity, scrupulosity and perfectionism. Psychological factors that maintain obsessions and compulsions include a sense of inflated responsibility for bad things happening; a tendency to thought-action fusion (where the individual having a thought about an action is like doing the action); and a desire to suppress unwanted thoughts – which simply makes them pop up even more. Even the act of checking causes further doubting that the checking has been done properly and simply creates more checking – a vicious cycle that only adds to the distress. At least some cases of OCD may be caused by deficits in cognitive functioning or brain abnormalities, although we're still awaiting definitive evidence that these factors actually cause OCD. However, one condition that is highly associated with OCD is autism spectrum disorder, where as many as one in three children with ASD can be diagnosable with OCD.

Finally, sub-clinical compulsions are something that we all indulge in. The more we're exposed to the stresses and strains of the modern world, the more compulsive activities offer some sanctuary from those anxieties. Our compulsions provide a much-needed sense of agency in a world that often seems out of our control, they help us to achieve the indigenous euphorias associated with activities such as repetitive exercise, and they are driven by the desire to re-achieve that dopamine rush that we know we'll get at some point if we keep on gaming, texting, dieting, shopping, gambling and all those other modern-day compulsions that fill our lives.

CHAPTER NINE

The Snake in the Grass

Panic & Its Disorders

'Nothing is terrible except fear itself.'

— Sir Francis Bacon, 1623

I've had two episodes in my life when I've experienced multiple panic attacks. Both episodes had quite different symptoms, but each set of symptoms was equally terrifying in its own way. The first occasion was in 1979, when I had my first encounter with depersonalisation. I was visiting a friend called Nigel and chatting to his mother in the kitchen about how to bake homemade lasagne when I suddenly became aware that my flow of immediate consciousness felt like it was being streamed on to a TV screen directly in front of me. This happened suddenly, and inexplicably. I was watching an IMAX 3D state-of-the-art film of the culinary conversation Nigel's mother and I were having – but in real time exactly as it was happening. This sudden switch in reality is what is terrifying, mainly because the people and the objects around you suddenly seem strangely distant – like you've just stumbled in on an ordinary domestic scene in which you're one of the central characters but you don't feel you have direct personal contact with them! Of course, you've no idea what's happening to you, and this simply magnifies the terror and triggers other symptoms of panic such as heart palpitations, sweating, trembling, dizziness and hyperventilating.

In a growing state of panic I watched myself continuing a mundane conversation about Italian cookery while trying desperately to understand what was happening to me and, more importantly, how this would end. Needless to say, I didn't go crazy, I didn't collapse from a heart attack, I didn't faint, I didn't throw up over Nigel's mother's exquisitely prepared dish of lasagne – and I didn't suddenly discover I'd swallowed the blue pill and was now living in a computer-simulated world where I could watch myself performing! The experience lasted for what felt like a couple of minutes and then slowly dissipated as normal service was resumed.

The experience left me quietly shaken, but how do you describe it to someone? I told Nigel I'd just felt a bit strange, that's all – although he was adamant he hadn't noticed anything odd about me during that conversation. But at that time I still didn't know how to explain it, and what became more disconcerting and frightening was the fact that I began to have more of these experiences. A panic attack is very frightening. Like a snake in the grass it creeps up without you knowing, and when it attacks unexpectedly you don't even recognise it as a snake. You think you're going crazy. But, if you think that's bad enough, then imagine this same experience every day, and in some cases, many times a day. That is panic disorder.

I've been quite specific about the date of my first panic attack – 1979. The significance of this is that as a recognisable mental health problem, panic disorder was not officially identified as a type of acute anxiety condition until around the time of the publication of the revised American Psychiatric Association diagnostic manual in 1980.

As my experiences continued I eventually visited my GP surgery. An elderly locum GP saw me. He listened to my experiences and told me I probably had an infection of the inner ear and to come back in a couple of weeks if the symptoms persisted. I was unimpressed. At that time, no one – including doctors – knew exactly what these acute attacks of anxiety were. But throughout history, there are regular reports of people having very similar experiences to my own.

In 1621, an English doctor, Robert Burton, described the effects of a specific type of fear: 'This fear causes in man, as to be red, pale, tremble, sweat; it makes sudden cold and heat to come all over the body, palpitations of the heart, syncope, etc. It amazed many men that are to seek or show themselves in public assemblies . . . Many men are so amazed and astonished with fear, they know not where they are, what they do, and which is worst, it tortures them many days before with continual affrights . . . '[1]

What is perhaps most debilitating about irregular panic attacks is that you simply don't know when the next sneaky attack is going to come along. It comes out of the blue, at any time, without regard to the company you're keeping, or the significance of your day's events. I'm sure you can see where this is leading. As soon as you begin to fear the next attack, you also begin to spend less time in circumstances where you think a spontaneous attack might have embarrassing or frightening consequences. And these circumstances usually involve busy places where you think you might embarrass yourself in front of other people or you don't feel that you can easily find a safe place if an attack strikes. This is the beginning of the condition known as agoraphobia – a condition that imprisons many sufferers in their own homes for fear of the possible consequences of a sudden panic attack.

This consequence of acute anxiety attacks was recognised in 1878 by the French psychiatrist Henri Legrand du Saulle who wrote

1 Burton, R. (2002) *The Essential Anatomy of Melancholy* [1621]. New York: Dover Publications.

about the 'fear of spaces' saying, 'Although we can observe now and previously that these patients fear open places, they can feel fear of theatres, churches, high balconies in buildings or whenever they are found near wide windows, or buses, boats or bridges.'[2]

In this insightful quote, du Salle recognises that agoraphobia is not simply a fear of open spaces, it's a fear of public spaces generally – and he also makes the interesting link between panic attacks and height phobia – a link that wasn't to be objectively established until over a century later.

Individual panic attacks themselves are not that rare and are probably experienced at some point in their life by one in four people[3]. These acute attacks are associated with a variety of physical symptoms, including heart palpitations, perspiring, dizziness, hyperventilating, nausea and trembling. In addition, you can also experience genuine feelings of terror and depersonalisation (a feeling of not being connected to your own body or in real contact with what is happening around you). Panic disorder is a condition that can develop out of individual panic attacks, and the criteria for a diagnosis of panic disorder indicate that the individual must experience recurrent panic attacks, and in addition must develop a persistent fear of future panic attacks. The frequency of panic attacks in panic disorder can vary considerably between individuals.

During my three months of panic disorder I would experience on average one panic attack a day, but for others it may be as few as just one attack a week. The disorder is associated with a number of fears and apprehensions that the sufferer develops. These include

2 Berrios, G. E. (1996) 'Anxiety and cognate disorders.' In G. E. Berrios. *The History of Mental Symptoms. Describing Psychopathology Since the Nineteenth Century.* Cambridge University Press.

3 Kessler, R. C., Chiu, W. T., Jin, R. J., Ruscio, A. M., Shear, K. & Walters, E. E. (2006) 'The epidemiology of panic attacks, panic disorder, and agoraphobia in the National Comorbidity Study.' *Archives of General Psychiatry*, 63, 415–424.

fears that the attacks indicate an underlying serious medical condition (e.g. cardiac disease, a seizure) – even though repeated medical tests indicate no life-threatening illnesses. Others feel they're losing control or 'going crazy'. Concerns about future attacks often result in the sufferer developing avoidance or safety behaviours that can lead to them becoming fearful of leaving their home, which may mean quitting their job and neglecting their social life.

Living with Panic

Marilyn is a thirty-three-year-old single woman who works for a local telephone company and lives alone in her apartment. Her first panic attack occurred when she was driving her car over a bridge on a very rainy day. She experienced dizziness, pounding heart, trembling and difficulty breathing. As a result of the symptoms she was terrified she would lose control of her car and crash. Since then she's frequently experienced both full panic attacks and limited-symptom attacks (where she feels dizzy and believes she's about to pass out). She became intensely fearful of her panic attacks and highly apprehensive about future panic attacks. As a result of these fears she now avoids waiting in queues, drinking alcohol, elevators, movie theatres, driving over bridges, driving on major roads, flying by plane, and heights (she won't now go out on her tenth-floor balcony). In addition, Marilyn is often late for work because she takes routes to work that don't involve driving on major roads[4].

Marilyn's experience is relatively typical for individuals who develop panic disorder. She has a spontaneous and unexpected panic attack, and she is overwhelmed by the physical symptoms. If panic attacks persist, she then comes to fear those symptoms and believes they may be indications of a severe medical condition or even the

4 Davey, G. C. L. (2014) *Psychopathology*. Wiley.

first signs of a mental illness. This then leads to the development of what we call 'safety behaviours' – these are behaviours designed to ensure that she doesn't have an attack in places where she believes this might be 'unsafe' or in public places where the attacks might be embarrassing for her. In her case, she avoids various public places, various forms of transport, and some places that she fears may not be safe if she's having an attack such as standing on the balcony of her tenth-floor apartment.

The lifetime prevalence rate for panic disorder is around 5 per cent – that is, one in twenty people will be diagnosable with panic disorder at some point in their lifetime[5]. But although panic attacks occurring at the onset of panic disorder appear to come completely 'out of the blue', this onset is usually associated with a period of stress in the individual's life. Psychiatrists Carlo Faravelli and Stefano Pallanti from the Institute of Nervous and Mental Diseases in Florence, Italy, assessed the life events of sixty-four panic disorder patients during the twelve months prior to the onset of the disorder, and compared these life events with those of seventy-eight healthy participants. They found that the panic disorder sufferers had more major life events, more stressful life events, more life events that they felt were beyond their control, and more loss events than the control participants[6]. So, once again, we can point to life stress as a precipitating factor in the aetiology of yet another anxiety disorder.

But the effect that stress has on the development of panic attacks is an insidious and gradual one – which is why the initial panic attacks seem so unexpected and frightening – and panic may only

5 Grant, B. F., Hasin, D. S., Dawson, F. S., Goldstein, R. B. et al. (2006) 'The epidemiology of DSM-IV panic disorder and agoraphobia in the United States: Results from the National Epidemiology Survey on alcohol and related conditions.' *Journal of Clinical Psychiatry*, 67, 363–374.

6 Faravelli, C. & Pallanti, S. (1989) 'Recent life events and panic disorder.' *American Journal of Psychiatry*, 146, 622–626.

be precipitated by certain kinds of stressors and not others. Ethan Moitra, a postdoctoral researcher in the Department of Psychiatry and Human Behavior at Brown University, discovered that certain kinds of stressful life events cause panic symptoms to increase gradually over succeeding months rather than spike immediately. He found that stressful life events in the categories of 'work' (such as a demotion or a lay off), or 'friends/family/household' (such as a family argument) would increase the probability of panic attacks gradually for at least three months after these events. Stressful events in other categories, such as crime or deaths, did not seem to affect panic symptoms at all[7].

The Nature of the Snake Bite

Panic is arguably the anxiety disorder that possesses the severest of physical symptoms – symptoms that include heart palpitations, breathlessness, dizziness, nausea and excessive perspiration. This is not just a psychological cascade of anxious thoughts and feelings – these are genuine physical symptoms. You can feel your heart pounding, see your hand shaking, hear your lungs gasping, and run your fingers through the beads of sweat on your forehead. This is not all in the mind – there is blood and guts physiology in these symptoms! This is because panic attacks represent an activation of our physiological fight/flight defensive reaction that's evolved to provide us with the immediate means to avoid danger. So during periods of stress or danger, our sympathetic nervous system is activated, and its major effect is to signal release of the hormones adrenaline and noradrenaline that release energy and prepare the body for action. These chemicals have the effect of generating an increase in

7 Moitra, E., Dyck, I., Beard, C., Bjornsson, A. S. et al. (2011) 'Impact of stressful life events on the course of panic disorder in adults.' *Journal of Affective Disorders*, 134, 373–376.

heartbeat that increases blood flow and improves delivery of oxygen to the muscles (the pounding heart experience), they increase the speed and depth of breathing to provide more oxygen to the tissues for action (this hyperventilation can make the individual feel dizzy or light-headed), and they increase perspiration which prevents the body from overheating (and makes it harder for a predator to grab you!). There are some other effects as well which give rise to panic-type symptoms, such as the redirecting of blood away from places where it's not needed (such as the stomach) towards places where it is needed (the muscles), resulting in feelings of nausea as a result of reduced activity in the digestive system. The pupils widen to let in more light, resulting in the blurred vision often experienced during a panic attack. Finally, adrenaline and noradrenaline also cause muscle groups to tense up in preparation for fight or flight, which can often give rise to sensations such as chest pains which many panic attack sufferers will interpret as signs of an impending heart attack or cardiac arrest. In this way, a panic attack is the activation of the sympathetic nervous system in such a way as to cause a general activation of a whole metabolic system. Once activated it takes some time for these effects of the hormones adrenaline and noradrenaline to die down, so you'll continue to feel aroused or apprehensive for some time – at least until your parasympathetic nervous system has restored normal service and you feel relaxed again.

Survival is an urgent business, so this whole metabolic cascade is so fast that a panic attack typically develops suddenly and reaches its peak within ten minutes. In the presence of a genuine proximal threat that needs to be avoided, this reaction is highly adaptive, and rapidly prepares the organism to fight vigorously or flee. However, during panic attacks that occur spontaneously in the absence of immediate threats or dangers, this response seems inappropriate and unnecessary. In the case of spontaneous panic attacks, it seems as if the threat or danger threshold which triggers the fight or flight reaction has been significantly lowered or that attacks may just simply be triggered at random. However, although it seems for the sufferer that panic attacks 'come out of the blue', there is evidence that such attacks are not without warning after all.

Psychologist Alicia Meuret at Southern Methodist University in Dallas monitored panic disorder patients around the clock. She found that in the hour prior to a panic attack these individuals were exhibiting increased physiological instability and the final minutes before onset were dominated by increases in hyperventilation – physiological effects that the patients were entirely unaware of[8]. We know that hyperventilation alone can trigger panic attack symptoms and hyperventilation is one particular response to stress and anxiety, so it is possible that Alicia Meuret's study indicates that increased levels of physiological instability and hyperventilation caused by stress or anxiety may be the unseen precursors to 'un-cued' panic attacks.

One of the 'usual suspects' in the brain that's been shown to become hyperactive during a panic attack is the amygdala, an area of the brain that plays a pivotal role in the neural networks concerned with fear and anxiety. In animal studies, behaviours similar to those of panic attacks have been observed when the amygdala is stimulated, and increased levels of amygdala activity have been found in patients with chronic panic disorder. This has led some researchers to speculate that altered structure and function in the amygdala may make some people vulnerable to developing panic disorder because of increased reactivity of the amygdala (particularly to spontaneous panic attacks occurring in the absence of external threat or danger).

8 Meuret, A. E., Rosenfield, D., Wilheim, F. H., Zhou, E. et al. (2011) 'Do unexpected panic attacks occur spontaneously?' *Biological Psychiatry*, 70, 985–991.

Although this looks like a promising avenue of research, to be fair, the evidence on this matter is still far from perfect[9].

But this is not all there is to the story. It's by no means all biology and body – there's a substantial degree of mind involved in the nurture and maintenance of an anxiety problem such as panic disorder.

Wind Blockage, Weak Kidneys and the Puerto Rican Syndrome

Ana's husband and extended family had become concerned for her and were bewildered by her symptoms. Ana is a twenty-year-old married Latina woman originally from a small town in central Mexico. She grew up in poverty but moved to the United States where she was undocumented[10]. She has a two-year-old daughter and a husband two years her elder and they live together in a one-bedroom apartment in the same complex as her husband's extended family.

Ana experienced her first symptoms while stressed and arguing with her husband, and noted that acute stressors, including stressful interpersonal interactions or feeling angry towards another person, triggered all of her attacks. She described the attacks as intense spells of nervousness, crying, difficulty breathing, heart palpitations, bodily weakness, trembles, difficulty speaking, sensations of heat travelling throughout her body, and a sense of being 'disconnected' and out of control. During the attacks Ana was encouraged by her husband to inhale alcohol fumes, a practice among some Latinos where alcohol is infused with herbs and fragrance and is rubbed on the face during an attack to bring the sufferer back to consciousness.

9 Kim, J. E., Dager, S. R. & Lyoo, K. (2012) 'The role of the amygdala in the pathophysiology of panic disorder: Evidence from neuroimaging studies.' *Biology of Mood & Anxiety Disorders*, http://www.biolmoodanxietydisord.com/content/2/1/20
10 Sanchez, A. & Shallcross, R. (2012) 'Integrative psychodynamic treatment of Ataque de Nervios.' *Clinical Case Studies*, 11, 5–23.

Ana is experiencing *ataques de nervios*. This is a culturally shaped syndrome found in Latinos and other Hispanic groups, and was originally labelled the 'Puerto Rican Syndrome' because it was first documented in Latino populations in the Caribbean. It represents a response to severe stress, particularly in relation to conflict or loss in the family, including arguments, funerals and accidents. Now, you'll probably have recognised that many of Ana's symptoms during her attacks were also symptoms of what we've described as panic attacks. But her responses include other emotional symptoms that are rarely found in panic attacks in many other cultural groups. These responses include shouting, aggression, anger, collapsing and even amnesia. What's interesting about *ataque de nervios* is that it's a culturally sanctioned reaction to stress that includes many forms of response that are both shaped by the Latino culture and accepted by it. It's basically a panic attack with some added on culturally relevant extras. For example, within European and white-American cultures panic attacks are certainly not experiences to make a song and dance about! We try to hide the symptoms and avoid places where we might publicly reveal our attacks – we seem ashamed of our panic and believe that others will view it as a sign of weakness. But in Latino culture, *ataque de nervios* fits the cultural pattern of expressing distress through the body – a process in which the connection between intrapersonal processes and the social world are mediated through the body[11]. Hence, external expressions of anger, shouting, and even loss of consciousness – which all fit the Latino cultural script.

What is also interesting in the case of *ataque de nervios* is that it may be a clinical syndrome that survives only as long as the cultural beliefs that support and shape it. *Ataques de nervios* appear to be significantly

11 Guarnaccia, P. J., Rivera, M., Franco, F., & Neighbors, C. (1996) 'The experiences of ataques de nervios: Towards an anthropology of emotions in Puerto Rico.' *Culture, Medicine and Psychiatry*, 20(3), 343–367.

more prevalent among Latinos age forty-five and older than among those younger than forty-five[12] – a sign perhaps of the globalisation of the modern world eroding the local cultural beliefs that have given birth to culture-bound syndromes such as *ataque de nervios*.

One of the more striking examples of culture shaping the phenomenology of panic has been identified in Cambodian refugees. According to Cambodian culture a wind-like substance (*khyâl*) moves through the circulatory system, and simply standing up may cause what is called '*khyâl* overload' – an upsurge of *khyâl* and blood that Cambodians believe could lead to asphyxia, neck vessel rupture, loss of consciousness, or death.[13] For Cambodians, dizziness that may be experienced when standing up is interpreted as potentially fatal and can regularly generate a feeling of terror and a panic attack – contemporary Westerners would probably view this experience as nothing more than a touch of low blood pressure. Similarly, unlike Westerners, Cambodians often report panic attacks in conjunction with neck pain. This results from any neck soreness being attributed to excessive 'wind' and blood pressure in the neck that the sufferer believes may rupture blood vessels. This gives rise to catastrophic cognitions about the sore neck that may often lead to neck-focused panic attacks[14].

Just one more example. In traditional Chinese medicine anxiety is often attributed to organ dysfunction, and the kidneys are believed to nurture the brain by producing marrow. Symptoms of 'weak

12 Guarnaccia, P. J., Rubio-Stipec, M., & Canino, G. (1989) '*Ataques de nervios* in the Puerto Rican Diagnostic Interview Schedule: The impact of cultural categories on psychiatric epidemiology.' *Culture, Medicine, and Psychiatry*, 13, 275–295.

13 Hinton, D. E., Hofman, S. G., Pitman, R. K., Pollack, M. H. et al. (2008) 'The panic attack-posttraumatic stress disorder model: Applicability to orthostatic panic among Cambodian refugees.' *Cognitive Behaviour Therapy*, 37, 101–116.

14 Hofman, S. G. & Hinton, D. E. (2014) 'Cross-cultural aspects of anxiety disorders.' *Current Psychiatry Reports*, 16, 450.

kidney' include frequent urination, incontinence, vertigo, night sweats, dry mouth, back pain, tinnitus, and – perhaps surprisingly – premature greyness and hair loss! The kidneys are also associated with the emotion of fear. As a result, many Chinese patients will associate back pain with catastrophic thinking about the range of symptoms believed to be associated with 'weak kidney', catastrophic thinking that can often precipitate a panic attack – especially since the kidney is believed to be intimately involved in anxiety and fear[15].

What these culturally distinct examples illustrate is that cultural scripts can determine not only what triggers a panic attack but also how cultural beliefs can determine the symptoms of panic attacks. The point to be made here is that responses to stress, such as a panic attack, are not simply and solely determined by the body and its physiology; local cultural practices and beliefs can influence the nature and outcome of the symptoms and even the types of bodily responses generated as reactions to stress. If our cultural beliefs can change the shape of anxiety responses, then our thoughts and beliefs are very powerful – powerful enough to influence the development, maintenance and recovery from panic disorder. And that is indeed the case.

Espresso to Stress-o

Chris Choi was grabbing his Veranda Roast grande (he takes it black) at an L Street NW Starbucks in downtown Washington on Monday morning, his first of the day. 'It's very trendy to drink coffee,' said Chris, twenty-three, 'You'll never be judged going out and getting coffee. You find more people into that.'[16]

15 Perhaps Chinese is not the only culture in which panic attacks can be triggered by catastrophic thoughts about premature baldness!

16 https://www.washingtonpost.com/news/business/wp/2016/10/31/look-how-much-coffee-millennials-are-drinking/?utm_term=.5cf1763c6809

I'm not a great coffee drinker, but I know many people are. One a day is often just enough for me. However, in the last couple of decades, the expansion of coffee shops and coffee capsule systems has seen an increase in the popularity of coffee consumption – especially among Millennials (nineteen to thirty-four-year-olds). Migration from the countryside to the cities in countries such as China has also led to many people trying coffee for the first time and finding they like it. But this increase in the popularity of coffee may be one of the factors fuelling our modern feelings of existential dread. Many people overlook the fact that caffeine indirectly increases noradrenaline and causes symptoms essentially indistinguishable from anxiety, including nervousness, irritability, trembling, palpitations, flushing and heartbeat irregularities. The more caffeine you consume in a day, the more these symptoms are likely – and not just in adults, but also in children.

A study by Gareth Richards and Andrew Smith at Cardiff University studied the weekly caffeine intake of 3,071 secondary school pupils. They found that after adjusting for effects of diet, demography and lifestyle, there were significant positive correlations between total weekly caffeine intake and measures of anxiety[17], with coffee being the major contributor to these school kids' caffeine intake.

Many people are clearly unaware of the relationship between caffeine and anxiety symptoms. In 1974, John Greden, then Assistant Professor of Psychology at the University of Michigan Medical Center wrote a brief but influential paper entitled 'Anxiety or Caffeinism: A Diagnostic Dilemma'. In this paper he reports the case of an ambitious thirty-seven-year-old army lieutenant colonel referred to a military medical clinic because of a two-year history of chronic anxiety. His daily symptoms included dizziness, trembling,

---

17 Richards, G. & Smith, A. (2015) 'Caffeine consumption and self-assessed stress, anxiety, and depression in secondary school children.' *Journal of Psychopharmacology*, 29, 1236–1247.

apprehension about his job performance, butterflies in the stomach, restlessness and difficulty sleeping. He was proud of the fact that his coffeepot was a permanent fixture on his desk, and admitted drinking eight to fourteen cups of coffee a day. It was suggested to him that coffee toxicity might be causing his symptoms. He responded with incredulity and refused to limit his intake of coffee, cocoa or cola. When his symptoms persisted, he then agreed voluntarily to reduce his caffeine intake, and almost immediately most of his physical symptoms improved, as did his scores on self-report measures of anxiety. His job apprehension still persisted, but he cynically observed that he was 'still working for the same S.O.B.'!

So why am I banging on about the link between caffeine consumption and anxiety symptoms? First, because our contemporary coffee culture may be genuinely contributing to modern feelings of pervasive 'existential dread' reported by writers such as Scott Stossel in his book *My Age of Anxiety* and blogging journalists who have noted the puzzling growth of anxiety in the modern age[18]. The sheer volume of coffee consumption may not be as great as it has been in the past (I think coffee consumption in the United States peaked as long ago as the 1940s), but it's a modern-day culturally popular beverage delivered by trendy coffee shops and convenient coffee capsule machines that we're told every home should have (yes, there's one in our house!). What's different in the modern era is that the current generation is much more aware of anxiety symptoms than were coffee drinkers twenty or thirty years ago. So we may be acutely aware today of our caffeine-induced anxiety symptoms but not necessarily aware that these symptoms may in part be attributed to our coffee consumption.

18 Journalists and columnists such as Jonathan Gornall, Will Hutton, Simon Copland and Louise Chunn amongst others.

But second, caffeine is regularly used in what are known as 'biological challenge procedures' used in research on panic disorder, and these studies tell us some interesting things about what triggers panic attacks and how panic disorder develops out of just a few isolated panic attacks. The million-dollar question is why some people experience isolated panic attacks, brush them off, and continue with life as normal, whereas others fall sharply into the snake pit of regular, debilitating attacks that stymie all aspects of life for months and even years.

A biological challenge procedure is where a provocative agent is used to induce panic attacks, and this can tell us whether individuals suffering panic disorder have a greater sensitivity to such agents. Dennis Charney and colleagues from Yale University School of Medicine administered 10mg of caffeine to twenty-one patients with a diagnosis of panic disorder and seventeen healthy control participants. Caffeine produced significantly greater increases in self-rated anxiety, nervousness, fear, nausea, palpitations and tremors in the panic disorder patients than the controls. Caffeine also induced symptoms identical to full-blown panic attacks in fifteen of the twenty-one patients[19], but not in the healthy controls. Other provocative agents that produce similar results include carbon dioxide (CO_2) inhalation, sodium lactate, the drug yohimbine, and even something as basic as voluntary room-air hyperventilation[20].

The face-value conclusion from these wide-ranging studies is that individuals with a diagnosis of panic disorder have a significantly greater sensitivity to provocative agents than do individuals

19 Charney, D. S., Heninger, G. R. & Jatlow, P. I. (1985) 'Increased anxiogenic effects of caffeine in panic disorders.' *Archives of General Psychiatry*, 42, 233–243.

20 Forsyth, J. P. & Karekla, M. (2001) 'Biological challenge in the assessment of anxiety disorders.' In M. M. Antony, S. M. Orsillo & L. Roemer (Eds.) *Practitioner's Guide to Empirically Based Measures of Anxiety*. Springer.

without a diagnosis of panic disorder. But that doesn't tell us where that added sensitivity resides. There are many who believe that this added sensitivity resides somewhere in the sufferer's biology – perhaps an added sensitivity in the brain's fear centre, the amygdala[21], or overactivity in the body's noradrenergic neurotransmitter system – the system that regulates arousal and our fight/flight reactions[22]. There is certainly evidence that's consistent with both these possibilities. But that evidence isn't conclusive, because most of the studies have identified these added biological sensitivities in individuals who already have panic disorder, so we don't know whether these added sensitivities are merely *consequences* of having panic disorder or whether they're a genuine *cause* of the disorder. So let's look somewhere slightly different. Let's try the mind rather than the body.

I Think Therefore I Panic

The Stealth roller coaster in Thorpe Park, Surrey, is the fastest roller coaster in the UK and the tallest launch coaster in the country. The ride begins with an American voice announcing, 'Place your heads back, face forwards, hold on tight and brace yourself'. Five red lights then light up in sequence – the lights abruptly turn green and the coaster accelerates to 80 mph in just 1.9 seconds. It quickly reaches the highest point on the ride, before abruptly turning 90 degrees to the left and falling steeply into another sudden 90-degree turn before encountering a bunny-hop hill that produces a brief moment of weightlessness. Roller coaster rides such as this generate many

21 Kim, J. E., Dager, S. R. & Lyoo, K. (2012) 'The role of the amygdala in the pathophysiology of panic disorder: Evidence from neuroimaging studies.' *Biology of Mood & Anxiety Disorders*, http://www.biolmoodanxietydisord.com/content/2/1/20

22 Redmond, D. E. (1977) 'Alterations to the function of the nucleus locus coeruleus: A possible model for studies of anxiety.' In I. Hanin & E. Usdin (Eds.) *Animal Models in Psychiatry and Neurology*. New York: Pergamon Press.

bodily sensations that make these rides what they are – fabulously exciting to some, scary and frightening to others, and a complete no-go to the rest. Basically, the same experience can be seen by one person as the most exhilarating experience in the world, and by another as the most terrifying.

To put this idea into a context relevant to panic disorder, one exercise that I would regularly carry out with my undergraduate students when discussing the causes of panic disorder was a brief experiment involving hyperventilation. I'd ask everyone in the lecture theatre to hyperventilate for just a few breaths (not too many, we didn't want anyone passing out!). Then I'd quickly ask them to think of a couple of words that described how they felt after hyperventilating. The main effects of a brief period of hyperventilation are mild breathlessness and light-headedness, but it was interesting to see how my students interpreted these. 'Breathlessness' was interpreted by some as 'agitated' or 'gasping', but by others as 'excited' or 'stimulating'. 'Light-headedness' for some was 'dizzy' or 'fainting', but for others it was 'chilled' or 'relaxed'. Exactly the same biological reactions, but interpreted in almost polar opposite ways by different people – one set of interpretations is good or even pleasurable, while the other set is bad and even unpleasant. Clearly, body sensations don't have the same connotations for everyone.

In the case of panic disorder, it appears there are important differences in how individuals interpret the symptoms of a panic attack, and many people who suffer anxiety generally tend to have relatively fixed ways of interpreting events around them and events that happen to them. Individuals who develop panic disorder are significantly more likely to interpret ambiguous bodily sensations as threatening than someone who doesn't develop panic disorder. Take the statement 'My heart is beating faster' – the meaning of this simple phrase is ambiguous, yet someone who develops panic disorder is likely to endorse a threatening interpretation ('I may be going to have a heart attack') rather than a benign interpretation ('I'm feeling excited'). A tendency to a negative interpretation bias – especially of body sensations – not only differentiates those with panic disorder from those without, but has also been shown to be a causal precursor of panic disorder[23].

Oxford University Clinical Psychologist David M. Clark has argued that this threat interpretation bias leads to a 'catastrophic misinterpretation' of bodily sensations that precipitates panic attacks and helps to turn isolated panic attacks into the regular occurrences that define panic disorder[24]. This view proposes that the bodily sensations that are misinterpreted are mainly those involved in normal anxiety responses (such as palpitations, breathlessness, dizziness, etc.), and the catastrophic misinterpretation involves perceiving these sensations as much more dangerous than they really are (e.g. that heart palpitations are evidence of an impending heart attack). Clark specifically uses the term 'misinterpretation' because he believes that many people who panic tend to misinterpret bodily sensations even when they're caused by non-anxious states such as exercise or caffeine consumption. This catastrophic misinterpretation process then creates a vicious cycle in which fearful misinterpretation generates more anxiety that in turn creates more bodily symptoms that are again fearfully misinterpreted, and this repeating cycle occurs very rapidly and escalates into a full-blown activation of the physiological fight/flight defensive reaction that characterises a panic attack. In this way, the mind has taken control of the body and our evolved

23 Woud, M. L., Zhang, X. C., Becker, E. S., McNally, R. J. & Margraf, J. (2014) 'Don't panic: Interpretation bias is predictive of new onsets of panic.' *Journal of Anxiety Disorders*, 28, 83–87.
24 Clark, D. M. (1986) 'The cognitive approach to panic.' *Behaviour Research and Therapy*, 24, 461–470.

physiological fight/flight reaction isn't being triggered by genuine threats, but by our 'beliefs' about what our bodily sensations mean.

There are at least three different types of beliefs here that contribute to catastrophic misinterpretation and to panic disorder – a belief that ambiguous bodily sensations should be *interpreted as threatening*; a belief that panic attacks should be *expected* once bodily sensations have been detected; and a belief that bodily sensations and their consequences should be *feared*.

So what exactly are these beliefs and where do they come from? First, maybe people who develop panic disorder have every right to be wary and fearful of bodily sensations if they have a history of physical illness. Well, there is a growing body of evidence suggesting that panic disorder often occurs concurrently with physical illnesses, particularly respiratory illnesses such as asthma, cardiovascular illnesses, irritable bowel syndrome (IBS), and diabetes[25]. The number of physical illnesses a person reports having suffered is also directly related to the likelihood of developing panic disorder[26]. It's still not clear in which direction this relationship runs, whether physical illness increases the risk for panic disorder, or panic disorder increases the risk of physical illness. But these recent findings are consistent with the view that many of those who suffer panic disorder may have experienced increased levels of physical illness that may make them more wary and fearful of their bodily sensations.

Second, 'nothing is terrible except fear itself' wrote Sir Francis Bacon in 1623, and it's a quote that could have been tailor-made

25 Meuret, A. E., Kroll, J. & Ritz, T. (2017) 'Panic disorder comorbidity with medical conditions and treatment implications.' *Annual Review of Clinical Psychology*, 13, 209–240.

26 Moreno-Peral, P., Conejo-Ceron, S., Motrico, F., Rodriguez-Morejon, A. et al. (2014) 'Risk factors for the onset of panic and generalized anxiety disorder in the general adult population: A systematic review of cohort studies.' *Journal of Affective Disorders*, 168, 337–348.

to describe modern-day panic disorder. Individuals suffering panic disorder fear their own bodily sensations, and in particular have a specific fear of anxiety symptoms. This fear of anxiety has come to be known as *anxiety sensitivity*, and it's a construct that's known to be a significant risk factor for panic disorder – if you score highly on measures of anxiety sensitivity then you are significantly more likely to develop panic disorder in the future.

Norman Schmidt and colleagues at Florida State University measured anxiety sensitivity immediately before 1,401 cadets entered the US Air Force Academy's highly stressful five-week 'boot camp' programme. Seventy-four of these cadets reported a spontaneous panic attack during the boot camp, and statistical analysis revealed that scores on the anxiety sensitivity measure predicted these attacks. Cadets in the top 25 per cent of anxiety sensitivity scores were twice as likely to panic during boot camp than were other cadets[27]. Being fearful of your bodily sensations – especially bodily sensations indicative of anxiety – seems to be a very important risk factor for experiencing panic attacks and developing panic disorder.

So where does anxiety sensitivity come from? Why are some people high on anxiety sensitivity and others seemingly unbothered about whether they're anxious or not? There are still relatively few comprehensive studies of the origins of anxiety sensitivity, but we do have some snippets that point to some possible causal candidates. One is genetics. Twin studies suggest that anxiety sensitivity is 'moderately' heritable (accounting for up to 61 per cent of the variance in anxiety sensitivity scores) and this genetic effect is generally stable over time, but there is also a clear indication that environmental

27 Schmidt, N. B., Lerew, D. R., Jackson, R. J. (1997) 'The role of anxiety sensitivity in the pathogenesis of panic: Prospective evaluation of spontaneous panic attacks during acute stress.' *Journal of Abnormal Psychology*, 106, 355–364.

factors can also influence anxiety sensitivity levels as well[28]. Stressful life events are associated with subsequent increases in anxiety sensitivity in adolescents, especially stressful events related to health (e.g. the individual or a member of the family being hospitalised) and to family discord (e.g. parents being divorced)[29]. In addition, our interactions with our parents may once again be a culprit in determining at least some of our sensitivity to anxiety. Various retrospective studies have reported that individuals high on anxiety sensitivity claim that their parents encouraged sick role behaviour in response to illness and anxiety symptoms[30], or showed concern about symptoms associated with minor illnesses such as rashes and colds[31].

David Clark's catastrophic misinterpretation account of panic disorder is now the most widely accepted explanation of panic disorder. It's a psychological account that has led to the development of highly successful CBT treatments for panic disorder – treatment programmes that enable the sufferer to identify their biased thinking and dysfunctional beliefs about the causes and consequences of bodily sensations and to change them[32]. When the mind controls

---

28 Zavos, H. M. S., Gregory, A. M., Eley, T. C. (2012) 'Longitudinal genetic analysis of anxiety sensitivity.' *Developmental Psychology*. 48(1), 204–212.

29 McLaughlin, K. A. & Hatzenbuehler, M. L. (2009) 'Stressful life events, anxiety sensitivity, and internalizing symptoms in adolescents.' *Journal of Abnormal Psychology*, 118, 659–669.

30 Watt, M. C., Stewart, S. H., Cox, B. J. (1998) 'A retrospective study of the learning history origins of anxiety sensitivity.' *Behaviour Research and Therapy*, 36, 505–525.

31 Stewart, S. H., Taylor, S., Jang, K. L., Cox, B. J., Watt, M. C., Fedoroff, I. C., Borger, S. C. (2001) 'Causal modeling of relations among learning history, anxiety sensitivity and panic attacks.' *Behaviour Research and Therapy*, 39, 443–456.

32 Otto, M. W. & Deveney, C. (2005) 'Cognitive-behavioral therapy for the treatment of panic disorder: Efficacy and strategies.' *Journal of Clinical Psychiatry*, 66, 28–32.

the body, the mind is the first place to look, not just for causes but also for solutions.

The Final Paradox

There is just one final conundrum that needs to be explained. What's intriguing about panic disorder is that some sufferers will have experienced hundreds of panic attacks over a period of months and sometimes years, yet they still misinterpret the bodily sensations associated with panic in a catastrophic way. The individual who thinks they're going to have a heart attack *still* thinks they're going to have a heart attack even though all their previous panic attacks have never resulted in this particular catastrophic outcome. So why don't these catastrophic thoughts about having a heart attack extinguish?

The answer is that those who develop chronic panic disorder tend to also develop what are known as 'safety behaviours'. In my own particular case, if I thought I might have a panic attack on the train on the way to work in London, I'd simply stay and work at home that day. If I was having a panic attack in the street on the way to work (nausea, dizziness and depersonalisation), I'd immediately go and lean on a nearby wall and take some papers out of my brief case to make it look as if I were checking something. I'd stay there until the attack had passed. By doing these things, I believed I'd 'saved' myself from some even worse outcome, such as fainting in the street or involuntarily throwing up over the train passenger sitting next to me. Other examples of safety behaviours include sitting down if the catastrophised outcome is a supposed heart attack, or moving slowly and looking for an escape route if the catastrophic outcome is losing control and acting foolishly[33]. Used in this way, safety behaviours

33 Helbig-Lang, S. & Petermann, F. (2010) 'Safety behaviors across anxiety disorders: Tolerate or eliminate?' *Clinical Psychology: Science and Practice*, 17, 218–233.

are effectively avoidance responses that prevent the individual from disconfirming their catastrophic beliefs – the effective outcome becomes 'I saved myself so I still believe that terrible outcome could still happen'. Disconfirming the catastrophic beliefs associated with panic symptoms is an important process in cognitive therapy for panic disorder, and this means attempting to eliminate these safety behaviours in some way – either by convincing the sufferer that the safety behaviours are not what they think they are, or by preventing the safety behaviours in such a way as to show the client that there is no catastrophic outcome following a panic attack, even when the safety behaviours are removed[34].

The Crux of the Matter

Panic attacks are hard to endure – especially when you've come to fear them and when they've mutated from the odd sporadic attack into the regular nightmare that becomes full-blown panic disorder. Explanations of anxiety problems such as panic disorder almost make them sound logical and paradoxically benign – but, of course, they're neither of those things to the sufferer. Those who suffer panic disorder are neither feigning nor dishonest – discovering that what you thought was going to be a heart attack was in fact a panic attack doesn't invalidate your suffering[35]. Unlike our Latino relatives who have no reservations about displaying their panic and anxiety in public, us Europeans and Westerners prefer to disguise our panic and hide it from view to the point where we end up also locking ourselves away, preferring to sit at home with our shortness of breath, trembling, blurred vision and feelings of nausea. As Daniel

34 Rachman, S., Radomsky, A. S. & Shafran, R. (2008) 'Safety behaviour: A reconsideration.' *Behaviour Research and Therapy*, 46, 163–173.

35 https://www.theguardian.com/society/2013/sep/15/anxiety-epidemic-gripping-britain

Smith wrote in *Monkey Mind*, his autobiographical account of his own anxiety, anxiety sufferers are 'stiflers' who learn to seal their anxiety off from public view, 'they learn to cork their anxiety within themselves like acid in a vial. It isn't pleasant. The human mind isn't Pyrex, it can corrode.'[36] Panic disorder is truly terrifying, and it's truly disabling, but if it's recognised for what it is – anxiety mischievously masquerading as something much worse – it is genuinely curable.

36 Smith, D. (2013) *Monkey Mind: A Memoir of Anxiety*. Simon & Schuster.

CHAPTER TEN

Social Anxiety

'You probably wouldn't worry about what people think
of you if you could know how seldom they do!'

— Olin Miller, 1937[1]

A s a boy I was constantly planning how I could get out of 'performing' in front of other people. These performances could
be something as seemingly simple as having to meet visiting relatives (I'd lock myself in my bedroom) or it could be an unthinkably
hideously public event like reading the lesson in assembly at school
(I'd feign illness the day before). Meeting relatives must seem like a
simple, everyday activity, but for me it was a performance in which I
was aware of my every muscle twitch and eye blink. I was considered
a shy child, but shyness isn't an explanation – it's just another word
to describe someone as socially reticent – so what's the problem with
social reticence?

It was one of the major sources of anxiety for me as a child and
a young adolescent. I recollect from my childhood sitting mortified
at my cousin's wedding reception with the contents of a bowl of
fruit salad and condensed milk soaking into my lap. I'd foolishly

1 Thank you to my fellow psychologist Peter McEvoy for bringing this
quote to my attention.

tried to cut up the fruit with an oversized dessertspoon and the bowl tipped over and emptied its contents into my lap – and it did it in full Technicolor slow motion before my very eyes. Everyone must have seen it and be quietly laughing to themselves at my incompetence. My first thought was to somehow sneak out without anyone noticing, get a bus home, and then lock myself in my bedroom. My second thought was to die there and then. Neither option was viable. I was petrified of the consequences of a social faux pas, and for the socially anxious person, a faux pas is a flashbulb memory moment that is never forgotten in a lifetime. And every time the memory is activated it drags up a scoop of dread from the pit of your stomach and stuffs it into your throat.

If you're socially anxious, you're going to be continually worried that you'll get something wrong, and for most children learning what's socially right and wrong is a central part of growing up. Learning what is right is obviously a good thing. But learning what is wrong can be a winding path that can take you to some strange places. Parents are well meaning people, but they can be less than explicit about how they define what's right and wrong. Before one outing I remember my mother telling me as a child to 'behave properly and don't pick your nose'. I do know what picking my nose is, but – dear mother – you hadn't quite defined for a five-year-old boy what 'behaving properly' was. So if I'm going to be a diligent son, all I can do is focus entirely on not picking my nose . . . and stay in the background!

Many parents do focus their parenting more on what's the wrong thing to do, and rather less on what's the right thing to do. I don't recall having a torrid time being parented as a child, but I do remember my mother regularly telling me 'not to show her up in public' before we went out. The only way I found out what I could and couldn't do was when I was chastised in the street for something – there seemed to be no rule book for this, and my mother was judge and jury, administering summary justice seemingly when she felt like it. This is one pathway to social anxiety and avoidance in later childhood and adolescence, and the words 'I must not do the wrong thing' still ring in my ears today.

Living with Social Anxiety Disorder

Human beings are basically social animals. We live in family groups, our normal means of reproduction is with the help of a partner, we relax together in social settings, buy our provisions in large warehouses full of other shoppers (called supermarkets), we regularly work together in organised groups, travel together on trains and buses, and in these modern times we even socialise indirectly via social media and instant smartphone connectivity. So being phobic of people is a disadvantage in almost all spheres of life. In severe cases of social anxiety this can inflict a lifetime of damage, as social anxiety sufferer Gary describes.

'You have to be a sufferer of social anxiety to understand the pure terror that a victim of this illness feels. You shake like a leaf, you blush, your mouth goes dry, you can't speak, you break out in a cold sweat, your legs feel so weak you think you're going to fall. Your thoughts become confused and disorientated. Forget butterflies in the stomach – your guts are twisted inside out with fear. Social anxiety made me sink so low I ended up cleaning public toilets for a living. I never married, I had no children, I never owned my own house. I was a smart-looking young man so I got some good jobs, but because of social anxiety no way could I hold them. Would you buy from a salesman who went a deep red, stammered, couldn't look you in the eye, and shook so much that even his head trembled? No – nor would the boss who in the end would say get lost, you're bad for business. Over the years I slid down and down the social ladder with long spells out of work and, of course, no money. By the time I was thirty I could only do work where I didn't have to deal with people, work like road sweeping, night work in factories, and in the end cleaning public toilets when closed at night. If I attempted going into a restaurant or café, I'd pick a table facing the wall and if anyone sat at my table my hands would shake so much I couldn't get the food into my mouth. I became the ultimate night person only going out late to walk the streets.'

Gary's story relates the terror inflicted by social situations and his subsequent social decline. The person who is socially anxious tries to avoid any kind of social situation in which they believe they may behave in an embarrassing way or in which they believe they may be negatively evaluated, and these types of situation can range from something as simple as having a conversation, eating or drinking in front of others, or performing in front of others (such as giving a speech or a presentation). So pervasive is anxiety of these socially based situations that it's also a predictor of several other debilitating problems such as depression and substance abuse[2].

The diagnostic manual DSM-5 describes some of the defining features of social anxiety disorder, which include situations in which the sufferer believes he or she will show anxiety symptoms that will be negatively evaluated (that is, they believe they'll be humiliated, embarrassed or rejected, or will offend others). They may fear public speaking because of concern that others will notice their trembling hands or voice. Or they may experience extreme anxiety when conversing with others because of fear they'll appear inarticulate. They may avoid eating, drinking or writing in public because of fear of being embarrassed by having others see their hands shake. Individuals with social phobia almost always experience symptoms

2 Rapee, R. M. & Spence, S. H. (2004) 'The etiology of social phobia: Empirical evidence and an initial model.' *Clinical Psychology Review*, 24, 737–767.

of anxiety in the feared social situations (e.g. palpitations, tremors, sweating, gastrointestinal discomfort, muscle tension, blushing, confusion), and, in severe cases, these symptoms may turn into a full-blown panic attack. As a result of their reluctance to engage with social situations, sufferers of social anxiety disorder also tend to underperform in education and in the workplace, have impaired social and romantic relationships, and reduced productivity[3].

Social anxiety disorder is the fourth most common mental health condition with about one in eight people (12 per cent of the population) being diagnosable with social anxiety disorder in their lifetime[4]. As you can probably imagine, social anxiety is an early starter, with the typical age of onset in the early to mid-teens as youngsters begin to struggle with their growing responsibilities in the world. Social anxiety is a common reason for school refusal in young children, and is the only mood or anxiety disorder that's been consistently associated with dropping out of school early[5]. There is also a modest gender imbalance, with a gender prevalence of 3:2 females to males[6].

I'm Lonely – Leave Me Alone!

I described in Chapter 3 how loneliness was reaching epidemic proportions in the modern world, and that loneliness is a significant cause

3 Kessler, R. C. (2003) 'The impairments caused by social phobia in the general population: Implications and interventions.' *Acta Psychiatrica Scandinavica Supplement*, 417, 19–27.

4 Kessler, R. C., Berglund, P., Demler, O. et al. (2005) 'Lifetime prevalence and age-of-onset distributions of DSM-IV disorders in the national comorbidity survey replication.' *Archives of General Psychiatry*, 62, 593–602.

5 Stein, M. B. & Kean, Y. M. (2000) 'Disability and quality of life in social phobia: Epidemiological findings.' *American Journal of Psychiatry*, 157, 1606–1613.

6 Xu, Y., Schneier, F., Heimberg, R. G., Princisvalle, K., Liebowitz, M. R., Wang, S. et al. (2012) 'Gender differences in social anxiety disorder: Results from the national epidemiologic sample on alcohol and related conditions.' *Journal of Anxiety Disorders*, 26, 12–19.

of anxiety. But there's an even more intimate relationship between loneliness and social anxiety. Loneliness is related to social anxiety like a rock is to a hard place. Loneliness is an ache that needs to be soothed by social contact and companionship, but social anxiety is the lock on the door that imposes continued isolation and exclusion. The twin demons of loneliness and social anxiety are a formidable pair and in effect reinforce each other. Social anxiety predicts future loneliness, and loneliness also predicts future social anxiety[7] – there's a vicious cycle ready to spiral out of control!

Now throw paranoia into the mix. Loneliness also predicts future states of paranoia as well as social anxiety – paranoia is social anxiety's long-forgotten sibling and many researchers have argued that paranoid thinking is one of the central processes that drive social anxiety[8]. Daniel Freeman and researchers at the Institute of Psychiatry in London have suggested that non-clinical paranoia may be a particular type of social fear that's associated with social anxiety, loneliness and feelings of isolation[9]. Paranoia is not just an attribute that's associated with psychosis and delusional states; it's a relatively common feature of many people's thinking.

In a study of paranoia in 8,576 individuals representative of the general population, researchers at the Institute of Psychiatry found that many examples of paranoid thinking were endorsed by up to 30 per cent of the population. These included worries over social inferiority, worries over criticism by others, feelings that people

7 Lim, M. H., Rodebaugh, T. L., Zyphur, M. J. & Gleeson, J. F. M. (2016) 'Loneliness over time: The crucial role of social anxiety.' *Journal of Abnormal Psychology*, 125, 620–630.

8 Martin, J. A. & Penn, D. L. (2001) 'Social cognition and subclinical paranoid ideation.' *British Journal of Clinical Psychology*, 40, 261–265.

9 Freeman, D., Gittins, M., Pugh, K., Antley, A. et al. (2008) 'What makes one person paranoid and another person anxious? The differential prediction of social anxiety and persecutory ideation in an experimental situation.' *Psychological Medicine*, 38, 1121–1132.

were generally against them and might use or hurt them, a reluctance to reveal too much in case people used it in adverse ways, and often perceiving hidden threats or insults in the things other people say or do[10]. In this age of negative news, fake news, and narcissistic self-promoting politicians, perhaps we're right to be just a little bit suspicious and acceptably paranoid. But just look at that list of paranoid beliefs – they look very much like the irrational fears of embarrassment, humiliation, rejection and criticism held by many people who are socially anxious.

In an imaginative study, Fabian Lamster and colleagues at the University of Marburg in Germany attempted to experimentally manipulate feelings of loneliness in a group of sixty participants (none of whom reported being particularly lonely people) and to measure the effect that this had on paranoid beliefs[11]. They asked their participants to complete a questionnaire on loneliness, but half the participants received items such as 'I *sometimes* feel isolated from others' which they were likely to endorse, the other half received items such as 'I *always* feel isolated from others' which they were not likely to endorse. After this, all participants were asked to rate the statement 'Right now I feel a bit lonely', and the first group reported feeling significantly more lonely than the latter group. Once they had manipulated their participants' feelings of loneliness in this way, they then discovered that paranoid beliefs were significantly higher in the group that felt lonelier. Experimental studies that manipulate loneliness in this way suggest that loneliness does indeed *cause* paranoid beliefs to increase, a factor which suggests that paranoid

10 Bebbington, P. E., McBride, O., Steel, C., Kuipers, E. et al. (2013) 'The structure of paranoia in the general population.' *British Journal of Psychiatry*, 202, 419–427.
11 Lamster, F., Nittel, C., Rief, W., Mehl, S. & Lincoln, T. (2017) 'The impact of loneliness on paranoia: An experimental approach.' *Journal of Behavior Therapy & Experimental Psychiatry*, 54, 51–57.

thoughts may need to be addressed in any interventions for both loneliness and social anxiety.

If social anxiety leads to loneliness, and loneliness leads to social anxiety and paranoia, then many socially anxious individuals can end up living lonely lives in illusory worlds that exist only in their heads. It's a world that's threatening and populated by judgemental critics who scrutinise every word and action. If you're socially anxious, it's hard work living only in your head when loneliness may also be stealing your breath and choking you.

Social Anxiety, Social Media and Smartphone Use

Social networking sites should be extremely attractive to shy people and those with a social anxiety problem because they're environments where face-to-face interaction can be closely controlled. This will at least dispel some of the concerns that sufferers have about being observed while socialising and also allow them to interact with others at a distance and at their own pace. This provides more time to be sure that you're not committing faux pas, and that nothing is posted that you might later regret.

Lonely and socially anxious individuals regularly use social networking sites in the belief that it will relieve them of their loneliness and anxieties – often to the point where their use becomes something of an addiction, and we discussed some of the evidence relating to this in Chapter 3. For example, real-life social interaction is negatively associated with excessive use of Twitter[12], and social anxiety and the need for social reassurance are also associated with

12 Ndasauka, Y., Hou, J., Wang, Y., Yang, L. et al. (2016) 'Excessive use of Twitter among college students in the UK: Validation of the Microblog Excessive Use Scale and relationship to social interaction and loneliness.' *Computers in Human Behavior*, 55, 963–971.

use of Facebook to the point where it's almost a daily addiction[13]. The use of social media in this way can often have the opposite effect of that desired, and may simply make the socially anxious person feel lonelier and more disconnected when they end up interacting with Facebook in a passive way merely to update their own activities or follow the activities of others – activities that will simply reinforce feelings of disconnectedness[14].

However, there is a significant difference in the use of social media between those who are socially anxious and those who are lonely. Lonely people bring their lack of real-life relationships with them to sites like Facebook. They're less likely to post photos of family and friends (perhaps they simply have fewer photos), and are less likely to comment on photos posted by other Facebook users[15]. Lonely people are also more likely to use passive features of Facebook (such as 'liking' or playing games) than they are to use active features (such as sharing or communicating with other users)[16].

In contrast, socially anxious individuals tend to use Facebook at least as much as non-socially anxious individuals (up to 1¼ hours per day on average). They share most Facebook activities at the same level as non-anxious users, and post as many photos as non-socially anxious individuals. But while socially anxious individuals are keen

13 Lee-Won, R. J., Herzog, L. & Gwan Park, S. (2015) 'Hooked on Facebook: The role of social anxiety and need for social assurance in problematic use of Facebook.' *Cyberpsychology, Behaviour and Social Networking*, 18, 567–574.

14 Marche, S. (2012) 'Is Facebook making us lonely?' http://www.theatlantic.com/magazine/archive/2012/05/is-facebook-making-us-lonely/308930/

15 Scott, G. G., Boyle, E. A., Czerniawska, K. & Courtney, A. (2017) 'Posting photos on Facebook: The impact of narcissism, social anxiety, loneliness, and shyness.' *Personality & Individual Differences*, http://dx.doi.org/10.1016/j.paid.2016.12.039.

16 Ryan, T. & Xenos, S. (2011) 'Who uses Facebook? An investigation into the relationship between the Big Five, shyness, narcissism, loneliness, and Facebook usage.' *Computers in Human Behavior*, 27, 1658–1664.

to be connected and to use social media sites, they may do this as a substitute for real life.

Psychologists Erin Murphy and Tamara Tasker at the Pacific University Oregon surveyed 388 participants for Facebook use and levels of social anxiety. They found a significant positive relationship between time spent on Facebook and overall social anxiety score. They also discovered a further significant positive relationship between the participants' ratings of the ease with which they could use online communication and their social anxiety scores. It's not clear in what direction these relationships run, but they are consistent with the idea that socially anxious individuals find it easier to communicate in online settings. Murphy and Tasker conclude 'communication done by computer allows the (socially anxious) individual more control over the situation than face-to-face communication. For example, individuals can slow conversation, allowing them to think through, edit and delete thoughts if desired. They can get up and leave the computer (and thus the conversation) if they wish. Additionally, overt physiological symptoms of blushing, sweating, trembling and voice quivering are safely hidden from view.'[17]

While socially anxious individuals appear highly attracted to social media sites, cell phone data tell a slightly different story – using cell phones to make voice calls may be just a little bit too much like real-life interaction for the social phobic. As we might expect, socially anxious individuals prefer to text rather than make voice calls. This allows them time to think about the wording of their message, and to disengage from the multiple attentional requirements of real-time social interaction required by a voice call. In addition, individuals high in social anxiety rarely make outgoing

17 Murphy, E. & Tasker, T. (2011) 'Lost in a crowded room: A correlational study of Facebook and social anxiety.' In J. Barlow (Ed) *Interface: The Journal of Education, Community and Values*, vol 11, 89–94. Forest Grove.

voice calls in the evening and receive less incoming calls at any time than non-anxious individuals[18]. In contrast, lonely individuals prefer to make voice calls than to text, and rate texting as a less intimate method of contact – lonely people clearly prefer talking over texting, presumably as a way of achieving a more intimate contact that might alleviate their loneliness[19].

For the socially anxious person, it's not socialising *per se* that's the anathema; it's the real-time component of socialising that causes the problems. Wherever the real-time component can be set aside, then social interaction is perfectly acceptable – acceptable if there is time to edit and change communications, to avoid multiple attentional requirements that might lead to mistakes or faux pas, to avoid being observed while interacting, and to allow an opportunity to exit the interaction at any time. Social media and text messaging serve most of these purposes perfectly.

To Blush or Not to Blush

Have you ever spilt coffee over your boss? Have you ever been confronted about stealing the company's paper clips? Has your boss ever praised you for your excellent work during the company's annual review? And have you ever been subjected to the indignity of singing 'Old MacDonald Had a Farm' to your workmates during an away-day team-building exercise? All a part of the normal trials and tribulations of the modern-day corporate employee! But each of these scenarios has a different emotional and psychological focus. In order of scenario they are: ineptitude, guilt, pride and self-consciousness.

18 Gao, Y., Li, A., Zhu, T., Liu, X. & Liu, X. (2016) 'How smartphone usage correlates with social anxiety and loneliness.' PeerJ, doi: 10.7717/peerj.2197

19 Reid, D. J. & Reid, F J. M. (2007) 'Text or talk? Social anxiety, loneliness, and divergent preferences for cell phone use.' *CyberPsychology & Behavior*, 10, 424–435.

Yet they all have one thing in common – they're all situations that are likely to make you blush. Blushing is entirely out of your control – you can't make yourself blush, and you can't stop yourself blushing. So what is it, and why is it important?

A blush is a reddening of the cheeks and forehead that, if you're unlucky, can also extend to the ears, neck and upper chest. A blush seems to be produced by a combination of factors. The face has an extensive network of veins in its subcutaneous layers that hold a large volume of blood, and these blood vessels are particularly close to the surface in the cheeks. Activation of the sympathetic nervous system triggers receptors in the facial area that in turn cause vaso-dilation. This increases blood flow and causes the blush area to redden. Blushing is very distinctive, and differs from many other forms of facial reddening caused by such things as physical exertion, alcohol consumption, or a Friday night lamb vindaloo at the local Indian restaurant. Blushing isn't triggered by one particular emo-tion, but it does accompany a range of self-conscious emotions such as shame, guilt, shyness and pride. It represents the psychological state of 'embarrassment', especially when accompanied by a feeling of self-consciousness and ambivalent arousal (ambivalent arousal is a tendency to want to flee from the embarrassing situation when this would be socially inappropriate).

Blushing has a particular relevance for those who are socially anxious, and is the main complaint of one in three people who seek help for their social anxiety[20]. Many individuals who are socially anxious fear blushing in social situations because they believe others will judge them negatively for blushing, and this is often a factor that leads them to avoid social situations. Even in other cultures, blush-

20 Fahlén, T. (1997) 'Core symptom pattern of social phobia.' *Depression and Anxiety*, 4, 223–232.

ing is often perceived negatively. For example, *taijin kyofusho* (TKS) is one of Japan's most common phobias. Literally translated it means 'the fear of interpersonal relations', but while blushing in social anxiety disorder relates to the fear of oneself being embarrassed in front of others, TKS sufferers are fearful of embarrassing others with their blushing. The difference in fear focus between Westerners and Japanese folk almost certainly originates in differences in the cultural focus in Japan and the West. Western societies espouse individualism, while Japanese and many other Asian cultures embrace collectivism. So the Westerner as an individual is the one who is embarrassed by his/her blushing because others are watching, but the Japanese blusher is concerned about the reactions of the group and worried about causing offence by blushing (which could bring shame on family and friends).

But the socially anxious person's perception of their own blushing may be largely in their head. Studies suggest that social anxiety is highly correlated with self-perceived blushing, but not with physiological measures of blushing. That is, the socially anxious individual believes they blush more than non-socially anxious individuals, but this isn't upheld by physiological measures of their actual blushing[21] – yet another example of how erroneous beliefs about the self and the world act to maintain anxiety.

Because blushing is closely associated with self-consciousness, it's often been assumed that children can't blush until they develop self-consciousness. But a study by Milica Nikolić and colleagues from the University of Amsterdam found differently[22]. They asked four-and-a-half-year-old children to sing a song of their choice in

21 Nikolić, M., Colonnesi, C. & de Vente, W. (2015) 'Blushing and social anxiety: A meta-analysis.' *Clinical Psychology Science & Practice*, 22, 177–193.

22 Nikolić, M., Colonnesi, C., de Vente, W. & Bögels, S. M. (2016) 'Blushing in early childhood: Feeling coy or socially anxious?' *Emotion*, 16, 475–487.

front of an audience. Their performance was video-recorded and played back to them in front of the audience. They asked parents to report their children's social anxiety levels and also took physiological measures of blushing during the performance and during the watching-back task. They found that blushing, in combination with a low number of positive shy expressions (shyness expressed in a positive way with a coy smile and aversion of gaze), was associated with heightened social anxiety. They concluded that blushing appears to be an early indicator of social anxiety in children as young as four-and-a-half years.

But studies such as this raise some interesting questions about the function of blushing. Nikolić and colleagues argue that both blushing and positive shy expressions serve an evolved appeasement function in social situations – they serve to weaken other people's negative reactions to the blusher's behaviour and to make observers bond and empathise with them. A blush as an appeasement signal has a number of effects. It tells others that we're ashamed or embarrassed, that we're aware that something is not right, and that we'd probably like to put things right. It shows that we're not a brazen or shameless person, that we're communicating appeasement and providing a nonverbal apology[23]. In the context of appeasement, blushing has a number of benefits for the blusher. A person who blushes after a mishap is often liked more than someone who doesn't blush, is considered more positively by others, and promotes trust between themselves and their audience[24].

So if blushing has such an adaptive function, why do so many socially anxious people hate blushing? Why is the act of blushing

23 Crozier, R. (2010) 'The puzzle of blushing.' *The Psychologist*, 23, 390–393.
24 Aan het Rot, M., Moskowitz, D. S. & de Jong, P. J. (2015) 'Intrapersonal and interpersonal concomitants of facial blushing during everyday social encounters.' PLOS One, DOI:10.1371/journal.pone.0118243.

both a source and a consequence of anxiety? This may be related to a heightened sensitivity to evaluation by others, with socially anxious individuals being biased towards believing that all evaluation by others is likely to be negative. It's not clear where this bias might come from, although blushing is frequently experienced by the blusher in situations considered as embarrassing or shameful, and perceived as embarrassing by the observer as well – emotional experiences that are likely to be evaluated as negative and to imbue the blush itself with negative valence. In addition, because blushing is often a source of shame and anxiety, many social anxiety sufferers believe that people interpret a blush as a sign of social incompetence, weakness or loss of control[25]. These acquired beliefs may often override the adaptive value of the blush, and lead to many individuals seeking to avoid social situations where they might blush, and to interpreting blushing catastrophically when it does happen. My advice? Blush with confidence! There are likely to be more benefits than costs.

The Origins of Social Anxiety

Like most anxiety-based problems social anxiety runs in families – if you're socially anxious then it's probable that one or both of your parents also have social anxiety issues. When a mental health problem runs in families it usually means at least one of two things – there's a genetic element to the problem that's passed on from parents to children, or there's a parenting issue. A recent analysis of twin studies reported heritability estimates of 41 per cent for social anxiety disorder, slightly higher than for many other anxiety

25 Edelmann, R. J. (1990) 'Embarrassment and blushing: A component-process model, some initial descriptive and cross-cultural data.' In W. R. Crozier (Ed.) *Shyness and Embarrassment: Perspectives from Social Psychology*, 205–229. Cambridge University Press.

problems and suggesting that there may well be important temperament factors that are genetically transmitted[26]. While indicating
the importance of genetic influences, this does beg the question
of what aspect of social anxiety disorder is inherited. Some studies
have been able to identify specific characteristics related to social
anxiety disorder that appear to have a genetic component, and
these include submissiveness, anxiousness, social avoidance and
behavioural inhibition[27]. For example, many children seem quiet,
isolated and anxious when confronted either with social situations
or with novelty, and this characteristic has come to be defined by the
term *behavioural inhibition* (BI). BI represents a consistent tendency
to display extreme fearfulness, withdrawal, reticence and restraint
in the face of novelty[28], and toddlers exhibiting BI will show overt
distress and cling to their mothers in unfamiliar or novel situations.
They are also reluctant to approach novel objects, peers and adults.
Pre-schoolers with BI seem quiet and are reticent to speak or play
spontaneously, and by age seven the reluctance to socialise is found
mainly in group contexts. BI is estimated to have quite a high level
of inheritability – between 50 and 70 per cent[29], and BI is considered
to be a specific risk factor for social anxiety disorder.

26 Scaini, S., Belotti, R., & Ogliari, A. (2014) 'Genetic and environmental
contributions to social anxiety across different ages: A meta-analytic approach
to twin data.' *Journal of Anxiety Disorders*, 28, 650–656.

27 Warren, S. L., Schmitz, S. & Emde, R. N. (1999) 'Behavioral genetic
analyses of self- reported anxiety at 7 years of age.' *Journal of the American
Academy of Child and Adolescent Psychiatry*, 38(11), 1403–1408.

28 Hirschfeld-Becker, D. R. (2010) 'Familial and temperamental risk
factors for social anxiety disorder.' *New Directions for Child and Adolescent Development*, 127, 51–65.

29 Smoller, J. W. & Tsuang, M. T. (1998) 'Panic and phobic anxiety:
Defining phenotypes for genetic studies.' *American Journal of Psychiatry*, 155,
1152–1162.

Figure 10.1 Behavioural inhibition is a largely inherited temperament characteristic in which a child displays extreme fearfulness and reticence in the face of novelty – often clinging to their mothers in unfamiliar or novel situations.

But environmental and experiential factors also appear to account for a significant proportion of the variance in levels of social anxiety, suggesting that social anxiety may also be influenced by parenting factors, the frequency of negative or traumatic life events, and adverse social experiences[30]. Let's start with one of the usual suspects – parenting!

Paula Barrett and colleagues at the University of Queensland asked children aged seven to fourteen years and their parents to separately interpret and provide plans of action for a couple of hypothetical scenarios[31]. These scenarios were ambiguous and could

30 Norton, A. R. & Abbott, M. J. (2017) 'The role of environmental factors in the aetiology of social anxiety disorder: A review of the theoretical and empirical literature.' *Behaviour Change*, 34, 76–97.

31 Barrett, P. M., Rapee, R. M., Dadds, M. & Ryan, S. M. (1996) 'Family enhancement of cognitive style in anxious and aggressive children.' *Journal of Abnormal Child Psychology*, 24, 187–203.

either be interpreted as negative or benign. For example, 'You see a group of children from another class playing a great game. As you (your child) walk over and want to join in, you notice that they are laughing. What do you think is happening?' They are then asked to choose between a benign interpretation of what's happening ('they will soon ask you to join in') and a negative interpretation ('they are telling secrets about you'). After the child and the parents had separately given their responses, they were asked to have a five-minute family discussion together and then provide a final response about what they would do in that situation. They found that anxious children were more likely to choose the negative interpretation of the scenarios as were the parents of those anxious children, but perhaps more interestingly, the anxious children chose even *more* avoidant plans of action after discussing the scenario with their parents. The researchers suggested that families provide the context in which children learn to interpret and respond to social situations, and that anxious thinking and anxious behaviour may be modelled, supported and reinforced by anxious parents. Consistent with this, socially anxious individuals are more likely to have anxious parents who tend to be less socially active and more inhibited, and may model social avoidance, as well as restricting or preventing social engagement or denying their offspring the opportunity to develop social skills.

Having the opportunity in childhood to experience social situations first hand, develop social autonomy and acquire social skills is critical for normal social development – something that over-controlling and overprotective parents may well stifle. We came across overprotective parents in Chapter 4 – those helicopter, bubble-wrap and snowplough parents who control and protect many aspects of their children's' lives, but in doing so provide the basis for a future of anxious thinking and avoidant behaviour. Over the past twenty years enough evidence has accrued on this issue to fill a large library. For example, adults with social anxiety tend to recall their parents being over-controlling and restricting their autonomy; parents of socially anxious children display more controlling behaviour during a challenging task with their children; higher maternal control at age seven years predicts social anxiety during adolescence; over-controlling and overprotective parenting communicates to a child that they lack the capacity to cope with challenging situations and require protection from a dangerous world; and over-controlling parents provide more negative feedback to their children, which may lead to them becoming hypervigilant for and preoccupied with the perceived likelihood of negative social evaluation. Need I go on? But having said this, overprotective and over-controlling parenting doesn't necessarily mean that a child *will* develop social anxiety, merely that it significantly increases the risk of this.

Finally in relation to parenting factors, an insecure attachment style is also a predictor of social anxiety – especially an anxious-ambivalent attachment style that is often the product of erratic and unpredictable parenting[32]. Such inconsistency in the parent–child relationship creates anxiety surrounding the availability of attachment figures that can lead to distrust in future relationships and a fear of social exclusion or rejection. Individuals with social anxiety will often exhibit a preoccupied attachment style that is associated with discomfort in close relationships, low levels of trust in others, and anxiety at the prospect of rejection or abandonment[33].

The over-controlling, less warm and more rejecting parent styles that we've seen to be risk factors for social anxiety also have their

32 Kerns, K., & Brumariu, L. (2014) 'Is insecure parent–child attachment a risk factor for the development of anxiety in childhood or adolescence?' *Child Development Perspectives*, 8, 12–17.
33 Eng, W., Heimberg, R., Hart, T., Schneier, F., & Liebowitz, M. (2001) 'Attachment in individuals with social anxiety disorder: The relationship among adult attachment styles, social anxiety, and depression.' *Emotion*, 1, 365–380.

impact in other indirect ways. Such parents also inflict greater levels of emotional and physical maltreatment on their children (through rejection or physical abuse of the child when the child does things that the parents disapprove of), and this has been shown to increase the severity of social anxiety in later life[34]. This is particularly true of physical abuse. A study by psychiatrists at the Hospital Parc Taulí in Barcelona found that family violence predicted greater social anxiety among Spanish university students[35], and this is consistent with other research finding that having an aggressive mother or father increases the risk of social anxiety, as does domestic physical abuse. There is also a long list of other negative family events that can increase the risk of social anxiety, and these include the death of a parent, parental marital discord, parental separation and divorce, and having to start a new school. But they are not specific risk factors for social anxiety alone and also predict other anxiety-based problems and mental health problems generally[36].

Are these risk factors for social anxiety on the increase? At least some of them certainly are. Risk factors such as overprotective parenting, childhood abuse, and parental divorce and separation are all on the increase. There are micromanaging and 'full-service' forms of parenting that have become increasingly popular since the 1980s because of factors such as the increased awareness of childhood

34 Bruce, L., Heimberg, R., Blanco, C., Schneier, F., & Liebowitz, M. (2012) 'Childhood maltreatment and social anxiety disorder: Implications for symptom severity and response to pharmacotherapy.' *Depression and Anxiety*, 29, 131–138.

35 Binelli, C., Ortiz, A., Muniz, A., Gelabert, E., Ferraz, L., Filho, A., Crippa, J., Nardi, A., Subira, S., & Martin-Santos, R. (2012) 'Social anxiety and negative early life events in university students.' *Revistra Brasileira de Psiquiatria*, 34, S69–S80.

36 Norton, A. R. & Abbott, M. J. (2017) 'The role of environmental factors in the aetiology of social anxiety disorder: A review of the theoretical and empirical literature.' *Behaviour Change*, 34, 76–97.

abductions, the growing taboo of leaving children alone, the need to supervise increasing homework loads and, in an increasingly busy world, the need to supervise and schedule a child's play and educational activities (see Chapter 4)[37]. In the context of childhood abuse, police forces in England and Wales have been dealing with growing numbers of child abuse incidents in recent years[38] (see also Chapter 4), and there has been a steadily increasing trend in parental marital discord and divorce over the past twenty-five years in Westernised countries such as the UK and the USA[39,40] (Chapter 3). So we should expect an already prevalent anxiety problem such as social anxiety to increase in prevalence over the next decade as the concoction of risk factors that precipitates this condition continues to affect more and more families.

'There's Nothing Crueller than a Bunch of School Kids' – The Rise of Cyber-Victimisation

I suspect that very few of you are aware that Sigmund Freud wrote a book about jokes – no, not the Sigmund Freud collection of hilarious after-dinner jokes and anecdotes. It's called *The Joke and its Relation to the Unconscious*, and it explores the psychological purpose of joke telling, wit, comedy and teasing[41], and he argues that jokes and witticisms are often socially acceptable ways of expressing views and emotions that otherwise would cause offence. A joke usually involves

---

37 http://uk.businessinsider.com/the-rise-of-the-helicopter-parent-2015-7

38 https://www.ons.gov.uk/peoplepopulationandcommunity/crime-andjustice/articles/abuseduringchildhood/findingsfromtheyearending march2016crimesurveyforenglandandwales#main-points

39 http://www.ons.gov.uk/peoplepopulationandcommunity/birthsdeaths andmarriages/divorce/bulletins/divorcesinenglandandwales/2013

40 https://www.cdc.gov/nchs/nvss/marriage_divorce_tables.htm

41 Freud, S. (2002) *The Joke and its Relation to the Unconscious*. Penguin Modern Classics.

a joke-teller, an audience or listener, and a butt or scapegoat, with the joke itself often directing hostility or cynicism towards the butt of the joke, but in a socially acceptable way that involves pleasure and laughter (at least for the joke-teller and the audience). The joke can represent a concealed form of aggression that bestows the joke-teller with some degree of dominance and social control, and the butt of the joke with stigma and rejection. Even entire countries are known for their own specific targets of 'put-down' humour[42]. The French poke fun at the Belgians; Canadians love to tell jokes about people from Newfoundland ('Newfie' jokes); and in the past the butt of English jokes has often been the Irish.

For school-aged kids, a joke often comes in the form of teasing or name-calling (which is only a short step away from verbal bullying), but even in a child's world a joke and a tease can still be a concealed form of aggression that can cause harm to its targets. Adults with social anxiety disorder are more likely to report having had a child-hood history of teasing, and one study reported that over 92 per cent of individuals they interviewed suffering from social anxiety disorder reported severe teasing in childhood[43]. The playground bully may cause as much damage with a well-directed cynical remark as with a slap or a punch.

Peer 'relational victimisation' can also be a significant risk factor for later social anxiety. Relational victimisation refers to such things as exclusion from a social group and also emotional bullying, and can result in the victim having fewer friends, less peer acceptance, and difficulty making new friends, and relational victimisation may

42 http://www.laughterremedy.com/article_pdfs/Negative%20%20 Humor.pdf

43 McCabe, R., Antony, M., Summerfeldt, L.., Liss, A., & Swinson, R. (2003) 'Preliminary examination of the relationship between anxiety disorders in adults and self-reported history of teasing or bullying experiences.' *Cognitive Behaviour Therapy*, 32, 187–93.

even have a greater impact on social anxiety than overt physical victimisation[44]. In addition, given that modern-day school children spend much of their time socialising via social media, there's growing evidence that cyber-victimisation can also lead to social anxiety[45], and kids who are peer-victimised in a traditional face-to-face context are often cyber-victimised by peers as well. If you're a blossoming bully, cyber-victimisation has a lot to recommend it. It has the potential for anonymity of the perpetrator and the ability to broadcast damaging information to a significantly wider audience than in traditional forms of playground bullying. Furthermore, turning off your laptop or smartphone doesn't prevent the cyber-attack from being seen by peers. Cyber-bullying offers little escape for the victim. Anyone with a laptop or a smartphone can be cyber-bullied. Whereas bullying used to happen in the confines of the school grounds, the Internet now enables bullying to occur at any time and in front of a potentially infinite audience. In schoolyard bullying, the victim is frequently the physically weaker kid preyed on by an older and bigger peer, but online, the ranks of the bully can now be joined by the weaker kids where computer prowess is more important than physical brawn[46].

Being bullied is a significant risk factor for subsequent social anxiety, but bullying is changing. It's moving from the schoolyard to the Internet, it's becoming relational rather than physical. In theory anyone with a smartphone and a belligerent inclination

44 Tillfors, M., Persson, S., Willen, M., & Burk, W. (2012) 'Prospective links between social anxiety and adolescent peer relations.' *Journal of Adolescence*, 35, 1255–1263.

45 Landoll, R., La Greca, A., Lai, B., Chan, S., & Herge, W. (2015) 'Cyber victimization by peers: Prospective associations with adolescent social anxiety and depressive symptoms.' *Journal of Adolescence*, 42, 77–86.

46 Rosewarne, L. (2017) '"Nothing crueler than high school students": The cyberbully in film and television.' *International Journal of Technoethics*, 8, 1–17.

can become a cyber-bully, and the audience that can observe these acts of cyber-bullying is potentially unlimited and geographically far-reaching. Unless we can find effective ways to manage cyber-bullying amongst school kids, we must accept that we'll have growing levels of adolescent and adult anxiety – especially in the form of social anxiety.

The Psychology of Social Anxiety

There's not a lot of socialising going on in social anxiety, but there's certainly a lot of thinking! People with social anxiety appear to have developed some very biased ways of thinking that maintain their social anxiety over time.

Let's begin with a simple demonstration. UK Clinical Psychologist Warren Mansell and colleagues conducted a very simple experiment with participants who were either high or low on measures of social anxiety. Each participant was asked to make a three-minute speech on a controversial topic to a TV monitor that they believed displayed six people who were watching their performance live. Two audience members exhibited only positive behaviours during the speech (nodding, leaning forward, smiling), two audience members exhibited only negative behaviours (yawning, looking round, shaking head), and the remaining two exhibited only neutral behaviours (adjusting seat position, playing with a pen).

After the speeches, the high social anxiety participants reported that overall the audience had judged their performance significantly more negatively than the low socially anxious participants. More specifically, high social anxious participants were selectively attending to audience members who were negatively evaluating them, and ignoring the positive or neutral behaviours of the remaining audience. The researchers concluded that socially anxious individuals base their judgements of being disapproved by others on limited processing of their social environment[47] – namely a biased processing of only potentially negative information about their performance.

The heads of the socially anxious are full of negative biases of this kind. This leads to excessively negative predictions about future social events, and this biased evaluation helps to support social avoidance behaviours. They are more likely to interpret ambiguous social information negatively, and interpret their own performances in social situations significantly more critically than non-sufferers and independent assessors who have objectively observed and rated their performance[48]. They themselves are their most hardened and destructive critics. In addition, the socially anxious have a genuine block when it comes to receiving and processing positive social feedback, and have an inability to take anything 'good' from a social performance[49]. These information-processing biases make it almost inevitable that the socially anxious are going to negatively evaluate themselves and their performance in social situations and severely underestimate their own social skills – self-judgements that are all grist to the mill of beating yourself up and avoiding the next social interaction.

So what facilitates this almost single-minded focus on negativity and poor self-evaluation? Well, socially anxious individuals tend to shift their focus of attention inwards on to themselves and their own anxiety when in social situations. I can remember many examples of

47 Perowne, S. & Mansell, W. (2002) 'Social anxiety, self-focussed attention, and the discrimination of negative, neutral and positive audience members by their nonverbal behaviours.' *Behavioural & Cognitive Psychotherapy*, 30, 11–23.

48 Dodd, H. F., Hudson, J. L., Lyneham, H. J., Wuthrich, V. M., Morris, T. & Monier, L. (2011) 'Self-ratings and observer-ratings of social skill: A manipulation of state social anxiety in anxious and non-anxious children.' *Journal of Experimental Psychopathology*, 2(4), 571–585.

49 Alden, L. E., Mellings, T. M. B. & Laposa, J. M. (2004) 'Framing social information and generalized social phobia.' *Behaviour Research and Therapy* 42(5), 585–600.

this from my own youth. On one school speech day I had to walk from the audience on to the stage to receive my prize. As far as I was concerned I felt like a condemned man walking towards the hangman's gibbet. The stage was an unfocused blur and all I could feel was a pair of wobbly legs taking me step by every tortuous step up the aisle nearer to what I felt was about to be a social catastrophe in a swelteringly hot assembly hall. As it happens, it wasn't a social catastrophe and I picked up my prize and shook hands with the distinguished somebody who was there to make the day important. But afterwards I vowed never to do that again because everyone must have seen me wobbling tentatively towards the stage on shaking legs and with a brow soaked in anxious sweat. But everyone I spoke to afterwards said they didn't see anything unusual. I wasn't a quivering jelly, I wasn't covered in sweat, and I didn't look anxious . . . but I didn't believe them. From my perspective I was a walking embarrassment.

This shift of attention inwards in socially anxious individuals is known as *self-focused attention* and leads those who are socially anxious to believe they may look as anxious as they feel inside[50]. It's interesting that those with social anxiety often recall social memories from an observer perspective rather than a personal perspective. In one study, socially anxious individuals were asked to recall a recent specific occasion when they felt anxious and uncomfortable in a social situation. They were allowed thirty seconds to image the scene and were then given the following instruction: 'Thinking about the image you've just had, is your predominant impression one of viewing the situation as if looking through your eyes, observing the details of what is going on around you or is the predominant impression one in which you are observing yourself as if you were outside yourself

50 Spurr, J. M. & Stopa, L. (2002) 'Self-focused attention in social phobia and social anxiety.' *Clinical Psychology Review*, 22, 947–975.

looking at yourself from an external point of view?' In memories of social situations, the socially anxious reported a marked observer perspective whereas non-socially anxious individuals took a field perspective (seeing the situation as if looking through their own eyes)[51]. Interestingly, my own memory of that school speech day is very much from an observer perspective – I'm hovering above the assembled throng watching myself walk unsteadily and anxiously up the aisle towards the stage. This rather odd perspective-taking is almost certainly a post-event mental construction (no one has yet convinced me that I can actually hover above crowds taking images of the scene below like a camera drone). If you're fully focused only on your internal reactions, you'll have no sensory memory of the external features of the social event from your own physical per-spective – only memories of your own feelings. It's presumably from these anxious feelings that I constructed my observer-based perspec-tive of an anxious perspiring figure hopelessly staggering through the lines of assembled parents attempting to reach the stage without any embarrassing mishap. A perspective seemingly not shared by anyone else in the audience.

Self-focused attention in social situations is itself a cause of anxiety, facilitates negative thoughts during the social interaction, and generates an expectation that others will rate you more nega-tively – and this occurs in both adults and children[52]. So switching to a self-focused mode is only likely to increase the severity of any anxiety feelings you have at the time.

51 Wells, A., Clark, D. M. & Ahmad, S. (1998) 'How do I look with my minds eye: Perspective taking in social phobic imagery.' *Behaviour Research and Therapy*, 36, 631–634.

52 Kley, H., Tuschen-Caffier, B. & Heinrichs, N. (2011) 'Manipulating self-focussed attention in children with social anxiety disorder and in socially anxious and non-anxious children.' *Journal of Experimental Psychopathology*, 2, 551–570.

Finally, even when the social interaction is over, the socially anxious individual can't leave it alone. If it's not bad enough predicting bad things happening prior to a social interaction, and then focusing on anxious feelings during the event, the socially anxious person will then ruminate on their performance excessively after the event. After each significant social interaction, socially anxious individuals become their very own highly critical appraisal manager. They indulge in excessive post-event processing of social events that includes critical self-appraisal and an assessment of the severity of their anxiety symptoms – a process that has the effect of maintaining negative appraisals of performance over time and maintaining social anxiety[53].

This concatenation of cognitive and information processing biases has a monumental effect on anyone who is socially anxious. It maintains the predominant focus on feelings of anxiety during social events, generates highly critical self-evaluations of performance, prevents the processing of positive feedback, and spawns hours of ruminative negative thought about previous social interactions – all of which feed the anxiety beast itself, maintaining social anxiety and supporting active avoidance of social situations. But because we've been able to identify each of these different elements contributing to social anxiety, the shining ray of positive light here is that we can develop effective cognitive-based interventions to help manage each of them and significantly reduce the symptoms of social anxiety, and many of these techniques are already being deployed by therapists and organisations offering CBT services[54].

53 Rachman, S., Gruter-Andrew, J. & Shafran, R. (2000) 'Post-event processing in social anxiety.' *Behaviour Research and Therapy*, 38(6), 611–617.

54 https://www.div12.org/psychological-treatments/disorders/social-phobia-and-public-speaking-anxiety/cognitive-behavioral-therapy-for-social-anxiety-disorder/

Thumbnail Sketch

I began this chapter with a quote – 'You probably wouldn't worry about what people think of you if you could know how seldom they do!' Indeed, your opinion of how much other people judge you is almost certainly hugely exaggerated – but I suspect you secretly knew that anyway. Because the fear of being judged or evaluated is a significant factor in many cases of social anxiety, those with social anxiety often view themselves as failing to meet what they perceive as the higher social standards set by others, and they may often see this as a flaw or failing in themselves – a flaw or failing that makes them reluctant to seek help for their problem. Another factor that will make the socially anxious reluctant to seek treatment is that seeking help is itself a social activity, and they may find it extremely difficult to interact with healthcare professionals, staff and other service users. In part because of these issues only about half of those with diagnosable social anxiety ever seek treatment, and those who do seek treatment do so only after suffering up to twenty years of symptoms[55]. Unless we find more acceptable ways of identifying social anxiety and facilitating accessible treatments, social anxiety is likely to be a significant part of the modern anxiety epidemic for many years to come.

Many of the risk factors for social anxiety are also on the increase. Loneliness is nearing epidemic proportions, and we know there's a reciprocal relationship between loneliness and social anxiety. Factors such as living alone, divorce and increased longevity are all contributing to the social circumstances that create loneliness, with the assumption that these will impact on social anxiety as well.

55 Grant, B., Hasin, D., Blanco, C., Stinson, F., Chou, S., Goldstein, R. B. (2005) 'The epidemiology of social anxiety disorder in the United States: Results from the National Epidemiologic Survey on Alcohol and Related Conditions.' *Journal of Clinical Psychiatry*, 11, 1351–1361.

Overprotective forms of parenting have also become increasingly popular since the 1980s, a fact that may leave us with an upcoming generation of socially anxious young adults. And our current generation of youngsters has a new technology that makes its own contribution to social anxiety. Smartphones and social media allow the socially anxious to conduct many of their social encounters outside of the real-time component that fuels much of their social anxiety – yet another reason for them to avoid real-life social situations and avoid seeking help. Smartphones and social media also provide a modern means to troll and bully others. These enable bullying to move from the schoolyard to the Internet. Anyone with a smartphone or a laptop can become a cyber-bully, and similarly, anyone can become a victim. The known link between being cyber-bullied and social anxiety makes this just another means of spreading the social anxiety epidemic.

CHAPTER ELEVEN

'Soldier's Heart'

The Effects of Trauma in the Modern World

'Some people's lives seem to flow in a narrative; mine had many stops and starts. That's what trauma does. It interrupts the plot. You can't process it because it doesn't fit with what came before or what comes afterwards.'

— Jessica Stern, *Denial: A Memoir of Terror*

In her book *Denial: A Memoir of Terror*, Jessica Stern goes on to quote a soldier friend of hers: 'In most of our lives, most of the time, you have a sense of what is to come. There is a steady narrative, a feeling of "lights, camera, action" when big events are imminent. But trauma isn't like that. It just happens, and then life goes on. No one prepares you for it.'

Janice Brooks from Brentwood in Essex was a personal assistant working on the eighty-fourth floor of the South Tower of the World Trade Center on the morning of 11 September 2001. It was 8.40 a.m. Her story, as reported in the *Daily Mail*, was that she was sitting at her desk after an early morning run along the Hudson River when she heard a very loud, dull thud, and then to her surprise saw thousands of scraps of paper swirling past the window. Someone yelled 'Everybody out!' But she stayed to phone her boss to let him know she was leaving. 'F**king hell, Janice, a plane has gone into the North Tower. Get the f**k out of there!' was all she remembers him saying.

She recounted how she made her way into a stairwell that was already full with people fleeing the building – she could already feel the heat from the intense fires burning in the other tower. Then, as she made her way through a fire door, she was halted abruptly as the walls and floor shook violently and almost knocked her off her feet. It was United Airlines Flight 175 hitting her tower and tearing through six floors directly above her – one of those floors was the eighty-fourth where moments earlier Janice had been sitting at her desk. Dust and debris swirled down the stairwell engulfing those fleeing. The ceiling tiles fell in and door frames buckled.

Janice can't speak about what happened next without crying. A woman came through a door leading on to the stairwell. Half her arm was hanging off as through it had been sliced through by a machete. Then a man appeared with huge shards of glass embedded in his chest. They tried opening fire doors but after they successfully prized open the first one, the staircase to safety had been blown away by the blast. Janice had lost her shoes and her feet were lacerated by grit and debris. Their flight through the thick smoke was accompanied by coughing, sobbing and, periodically, blood-curdling screams.

Eventually they found an undamaged staircase. Janice realised that blood was seeping between her toes as she trod in the footsteps of those who'd gone before. They finally reached the ground floor plaza and Janice realised the enormity of what had happened. It was 9.39 a.m. A policeman hurried her to the street exit adding, 'Don't look up. Just keep your head down and run!'[1] She ran for her life. The first and only time she'd experienced the terror of running to save her life.

1 From http://www.dailymail.co.uk/news/article-136382/9-11--Survivors-Twin-Towers.html

In life, some of us are dealt extreme experiences that we'd never wish on anyone. These events often threaten our very existence or result in serious injury, physical attack or sexual violation. Such traumas challenge our very concept of feeling safe to the point where we believe we can never truly feel safe again. In 2001 the terrorist attack on the twin towers of the World Trade Center in New York was just one such event, and these events seem so extreme in their nature that we assume they must be quite rare, but in fact around 50 per cent of all adults experience at least one event in their lifetime that can be considered equivalent to 9/11 in terms of its perceived threat to the individual's own life and physical safety[2]. These events can occur in many forms, including natural disasters like earthquakes, floods and tsunamis. They can be the consequence of international conflict and include torture, prisoner-of-war experiences and combat trauma. Physical abuse such as rape and other forms of physical violence are common causes of trauma, and even personal accidents such as involvement in a motor vehicle accident can have a long-lasting effect on a person's mental health.

But anxiety as such wasn't a relevant precursor of 9/11 because that event was certainly not one that would have been predicted by those who left home for work in the twin towers on 11 September 2001. There would have been no anticipatory apprehension. But what about the consequences for those who survived?

After extreme traumatic life events such as these, many survivors live with the painful and distressing symptoms of post-traumatic stress disorder. They cannot sleep. They are continually replaying the events of the trauma in their mind. Their experiences are relived in vivid nightmares. They have difficulty concentrating, are jittery

2 Ozer, R. J. & Weiss, D. S. (2004) 'Who develops posttraumatic stress disorder?' *Current Directions in Psychological Science*, 13, 169–172.

and easily startled by sudden movements or loud noises. They live with feelings of shame and guilt, and an enduring inability to cope with the future. They avoid anything that might remotely remind them of the events associated with the trauma.

The psychological effects of extreme events such as 9/11 have their own diagnostic category in the American Psychiatric Association's manual of psychiatric disorders[3] – *post-traumatic stress disorder*, or PTSD for short. Although PTSD is officially classified as a stress- or trauma-related disorder, anxiety has its grubby fingerprints all over this condition. We've already encountered Frank in the Waiting Room in Chapter 1. Frank was someone who had already experienced some non-life-threatening trauma in the form of painful dental treatments, and the anxiety symptoms generated prior to future visits to the dentist were very similar to many of the symptoms that define PTSD – but these were anxiety responses that were primarily restricted to those times when Frank was required to enter the dentist's waiting room once again.

Now imagine something slightly different. First, much of the anxiety we've discussed previously may be delusional in the sense that the anxious individual has never yet experienced the anticipated threats that fuel their anxiety, and many of the events that make them anxious are often very unlikely to happen. But what if you know from first-hand experience the horrifying severity of the threat that's on your mind because you've already experienced it? This is the plight of the PTSD sufferer, living day and night with the vivid memories of the trauma in a world whose benevolence and safety has been severely thrown into doubt – a life now lived with an anxiety of life itself.

3 American Psychiatric Association (2013) *Diagnostic and Statistical Manual of Mental Disorders* (5th edition). Washington, DC: American Psychiatric Association.

The distinctive symptoms of PTSD are usually grouped into four categories: (1) uncontrollable, intrusive symptoms such as vivid visual flashbacks and intrusive thoughts about the experienced event; (2) our old enemy avoidance responding, including active avoidance of thoughts, memories or reminders of the trauma; (3) increased arousal and hypervigilance and exaggerated startle responses to sudden events; and (4) negative changes in mood including persistent feelings of fear, horror, anger, shame or guilt, and persistent negative beliefs about oneself, other people or the world itself. This is a formidable package of symptoms, but what most perplexes researchers into the causes of PTSD is that not all of those who experience an extreme life-threatening event develop PTSD. Just over one in three people who experience severe trauma go on to develop actual symptoms[4], so what is it about PTSD sufferers that makes them so vulnerable to this debilitating condition?

Soldier's Heart, Shell Shock and Post-Vietnam Syndrome

Some of the most brutal life-threatening events come in the context of war and conflict, so we can trace the history of PTSD symptoms in combat troops who've been involved in wars throughout the centuries. Interestingly, PTSD only appeared as a defined diagnostic category in 1980, but the symptoms of PTSD had been known for some time – especially in relation to the psychological problems exhibited by combat veterans. It's been given various names including 'Combat Stress Reaction' in World War II, 'Shell Shock' during World War I, and 'Soldier's Heart' in the post-American Civil War era when it was recognised that many veterans had been significantly changed by their combat experiences.

4 http://www.ptsdunited.org/ptsd-statistics-2/

'Soldier's Heart' was a term coined by the American cardiologist Jacob Mendes Da Costa to describe a form of cardiac neurosis in which the cardiovascular system of returning Civil War veterans had seemed to be significantly changed by their experiences[5]. But at this time the frightening visual flashbacks experienced by sufferers were not considered to be the result of anxiety, trauma or neurosis, but of nostalgia! If a Vermonter had an uncontrollable flashback of marching through Georgia with Sherman's Army, this was assumed to be because he was nostalgic for being back in Vermont! Such are the politics of war that even the bad things need to be given a positive spin.

It was only after tens of thousands of Vietnam veterans returned to the USA scarred by their experiences during that twenty-year Asian war that the scale of the psychological effects of combat became evident. The nature of the Vietnam War threw together a relatively new mix of combat events, political circumstances and psychological factors that traumatised many of the veterans who served there. Many who served in Vietnam were reluctant soldiers because of the draft, and were thrown directly into combat after a brief period of training. In addition, the nature of the warfare in Vietnam made it hard for the Americans to know who the enemy were. Americans fought alongside the South Vietnamese Army, but the rebel Viet Cong were also recruited from amongst the South Vietnamese population and controlled many of the towns in the south. Fighting in dense jungle against an enemy that was difficult to identify significantly degraded a soldier's psychological well-being. The political background to the war also prolonged the veterans' post-war stress. A significant proportion of American citizens disapproved of the war, and veterans were not welcomed home as

5 Wooley, C. F. (1982) 'Jacob Mendes Da Costa: Medical teacher, clinician, and clinical investigator.' *American Journal of Cardiology*, 50, 1145–1148.

heroes but often as murderers, and were not encouraged to talk about their war experiences in the way that veterans of previous conflicts had been. The rotation patterns used during the Vietnam War prevented soldiers from working through their combat experiences before being thrown back into American society. If they survived their year of duty they were flown home on a commercial airliner – often still wearing their muddied fatigues, leaving behind their army buddies – and in a severely jet-lagged state were dropped into the chaos of an American urban traffic jam to fend for themselves[6].

Mike was a Navy corpsman (an enlisted medical specialist) who sailed to Vietnam in 1967[7]. 'I was surrounded by death in Vietnam. No one needs to tell me how lucky I was. Statistics weren't on my side. I was a field corpsman, a prized target.' There were no frontlines in Vietnam. If you were there, you were in it. Everyone had the opportunity to get killed. 'I knew at least a dozen corpsmen who died there. I still wonder why I survived and those others didn't. I've been dealing with this for decades. It's called "survivor's guilt", a symptom of PTSD. When I came home, I thought I was fine. But over time I became short-tempered and paranoid. I was always on edge and alert – "hypervigilant" they call it. I thought that was a good thing. You know why? Because that's what can save your life in a war. Ten years ago, I'd been homeless for three-and-a-half years, living under a tree in a vacant lot. My PTSD was raw. I was hurting. My anger built up, and my alcohol abuse exploded. I was becoming a danger to others and myself.'

Mike finally built up courage to attend a Vet Center for counselling directed at his anger and low self-esteem, and eventually became a retired gardener living in Concord, California.

6 Brinson, T. & Treanor, V. (2005) 'Vietnam Veterans and Alcoholism.' *The VVA Veteran* March/April 2005 http://www.vva.org/archive/TheVeteran/2005_03/feature_alcoholism.htm
7 http://www.anothersource.org/torment_1.html

The term *Post-Vietnam Syndrome* was used to describe returning soldiers with trauma symptoms, but many were not given either treatment or compensation if their symptoms occurred within six months of returning home because it was then assumed it was a pre-existing condition that preceded combat experience[8]. In the absence of any compensation, support and treatment for their condition, many Vietnam vets turned to self-medication as a solution, and amongst Vietnam veterans subsequently seeking treatment for PTSD, between 60 and 80 per cent had alcohol-use disorders[9].

Even though the experiences of returning Vietnam War veterans were far from acceptable, subsequent understanding of their symptoms did contribute to the diagnostic criteria for PTSD being defined for the first time in 1980, and PTSD was identified as a diagnostic category that extended well beyond the battlefield to a range of extreme experiences that inflicted life-threatening horrors on the sufferer.

Since the days of Vietnam, a good deal of research has been focused on the reactions of American combat troops in subsequent conflicts such as the Gulf War, the Iraq War and Afghanistan. The statistics don't encourage us to believe that experiences of post-traumatic stress are on the decrease in combat zones – even though we may be led to believe that war is in fact becoming a more sanitised process in which technological advances have improved battlefield conditions for frontline troops. We now have direct drone strikes, non-lethal weapons, precision bombing and autonomous killing machines – all of which are supposed to minimise non-combat casualties and protect combat soldiers. But as US Civil War General Robert E. Lee once said, 'It is well that war is so terrible, otherwise we should grow too fond of it.'

8 http://historyofptsd.umwblogs.org/vietnam/
9 https://www.recoveryfirst.org/blog/addiction-and-alcoholism-in-vietnam-war-veterans/

However, even in these modern times, combat zones still feel the horror of barrel bombs and chemical weapons. A war is not yet a clinically intellectual game of chess and never will be. It's a matter of life and death. Not only for those in the combat zone, but often for those waging the war. There's good reason for the combatants to make the experience of war as terrifying as they can because it's all about subduing opponents and crushing their will to fight (very few ever wage a war half-heartedly). Sanitised or not, the experience of putting yourself in the front line of a war zone will be nonetheless traumatic.

So is war less dangerous for a soldier in the modern era? The death rate for Union soldiers during the American Civil War was 16.4 per cent of soldiers deployed. The American military death rate during World War II was 2.5 per cent. During the Vietnam War this rate dropped to 0.6 per cent. For the Gulf War this was 0.017 per cent[10], and for American troops deployed in Iraq and Afghanistan up to 2012 it was 0.27 per cent[11]. So, the good news for military personnel is that in modern times your risk of being killed in combat is significantly reduced, but this doesn't seem to have affected the levels of PTSD reported in military personnel generally. Levels of PTSD in Gulf War veterans are estimated at between 4 and 9 per cent[12], and in veterans of the wars in Iraq and Afghanistan around 8 per cent[13].

10 Leland, A., & Oboroceanu, M -J. (2010). American war and military operations casualties: lists and statistics. Washington, DC: *Congressional Research Service*. www.crs.gov RL32492.

11 www.defense.gov/news/casualty.pdf

12 Wolfe, J., Brown, P. J. & Kelley, J. M. (1993) 'Reassessing war stress: Exposure and the Persian Gulf War.' *Journal of Social Issues*, 49, 15–31.

13 Smith, T. C., Ryan, M. A. K., Wingard, D. L., Slymen, D. J., Sallis, J. F., Kritz-Silverstein, D., & Millennium Cohort Study Team (2008) 'New onset and persistent symptoms of post-traumatic stress disorder self-reported after deployment and combat exposures: Prospective population based US military cohort study.' *British Medical Journal*, 336, 366–371.

These are conservative estimates based on more detailed diagnostic assessments, but many other studies report levels of post-traumatic stress symptoms in up to 18 per cent of deployed military personnel in Vietnam[14], and over 15 per cent in the Gulf War[15]. The lifetime prevalence rate for PTSD in the general population is much lower at between 1 and 3 per cent, so military personnel are at least three to four times at greater risk of developing PTSD than the average person – even in this era of so-called 'sanitised' modern warfare[16]. This greater risk experienced by military personnel has a long-term legacy. These are not mental health issues that simply go away, and it's been estimated that forty years after the end of the Vietnam War around 271,000 Vietnam theatre veterans have current full PTSD symptoms – figures that underscore the need for mental health services for veterans for many decades after a conflict has ended[17].

Finally, is there something unusual about being in the US military at the present time that increases the risk of stress-related disorders such as PTSD beyond what might be expected given the current risk of trauma in combat? Something is surely up, given that suicide rates among US Army personnel have increased by more than 80 per cent between 2004 and 2008 (currently higher than the matched civilian rate) – and with a third of those suicides occurring in soldiers

14 Dohrenwend, B. P., Turner, J. B., Turse, N. A., Adams, B. G., Koenen, K. C., & Marshall, R. (2006) 'The psychological risks of Vietnam for U.S. veterans: a revisit with new data and methods.' *Science*, 313, 979–982.

15 Perconte, S., Wilson, A., Pontius, E., Dietrick, A. et al. (1993) 'Unit-based intervention for Gulf War soldiers surviving a SCUD missile attack. Program description and preliminary findings.' *Journal of Traumatic Stress*, 6, 225–238.

16 There are factors other than combat experiences that may have inflated the risk of PTSD in military personnel and I'll discuss these later in this chapter.

17 Marmar, C. R., Schlenger, W., Henn-Haase, C. et al. (2015) 'Course of posttraumatic stress disorder 40 years after the Vietnam War.' *JAMA Psychiatry*, 72, 875–881.

who had never been deployed[18]. Maybe being in the Army is just a stressful job all round? Well, after analysing eleven factors relating to everyday job stress, including deadlines, competition, career growth and physical demands, the Internet career site CareerCast concluded that in 2017 'enlisted military ranks' was the world's most stressful job field[19]. So maybe the downside of a modern-day soldier's lot is not just confined to trauma, killing and death, it's also about everyday job stress in its broadest sense. It's a goddam demanding day job that the US Armed Forces certainly need to take closer scrutiny of for the sake of the mental health of its employees. A view that may well apply to many other armed forces around the world.

The Effects of Trauma

Somehow extreme trauma can create a jumble of physical and cognitive symptoms that we've come to collectively know as PTSD. These include vivid and uncontrollable intrusive flashbacks about the trauma, a debilitating hypervigilance to everything going on around, a stressful heightened startle response to sudden stimuli, nightmares, and sudden changes in mood that may range from severe depression to uncontrollable anger. These are likely to be accompanied by feelings of guilt, shame and low self-esteem. To add to the complexity of these symptoms, they may begin to occur immediately after the trauma or there may be a slow and delayed onset of anything up to six months or a year before symptoms appear. The social consequences are often catastrophic. The sufferer may lose interest in all activities they had previously enjoyed, job loss and

18 Bachynski, K. E., Canham-Chervak, M., Black, S. A., Dada, E. O., Millikan, A. M., & Jones, B. H. (2012) 'Mental health risk factors for suicides in US Army, 2007–2008.' *Injury Prevention*, 18, 405–412. http://dx.doi.org/10.1136/injuryprev-2011-040112

19 http://www.careercast.com/jobs-rated/most-stressful-jobs-2017

subsequent unemployment is common, and drifting into substance abuse as a form of self-medication is widespread.

PTSD symptoms are such a mixture that each individual symptom may be generated by the effect of trauma on quite different cognitive or physiological mechanisms. First, let's investigate the very disturbing and vivid intrusive flashbacks of the trauma experienced by sufferers. Andy is an ex-fire officer who was in charge of a fire truck at a house fire twenty years ago where three people died. His job was to remove the human remains from the house. He became distressed and started crying and feeling upset a few days later. Suddenly, at another similar incident seventeen years later his mind suddenly became occupied by a flashback to the original incident. After this he began experiencing three to four flashbacks a day. The flashbacks were so vivid and sensory he could feel the heat of the fire across his face and experience the acrid smells in his nostrils[20]. These are typical symptoms of PTSD – intense flashbacks that are uncontrollable and distressing.

So with this in mind we go back to one of the original conundrums of PTSD – why do some people who experience trauma develop vivid, distressing flashbacks and others don't? One factor may well be the level of corticosteroid hormones normally secreted from the adrenal glands following a stressful experience. Those who go on to develop PTSD symptoms – especially intrusive vivid memories – have been found to have significantly lower cortisol levels immediately after the traumatic experience than individuals who don't develop PTSD[21]. This is important because high levels

20 https://www.nhs.uk/conditions/post-traumatic-stress-disorder/pages/realstoriespage.aspx
21 Delahanty, D. L., Raimonde, A. J., & Spoonster, E. (2000) 'Initial post-traumatic urinary cortisol levels predict subsequent PTSD symptoms in motor vehicle accident victims.' *Biological Psychiatry*, 48(9), 940–947.

of cortisol can interfere with the laying down of memories of trauma, so low levels of cortisol will do the opposite and result in the over-consolidation of traumatic memories[22] – an over-consolidation that retains the vivid detail of the experience and retains this detail over a long period of time. Even more intriguing is the finding that low levels of cortisol in pregnant mothers who experience trauma and develop PTSD can also be passed on to their unborn children.

Rachel Yehuda and colleagues from the Mount Sinai Medical Center in New York took saliva samples from thirty-eight pregnant women who were either at or near the World Trade Center at the time of the 9/11 terrorist attacks. They found that those women who developed PTSD symptoms after the attacks had significantly lower cortisol levels in their saliva than those who were in the area of the attacks but did not develop symptoms. But when following up these findings a year later, those children born to the mothers who developed PTSD also had significantly lower cortisol levels and exhibited increased stress responses when shown novel stimuli.

Subsequent research has suggested that the effects of trauma can be passed on to later offspring through a process known as *epigenetics*. That is, the trauma experience doesn't affect DNA sequences as such, but does affect gene activity by switching specific genes 'on' or 'off', and some of this chemically altered activity is inherited from one generation to another. Trauma can especially activate genes that regulate the function of glucocorticoid receptors in the brain which in turn regulate the levels of stress hormones such as cortisol. In this way, trauma experiences can influence gene expression that in turn become inherited attributes passed on to the trauma victim's offspring.

22 Chou, C.-Y., La Marca, R., Steptoe, A. & Brewin, C. R. (2014) 'Biological responses to trauma and the development of intrusive memories: An analog study with the trauma film paradigm.' *Biological Psychology*, 103, 135–143.

In subsequent studies, Yehuda and other researchers have identified gene expression patterns caused by trauma in 9/11 survivors, in adult offspring of female Nazi holocaust survivors[23], and offspring of female veterans of the Iraq war[24]. These inherited characteristics of trauma do appear to make the offspring of trauma survivors themselves more vulnerable to trauma, PTSD and mental health problems. But it's not likely to be all one way; the most recent research on epigenetics does suggest that the offspring of trauma survivors may also inherit other kinds of traits that may promote resilience as well as vulnerability – and that would make sense if the process of trauma inheritance has evolved because it's ultimately an adaptive one.

So how do over-consolidated memories of trauma in PTSD sufferers come to be activated so regularly and uncontrollably? Probably because they can be activated by almost any similar or relevant stimulus. Charles Figley, Professor of Disaster Mental Health at Tulane University, has argued that one reason memories of the trauma are so hard to shake off is because they become entwined in the fabric of everyday life after the trauma[25]. A hill on the horizon may have been the place where you proposed to your wife, but after your combat trauma it has also become the distant hill in Afghanistan where you saw friends and comrades die. You've returned home, but home itself contains many images that can remind you of those distressing memories. Even home no longer feels like a safe place.

In PTSD sufferers there is also at least one other process operating that prevents trauma memories being degraded and this is active

23 Yehuda, R., Bell, A., Bierer, L., & Schmeidler, J. (2008) 'Maternal, not paternal PTSD, is related to increased risk for PTSD in offspring of Holocaust survivors.' *Journal of Psychiatric Research*, 42(13), 1104–1111.

24 http://fisherpub.sjfc.edu/cgi/viewcontent.cgi?article=1007&context=dnpforum

25 Figley, C. R. (1978) *Stress Disorders Among Vietnam Veterans: Theory, Research and Treatment*. Brunner/Mazel.

avoidance of anything that reminds them of the trauma. Memories will only tend to degrade once they've been consciously activated, reviewed and restructured, and this process is one that is a central feature of many psychological interventions for PTSD, especially eye-movement desensitisation and reprocessing (EMDR) and cognitive restructuring therapy.

Other common features of PTSD reflect more global psychological issues that the sufferer develops. These include low mood, feelings of guilt and shame, low self-esteem and loss of interest in activities that were previously enjoyed, and even a lack of interest in life generally. Clinical Psychologists Anke Ehlers and David Clark from the University of Oxford have suggested that there is a specific psychological attribute that's important in making some people vulnerable to PTSD after a trauma and which maintains some of these more diffuse symptoms[26]. This is a specific frame of mind they've called *mental defeat*. Such individuals tend to process information negatively, view themselves as unable to act effectively, and feel unable to cope with what has happened to them or to protect themselves from future traumas. They may also blame themselves for what has happened to them, or for what happened to others during the trauma, and blame themselves for surviving when others died. These factors generate a view of the world as an unsafe place and one that they feel they cannot influence or protect themselves from – to all intents and purposes the sufferer views himself or herself as a helpless victim.

This mental state that is associated with PTSD symptoms may often arise out of the way in which the trauma is processed in the context of the individual's self-identity. Identity is a collective term

26 Ehlers, A. & Clark, D. M. (2000) 'A cognitive model of posttraumatic stress disorder.' *Behaviour Therapy and Research*, 38, 319–345.

for the roles, goals and values that we adopt to give our lives direction and purpose[27]. If we already possess a self-identity that defines us as a victim in life, or if an experienced trauma changes our view of ourselves into one of being a victim, then both these scenarios increase the risk of PTSD symptoms. As Steven Berman at the University of Central Florida has pointed out, prior self-identity can significantly affect how a trauma is processed. For example, being a refugee trying to escape war and conflict is likely to be viewed through the lens of being a victim because of who you are and the circumstances you're in, and war-related traumas may be closely associated with who the refugee has come to define themselves as. If traumatic events are centrally related to who you believe you are, then this can significantly increase the risk of PTSD[28], and the PTSD prevalence rates for individuals living in war zones has been estimated as high as 12 per cent in some studies[29].

The relationship between trauma and identity is complex and still unclear, and as the quote at the beginning of this chapter implies, extreme traumatic events don't always come along as part of the ongoing life story, they can often interrupt the story, and they simply don't fit into what had gone before or what might have been expected to come afterwards. If you're lucky, then you may be able to view the trauma as an isolated event in an otherwise coherent life progress. But for others it can be an event that shatters the unity of that person's self-identity, and fragmented self-identity often comes

27 Erikson, E. H. (1959) *Identity and the Life Cycle: Selected Papers*. International Universities Press.

28 Blix, I., Solberg, Ø., Heir, T. (2014) 'Centrality of event and symptoms of posttraumatic stress disorder after the 2011 Oslo bombing attack.' *Applied Cognitive Psychology*, 28, 249–253.

29 Charlson, F. J., Steel, Z., Degenhardt, L., Chey, T. et al. (2012) 'Predicting the impact of the 2011 conflict in Libya on population mental health: PTSD and depression prevalence and mental health service requirements.' PLOS One, 7, e40593.

along with lack of confidence, a view of the world as an unpredictable place, and doubts about one's ability to cope. All grist to the mill of the broader psychological problems that are associated with PTSD.

Close Encounters of the Fourth Kind

Extreme trauma comes in many shapes and forms, and one form – believe it or not – is abduction by aliens. Alien abduction involves reports of 'being taken against one's will by non-human entities and subjected to complex physical and psychological procedures'. People who claim to have been abducted are known as 'abductees' or 'experiencers' and many describe their encounters as highly traumatising and terrifying, and many develop symptoms similar to PTSD.

The earliest publicised report of alien abduction became known as the Barney and Betty Hill Abduction in a rural area of New Hampshire in 1961. They were driving back home from a vacation in Montreal when Betty spotted an odd moving light in the sky. Because her sister had told her about flying saucers some years earlier, that's what Betty thought she might be observing. They report the object rapidly descending towards their vehicle. Barney stopped the car and got out and reported seeing what he thought were a dozen or so humanoid figures through the craft's windows. Barney raced terrified back to the car shouting at Betty that the aliens were going to capture them. He drove away at high speed with what seemed like a series of beeping and buzzing sounds bouncing off the car. At this point they claim to have entered an altered state of consciousness, and found that they'd seemingly driven over thirty-five miles before regaining full consciousness.

Ten days after the encounter, Betty began to have vivid dreams in which she recalled being forced by human-like figures around five feet tall with black hair, dark eyes, grey skin and prominent noses to walk through the forest and up a ramp into a disc-shaped craft.

Barney was also marched through the forest behind her. Once in the craft she and Barney were taken to separate rooms. Betty was sat in a chair and the alien she called 'the examiner' shone a bright light on her, examined her legs and feet, took samples of her hair and fingernails and scraped a sample of skin. He then forced a needle into her navel that caused her excruciating pain. The Hills were then escorted from the craft, taken to their car, and allowed to resume their journey.

In subsequent hypnosis sessions, both Betty and Barney separately recalled their abduction experiences. These sessions convinced Barney that aliens had abducted both him and Betty, but their hypnotherapist, Benjamin Simon, speculated that Barney's recollections had been inspired by Betty's dreams. Although they'd been traumatised by their abduction experiences, the Hills were happy to speak about them, but rarely sought publicity and eventually returned to their regular lives.

Since this first report of alien abduction, there have been many more, and some estimates suggest that as many as 6 per cent of the general population may have reported abduction experiences[30]. But hard evidence of alien abduction is difficult to pin down. So are abductees deluded? Are they cranks, or mere pranksters? Well no. Many of those people who claim to be alien abductees are seemingly sincere, psychologically healthy, non-psychotic people[31].

Professor Richard McNally and his colleagues at Harvard University have spent over ten years researching the psychology of alien abductees, and in particular why it is that some people embrace

30 Appelle, S. (1996) 'The abduction experience: A critical evaluation of theory and evidence.' *Journal of UFO Studies*, 6, 29-78.
31 McNally, R. J. (2012) 'Explaining "memories" of space alien abduction and past lives: An experimental psychopathology approach.' *Journal of Experimental Psychopathology*, 3, 2–16.

the identity of 'alien abductee' even when they report that their experiences have been traumatic and terrifying. His research has isolated a number of traits possessed by 'alien abductees' each of which he argues contributes to the experiences they recall when 'being abducted' and to the desire to cling on to their belief that aliens were responsible for their abduction experiences. Let's look at each of these five traits in turn.

First, many people who have reported alien abduction suffer episodes of early-morning sleep paralysis. On awakening from this paralysis, their terror gives rise to hallucinations of flashing lights and buzzing sounds. Some experience feelings of 'floating' around the room or seeing figures in the room. While many people interpret these post-sleep paralysis experiences as dreaming, some people interpret these experiences as seeing figures, ghosts or aliens.

Second, in an elegant set of experimental studies, McNally and colleagues found that individuals who claimed to have been abducted by aliens were prone to what is known as 'false memory syndrome' (see a later section in this chapter). That is, alien abductees regularly claimed to recall words, items, sentences, etc. in memory tests that they had never actually seen before[32]. If this 'false memory' effect can be generalised to autobiographical memories, then individuals who claim to have been abducted by aliens would be twice as likely to 'falsely remember' things that had never happened to them than would non-abductees.

Third, alien abductees also score significantly higher than most people on the mental characteristic known as 'absorption'. This is a trait related to fantasy proneness, vivid imagery and susceptibility to hypnosis and suggestion. Because of this it's probably not surprising

32 Clancy, S. A., McNally, R. J., Schachter, D. L., Lenzenweger, M. F. & Pitman, R. K. (2002) 'Memory distortion in people reporting abduction by aliens.' *Journal of Abnormal Psychology*, 111, 455–461.

that many alien abductees recall their experiences under hypnosis, where memories of abduction can be induced through suggestibility – especially if the person leading the hypnosis session asks particularly leading questions about abduction.

Fourth, being whisked up into spaceships by tractor beams or light sources is not something that happens every day – nor is it something that is easily explainable within our existing knowledge of physics. Similarly, being subjected to imaginative medical procedures requires a tendency to accept unusual and non-mainstream ideas. This is also a trait possessed by 'alien abductees'. They score highly on measures of magical ideation and endorse New Age ideas that encompass beliefs about alternative medicines and healing, astrology and fortune telling. Such beliefs would certainly allow the individual to accept things happening to them that would be dismissed by existing scientific knowledge.

Finally, as a cultural phenomenon, alien abduction has entered folklore and the images and descriptions of aliens and their spacecraft have become familiar to many people. Alien abductees tend to be very familiar with this cultural narrative which is one possible reason why their descriptions of aliens and their spaceships are so similar – being fuelled as they are by sci-fi films and numerous books about aliens and alien abduction.

All of these studies of 'alien abductees' were carried out after their abduction experience, so it's difficult to know whether these five traits are consequences of the experience or were – as McNally suggests – factors that led individuals to interpret rather earthly experiences (such as sleep paralysis and memory irregularities) as evidence of abduction. But then – perhaps fantastically – can we genuinely rule out the possibility that such experiences are genuine?

When I posted this piece about the psychology of alien abduction on my *Psychology Today* blog I received scores of vitriolic comments belittling my pathetic attempts to discredit the reality of alien abduction[33]. I was, they claimed, obviously a part of the conspiracy to cover up what they already knew – that alien life forms existed and were regular interactive visitors to our planet. At the very least, such commentaries testify to the strength with which beliefs about aliens and alien abduction are held by many people, despite my so-called feeble attempts to explain them using psychological science! But then, as McNally shrewdly points out, experiences of alien abductions are not just superficial, two-dimensional hallucinations, they are also experiences that often deepen spiritual awareness and give shape to the identities of abductees and provide a basis for their beliefs about the world and the universe.

Professor McNally told me about the reaction of one female participant in his psychological studies of alien abduction. After a lengthy debriefing explaining to her the psychological processes that had given rise to her having 'memories' of alien abduction, she sat back looking intensely at him before uttering something along the lines of 'Well, Mr Professor, all of that shows just how little you know!' Either this feisty lady did know more than a distinguished Harvard professor, or in a strange roundabout way, her dismissal of science was an indication that 'alien abductees' are going to stick with their beliefs even in the face of meticulously researched psychological explanations. Nevertheless, whether the experiences of abduction are real or not, the experiences and the interpretations adopted by 'alien abductees' are often psychologically helpful and can be spiritually comforting.

The moral of this story is that, whether alien abductions are real or merely psychological, they can generate life-altering experiences

33 https://www.psychologytoday.com/blog/why-we-worry/201207/five-traits-could-get-you-abducted-aliens

that in some people will be terrifying enough to generate symptoms of PTSD, but in many others will provide experiences that can enable spiritual growth and generate beliefs about the world that form a significant part of that person's self-identity. This is also true of trauma generally, where trauma can act to increase spiritual development and trigger the search for purpose and meaning in life[34]. This process may not always be immediately successful when it comes to improving psychological functioning, but it can provide the basis for recovery from trauma through structured psychotherapy.

Repressed Memories, Recovered Memories and False Memories

For many people, trauma is not simply a terrifying event that happens unexpectedly to punctuate an otherwise uneventful, benign lifetime, it can represent events that someone has been consistently subjected to while vulnerable and at risk. Childhood adversity is one such example, and it can take many forms. At its most serious, childhood trauma represents exposure to a number of forms of interpersonal violence, including physical abuse, sexual assault, rape and molestation. We've known for some considerable time that childhood adversity is a strong determinant of psychopathology in adulthood, and can double the risk of a psychiatric disorder in adolescence[35].

Some of these violent childhood experiences may be so traumatic that many therapists and clinicians believe that individuals can effectively 'forget' these events for significant periods of their lives. This view stems back to the original works of Sigmund Freud

34 Decker, L. R. (1993) 'The role of trauma in spiritual development.' *Journal of Humanistic Psychology*, 33, 33–46.

35 Dunn, E. C., Wang, Y., Tse, J., McLaughlin, K. A. et al. (2017) 'Sensitive periods for the effect of childhood interpersonal violence on psychiatric disorder onset among adolescents.' *British Journal of Psychiatry*, DOI: 10.1192/bjp.bp.117.208397.

who believed that severe trauma was repressed to the unconscious mind because it was too painful to tolerate. However, attempting to confirm that memories have been repressed is a difficult process. For example, it's often difficult to find corroborative evidence even when repressed memories of abuse seem to have been recovered, because many of the recovered memories may be of abuse that the perpetrators will be unwilling to substantiate.

Can memories of childhood trauma or abuse be repressed? In 1995 Linda Meyer Williams from the University of New Hampshire used hospital files to identify 206 women who, as children, had received medical treatment for sexual abuse in the 1970s. Twenty years later, she located those individuals and interviewed them about a range of topics, including childhood sexual abuse. Of those interviewed 38 per cent did not report the incident of sexual abuse for which they were hospitalised, but did report other incidents, suggesting they were not simply holding back sensitive information. Of those who did report the sexual abuse incident, 16 per cent reported that there were effectively times in their lives when they'd forgotten it[36]. But is this a specific act of repression of painful memories, or is it just the normal process of forgetting?

There's conflicting evidence on this. While there are some studies that have reported no evidence of repressed memories for well documented traumatic events such as kidnap or Holocaust experiences[37], there may be some forms of trauma that are more likely to be repressed. Psychologist Jennifer Freyd at the University of Oregon has argued that childhood sexual abuse is often perpetrated

36 Williams, L. M. (1995) 'Recall of childhood trauma: A prospective study of women's memories of child sexual abuse.' *Journal of Consulting and Clinical Psychology*, 62, 1167–1176.
37 Zola, S.M. (1998) 'Memory, amnesia, and the issue of recovered memory: Neurobiological aspects.' *Clinical Psychology Review*, 18(8), 915–932.

by a trusted caregiver, such as a parent or close relative, and this gives rise to what she's termed 'betrayal trauma'. Betrayal trauma theory argues that there is a social benefit to remaining unaware of abuse when the perpetrator is a caregiver, and broadcasting a betrayal of this kind may be counter-productive to survival[38]. This has been termed 'betrayal blindness', which is the unawareness or forgetting exhibited by people towards betrayal by caregivers, and it may be a basis for the repression of memories of abuse – but only abuse perpetrated by otherwise trusted caregivers.

During the 1980s and 1990s many therapists came to believe that a wide range of psychiatric symptoms were caused by past sexual abuse that had been repressed in the memories of the victims. They also believed that a range of therapeutic methods could be used to recover these repressed memories, and these included hypnotism and directive psychotherapy. These approaches generally came to be known as 'recovered memory therapy', and proponents of this approach had a crusading belief that a wide range of psychiatric symptoms was indicative of childhood sexual abuse.

Much of the impetus for this loose therapeutic movement came from a book called *The Courage to Heal*, written in 1988 by two feminist counsellors, Ellen Bass and Laura Davis[39]. They argued that a large number of people are the victims of childhood sexual abuse but do not realise they were abused, and that a list of symptoms (e.g. being held in a way that made them feel uneasy) may well be indicative of actual childhood abuse. Their overriding principle was 'If you feel something abusive happened to you, it probably did!' Therapists who subsequently adopted this approach to treating psychopathology were thus given free rein to indulge in a directive

38 Freyd, P. (1996) 'False memory syndrome.' *British Journal of Psychiatry*, 169(6), 794–795.
39 Bass, E. & Davis, L. (1988) *The Courage to Heal*. William Morrow.

approach attempting to uncover evidence of suppressed memories of childhood abuse – even to the point where clients were told they were 'in denial' if they couldn't remember instances of abuse. Under such conditions it's almost inevitable that clients may begin to 'recall' instances of abuse that did not actually happen.

Julia Shaw is a criminal psychologist at London's South Bank University specialising in how false memories may be formed in the brain, and she's regularly called to testify in criminal cases involving the recall of repressed memories. In one such case in 2016, two sisters had accused a close female relative of sexually abusing them forty years earlier in the 1970s[40]. Shaw looked for clues in the sisters' evidence to see if these memories of abuse were genuine recovered memories or whether they were erroneous reconstructions. Shaw noticed that the older sister would say things such as 'My childhood was rough and I buried so much. I think it was my coping mechanism – I must have just blocked it' – a statement that suggests an assumption of repression on the part of the elder sister. The younger sister couldn't remember much of what had happened, but simply agreed with her sibling's version of events. Shaw viewed this as a form of social contagion – a process where testimonies are shaped by others' accounts of what had happened (a process that may have been involved in the shaping of the alien abduction experiences of Betty and Barney Hill earlier). The transcripts of the sisters' evidence also gave the impression that the elder sister appeared to be guessing at the details of these experiences, using phrases like 'I can't remember, I just had this really weird feeling that she used to make us do stuff to each other'.

The case was eventually dropped because of new evidence that the defendant was able to provide indicating that the alleged abuse

40 http://www.wired.co.uk/article/false-memory-syndrome-false-confessions-memories

was unlikely to have occurred. Shaw points out that our knowledge of memory processes has progressed to the point where we know that human memories are malleable, open to suggestion, and often unintentionally false: 'In everyday situations we don't really notice or care that they're happening. We call them mistakes, or we say we misremembered things, but in the criminal justice system these mistakes can have grave consequences.'

This debate on whether recovered memories of trauma are genuine or false is still ongoing. There is no doubt that *some* people probably do repress memories of childhood abuse, *some* probably recover these memories – either with or without therapy – and *some* probably recall memories of childhood abuse that never actually happened but are unintentional *post hoc* reconstructions perhaps shaped by the suggestions or narratives of others.

Is There a PTSD Disability Compensation Epidemic?

Throughout many of the chapters in this book I've alluded to the possibility that increased awareness of mental health problems may be one factor contributing to the modern anxiety epidemic. People are more aware of mental health symptoms, contemporary views of these symptoms have often tended to label them as abnormalities in need of treatment rather than normal everyday emotions, and the average member of the public is becoming more aware of how to seek treatment and disability compensation for mental health problems. There's nothing wrong with these developments (except perhaps the continuing over-medicalisation of everyday emotions), and it will enable more people suffering mental health problems to receive appropriate treatment for their symptoms. But for some people the very nature of their occupations puts them at greater risk of experiencing trauma, and as a consequence, at greater risk of developing PTSD.

We've already mentioned members of the armed forces as one group; others include members of the rescue services such as fire-fighters and emergency medical personal, disaster first-responders, police officers and even trauma-counsellors themselves. Developing PTSD symptoms because of the nature of your job will have led to many of these at-risk professions developing disability processes to compensate their employees and provide access to suitable treatment programmes. But this can give rise to some unusual anomalies.

As psychologists Richard McNally and Christopher Frueh have pointed out, the wars in Iraq and Afghanistan have produced historically low rates of fatalities and injuries, and moderate rates of PTSD among US combatants[41]. But despite this they've generated unprecedented high rates of PTSD disability compensation-seeking from the US Department of Veteran Affairs (VA). Why is this? At least part of the answer is that the VA actively pursues veterans who have shown signs of PTSD, it has used public awareness campaigns to highlight the symptoms of PTSD, and it routinely screens veterans for symptoms – all admirable developments. But does this high profiling of PTSD encourage symptom-faking and malingering? It may be that some veterans do exaggerate their symptoms, and one study discovered that over half of the veterans in the study who were seeking treatment for PTSD showed clear evidence of symptom exaggeration[42], but there was somewhat less evidence for downright faking of symptoms[43].

41 McNally, R. J. & Frueh, B. C. (2013) 'Why are Iraq and Afghanistan war veterans seeking PTSD disability compensation at unprecedented rates?' *Journal of Anxiety Disorders*, 27, 520–526.

42 Freeman, T., Powell, M., & Kimbrell, T. (2008) 'Measuring symptom exaggeration in veterans with chronic posttraumatic stress disorder.' *Psychiatry Research*, 158, 374–380.

43 But see https://www.theguardian.com/uk-news/2016/jan/23/many-mili tary-veterans-ptsd-claims-fabricated-or-exaggerated for an up-to-date account of PTSD symptom faking and exaggeration in UK veterans.

However, one interesting finding is that response to treatment of PTSD in veterans is unrelated to disability status[44]. That is, we might expect that the less severe your symptoms, the more likely you are to recover – but that isn't the case with PTSD in veterans. This may seem strange but as McNally and Frueh point out, veterans who have been awarded disability continue to have significant incentives to maintain (or increase) their disability status and their disability benefits. For example, those who have received disability compensation awards that were less than 100 per cent continue to complain of symptoms and continue in treatment until they finally attain a disability rating of 100 per cent – at which point mental-health visits by sufferers plummet[45].

It's the case that many veterans returning from combat find it difficult to adjust to their new lives. Some find themselves unemployed after proudly serving their country, some struggle to transfer their skills to a civilian job market, and many more have difficulty readjusting to a normal family life again. As a consequence of these re-adjustment issues, many use the VA's flawed disability procedures to offset financial need rather than secure treatment and subsequent recovery from a disability such as PTSD.

The point being made here is not that war veterans do not deserve their disability payments – they most certainly do! Progress has been made in ensuring that many more deserving veterans receive appropriate disability compensation than ever before. But the overall number of people suffering mental health problems may be inflated

44 Belsher, B. E., Tiet, Q. Q., Garvert, D. W., & Rosen, C. S. (2012) 'Compensation and treatment: disability benefits and outcomes of U. S. veterans receiving residential PTSD treatment.' *Journal of Traumatic Stress*, 25, 494–502.

45 Veterans Affairs Office of the Inspector General (2005) Review of state variances in VA disability compensation payments. VA Office of Inspector General report no. 05-00765-137. Retrieved from http://www.va.gov/ foia/err/ standard/requests/ig.html.

by the unusual dynamics of the disability policies currently offered by governments and employers – policies that may very often offer incentives to exaggerate symptoms and to avoid full recovery. This isn't a process that's peculiar to mental health problems, it's been a recurrent issue with disability policy generally – but mental-health awareness is relatively new, and so we're only just beginning to see these consequences of disability policy in areas such as stress, anxiety and depression.

There's Nothing New Under the Sun

Some of the events that come along in a lifetime challenge our very concept of being safe. They are extreme stressors that endanger our existence or violate our sense of self-identity. These events don't fit comfortably into what has gone before in our lives, and neither can we easily fit them into what we would wish for our future. They are usually entirely unpredicted, shocking in their severity, and devastating in their ability to disrupt even the most stable of lives. They are earthquakes, tsunamis, floods, fires, train crashes, car accidents, rape, torture, military combat, terrorist attacks, physical violence, and many other events that make us fear for our lives.

A common outcome for many people who experience these events is PTSD – a disabling condition that bestows on survivors a hotchpotch of symptoms including vivid flashbacks, nightmares and hyperarousal, together with feelings of shame, guilt, anger and anxiety. These symptoms are often accompanied by an enduring inability to cope with the future, the belief that the world is an uncertain and unsafe place, and a lack of interest in life itself.

Even though PTSD didn't appear in diagnostic manuals until 1980, we haven't just invented it – it's been around for a long time, known as Soldier's Heart, Shell Shock, and Combat Stress Reaction in earlier generations. Study of ancient manuscripts by Professor

Jamie Hacker Hughes of Anglia Ruskin University has revealed that the first evidence of traumatic symptoms as a result of battle or combat dates back to ancient Mesopotamia during the Assyrian Dynasty between 1300 and 609 BC, well before the Greek and Roman eras[46]. Writings tell of soldiers in the aftermath of battle suffering 'psychogenic mutism' or disturbances of the mind – often explained away as 'the spirits of those enemies whom the patient has killed'. Even without the technological horrors of modern warfare, ancient warriors would still have been subjected to psychological trauma in battle with the high risk of death, witnessing other soldiers suffering death and severe injury, and the risk of injury from the iron-hardened tips of arrows, showers of sling-stones, and razor-sharp swords.

As the title of Jamie Hacker Hughes' article suggests, there is 'nothing new under the sun'. In the modern era, we are simply better at defining and diagnosing the effects of trauma, understanding their causes, and helping sufferers to recover.

46 Abdul-Hamid, W. K. & Hacker Hughes, J. (2014) 'Nothing new under the sun: Post-traumatic stress disorders in the ancient world.' *Early Science & Medicine*, 19, 549–557.

CHAPTER TWELVE

Managing Your Stress and Anxiety

'If you always do what you've always done, you'll always get what you've always got.'

One consequence of the modern anxiety epidemic is that there are almost as many anxiety self-help books in the bookshops as there are stars in the sky! Most offer good advice about how to manage your anxiety and stress, and I recommend you browse some of the more popular and successful ones. In this chapter, my aim is to offer some easily usable tips to help you manage your stress and negative moods on a daily basis, and also to provide you with some more analytical approaches to understanding your anxiety in more detail which will hopefully help you to modify the way you think and behave in relation to your anxieties. Finally, if you're at a stage where you think you want to move on from anxiety and improve your life, there are some simple tips on this towards the end of the chapter.

But please don't start reading this book at this chapter! Much of the battle against anxiety is won if you understand the causes of your anxiety – the external factors that give rise to your anxieties and worries, and the cognitive and physiological processes that generate your anxiety. I've spent some considerable time in the earlier chapters describing what I hope are accessible and engaging explanations of how anxiety is caused. Understanding these causes – especially in relation to individual anxiety disorders – can be a liberating process in itself, and some of the greatest successes I've had managing my own anxieties have come through insightful understanding of the causes of that anxiety. Most importantly, this understanding will certainly help you to apply some of the anxiety management tips and methods described in this chapter. But first, let's just set the scene: anxiety isn't a mugger you're trying to fight off, it's a part of you – it's your anxiety, and that mindset is important when it comes to managing your anxiety.

Anxiety: the Myth of the Body Snatcher

Invasion of the Body Snatchers is a famous 1956 science-fiction film (remade several times) in which alien seeds invade Earth and replace sleeping people with physical duplicates. Let's be clear, that's not how anxiety works. Anxiety is not an alien body snatcher that's attacked you, overwhelmed you, and replaced your thoughts and feelings with distressing imposters that you find almost impossible to cast out. Anxiety is not a bat that's got caught up in your hair, a leech that's stuck to your body, or a rabid stray dog that's hounding you as you go about your daily business. But there are still many cultures in the world that view mental health problems such as anxiety as if it were the result of something, such as an evil spirit, possessing, attacking or taking over the sufferer.

I've discussed the issue of 'spirit possession' and mental health in one of my *Psychology Today* blog posts[1]. Explanations of mental health

1 https://www.psychologytoday.com/blog/why-we-worry/201412/spirit-possession-and-mental-health

problems in terms of 'possession' have taken many forms over the course of history, and it's a form of explanation that's meant that many who have been suffering debilitating and distressing psychological problems have been persecuted and physically abused rather than offered the support and treatment they need. Many ancient civilisations, such as those in Egypt, China, Babylon and Greece believed that those exhibiting symptoms of psychopathology were possessed by bad spirits (this is known as *demonology*), and the only way to exorcise these bad spirits was with elaborate ritualised ceremonies that frequently involved direct physical attacks on the sufferer's body in an attempt to force out the demons (e.g. through torture, flogging or starvation). Not surprisingly, such actions usually had the effect of increasing the distress and suffering of the victim.

In Western societies demonology survived as an explanation of mental health problems right up until the eighteenth century, when witchcraft and demonic possession were common explanations for psychopathology. Nevertheless, demonic or spirit possession is still a common explanation for mental health problems in some less developed areas of the world – especially where witchcraft and voodoo are still important features of the local culture such as Haiti and some areas of Western Africa[2].

The point here is to contrast the view of anxiety as an 'invading demon' with our modern-day view of anxiety, which is that it comes from within rather than invades you from without. It's a natural part of your biology, and it's grown out of the way you come to think about yourself and the world generally. So dealing with anxiety and stress is not about trying to beat something alien out of you, it's about retuning your engine – both your physical and psychological

2 Desrosiers, A. & St Fleurose, S. (2002) 'Treating Haitian patients: Key cultural aspects.' *American Journal of Psychotherapy*, 56, 508–521.

engines – to get the right balance of thoughts and adaptive behaviours that will reduce your levels of anxiety and stress. And there are many ways of doing this successfully.

Anxiolytic medications can be helpful when it comes to retuning the engine – especially in the short term. These can reduce your arousal and help you to manage your body's reaction to anxiety triggers and stressors. But pharmaceuticals won't directly change the way you think, nor will they significantly change your behaviour in relation to your anxiety – and the way you think and how you react to your anxiety are important causal determinants of how your anxiety develops and is maintained.

There are also some obvious downsides to medications. They can have unwelcome side effects, such as weight gain or drowsiness, and they can also generate a behavioural dependence that can prevent your anxiety from extinguishing. During one of my own bouts of panic attacks I very much appreciated the arousal-reducing effects of beta blockers (beta-adrenergic blocking agents) – they helped me to control my blood pressure and adrenaline levels, and made me feel just that bit more relaxed. Excellent! But what happened next wasn't. I began to feel so reliant on the arousal-reducing effects of the drugs that I began to carry them around with me everywhere – just in case I felt a panic attack coming on. This was my anxiety head taking charge again to the point where carrying the drugs around with me had become a 'safety behaviour' – and if you take a look back at Chapter 9 we know what safety behaviours do; they're avoidance responses that prevent the anxiety from extinguishing. The unconscious inference your brain takes from this is 'You're still carrying those pills around with you, so you must still be anxious!' The mind works in some mysterious ways. I'm not sure whether this obsession with carrying the beta-blockers around with me actually prolonged my panic attacks, but I certainly felt like panicking if I discovered I'd forgotten to take them out with me! The day I felt comfortable going out and leaving them in the medicine cupboard was the day I began to feel cured.

If you're unsure whether you should take medications for your anxiety problems, you should consult your GP or physician – they are the best person to advise you. They may even be able to refer you to the local mental health services for longer-term counselling or psychotherapy if your anxiety is particularly distressing and prevents you from working or studying.

As I've described in earlier chapters, your anxiety can often emerge out of a toxic brew of negative moods, dysfunctional beliefs about yourself and the world, biased thinking and avoidant behaviour, and each of these need attention if anxiety is to be managed. The beliefs, biased thinking and avoidant behaviour will need some longer-term attention, but your current moods are usually something you can tackle relatively immediately.

Boosting Your Mood

We've seen in many of the previous chapters that your current mood – especially negative mood – contributes directly to the generation of anxious thoughts and the perseveration of worries; it facilitates threatening interpretations of events, and unconsciously directs attention towards threats. In addition, negative mood is not a particularly pleasant experience, so there are a number of good reasons for trying to boost your mood and alleviate negative mood. Negative mood covers a range of bodily and cognitive states, including feeling stressed, feeling anxiety itself, sadness, anger, tiredness and pain. Maybe things keep going wrong, you shout at the kids, and you have to multitask after a long day. Here's some evidence-based tips for improving your mood, at least some of which can turn around your negative mood in less than ten minutes.

Listen to upbeat music: Yuna Ferguson, a psychologist from the University of Missouri, has conducted a number of studies showing that listening to upbeat or positive music can immediately boost your mood[3]. The music has to be positively valenced (e.g. Copland and not Stravinsky), and you need to listen to the music with the intention of improving your mood, but without constantly saying to yourself 'Am I happy yet?' – if you do that, it doesn't work!

We've conducted many lab studies where we've used positive music to make participants feel happier and less anxious, and this works well for improving mood in the short term. Just one note of caution, in the 1990s our 'happy' music was Mozart's upbeat 'Eine Kleine Nachtmusik' – what could be more jolly than that? But over the course of a couple of years we found that this piece of music was losing its effect – it was no longer making people feel happier. The reason? We discovered that it was regularly being used as the holding music when people were phoning customer service numbers and as a result had acquired a rather different connotation – it had become very closely associated with regular feelings of frustrated anger felt by unhappy customers unable to talk to a customer service representative! But don't take my word for what might be upbeat music. Dr Jacob Jolij, a cognitive neuroscientist at the University of Groningen, has developed a scientific formula for identifying the top ten feel good songs[4]. Here they are from number one down to number ten: Queen – 'Don't Stop Me Now'; Abba – 'Dancing Queen'; The Beach Boys – 'Good Vibrations'; Billie Joel – 'Uptown Girl'; Survivor – 'Eye of the Tiger'; The Monkees – 'I'm a Believer'; Cyndi Lauper – 'Girls Just Wanna Have Fun'; Jon Bon Jovi – 'Living on a Prayer'; Gloria Gaynor – 'I will Survive'; Katrina & the Waves

3 Ferguson, Y. L. & Sheldon, K. M. (2012) 'Trying to be happier really can work: Two experimental studies.' *Journal of Positive Psychology*, 8, 23–33.
4 http://www.jolij.com/?p=362

– 'Walking on Sunshine'. Is there anyone in the world who can listen to 'Don't Stop Me Now' without joining in on the title line? Anyway, take you pick and enjoy upbeat happiness!

Take a walk around the block: Not only does this physically disconnect you from your current environment that could be fuelling your negative mood, but even the mildest of exercise can improve your mood. If it's during the day, you'll also get the benefit of some daylight exposure, which we know can improve sleep problems and reduce depression. A study by Gregory Panza, an exercise physiologist at the University of Connecticut, tracked the physical activity of 419 generally healthy middle-aged adults. Even light physical activity, such as a ten-minute walk around the block with no noticeable increase in breathing, heart rate or sweating, was associated with an increased sense of well-being and lowered levels of depression[5].

Make yourself laugh: Laugh your worries away – when stress builds up laughing can instantly elevate your mood, reduce pain and stress, and – as an added bonus – boost immunity by decreasing stress hormones and increasing immune cells and infection-fighting antibodies. Laughing does this by releasing the natural opiate dopamine in the nucleus accumbens area of the brain – this is the reward centre in the brain, and has the effect of instantly making you feel less stressed and more positive. So, on your laptop, bookmark some YouTube videos that make you laugh so you can immediately access them when you need to. Alternatively, keep some classic comedy programmes on the hard drive of your TV box. Laughter really is one of the best medicines[6].

5 Panza, G. A., Taylor, B. A., Thompson, P. D. et al. (2017) 'Physical activity intensity and subjective well-being in healthy adults.' *Journal of Health Psychology*, https://doi.org/10.1177/1359105317691589.
6 P.S. Tickling yourself doesn't work – get someone else to do it!

Surround yourself with calming aromas: Light a fragrant candle or use a diffuser to create relaxing aromas around the house. Janice Kiecolt-Glaser and psychiatrists from the University of Ohio examined the psychological and physiological effects of a relaxant odour (lavender), a stimulant odour (lemon), and a no-odour control (water) after a stressful event (having to plunge one's hand into a bucket of ice water)[7]. A series of mood assessment tests showed that lemon (but not lavender) had a positive effect on mood regardless of expectancies or previous use of aromatherapy.

Take a bath or shower: Zoning out is a good thing if you can immediately create your own bit of space where you can relax peacefully. So what better than the privacy of the bath or a shower? In many cultures bathing has been a means of relaxing and purifying the body, but lying in a hot bath can have a whole number of important benefits. It improves our circulation, helps us to fall asleep and, if you're lucky enough to have a hot tub, spending ten minutes in there lowers blood pressure in people with hypertension[8]. If you're bathing at the end of the working day, then it's a relaxing and suitable place to think through your achievements of the day to give the day a positive ending.

There are many more suggestions for ways in which you can boost your mood – most can be found on health and well-being websites. I've highlighted just a few activities for which there is some reliable scientific evidence for their effectiveness. But since everyone is different, there may be many more activities that might suit just you. Some include looking through old photographs, clearing away clutter in your immediate environment, cooking, chatting to a close

7 Kiecolt-Glaser, J. K., Graham, J. E., Malarkey, W. B., Porter, K. et al. (2008) 'Olfactory influences on mood and autonomic, endocrine, and immune function.' *Psychoneuroendocrinology*, 33, 328–339.

8 Shin, T. W., Wilson, M. & Wilson, T. W. (2003) 'Are hot tubs safe for people with treated hypertension?' CMAJ JAMC, 169, 1265–1268.

friend, writing about your worries or negative feelings, or simply just smiling[9].

Ten Tips for Managing Your Anxiety

Next, here are ten general points to keep in mind when it comes to managing your anxiety. These will help you keep an informed perspective on what anxiety is and provide some very basic dos and don'ts when it comes to dealing with your anxiety.

Accept that anxiety is a normal emotion and can be helpful: Anxiety often generates additional layers of anxiety – especially if you become anxious about being anxious. Anxiety isn't unnatural – it's a normal emotion that has evolved to be helpful. In Chapter 1 I described many of the ways in which anxiety can help you deal with anticipated threats and challenges, and that's basically what it's there for. It can help you stay focused in an interview, and help to speed you home on a dark night. Bouts of anxiety usually don't last very long, so try not to fight off your feelings of anxiety, but accept them and say to yourself that it's okay to be anxious. Message to self: 'It's okay to be anxious.'

Understand that anxiety can't harm you: Experiencing anxiety doesn't mean you're going crazy, it means you're normal. Anxiety can't harm you; it's usually you that wrongly interprets signs of anxiety as being possibly harmful. Anxiety is not necessarily a pleasant feeling, but the physiological indications of anxiety such as perspiring, increased heart rate and trembling, are not harmful, nor are they signs of impending illness. Message to self: 'Anxiety can't harm me; I can still do what I need to do.'

---

9 Kaiser, J. & Davey, G. C. L. (2017) 'The effect of facial feedback on the evaluation of statements describing everyday situations and the role of awareness.' *Consciousness & Cognition*, 53, 23–30.

Avoid avoidance: We talked a lot in Chapter 4 about how avoidance is arguably the main factor that allows anxiety to develop and propagate. Avoiding highly dangerous things – such as running in front of moving cars – is quite sensible and reasonable. But if you're avoiding things that most other people think are safe, then you may need to deal with what may be inappropriate anxiety. Avoiding the things that make you anxious never allows you to find out the reality of the threat – it may not be a threat at all. But you don't discover there's no monster in the closet if you continue to avoid opening the closet door. There's some advice later in this chapter on how to face your anxieties in a structured step-by-step way. Message to self: 'Anxiety feeds off avoidance; I'll try and find a way to face my fears.'

Check that your anxiety is justified: Very often you should reality check your anxieties – is what you're anxious about really a significant threat or challenge, and are other people anxious about the things you are? Often the thing causing your anxiety may not be as dangerous or threatening as you think. This is certainly the case with many anxiety-based disorders where the level of anxiety elicited has grown way beyond what is reasonable for the threat that the sufferer perceives. Check your anxiety against reality by using a 'Disaster Prediction Fact Checker' similar to the example provided for Donna in Figure 12.1[10]. Message to self: 'Is my anxiety justified?'

Consider being adventurous rather than avoiding risk and uncertainty: Life is basically an adventure. There are no plans set out to be followed from the beginning; you can get as much out of life as you want to. There is nothing that stymies an adventure more than trying to avoid risk and uncertainty, so try to tip the balance from avoiding risk to seeking out new experiences. There is nothing

10 From Davey, G. C. L., Cavanagh, K., Jones, F., Turner, L. & Whittington, A. (2012) *Managing Anxiety with CBT for Dummies*. Wiley. Chapter 5.

Disaster Prediction Fact Checker

Stage	Donna's Response
Disaster prediction	When I eat at the restaurant with my family, I will get so nervous that I'll throw up at the table and people will think I am disgusting.
How anxious do I feel about now? (0–100%)	80%
Facts that support the prediction being true	I get nervous about eating at a restaurant. I feel sick when I get nervous. I saw someone throw up on a ferry and I found this disgusting.
Facts that don't completely fit with the prediction being true	**1. How likely is it really?** I have never actually been sick from nerves. I was sick once at a restaurant but that was probably because I had heatstroke. **2. How awful would it be really?** When I was sick in the restaurant from heatstroke, I did have time to get to the toilets, so no one really knew about it until I came out and told them. **3. How would I cope really?** If I was sick at the table, I would need to just apologise and leave. I would probably not go back to that restaurant, but that wouldn't be the end of the world.
Alternative, balanced prediction	When I eat in a restaurant with my family I may feel sick, but I'm unlikely to actually be sick. Even if I am, I'll probably have time to get to the toilet. Even if the worst did happen, I wouldn't be the end of the world. **How much do you believe this alternative prediction (0–100%)** 50%
How anxious do I feel about now? (0–100%)	40%

Figure 12.1 This Disaster Prediction Fact Checker shows the responses provided by someone who's fearful of eating in a restaurant. You can use this template to check your own anxiety disaster predictions (adapted from Davey, G. C. L., Cavanagh, K., Jones, F., Turner, L. & Whittington, A. (2012) *Managing Anxiety with CBT for Dummies*. Wiley).

that fuels anxiety like trying to control risk and uncertainty, so try to counteract this by doing something you consider adventurous at least once a week – things like going into a new situation where you don't know what will happen, or doing things without seeking reassurances from others first. Message to self: 'I will do something adventurous every week.'

No one is perfect – take a break from the rigid rules that make you anxious: Setting the highest standards for everything, all the time, is a recipe for stress and anxiety. So try to analyse the kinds of rigid rules that you yourself apply and replace these with more realistic expectations. These rigid rules are things like 'I must always be loved by everyone', 'I must never let anyone down', 'Life should always be fair', and 'I need to be fully in control of everything I do'. Write down some of the rigid rules you live your life by and try to think of some more reasonable alternatives. For example, 'I need to be fully in control of everything I do' could become 'I will do my best, but accept that some things are out of my control.' Message to self: 'No one is perfect – I will live my life using realistic rules.'

Refuse to let anxiety hold you back: Anxiety will regularly prevent you from doing things that you want to. But at some point you'll need to feel the fear if you're to move on. To overcome anxiety you'll have to undertake some challenges that initially make you feel anxious, but this can be an uplifting and valuable experience if you eventually manage to prove your anxiety wrong. Most things that make us anxious are usually not as bad as our anxiety told us they might be. Trying new things, taking challenges and solving problems all add up to a healthier and more productive life. Message to self: 'I will not let my anxiety hold me back'.

Recruit help to change: Moving on from anxiety will require you to change a lot of things you do and the way you do them, so it's always helpful to enlist the help of family or friends to try to achieve these changes. Friends may help you to attempt things you've never done before because of your anxiety – an assisting hand and some positive encouragement from another person will always be helpful. It's also good to know that other people understand your anxiety problems and are willing to help you. But beware – there are some forms of help from others that can reinforce your anxiety. For example, try not to seek reassurances from others that things will be okay. If you're seeking reassurances then this confirms you're still anxious, and it may prevent you from facing up to your fears. Similarly, if you're anxious about something like going to the shop, don't ask someone else to do it for you – you need to learn that with some perseverance and support you too can go to the shop without feeling anxious. Message to self: 'I'm happy to ask friends and family to help me to achieve changes that will reduce my anxiety.'

Be aware of the bigger picture: You're not just simply your anxiety – believe it or not, there is a lot more to you. You're a living, breathing human being whose life consists of many more things than just being anxious. But aspects of your broader lifestyle may be colluding with your anxiety, maintaining it, and even preventing you from moving on. For example, anxiety and sleeping problems are close allies, as are depression and anxiety. Try to organise your life so that you're able to get a regular good night's sleep, and if you also feel depressed, try to get help to relieve your depression because tackling your depression may leave you more confident to overcome your anxiety. Becoming over-reliant on anxiety medication or even choosing to drown your anxiety in alcohol are also unlikely to help you move on from anxiety. Medication or a stiff drink can take the edge off your anxiety in the short term, but they won't teach you the social or problem-solving skills you need to learn to alleviate your anxiety. Problematic drinking can leave you with next-day hangovers that mean you miss work or college, it depletes the feel-good brain chemical serotonin, increases secretion of the anxiety-generating hormone cortisol, and physically creates low mood and feelings of nausea and confusion – all sensations that trigger anxious thinking and anxious cognitive processes. Finally, you should encourage yourself to embrace healthy living. Regular exercise is known to reduce anxiety, and a healthy diet is associated with better mental health. Message to self: 'I'll try to embrace a more healthy lifestyle and move on from anxiety.'

Seek professional help if you feel you need it: Tackling your anxiety problems on your own can be a daunting and overwhelming prospect, and you shouldn't be afraid to seek more structured support from a CBT therapist, a psychotherapist or a counsellor. If your anxiety is particularly distressing or you believe you have patterns of anxiety that resemble one or more of the anxiety disorders I've described in Chapter 4, it would be sensible to seek professional help. You may be able to find suitable psychotherapeutic help privately, or alternatively you can approach your local health services or your GP or physician for advice.

I hope you can find some useful advice in these general tips that'll help you to manage your anxiety and move on. If you'd like more detail on how to implement these tips I would recommend CBT self-help books in general, including my own co-authored CBT self-help book *Managing Anxiety with CBT for Dummies*[11], as well as Helen Kennerley's *Overcoming Anxiety*[12].

Ten Tips to Manage Your Worrying

Sticking with basic tips for the time being, let's now look at some tips

11 Davey, G. C. L., Cavanagh, K., Jones, F., Turner, L. & Whittington, A. (2012) *Managing Anxiety with CBT for Dummies*. Wiley.
12 Kennerley, H. (2014) *Overcoming Anxiety* (2nd Edition). Little Brown Books.

for managing your worrying. Uncontrolled worrying can take you over at almost any time of the day or night, it increases your stress and anxiety levels, it can make the things you worry about seem significantly worse than they were before you started worrying, and it can lead you to worry about things that are simply never likely to happen – the good-old worrier's 'What if . . . ?' questioning style.

If you consider yourself a worrier, then you're not alone. Almost one in ten people find uncontrollable worrying a distressing affliction that feels as though it has become an inseparable part of their personalities and character. Chronic worrying is often driven by a need to worry to 'make sure things will all be OK', it will affect your mood, and it will also have detrimental effects on your relationships, your work productivity and your social life. But before you begin to have a look at some of the tips below, go back and have a read of Chapter 7 about the causes of the worry monster. This will help you understand some of the reasons why worrying can become compulsive, debilitating and uncontrollable, and will put some of the tips below into the context of how chronic worrying is caused.

Problem-solve, don't worry: Worrying is often a very inefficient attempt to problem-solve. So when you worry, try to turn this into useful problem-solving by considering what you need to do now to deal with the problem. Try to focus on the following steps: (1) identify the problem – try to give yourself a very precise description of what your worry is and why it's a problem; (2) define your goal – ask yourself what you want to change or achieve right now in relation to your worry, and make this a realistic concrete goal (not 'I want to feel better' – that's very difficult to define, feeling better will come with defining potential solutions); (3) brainstorm some alternative solutions and write them down, think of how you've solved similar problems in the past and adapt those to your current worry; (4) think about ways you can implement your solutions – this is important because many worriers can think up perfectly good solutions to problems, but don't feel they have the confidence to implement them. So this is a significant part of the problem-solving process, consider the practicalities and make plans to implement your solutions. Don't be put off.

Don't waste time on 'What ... if?' questions: Don't waste time thinking up situations that 'might' happen, but in reality are quite unlikely to happen – that's just a misuse of good brain time! Try to spot when you start asking yourself 'What if ... ?' type questions. The vast majority of the scenarios you create using this approach are never likely to happen – so why waste time thinking about them? To give yourself a sense of control over a 'What ... if?' worrying style, it's a good first step to record the 'What ... if?' questions that you ask yourself. Even just writing them down and reading the list periodically can help you to reduce the frequency of these types of thoughts.

Don't kid yourself that worry is always helpful: Don't be fooled into thinking that your worry will always be helpful. If you're a persistent worrier you've probably come to use worrying simply to kid yourself that you're doing 'something' about a problem. This is not an alternative to tackling the problem now in practical ways. Have a look back at Chapter 7 where I've described how most chronic worriers have developed a set of dysfunctional beliefs that worrying is a necessary and useful thing to do to prevent bad things happening. These beliefs drive the worrier's worrying about almost everything. See if you can identify these beliefs in yourself and find arguments as to why they may not be as useful as you think.

Learn to accept uncertainty: Uncertainty is a fact of life, so try to accept that you'll always have to live with and tolerate some uncertainty. Unexpected things happen, and accepting this in the longer term will make your life easier and reduce your anxieties. Try replacing very specific expectations about the future with some plans about achieving what you want in the future. For example, I worry that I might feel lonely if I move to a new city to take up a new job. But it's not useful to think of my move solely in terms of the uncertainty of whether I'll be lonely or not. It's healthier to create some plans about what I'll do when I get there – plans that'll help me to meet new friends and do things. Don't fall into the quicksands of uncertainty – plan your way positively around them. Focus on what you can control in a situation, and develop some positive plans to do just that.

Always try to lift your mood: Negative moods fuel worrying. Negative moods include anxiety, sadness, anger, guilt, shame and even physical states such as tiredness and pain. If you must worry, then try not to do it when in these negative mood states because your worrying will be more difficult to control and more difficult to stop. If you find yourself worrying in a negative mood, immediately try to do something to lift your mood. We've already covered some suggestions about how to boost your mood earlier in this chapter.

Don't suppress unwanted worries: When you do start to worry – don't try to fight or control those thoughts. It's helpful to notice them rather than try to suppress them, because actively trying to suppress thoughts simply makes them bounce back even more! So acknowledge those worrisome thoughts but then move on to doing something more useful.

Manage the times when you worry: Become a 'smart' worrier. If you find that worrying can be useful but that it just gets out of control, then try to manage your worry by setting aside specific times of day to engage in worrying as well as a specific place where you'll do it. But also take the time to soothe yourself when this period is over, just to get yourself back into balance. First, choose a time when you know you're unlikely to be busy doing other things – such as fifteen minutes during lunchtime or half an hour after you get home from work. Then choose a place. Make sure it's somewhere that isn't too cosy or comfortable – if you're going to spend some time worrying, you don't want that place to be too cosy or comfortable otherwise this could unwittingly reinforce any negative thinking or worrying you do. Somewhere outside may be suitable – such as the fire escape outside your office[13]. Or you could use that scruffy, old armchair that's been relegated to the garage. Similarly, it needs to be a place where all you do is worry – no answering your texts, eating, drinking or writing your shopping list, or anything else. We're trying to create a form of stimulus control, so that only your worry place is associated with worrying, and worrying is no longer elicited by places such as your work desk, your kitchen or your bedroom, but only by your worry place. So, whenever you catch yourself worrying, make a note of the worry, and reserve it for your worry time and worry place. Once your worry time is over make sure you reward yourself. Go and do something pleasant or relaxing, listen to some music, or chat with a friend.

Change 'What . . . if?' worries to 'How can I?' worries: To be able to manage your worries, you need to understand exactly what they are. Try keeping a worry diary for a week or so. Write down each worry when it occurs – just a sentence to describe it will do. Then later, try and see how many of your worries are 'What if . . . ?' type questions. As we mentioned earlier, 'What if . . . ?' worries are not helpful. You can try to turn these worries into 'How can I . . . ?' worries, which is more likely to lead you on to practical solutions (e.g. you could turn a 'What if I forget what to say in my interview?' worry into 'How can

---

13 Potter, B. A. (1997) *The Worrywart's Companion*. Council Oak Books. Chapter 8.

I prepare myself to remember what I need to say in my interview?'). You can also go back to Tip No.2 and use some of the strategies there for handling 'What if . . . ?' worries.

How not to lose sleep by worrying: Very often your worries may stop you sleeping. You may find yourself running through every possible problem that could arise and spend time trying to think up solutions. All this will do is keep you awake longer, and you'll end up feeling tired (and probably anxious) the next day. One solution to worries that keep you awake at night is to keep a pen and paper next to the bed. When you wake up worrying, simply write a list of things you need to do tomorrow (including dealing with the worry). You may well find that once the worry has been transferred to that piece of paper, there's now no longer any need to keep it in your head as well. It can be dealt with tomorrow. But the best solution to prevent worrying at night is to ensure that the bedroom is a discriminative stimulus that has come to elicit only sleeping. So don't treat the bedroom like an extension of the rest of the house, try not to use your smartphone or laptop in the bedroom, no TV, no nibbling that leftover pizza under the duvet! Save your bedroom for sleep – and, of course, sex!

Stay in the moment: Spending most of your time worrying about things that might happen in the future means that you'll spend less time enjoying the present and staying in the moment. Acknowledge the worries that enter your head, but don't engage them, try to refocus on what you're doing in that moment – watching a TV programme, reading a good book, playing with your children. Mindfulness exercises are helpful in this respect, and more of that next.

Five Tips to Manage Your Anxiety with Mindfulness

Anxiety is the emotion that forces you to live your life considering the future while you sacrifice the simple beauty of experiencing the present moment. Mindfulness is an approach to engaging with the present moment that helps you to connect with your body and become more aware of what's going on around you rather than fretting about what might happen in the future. It's about paying attention to what's going on in the here and now in a non-judgemental way. Mindfulness has been around for thousands of years, but it's only recently that it's become popular in Western cultures and in the past couple of decades it's been researched as an approach to managing a whole range of psychological and physical health problems. Studies of the effects of mindfulness-based therapy suggest that it can significantly improve anxiety and mood symptoms[14] as well as helping to alleviate vulnerabilities to stress[15]. Mindfulness allows you to calm your mind, begin to deal with your emotions rather than ignoring or rejecting them, improves your focus and concentration, and helps you to react less automatically and negatively to events. Here are a few simple tips that will introduce you to mindfulness and some exercises that will help you to manage your stress and anxiety.

Be aware of nature: How often do we get so caught up in everyday living that we don't even see the world around us? Becoming aware of nature in particular is a good way to start appreciating the present moment. Make a point of looking at the trees in the street on your way to work, or arrange a trip into the countryside on a regular basis. If it's a clear night, take a moment to gaze at the stars and experience the beauty of the universe.

14 Hofmann, S. G., Sawyer, A. T., Witt, A. A. & Oh, D. (2010) 'The effect of mindfulness-based therapy on anxiety and depression: A meta-analytic review.' *Journal of Consulting & Clinical Psychology*, 78, 169–183.
15 Armstrong, L. & Rimes, K. A. (2016) 'Mindfulness-based cognitive therapy for neuroticism (stress vulnerability): A pilot randomized study.' *Behavior Therapy*, 47, 287–298.

Reconnect mindfully with your body: Most people would admit they live most of their lives in their head – especially if they're an anxious type. As a result we become disconnected from our bodies, and are aware of our bodies only when we experience things like pain or hunger. A basic mindfulness exercise can help you to become more aware of your body. This has two benefits. It helps you to tune in more easily to the present moment, and it also allows you to begin accepting emotions instead of suppressing them. Figure 12.2 provides some simple instructions for a five-to-ten-minute exercise that will facilitate bodily awareness[16].

Breathing mindfully: Another ten-minute exercise that you can do anywhere is breathing mindfully. Close your eyes and focus on your breathing – don't try and change your breathing, just experience it as it is. You can focus on your breath going into your body, your throat or your lungs and tummy; if your mind wanders, gently guide it back to your breathing. When you've finished open your eyes and just consider how you feel.

Mindful listening: We tend to miss so many of the sounds around us and often can't remember most of the conversations we've been involved in during the course of a day. You can increase your awareness of the sounds around you by focusing on your breathing for a few minutes. Become aware of the sounds you can hear and their volume and pitch, and perhaps more importantly become aware of the silences between the sounds you hear.

Cooking mindfully: You can increase your awareness of any activity you're involved in by tuning into the sensations created by your body and focusing on the nature and characteristics of the external elements involved in that activity. For me, cooking is one particularly

16 Marshall, J. J. (2015) *Managing Anxiety with Mindfulness for Dummies*. Wiley.

Mindfulness exercise

Allow 5–10 minutes for this meditation:

---

1. **Place a hand on your stomach.**

   Become aware of your breath as your stomach rises and falls. Try to accept the breath as it is without forcing it.

2. **Imagine the breath going all the way down the body into both legs and both feet.**

   If you find this difficult, just bring a mindful awareness to both feet. What do they feel like? What does the contact feel like with the bed or the floor?

3. **Picture the breath rising up from your body, from both feet and up the legs.**

   Become aware of both knees and any sensations there. Similarly, become aware of both hips when you reach that point.

4. **Focus your breathing and mindful awareness on your tummy area and lower back.**

   Become aware of any sensations, remembering to bring a sense of curiosity and acceptance as much as you can.

5. **Bring the breath and mindful awareness to your chest and upper back.**

   Remember if the mind wanders off, just gently guide it back to the breath and whatever you're focusing on.

6. **Guide your breath gently down both arms to the fingertips and back up to the shoulders.**

   Observe any sensations in the wrist and elbow as you go.

7. **Focus your awareness on the neck, slowly moving up to the head.**

   Become aware of facial expressions and any tension in your face.

8. **Bring a sense of gratitude for your amazing body.**

   Also, bring kindness toward yourself for taking care of your health in this way.

9. **Open your eyes gently.**

Figure 12.2 Follow these instructions for a five to ten minute exercise that will facilitate bodily awareness (Adapted from Marshall, J. J. (2015) *Managing Anxiety with Mindfulness for Dummies*. Wiley).

engaging and relaxing pastime that involves activities such as chopping, whisking, kneading, stirring, sampling yummy tastes, and experiencing delicious smells and odours as well as a range of luscious food textures. Whatever the activity you choose to conduct mindfully, begin by feeling your breath and the sensations in your body before you begin, and then continue to experience the changes in your bodily sensations as you progress through the activity. In the case of cooking mindfully, this includes noticing how the texture of the food you're cooking may change, being aware of new smells and tastes, and – of course – enjoying the end product in a relaxed meal with friends or family.

Mindfulness can help your anxiety in a number of ways. Anxious people often try to avoid their feelings, and mindfulness guides you back to acknowledging them and accepting them, and this acceptance of your anxious feelings is a first step towards managing them. Mindfulness also enables you to experience many sensations other than anxiety, and this is a step towards realising that you are much more than just your anxiety. Mindfulness enables you to become more aware of your thoughts and to identify negative or unhelpful automatic thoughts that may trigger your anxiety. And your mindfulness training will allow you to shift your focus away from these negative thoughts and on to more neutral experiences such as your breathing. But perhaps most of all, mindfulness gives you back a sense of control, providing a first glimpse of how you can shift your focus away from anxious feelings and thoughts, and instilling a belief that you are a living, breathing, experiencing human being and not simply a walking, talking bundle of anxieties!

Creating a Map of Your Anxiety

One important theme throughout this book has been the notion that understanding the causes of your anxiety is a significant step in the direction of successfully managing that anxiety. So in this section, the intention is to help you to get a better picture of your own specific anxieties by creating a map of your anxiety that links together your anxiety triggers, your anxious thoughts, your behavioural responses to anxiety, and the bodily sensations that are associated with your anxiety.

First, think back over the past couple of weeks and write down some specific examples of when you've been anxious. Choose one of these examples – preferably one that's clear in your mind – and follow these subsequent steps.

Identify the triggers for your anxiety: What was it that happened to trigger your anxiety? Was it a sudden fearful thought that entered your head, something external that you encountered like a spider, an unexplained bodily sensation, or something that you can't resolve straight away such as the thoughts of a heavy workload?

What anxious thoughts and images went through your mind when you were anxious? Did you fear what might happen next, were you worried you wouldn't be able to cope, were there any frightening images that came to mind, and did you suddenly envisage a very bad worst-case scenario? If you thought something bad was going to happen, can you rate how probable you thought it was likely to happen on a 100-point scale, where 0=not likely to happen at all, and 100=certain to happen.

What did you do? Did you do something to try and make yourself safe, or to avoid the situation? Think of things that you actually *did* rather than what you *thought*.

How did your body feel at the time? Make a note of any bodily sensations you experienced at the time. Things like chest pains, trembling, nausea, hot flushes, dry mouth, headaches or dizziness.

Figure 12.3 provides the template of an anxiety map and you can transfer your responses to the four questions above into the appropriate boxes in the map[17]. The bottom half of the figure shows an example of a completed map to help you to fill in your own map. Once you've done this, now begin to think about how the events in each of the boxes were linked. If you think the anxiety triggers lead to anxious thoughts, then draw an arrow between the 'triggers' box and the 'thoughts and images box'. Do your feelings of anxiety lead to bodily sensations? If so, draw an arrow between the 'feelings of anxiety' box and the 'bodily sensations' box. Think back to your own anxiety example and try to add all the causal links you think happened in that anxiety episode. Use the example at the bottom of the figure to help you draw the map of your own anxiety episode.

You can now use this map to help you manage your anxiety. First, your map will probably show the important effect that your thoughts have on your feelings of anxiety. Consider how realistic these thoughts are (for example, did you think something terrible was going to happen, but in fact it didn't?), and also think about replacing these unhelpful thoughts in the future with more helpful and less anxiety-provoking ones (have a look over the tips to manage your anxiety and your worrying earlier in this chapter to help you with this).

Second, your map will also probably show how the things you do in your anxiety episode influence that anxiety. For example, as I explained in Chapter 4, avoiding your anxieties may make you feel better in the short term, but in the longer term it will probably make your anxiety worse (see Chapter 4 for an explanation of how this works). Facing up to your fears in a managed and gradual way will help you to rid yourself of avoidance behaviours and will enable your

17 Adapted from Davey, G. C. L., Cavanagh, K., Jones, F., Turner, L. & Whittington, A. (2012) *Managing Anxiety with CBT for Dummies*. Wiley. Chapter 2.

Making a Map of Your Anxiety

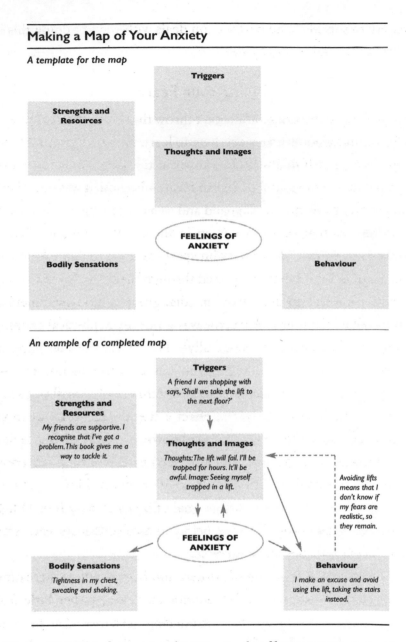

Figure 12.3 This figure provides an example of how to create an anxiety map (lower half) and shows a template that you can use for creating your own anxiety map. See text for further instructions (Adapted from Davey, G. C. L., Cavanagh, K., Jones, F., Turner, L. & Whittington, A. (2012) *Managing Anxiety with CBT for Dummies*. Wiley).

anxiety to subside. The next section deals with ways of doing this in a structured and managed way.

Facing Your Fears

If your best friend can't swim, don't throw them into the deep end of the swimming pool and expect them to learn to swim there and then! I was born and brought up in a town in the East Midlands whose motto was '*Coeur Anglais*' – English Heart – because it was effectively the geographic centre of England and as a consequence was further from the sea than any other town in the country. This left rather few opportunities to learn to swim apart from the foul-smelling and unappealing local canal that passed through the town. So as a young teenager I ended up in a small remedial group of non-swimmers at school. Our swimming instructor was an ex-army physical training instructor called Mr Seal (yes, really!). His approach to teaching us so-called water-phobes how to swim was to throw us one by one into the deep end of the municipal swimming pool. Needless to say, it merely terrified us. It was in effect a literal and brutal example of the behaviour therapy technique known as flooding! But facing your fears is not about jumping into deep ends of swimming pools (or even being pushed for that matter), it's about making structured and achievable steps towards your goal of being anxiety free. When constructing any programme to help you face your fears, each step must be manageable and achievable.

This is known as *graduated exposure* and begins with you creating a fear hierarchy starting with scenarios that cause rather little fear and anxiety and step by step introducing scenarios that become more worrisome and anxiety-provoking. The examples below show how to create a fear hierarchy related to fear of flying, but, of course, this should enable you to do the same with your own fear or anxiety.

Your fear hierarchy will contain scenarios that you've actually experienced, but it will also contain scenarios that you haven't encountered but fear that you might. In the case of fear of flying, an anxiety scenario you may have encountered might be 'standing in the queue to check in at the airport' but an anxious scenario that you may not have encountered but thought about may be 'travelling in the aircraft when it had to turn round and return to the airport because an engine was on fire'. But first a note of caution: simply thinking about your anxieties may be anxiety provoking. If this is the case, then try saying to yourself 'This is something I need to do to help myself and it'll be worth it'. However, if your anxiety is more intense, you may want to begin by working your way through a few of the tips earlier in this chapter or a suitable self-help book that will introduce you in a more measured way to some exercises that will begin to alleviate your anxiety. However, if your anxiety causes you real distress, then a visit to your family GP or physician to discuss your symptoms is a recommended first step.

Creating your anxiety hierarchy: First, try to create around fifteen scenarios related to your anxiety, and describe each one in detail so that you'll later be able to imagine them vividly. Write down each one on a separate index or postcard. When you've done this, then grade each scenario on a scale of 0–100 where 100 is the highest level of anxiety you can imagine and 0 is not at all anxiety-provoking. Write your rating on the back of each card. Now sort your cards into five separate piles: a Low Anxiety pile – ratings 1–19; a Medium/ Low Anxiety pile – ratings 20–39; a Medium Anxiety pile – ratings 40–59; a Medium/High Anxiety pile – ratings 60–79; and a High Anxiety pile – ratings 80–100. The aim is to have at least two cards in each pile. If that works out – that's fine. If not, try and create some more scenarios. Here's a hypothetical fear hierarchy for fear of flying, going from least anxiety-provoking to most anxiety-provoking:

Packing Luggage
Making Reservations
Driving to the Airport
Checking In
Boarding the Plane
Waiting for Boarding
Taxiing
In-Flight Service
Moving Around the Cabin
Climbing to Cruising Altitude
Descending
Waiting for Departure
Taking Off
Landing
Turbulence

Tackling your anxiety hierarchy: First, set yourself what you believe will be an achievable timetable for tackling your fear hierarchy. An example might be getting through the Low and Medium/Low Anxiety scenarios by the end of week two, getting through the Medium and Medium/High Anxiety scenarios by the end of week four, and completing the High Anxiety scenarios by the end of week six. Before you start tackling any of the fears in your hierarchy, try to enlist the support of a friend or family member who knows what you're doing and can offer support when you need it and encouragement and praise when you're doing well.

Working your way through your anxiety hierarchy: Start with the lowest graded scenario. If it's an activity you can carry out – such as looking at a cat if your anxiety is being around cats – then do so, but don't actively try to reduce the feeling of anxiety, that will slowly subside as you learn to be comfortable with the activity.

If you can't easily carry out the activity – such as being in turbulence on an aircraft – then try to imagine the scenario as vividly as you can. Keep repeating the activity, perhaps two or three times a day. Each time you engage in the activity, try to keep at it until you feel your anxiety levels coming down and rate how anxious you feel at the very end of the exercise on a 100-point scale where 0=not anxious at all, and 100=the highest anxiety you can imagine. When you feel you've conquered your anxiety for that scenario, then move on to the next scenario in the hierarchy – but only move on when you feel confident that you've mastered the previous one.

Don't try to jump steps, and don't try to rush yourself through the scenarios – remember this is a learning exercise, and you need to ensure that learning is completed fully and properly. Good luck!

Moving on from Your Anxiety

Managing your anxiety is only part of the solution – it's also important to take steps to prevent anxiety returning to your life once you feel you've got on top of it. Often this requires some lifestyle changes and a switch in focus towards self-development. This may involve introducing some new activities into your life, creating a clear vision of how you want your life to develop over the next few years, ensuring that you live healthily, and finding time to continue practising some of the anxiety management and mindfulness tips that you feel benefit you.

First, try developing a five-year plan for yourself. This is your vision of how you want your life to progress and how you might achieve your goals. In doing this, you need to balance realism and idealism. Try to imagine what you'd like to be doing in five years' time and write down some of these aspirations. It might help to ask yourself questions such as 'Where will I be living?', 'What will I be doing?', 'Who will I be with?' Now break each of your aspirations down into the manageable steps you might need to undertake to achieve these aspirations. These steps should be realistic and achievable, as should your hopes for the future. But be optimistic – basically you're saying to yourself, 'What do I need to do to achieve my aspirations if life has gone well?'

Second, live healthily. Poor health and bad living are breeding grounds for anxiety and stress. Looking after your body is good for your mental health, and I mentioned the benefits of even small amounts of exercise earlier in this chapter. Eating a balanced diet and getting a good night's sleep are also important. Hunger and tiredness are themselves negative mood states that can generate anxious and worrisome thoughts, facilitate threatening interpretations of events, and unconsciously direct attention towards threats and challenges. Also, try to drink alcohol and caffeine in moderation; excessive amounts of alcohol can lower the levels of serotonin in the brain and create feelings of anxiety the next day, and caffeine stimulates the release of norepinephrine that causes symptoms indistinguishable from anxiety. If you're unsure how to move on towards more healthy living, you could begin by making small changes to your diet, sleeping habits and exercise regimes, and monitoring how these affect your mental and physical well-being.

Third, introduce some new activities into your life or reclaim an interest you might have lost as a result of your anxiety. Think back to a good time in your life and spend about fifteen minutes trying to recall activities that you enjoyed at that time. Add to this list some activities that you've never done but think you might like to, things such as travelling, new hobbies and new forms of exercise, joining a group or a club, or dining out or eating new foods. Then try to put together a practical plan describing how you might go about starting your new activity. If you feel anxious

369

about trying something new, then use some of the exercises and tips earlier in this chapter to help you manage those anxieties (e.g. tackling your anxiety using the anxiety hierarchy, or seeing if you can put some of the ten tips for managing your anxiety into practice here).

Finally, soothe yourself through the normal daily stressors that you're bound to encounter by regularly practising the mood boosting tips I offered earlier in this chapter or by learning more about mindfulness[18]. Even when you're not feeling the debilitating symptoms of anxiety and stress it's worth having a regular daily routine for promoting relaxation and positive mood, and enjoying present-moment experience.

Remember, life is usually a very long thing. So there's often plenty of time to recover from your anxiety and to live a fulfilling life if you put your mind to it. But it's not about that elusive commodity called 'will power', it's more about restructuring your daily routines to ensure you promote healthy living and prevent bad habits that could foster anxiety. I'll finish with a salute from a famous character from the planet Vulcan who never experienced anxiety – or any other emotion for that matter – 'Live long and prosper'.

18 A good place to start would be Williams, M. & Pennman, D. (2011) *Mindfulness: A Practical Guide to Finding Peace in a Frantic World*. Piatkus.

EPILOGUE

In this book I've described the many ways that the modern world creates stress and anxiety. The way that anxiety manifests itself has not really changed over the centuries and we're still plagued by the same forms of anxiety disorder as our ancient ancestors, but the things that trigger our anxiety have certainly changed. We still experience many traditional causes of anxiety such as poor health, difficult relationships, unemployment, poverty and disadvantage, loneliness, work stress, and exposure to violence, trauma and conflict. Even in our modern world, some of these traditional sources of anxiety are on the increase. These include loneliness; relationship factors such as divorce; violence and abuse – including childhood abuse and neglect; increased working hours and more stressful work procedures; and a general sense of lack of control over our own destinies – especially amongst our youngsters who are introduced to the possibility of failure earlier and earlier in their lives as a result of increased systematic educational testing. Thankfully, some of the traditional causes of anxiety are generally on the decline, factors such as poverty, poor health and to some extent unemployment. But they leave in their place some new anxieties, such as income inequality, living with long-term disability, and the stresses of modern-day job-seeking.

In addition, modern technology has provided some entirely new sources of anxiety for the present generations. These include twenty-four-hour perpetual connectivity, the need to multitask across a range of different activities, and regular increasingly emotive news alerts and doomsday scenarios. Very soon almost every appliance in our houses will be connected to the Internet, fuelling fears of identity theft, data hacking, phishing, grooming and trolling. Even that bastion of modern-day living, the computer, brings with it daily worrisome hassles that include crashing hard drives, forgotten passwords, and the frustration of daily transactions that begin to seem strangely distant when all we'd like to do is speak to a real person.

Riding on the back of our daily computer stresses comes the perpetual connectivity provided by social media. The first recognisable social media sites were created in the mid-1990s, so most youngsters under the age of twenty will never have lived without the curse of social media. And a curse it can be. Social media use is closely associated with social anxiety and loneliness and can generate feelings of disconnectedness when we view what seem like the rich lives and social successes of others. A consequence of social media use is that youngsters count their social success in terms of metrics such as the number of friends they have on sites like Facebook, not the number of genuine confidants they have – confidants who would be true friends in times of difficulty and need.

To supplement this rash of new, modern anxieties is a gradual shift in the social ethos surrounding anxiety. This change has been almost contradictory in the messages it sends to us. We're told anxiety is a legitimate response to the stresses of modern living, and anxiety is almost considered a status symbol that signals how busy and successful you are. But we're increasingly told that anxiety is an emotion in need of treatment. Diagnostic categories for anxiety problems have burgeoned over the past thirty years, the pharmaceutical industry is keener than ever to medicalise anxiety and sell us a pharmaceutical solution for it, and increasing numbers of social campaigns increase awareness of mental health problems such as anxiety, valiantly attempt to destigmatise it, and then help us to identify it and seek treatment for it.

But it would be irresponsible of me to claim that all is doom and gloom on the anxiety epidemic front. Roughly one in five people regularly suffer distressingly high levels of anxiety but there's no significant evidence that this ratio has increased over the years[1]. But even if that ratio stays the same, as populations grow, more and more people will suffer anxiety and will be seeking treatment for it as awareness of mental health problems increases. On the other side of the coin, two out of five people tend to experience only low levels of anxiety, and will rarely need to seek treatment unless they encounter extreme life events that elicit extreme responses.

New psychosocial treatments for anxiety are continually being developed, and we now have specialised CBT programmes for most if not all of the main anxiety disorders[2]. In addition, access to basic forms of CBT for common mental health problems such as anxiety has increased significantly in a number of countries with the successful introduction of programmes such as IAPT (Improving Access to Psychological Therapies)[3], and computer-based CBT for anxiety is an increasingly effective medium through which sufferers can be helped to recover[4]. But even with the most successful

1 Baxter, A. J., Scott, K. M., Ferrari, A. J., Norman, R. E. et al. (2014) 'Challenging the myth of an "epidemic" of common mental health disorders: Trends in the global prevalence of anxiety and depression between 1990 and 2010.' *Depression & Anxiety*, 31, 506–516.

2 Kaczkurkin, A. N. & Foa, E. B. (2015) 'Cognitive-behavioral therapy for anxiety disorders: An update on the empirical evidence.' *Dialogues in Clinical Neuroscience*, 17, 337–346.

3 http://digital.nhs.uk/catalogue/PUB24016

4 https://adaa.org/learn-from-us/from-the-experts/blog-posts/pro fessional/computer-assisted-cognitive-therapy-viable

evidence-based psychotherapy and pharmaceutical procedures, we're still some way from helping 100 per cent of people to recover from anxiety disorders, and some anxiety disorders such as OCD and GAD can be debilitating life-long conditions resistant to both current medications and psychotherapies[5].

To improve the range of interventions available we need significantly more funding for mental health research. The level of funding for mental health research is pitiful when compared with that provided for research into other medical problems (see Chapter 4)[6], and arguably much of the funding that is available goes to medical and neuroscience programmes rather than the psychological research that would be needed to develop more effective, evidence-based talking therapies[7].

So, is there an anxiety epidemic? Contemporary definitions of the term 'epidemic' no longer allude to disease as a necessary condition, and consider an epidemic anything that negatively impacts on the health or welfare of a large number of people in a population[8]. One in five people in the UK suffer high levels of anxiety at any one time[9]; one in nine people worldwide will experience an anxiety disorder in any one year[10]; anxiety prevents you from working, learning, or performing your social and family responsibilities to your full potential;

5 https://www.psychologytoday.com/blog/why-we-worry/201211/the-lost-40

6 https://blog.wellcome.ac.uk/2015/04/21/mental-health-how-much-does-the-uk-spend-on-research/

7 http://www.papersfromsidcup.com/graham-daveys-blog/-the-funding-of-mental-health-research-in-the-uk-a-biased-and-flawed-system

8 Martin, P. & Martin-Grane, E. (2006) '2,500-year evolution of the term epidemic.' *Emerging Infectious Diseases*, 12, 976–980.

9 https://www.ons.gov.uk/peoplepopulationandcommunity/wellbeing/datasets/measuringnationalwellbeinganxiety

10 Baxter, A. J., Scott, K. M., Vos, T. & Whiteford, H. A. (2012) 'Global prevalence of anxiety disorders: A systematic review and meta-regression.' *Psychological Medicine*, 43, 897–910

anxiety and stress account for over a third of all work-related ill health[11] and costs over £100 billion in England each year in lost productivity and reduced quality of life[12]; and anxiety can kill – even sub-clinical levels of anxiety can increase the risk of mortality by 20 per cent[13]. So, yes, we do have a modern anxiety epidemic, but then so have most previous generations. The difference is that in our modern era we have a whole set of new and evolving anxieties and a growing awareness of anxiety as a potentially distressing and disabling state. We'll need to rise to the contemporary challenges that this presents in terms of understanding the causes of anxiety and the suffering it can convey, dealing with the economic cost to society that anxiety problems impose, developing new and more effective evidence-based intervention and prevention programmes, and providing more realistic levels of funding for mental health services and research.

11 http://www.hse.gov.uk/statistics/causdis/stress/

12 https://www.centreformentalhealth.org.uk/economic-and-social-costs

13 Russ, T. C., Stamatakis, E., Hamer, M., Starr, J. M. et al. (2012) 'Association between psychological distress and mortality: Individual participant pooled analysis of 10 prospective cohort studies.' *British Journal of Medicine*, doi: 10.1136/bmj.e4933

INDEX

absorption 327
accident phobia 174
activities, finding new 369–70
adaptive fallacy 168, 169
addiction
  gambling 30–1
  Internet 29
  social media 35, 75–6, 78, 80, 95,
    286–7
adrenaline 10, 131, 260–1
adventurous, being 348, 350
Afghanistan, war in 316, 317, 335
age cohorts, anxiety and 58–9, 94
agoraphobia 117, 150, 184, 224,
  256–7
alcohol 82, 351–2, 369
alien abduction 325–30, 333
ambivalent arousal 290
American Civil War 153, 313, 314,
  317
American Psychiatric Association
  50, 52, 123
  see also Diagnostic and Statistical
    Manual (DSM)
amygdala 14, 102, 103, 262, 270
anger 57, 137, 206, 271
animal hoarding 231–2
animal phobias 162, 170, 178–82,
  183
  see also specific phobias

anxiety
  adaptive and helpful 4, 19, 20–5,
    179, 347
  age groups 58–9, 94
  anxiety hierarchy 366–8
  anxiety and stress, distinguished
    18–19
  Disaster Prediction Fact Checker
    348, 349
  as emotional experience 3, 4, 11,
    12, 13, 14, 15, 16, 17, 88, 89,
    137, 347
  'epidemic' 2–3, 53, 54, 59–60,
    374–5
  Freudian analysis 146–7
  gendered experience of 56–7
  historical perspectives on
    134–55
  ingredients 15–16
  learnt emotion 15, 16, 17
  managing 347–52, 357–61
  mapping 362–5
  moving on from your anxiety
    368–70
  prevalence of 49, 55–60
  response to anticipated events
    10–11, 13
  risk factors for 101–15, 132–3
  what it is 9–18
  see also causes of anxiety

exercise 249–50, 345, 352
existential dread 3, 268
exposure therapies 131, 148
eye-movement desensitisation and
    reprocessing (EMDR) 323
Eysenck, Hans 148–9

Facebook 35, 54, 74, 76–8, 80, 95
    addiction to 76, 77, 287
    Facebook-induced stress 77–8
    negative impacts 76–7
    news feeds 48
    passive interactions with 79, 287
    socially anxious individuals and
        287–8
facial expressions for anxiety 12–13
failure, sense of 62, 63
fake news, psychological effects of
    47–8
false memory syndrome 327, 333–4
family and friends, help from 350–1
fantasy proneness 327
fear
    of bodily sensations 274
    facing 365–8
    fear hierarchy 365–6
    'fearcasting' 197
    graduated exposure 365
    historical perspectives on 137,
        138, 141, 256
    ingredients in anxiety 15, 17
    reflexive reactions 9–10, 15
    vicarious acquisition of 111–13
fear of fear see anxiety sensitivity
fight-flight response 7, 216, 250,
    260, 261, 262, 270, 272, 273
financial crisis (2007–2008) 58,
    81–2, 95
five-year plan for yourself 368–70
flashbacks 8, 118, 153, 313, 314,
    319, 320–1
flooding 148, 365
FOMO (fear of missing out) 2, 29,
    60, 75

freezing 15, 216
Freud, Sigmund 144–8, 223, 299,
    330–1
friendship networks
    genuine confidants 78, 95, 372
    loneliness and 70, 74
    quantifying 75
    see also social media

gambling addiction 30–1
gender differences in experience of
    anxiety 56–7, 203
    young people 61–2
Generalised Anxiety Disorder
    (GAD) 24, 57, 118, 154, 203–
    10, 374
    brain processes 209–10
    children 206–7
    deluded worldview 130
    diagnostic criteria 118, 151
    gender and 203
    heritability 208–9
    historic perspectives 147, 151
    negative life events and 203–4,
        208
    origins of 205–10
    parenting experiences and 205–8
    pathological worrying 147, 151,
        197, 206, 217
    physical symptoms 118, 203,
        216–17
    prevalence of 203
    risk factors for 88, 205
genetic inheritance see heritability
graduated exposure 365
Greco-Roman times, anxiety in
    135, 137–8, 150–2, 154
Gulf War 316, 317, 318
'gut' feeling of anxiety 18, 188

hair pulling see trichotillomania
health status
    anxiety and 24, 25, 55, 59, 71, 86,
        91–4, 95–6